*Edmund Spenser's*

# AMORETTI AND EPITHALAMION
## A CRITICAL EDITION

# Medieval & Renaissance

# Texts & Studies

VOLUME 146

*Edmund Spenser's*

# AMORETTI AND EPITHALAMION
# A CRITICAL EDITION

## Kenneth J. Larsen

ᗰEᗺIEVᗩᒪ & ᖇEᘉᗩISSᗩᘉᑕE TE᙭TS & STᑌᗺIES
Tempe, AZ
1997

**Library of Congress Cataloging-in-Publication Data**

Spenser, Edmund, 1552?–1599.
    [Amoretti]
    Edmund Spenser's Amoretti and Epithalamion: a critical edition
  / Kenneth J. Larsen.
    p.   cm. — (Medieval & Renaissance Texts & Studies ; v. 146)
    Includes bibliographical references and index.
    ISBN 0-86698-186-1 (alk. paper)
    1. Love poetry, English–Criticism, Textual.   2. Sonnets,
English–Criticism, Textual. 3. Marriage–Poetry. I. Larsen, Kenneth
J. II. Spenser, Edmund, 1552?–1599. Epithalamion. III. Title. IV.
Series.
PR2360.A5  1997
821'.3—dc21                            96-53914
                                                    CIP

∞

This book was produced by MRTS
at SUNY Binghamton.
This book is made to last.
It is set in Goudy,
smythe-sewn and printed on acid-free paper
to library specifications.

# Contents

My gratitude is due to Professor A. C. Hamilton for early encouragement and later enthusiasm; to my colleagues in the English Department, University of Auckland; to the staff of the Folger Shakespeare Library for much courtesy and patience; and finally to the fourth Elizabeth of this sequence, my wife, and to Daniel and Alexander, all of whom bore the brunt.

Formal acknowledgement is also made to the Master and Fellows of Trinity College Cambridge for their kind permission to reproduce Spenser's Amoretti, 1595: Capell * 18 f.G.3r.

# Abbreviations

EHR = *English Historical Review*
ELR = *English Literary Renaissance*
ELH = *English Literary History*
ES = *English Studies*
JEGP = *Journal of English and Germanic Philology*
JMRS = *Journal of Medieval and Renaissance Studies*
LCL = Loeb Classical Library, published by William Heinemann,
        London & Harvard Univ. Press
MLN = *Modern Language Notes*
MLQ = *Modern Language Quarterly*
MLR = *Modern Language Review*
MP = *Modern Philology*
N&Q = *Notes & Queries*
PQ = *Philological Quarterly*
RQ = *Renaissance Quarterly*
Ren. & Ref. = *Renaissance and Reformation*
RES = *Review of English Studies*
SEL = *Studies in English Literature*
SPh = *Studies in Philology*
SpS = *Spenser Studies*
TSLL = *Texas Studies in Literature and Language*
YES = *Yearbook of English Studies*

The framed device, inserted by Peter Short, the master printer, before both *Amoretti* and *Epithalamion* in the 1595 edition.

# Introduction

The volume containing Edmund Spenser's sonnet sequence and epithalamion was published in 1595 by William Ponsonby in London under the title,
"*Amoretti and Epithalamion. Written not long since* by Edmunde *Spenser.*" Of
the two larger works in the volume — it comprises a sequence of eighty-nine
sonnets, some short intervening anacreontic verses, and an epithalamium —
*Epithalamion* has customarily received the greater acknowledgement, although recent work on the sonnet sequence, *Amoretti*, by Dunlop, Johnson,
and Gibbs,[1] has gone some way towards redressing the balance. The discoveries presented in the following pages, concerning *Amoretti* in particular, are
exciting both for the insight they provide into Spenser's compositional
habits and for the way they present the sonnets in a more intimate light,
showing them to be expressive of a range of mood: frequently delicate and
tender, often daring, sometimes risqué.

Spenser's reputation was already secure prior to the publication of the
volume. Much of his poetry had already been published, although the
second installment of *The Faerie Queene* did not appear until the following
year, and only *Prothalamion* and the final two hymns of the *Fowre Hymnes*
are of probable later composition. Since this edition will show that the
sonnets comprising *Amoretti* were written for consecutive dates which fell
during the first half of 1594, the volume can only be the work of a mature
poet, whom an aside in *Amoretti*, "then al those fourty which my life
outwent,"[2] suggests was in his early forties.

---

[1] Alexander Dunlop, "Introduction to *Amoretti and Epithalamion,*" in William A. Oram
*et al.*, eds., *The Yale Edition of the Shorter Poems of Edmund Spenser* (New Haven: Yale
Univ. Press, 1989), 583–97; William C. Johnson, *Spenser's Amoretti: Analogies of Love*
(Lewisburg: Bucknell Univ. Press, 1990); Donna Gibbs, *Spenser's Amoretti. A Critical Study*
(Aldershot, Hants.: Scolar Press, 1990).

[2] *Am.* 60.8. For Spenser's works, apart from *Amoretti and Epithalamion*, the text
throughout is *Spenser, Poetical Works*, eds. J. C. Smith and E. de Selincourt (Oxford:
Oxford Univ. Press, 1969). *Amoretti*, requiring a singular verb, has been used as a title of

In writing a sonnet sequence Spenser was observing a Renaissance convention which had grown popular in England during the prior decade. Thomas Watson's *Hecatompathia* had appeared in 1582 and had been followed by among others John Southern's *Pandora* (1584), Samuel Daniel's *Delia* (1592), Barnabe Barnes's *Parthenophil and Parthenophe* (1593), Thomas Lodge's *Phillis* (1593), Giles Fletcher the Elder's *Licia* (1593), Michael Drayton's *Ideas Mirrour* (1594), Henry Constable's *Diana* (1594), and William Percy's *Coelia* (1594), while the anonymous *Zepheria* had also appeared in 1594 and Spenser, in *Amoretti* 8, shows some knowledge of Fulke Greville's *Caelica* 3, even though *Caelica* was published later.

Petrarch's *Rime* had established the mode in which poems employ a number of what were to become conventional *topoi*, all of which in their discrete way explain the poet's difficulties in the face of various facets of love. In *Amoretti* Spenser often uses the established *topoi*, for his sequence imitates in its own way the traditions of Petrarchan courtship and its associated Neo-Platonic conceits. His debt to Petrarchist *exempla* and to the unifying tendencies of continental philosophies is always clear. Yet suggestions of his continental predecessors, Tasso, Ariosto, du Bellay, Desportes, Marot, Cazza, and Serafino, would have been more evident in *Amoretti* to his contemporaries than they are to the modern reader. Spenser seldom imbues a sonnet with a clear Neo-Platonic cast (*Amoretti* 45 and 88 are possible exceptions) and generally accepts Neo-Platonic doctrines as conceits to be exploited. His essentially syncretic cast of mind shapes these conceits as non-specific rather than explicit imitations.

*Epithalamion* is a poem which gives a ritualized and public effect to the personal on a number of levels, cosmographical, mythological, publicly prayerful and euchological. As arguably the first epithalamium in English it set a precedent; its sources are principally classical, for Spenser imitates the detail of the epithalamia of Statius and Claudian as well as the epithalamial hymns of Catullus. It also shows a familiarity with the epithalamia of Spenser's immediate French predecessors, Marc-Claude Buttet and Rémy Belleau. But Spenser, who married Elizabeth Boyle on 11 June 1594,[3] moves apart from his predecessors by proposing in *Epithalamion* that a resolution to the sonneteer's conventional preoccupations with love may be found within the bounds of Christian marriage. The poem's recognition that the tension which had occurred in earlier *amoretti* between the physical and spiritual dimensions of love can be solved in matrimony is an argument for

---

the whole sequence, while *amoretti* has been used to describe the sonnets as individual units, but always in the plural.

[3] For the date of Spenser's marriage, see A. C. Judson, *The Life of Edmund Spenser* (Baltimore, 1945), 166.

the volume as a whole to be considered an integrated work. It also affords the work a strong Protestant character, because it reflects the doctrine that Spenser's Protestant contemporaries were developing, that the covenant of marriage, itself of the spiritual realm, was sealed and made manifest by physical consummation. It is to this doctrine that the later *amoretti* and the *Epithalamion* constantly return.

William Ponsonby, the volume's publisher, in his "Epistle Dedicatory" describes the *amoretti* as "sweete conceited Sonets," an appellation not unlike that ascribed to Shakespeare's sonnets by Meres, "sugred Sonnets." Shakespeare's sonnets have subsequently been seen with all their diversity and riches to have loosed themselves from the description. In this edition, it is hoped, Spenser's will be similarly delivered through the discovery that the eighty-nine sonnets are shaped as an artifact modeled after the liturgy. The detail provided by this edition's annotations confirms not only the importance of structure to the Renaissance sonnet sequence in general and the English in particular, but also the multi-faceted — and not exclusively poetic — nature of those structures. The findings also lay the groundwork for further understandings of Spenser's poetry: his wit is revealed in the following pages as one of elegant erudition, which enjoyed those etymological and scriptural puns and pleonasms most becoming of an educated Renaissance mind.

## I. Sources

### A. Liturgical

The eighty-nine sonnets of the *Amoretti*, as numbered in the 1595 octavo edition, were written to correspond with consecutive dates, beginning on Wednesday 23 January 1594 and running, with one interval, through to Friday 17 May 1594: they correspond with the daily and sequential order of scriptural readings that are prescribed for those dates by the liturgical calendar of the Church of England. Their conceits, themes, ideas, imagery, words, and sometimes their rhetorical structure consistently and successively match like particulars in these daily readings. Consequently the final structure of *Amoretti and Epithalamion* has been shaped by Spenser as a liturgico-poetic artifact.[4]

The generally accepted date of Spenser's marriage to Elizabeth Boyle on 11 June 1594, the feast of St. Barnabas, implies a final date for the comple-

---

[4] Anne Lake Prescott, in "The Thirsty Deer and the Lord of Life: Some Contexts for *Amoretti* 67–70," *SpS* 6 (1985): 58, has suggested that the presenting of calendrico-poetic sequences as gifts to women was not without precedent and cites as earlier examples du Bellay's *Olive* with its early Nativity poem and late Good Friday poem, and Giles Fletcher's *Licia* with its fifty-two sonnets and its 366 'days.'

tion of the work and suggests that the volume's inscription, *"Written not long since,"* should be accepted as factual. It is reasonable to assume that the volume's manuscript had been forwarded to England from Ireland on the same ship as Sir Robert Needham, who had departed for England on 25 September 1594; in his dedicatory letter to Needham, William Ponsonby, the volume's publisher, alludes to the manuscript "crossing the Seas in your happy companye." The volume was entered in the Stationers' Register on 15 November 1594.

Within the sequence the forty-six sonnets between *Amoretti* 22, with its reference to Ash Wednesday, the beginning of Lent ("This holy season fit to fast and pray"), and *Amoretti* 68, which celebrates Easter Sunday ("Most glorious Lord of lyfe that on this day, / Didst make thy triumph ouer death and sin"), suggest themselves as sonnets corresponding to the forty-six Lenten days which intervene between the two days. Dunlop, and particularly Johnson,[5] have already proposed that the key to locating the year with which the sequence corresponds lies with another sonnet within the forty-six, *Amoretti* 62, in which Spenser refers to the beginning of the year, "The weary yeare his race now hauing run, / The new begins his compast course anew." Since *Amoretti* 68, six sonnets later, is the Easter sonnet, then any year with which the sequence might correspond needs to be a year when Easter Day fell on 31 March, six days after 25 March, the beginning of the ecclesiastical year according to the old style calendar.[6] 1594—the year of Spenser's marriage and of the registration of the work—was the only year close to the time of composition when this occurred.[7] The *amoretti*, evidently, were written for the period leading up to Spenser's marriage on 11 June 1594, including the season of Lent. Moreover, if *Amoretti* 22 was written for 13 February 1594, the date on which Ash Wednesday fell in 1594, then *Amoretti* 23 might be ascribed to the Thursday following Ash Wednesday, 14 February 1594, *Amoretti* 24 to Friday 15 February 1594, and so on until *Amoretti* 68, Easter Sunday, 31 March 1594. Likewise, the

---

[5] Alexander Dunlop, "Calendar Symbolism in the *Amoretti*," *N & Q* 214 (1969): 24–26, and William C. Johnson, "Spenser's *Amoretti* and the Art of the Liturgy," *SEL* 14 (1974): 47–61.

[6] *Book of Common Prayer* (London, 1572), Ciii^v, "Note that the supputation of the yeere of our Lorde, in the Churche of Englande, beginneth the .xxv. day of Marche, the same day supposed to be the first day vpon whiche the worlde was created, and the day when Christe was conceyued in the wombe of the virgine Marie."

[7] The only other year when Easter Sunday fell on 31 March during Spenser's life was 1583. But the sequence's references to the already composed "six books" of *The Faerie Queene* (*Am.* 80.2) and to Elizabeth his betrothed (*Am.* 74.9–12) discount 1583 as a year of possible composition.

sonnets preceding *Amoretti* 22 might be ascribed earlier consecutive dates, and those following *Amoretti* 68 subsequent consecutive dates.

Johnson also proposed that each seventh sonnet, beginning with *Amoretti* 26 (Am. 26, 33, 40, 47, 54, 61) and concluding with *Amoretti* 68, corresponds with a Lenten Sunday and found parallels between the Epistles and Gospels of these days and corresponding sonnets. Sometimes he is correct; for example, he rightly sees the light motif in *Amoretti* 40, which coincides with the Third Sunday of Lent, 3 March in 1594, as echoing the day's Epistle, Ephesians 5.1–15. Sometimes his proposed connections are more tenuous; for example, he sees a parallel between the Collect of the Fifth Sunday of Lent, "We beseech thee almighty God, mercifully to *look vpon thy people*," and the opening of *Amoretti* 54, "Of this worlds Theatre in which we stay, / My loue lyke the Spectator ydly sits." The connection is slight, particularly since it is of the nature of nearly all Collects to ask God to "*look vpon thy people*." Furthermore, Johnson's claim that the Sunday sonnets differ from the weekday sonnets, and are marked by a respite from the poet's weekday troubles, is not borne out by close scrutiny.

Such calendrical and liturgical proposals are, however, totally dependent on the coincidence in 1594 of 25 March being the beginning of the ecclesiastical year and occurring some six days before Easter Sunday. Linking the *amoretti* to the Sundays' Epistles and Gospels, as Johnson proposed, is likewise dependent upon the same coincidence because the Sundays and feasts of the liturgical year are not secured to a particular date. The date of 25 March as the beginning of the ecclesiastical year was, in fact, contested by Bennett and Kaske.[8] However, the key to establishing definitely the year and days for which the sonnets were composed lies with other series of scripture readings that were appointed to be read on the days of 1594 by the *Book of Common Prayer*.

The calendar of the *Book of Common Prayer* appointed for each day a series of readings and psalms, the combination of which provided each year with its own distinctive interlocking grid of readings. The grid comprised

---

[8] Josephine Waters Bennett, "Spenser's *Amoretti LXII* and the Date of the New Year," *RQ* 26 (1973): 433–36, and Carol V. Kaske, "Spenser's *Amoretti and Epithalamion* of 1595: Structure, Genre, Numerology," *ELR* 8 (1978): 294: "March 25 does not begin the liturgical year, as Dunlop asserts; the first Sunday in Advent does." In rebuttal see substantive evidence adduced by A. Kent Hieatt, "A Numerical Key to Spenser's *Amoretti* and Guyon in the House of Mammon," *YES* 3 (1973): 19, where he cites a number of authorities: Reginald Lane Poole, *Medieval Reckoning of Time* (London, 1921), and "The Beginning of the Year in the Middle Ages," *Proceedings of the British Academy* 10 (1921): 113–37; A. F. Pollard, "New Year's Day and Leap Year in English History," *EHR* 55 (1940): 177–93; Christopher R. Cheney, *Handbook of Dates for Students of English History* (London, 1945).

three cycles. The *ferial* cycle was the basic cycle: it followed the calendar year beginning on 1 January and provided lessons at morning and evening prayer. It also provided each office with its proper psalms: the psalter was divided up so that the 150 psalms were read consecutively throughout a monthly cycle of thirty days, each day being appointed its proper psalms at both morning and evening prayer, with further rules governing the unequal length of months.[9] (There were special proper psalms for both Easter Sunday and Ascension Thursday.) The *temporal* cycle followed the church's liturgical seasons, Advent, Christmas, Epiphany, Lent, Easter, Pentecost, and Time after Trinity. The major liturgical feasts of the *temporal* cycle had both an Epistle and a Gospel for the Communion Service and special lessons at morning and evening prayer, which took precedence over those provided by the *ferial* cycle. The ordinary Sundays of the *temporal* cycle had their own Epistle and Gospel, but took their lessons at morning and evening prayer from the *ferial* cycle. The third cycle, the *festive*, comprised those feast days, such as the Conversion of St. Paul (25 January) or the Annunciation (25 March), which were not attached to the church's liturgical seasons and which fell on the same date each year. These feast days had their own Epistle and Gospel and generally, but not always, special lessons at morning and evening prayer, which also took precedence over the *ferial* lessons. Whenever they had no special lessons of their own, they took their lessons from the *ferial* cycle.

The scriptural selections used on a particular day could, therefore, derive from several sources: from the Epistle or Gospel if a day were a Sunday or feast day, from a day's proper psalms and from its two lessons at morning prayer and two lessons at evening prayer. In fact, Spenser, though infrequently making his sonnet correspond to a day's first lesson at either morning or evening prayer, which were always Old Testament readings, has usually matched them either with the daily psalms or the New Testament readings, whether they be the Epistle—on all but two occasions a New

---

[9] *The booke of Common prayer* (London, 1578), aii: "And because Ianuarie and March hathe one daye aboue the said number, and Februarie which is placed betwene them bothe, hathe only .xxviii. dayes: Februarie shal borrowe of either of the monthes (of Ianuarie and March) one daye. And so the Psalter which shalbe read in Februarie, must begin the last daye of Ianuarie, and ende the first daye of March. And whereas May, Iuly, August, October, and December, have .xxxi. dayes apiece: it is ordered that the same Psalmes shalbe read the last daye of the said Monthes which were read the daye before." Such a complicated system sometimes lead to slight mistakes. The psalms prescribed in the calendar preceding the 1572 Bishops' Bible, for example, mistakenly observed the rule laid down for all months other than January, and appointed a repeated Day 30 to 31 January, and Spenser, as I show later, has apparently followed this mistake. The 1572 calendar did, however, give 1 February its correct Day 2.

Testament reading—or the Gospel from the Communion Service, or the second lesson at morning or evening prayer.

For the *ferial* cycle these second lessons were always a chapter from the New Testament, which ran continuously throughout the year and fell on the same date each year. The second lesson at morning prayer on 2 January was Matthew, Chapter 1, on 3 January was Matthew 2, on 4 January was Matthew 3, and so on, until all four Gospels and the Acts of the Apostles were exhausted. Matthew started again with Chapter 1 on 3 May and a third series started on 31 August. Similarly, the chapters of the New Testament Epistles comprised the daily readings for the second lesson at evening prayer. It is the dovetailing of the daily psalms and lessons from the *ferial* cycle with the further readings from the *temporal* and *festive* cycles which provides each year with its individual pattern of readings. Obviously the Epistle and Gospel for a particular Sunday or feast day are the same whatever the year, but the proper psalms and second lessons at morning or evening prayer for a Sunday depend on the date upon which the Sunday falls. Psalms 9–11 and Luke 14 will be read on the Third Sunday in Lent and will be associated with the Sunday's Epistle, Ephesians 5.1–15, only in 1594, because only in 1594 does the Third Sunday in Lent fall on 10 March for which date they are the proper psalms and the second lesson at morning prayer. It is this arrangement of prescribed lessons and psalms at morning and evening prayer for the year 1594, together with the Epistles and Gospels of the Sundays and feast days, which provides consecutive topical and imagistic correspondences for nearly all the *amoretti* and confirms 1594 as the year for which they were composed. (A table of the scripture readings and lessons prescribed by the *Book of Common Prayer* for the period in 1594 with which the sonnets correspond is given in the Appendix.)

The sonnets preceding *Amoretti* 22, the Ash Wednesday sonnet, begin with *Amoretti* 1 for Wednesday 23 January 1594, the beginning of Hilary Term,[10] whose name can be discerned in the sonnet's threefold repetition of its opening "Happy," and whose phrase, "hands ... shall handle," echoes closely 23 January's evening prayer Psalm 115.7, "They haue handes and handle not."[11] *Amoretti* 3 corresponds to 25 January, the feast of the

---

[10] *The booke of Common prayer* (1578), aiii: "Hillarie Terme beginneth the .xxiii. or .xxiv. day of Ianuari [sic], and endeth the .xii. or .xiii. day of Februarie." Spenser, who in 1594 sat in the County of Cork as a Justice of the Queen, would have been conscious of the dates of the Terms.

[11] There exists another, slightly halting, version of *Am.* 1 (cf. Israel Gollancz, "Spenseriana," *Proceedings of the British Academy* [1907–8]: 99–102). The correspondence between the day's psalm verse and *Am.* 1, however, disallows the claim, asserted by Gollancz with hesitant support from Judson, that the variants between the two versions are

Conversion of St. Paul, and subsequent sonnets coincide with the weeks of Septuagesima, Sexagesima and Quinquagesima, the Sundays preceding Ash Wednesday, with which *Amoretti* 5, 12, and 19 correspond and whose dates in 1594 were 28 January, 3 February and 10 February. The first twenty-one sonnets can thus be awarded the twenty-one days of Hilary Term, whose conclusion, Tuesday 12 February, fitted exactly in 1594 with the beginning of Lent, Wednesday 13 February. The sonnets reflect either the daily psalms or the scriptural readings of the second lessons at morning or evening prayer of the *ferial* cycle, although, when a Sunday or midweek feast day occurs, Spenser often reflects its Epistle or Gospel in his corresponding sonnet.[12]

---

probably sufficient to confirm that the mauscript is an earlier version of *Am.* 1. The version is certainly not an autograph of *Am.* 1, as Gollancz asserts, see A. Judson, "*Amoretti*, Sonnet I," *MLN* 58 (1943): 548–50.

[12] *Amoretti* contains a number of initially incompatible references to the calendar year or to seasonal occurences. *Am.* 4 makes reference to the "New yeare." *Am.* 19 refers to spring as does *Am.* 70. *Am.* 62 is concerned with the new year and *Am.* 23 and 60 with the year past. Finally *Am.* 76 refers to May. All these references can be reconciled, in the cases of *Am.* 19 and 70 the solutions being neat.

*Am.* 4 opens, "New yeare forth looking out of Ianus gate," a line that implies on first reading the beginning of the year. Yet the sonnet could as equally celebrate the month of January as the beginning of January and its phrase "his passed date" (3), if it is a reference back to "New Yeare" (1), is a temporal referent looking back to 1 January. In fact details of the sonnet correspond to the 26 January's second lesson at evening prayer, 1 Cor. 7, in a way that brings out one of the most delightful jokes in all the *amoretti.*

*Am.* 19's opening reference to spring, "The merry Cuckow, messenger of Spring, / His trompet shrill hath thrise already sounded," observes the *Book of Common Prayer*'s calendar in an unmistakable manner. In most sixteenth century editions of the *Book of Common Prayer* a series of footnotes is appended to the calendar; attached to 8 February is the footnote: "As vpon this day, the Romanes began their spring, after Plinie." Spenser has observed the calendar's instruction and included it in the sonnet he has written for the subsequent third day. On 10 February the cuckoo has already thrice sounded the coming of spring (the sonnet also reflects other scriptural features causing it to celebrate a subsequent third day).

*Am.* 62 commemorates the beginning of the new year on 25 March. But in contrasting the old and new year it has also observed the day's scriptural and liturgical *topos* of the Monday before Easter, because the day's Epistle, Isa. 63, which was read on 25 March only in 1594, celebrated the old year past and the new year to come, Isaiah proclaiming, "the yere of my redemed is come" (v. 4), and continuing to contrast the "olde time" with the present days. Nor do the allusions to the past year in *Am.* 23, "and with one word my whole years work doth rend" (12), and in *Am.* 60, need be reconciled or construed literally, for they merely state that Spenser's love, not the *amoretti*, has now run the course of a year: "So since the winged God his planet cleare, / began in me to moue, one yeare is spent." *Am.* 70's opening, "Fresh spring the herald of loues mighty king," is an appropriate conceit for 2 April 1594, on which date was celebrated the feast of the Annunciation, transposed from 25 March, as well as Easter Tuesday, both of which in differing ways celebrate the rising of a new nature and birth to new life. The sonnet's theme of *carpe diem* matches precisely the special lessons prescribed for the Annunciation. The day was also the first available in April on which to commemorate spring's coming, because 1 April, being Easter Monday, required another type of sonnet. Lastly, the tem-

The sequence of correspondences continues to run with minor exceptions through the weeks of Lent, through the days of Easter Week, arriving
finally at Low Sunday, in 1594, Sunday 7 April.[13] However, *Amoretti* 75,

---

poral reference in *Am.* 76, "like early fruit in May," a departure from Tasso's "Nel dolce
april," has been made to make the sonnet specifically correspond to a date in early May.

[13] Within the sequence two small groups of *amoretti* are not related to a day's psalms
or scriptures readings, which suggests Spenser's absence from home and customary
scriptural resources. (Such absence is impossible to confirm, the only two pieces of biographical data available for 1594 being the days 23 May and 16 September, when Spenser
was sitting at Mallow as Justice of the Queen for the country of Cork, and neither date
falls within the compass of the *amoretti* [Henry F. Berry, "The English Settlement in
Mallow," *Journal of the Cork Historical and Archaeological Society* 2nd Series, 12 (1906): 2].
Most bibles, particularly the frequent large folio editions, were not meant to be carried
around.)

*Am.* 28–33, the first group, bear no resemblance to the coincident scripture readings
for the days, Tuesday 19 February to Sunday 24 February. Instead, Spenser has written a
series of sonnets which are broadly reminiscent of continental *exempla*, which suggests that,
having no Bible to consult, he composed a range of sonnets which work standard Petrarchist conceits in unspecific ways: *Am.* 30 works the ice/fire *topos*, *Am.* 28, the "laurell," *Am.*
29, the "bay," while *Am.* 32 opens, "The payneful smith." In *Am.* 33, Spenser apologizes
to his friend, Ludowick Bryskett, for not having finished *The Faerie Queene*, but the sonnet's autobiographical realism suggests the possible companionship and hospitality of Bryskett and infers Spenser's temporary absence from home and Bible during the preceding days.

Friday 15 March and Saturday 16 March is a further period when sonnets are not
related to a scriptural source. *Am.* 53 is constructed around the image of the "Panther."
*Am.* 52 makes absence explicit: its lines, "from presence of my dearest deare exylde," and
"So I her absens will my penaunce make," suggest separation and travel.

Three further sonnets also seem initially to lack a relationship with a corresponding
day's scriptural readings, although close examination reveals their resemblances. *Am.* 2
bears no relationship with Matt. 22, the second lesson at morning prayer for Thursday 24
January, with which *Am.* 2 corresponds. It does, however, exhibit particularly striking
correspondences with Matt. 23, which suggests that Spenser has mistakenly read the wrong
chapter. His confusion may be explained by one of the few errors in the *Book of Common
Prayer* calendar, because the entry which should read Matt. 23 was frequently absent, being
replaced by Matt. 13.

A like case occurs with *Am.* 9, the elements of whose *expeditio* exactly imitate the
detail of Pss. 147 and 148. These psalms were not correctly psalms read at evening prayer
for Thursday 31 January with which the sonnet corresponds. Since, however, the calendar
of the *Book of Common Prayer* sometimes, erroneously, prescribed for 31 January a repetition of the psalms for Day 30 (Pss. 144–46 and 147–50), the prescription for all other
months of 31 days, Spenser has apparently either made a mistake or followed a mistaken
calendar.

*Am.* 8 poses a peculiar problem because what appear to be three (and part of a fourth)
earlier versions of it exist in manuscript. Its first three lines are virtually identical to the
first three of Fulke Greville's *Caelica* 3, while its Surreyan form distinguishes it from all
other sonnets in the sequence. Yet the revisions to the prior versions that Spenser has
made for the final published version locate it firmly within the grid of daily scriptural
correspondences. The beginning of the final couplet, for example, which in all manuscript
versions had been variable and never satisfactorily rendered, has been newly cast as, "Dark
is the world." The recasting enables the sonnet to correspond with the detail provided by

the sonnet for Low Sunday, is the last day of the run of sonnets that can be ascribed a definite correspondence. The remaining sonnets, *Amoretti* 76–89, betray no verbal or topical correspondences with any of the proper psalms or second lessons for the days immediately subsequent to Low Sunday, or the Epistles or Gospels for the following Sundays.

Evidently Spenser's early intention was to bring the sequence of sonnets to a conclusion with *Amoretti* 75. His intention to observe a liturgical framework in the sequence would have been nicely rounded off with a sonnet that corresponds with the Sunday which brings the Easter festivities to completion. Low Sunday, the octave of Easter Sunday, eight days after the feast, known also as *Dominica in albis* [*depositis*], technically concludes the Easter ceremonies and celebrates the neophytes finally discarding the white garments in which they had been baptized at Easter. *Amoretti* 75 reflects the baptismal associations of the day with its *topoi* of water, washing, naming and eternal life, and acknowledges that the lady's name will be inscribed immortally in the heavens through the poet's verses, "you shall liue by fame: / my verse your vertues rare shall eternize, / and in the heuens wryte your glorious name" (10–12). The poet's concluding intent is intertwined in the sonnet with the strongest echoes in the sequence of the concluding lines to Ovid's *Metamorphoses* (15.871–79), in which Ovid prophetically intimates the gaining of his own immortality through verse. (An allusion to Ovid's lines is also used as the emblem with which E. K. brings *The Shepheardes Calendar* to conclusion.) Spenser's claim that the lady "shall liue by fame" eternally (9) imitates Ovid's identical claim, "perque omnia saecula fama . . . vivam"—even if the earthly body is subject to death. As the lady's name will not be "wyped out" (8), nor can Ovid's, for it is indelible, "nomenque erit indelibile nostrum." Both names will be written eternally in the heavens "super alta perennis astra"; finally Spenser's concluding couplet, "whenas death shall all the world subdew," is a direct rendering of Ovid's "domitis terris" (= the subdued world).

The Ovidian echoes confirm that Spenser was here imitating the *locus classicus* of poetic conclusions and his final lines asserting that the betrothed will finally enjoy a marriage in heaven ("and later life renew" [14]) is an appropriate conclusion for a period of betrothal in which marriage is seen as persisting in the world to come.

However, Spenser changed his mind and decided to append another fourteen sonnets to his sequence after *Amoretti* 75. He began composing sonnets again for the days subsequent to 3 May and leading up to the Vigil

---

Matt. 27, the second lesson at morning prayer for Wednesday 30 January, the account of the crucifixion when there was "darkenes ouer all the land" (v. 45).

of Pentecost, 19 May. He was moved to do this partly because 3 May stands
out in the liturgical calendar as a fresh beginning: on that day a new cycle
of second lessons at morning prayer commences with Matthew 1. It is a
characteristic of these later sonnets that their indebtedness to the days'
readings is more pronounced than in the preceding section of *Amoretti*.
*Amoretti* 76 exhibits oblique references to the Annunciation of Matthew 1
("the sacred harbour of that heuenly spright" [4]), and contains an apposite
temporal referent, "like early fruit in May"—a specific departure, already
noted by Lever,[14] from the original "Nel dolce april" of Tasso's "Non son
sì belli i fiori onde natura." The two weeks following Friday 3 May contain
the feast of the Ascension, Thursday 9 May 1594, when the scriptures
recount Christ was "lifted vp on high." *Amoretti* 82, written for the feast,
is loaded with allusions to the Ascension, including an appropriate final
couplet: "Whose lofty argument vplifting me, / shall lift you vp vnto an
high degree." Likewise the Sunday between the Ascension and Pentecost,
Sunday 12 May, through its second lesson at morning prayer, Romans 11,
which contains the principal scriptural account of the doctrine of election,
is characterized in 1594 by its celebration of 'election.' *Amoretti* 84, which
corresponds with the Sunday, concludes, "Onely behold her rare perfection,
/ and blesse your fortunes fayre election," one of only two occasions when
Spenser uses the word and the only time in *Amoretti*.

The final three sonnets of *Amoretti*, 87–89, are marked by their sense of
absence, their comfortlessness, and their "expectation." *Amoretti* 87 opens
its sestet with the line, "Thus I the time with expectation spend." *Amoretti*
88 opens with a reference to comfort and light, "Since I haue lackt the
comfort of that light," and *Amoretti* 89 opens with the simile of the dove,
"Lyke as the Culuer," which it later repeats, and also contains a reference
to comfort. The references can be read as liturgical and as alluding to
'Expectation Week,' which are those days between Ascension and Whit
Sunday, when the disciples were in earnest expectation of the Comforter,[15] while the repeated allusions to "comfort" anticipate the coming of
the Comforter as light at Pentecost, and the dove is the bird associated with
the Holy Spirit. These liturgical cues confirm that the three concluding
*Amoretti* 87, 88, and 89 correspond respectively to Wednesday 15, Thursday
16, and Friday 17 May, the days immediately preceding the Vigil of Pentecost, which in 1594 fell on Sunday 19 May. Furthermore the days immedi-

---

[14] J. W. Lever, *The Elizabethan Love Sonnet* (London: Methuen, 1956), 110.

[15] Anthony Sparrow, *A Rationale upon the Book of Common Prayer* (London, 1655), 170,
"This is called *Expectation-week*; for now the Apostles were earnestly expecting the fulfilling of that promise of our Lord, *If I go away, I will send the Comforter to you*, S. John
16.7."

ately prior to Ascension Thursday are Rogation Days, beginning with
Rogation Sunday 5 May, and continuing through Rogation Monday,
Tuesday, and Wednesday. As the next series of penitential days after Lent,
their celebration would have confirmed Spenser in his resolve to write these
added fourteen sonnets.[16]

In appending the extra sonnets Spenser had the overall structure of the
*Amoretti* in mind. The restructuring that ensued by the inclusion of a
further fourteen sonnets makes, for example, *Amoretti* 45, the mirror sonnet,
the middle sonnet of the sequence. As well, as Dunlop and Fowler have
pointed out,[17] the twenty-one sonnets that precede the Ash Wednesday
sonnet, *Amoretti* 22, which introduces the sonnets of the Lenten period, are
now matched by a further twenty-one sonnets after *Amoretti* 68, the Easter
Sunday sonnet which concludes Lent. Such uniformity and matching detail
clearly appealed to Spenser's mind which would have delighted in the
precision attained.

The extra sonnets also cause the sequence to move closer to the euchological design that Spenser ultimately intended for it. The final three
*amoretti* acknowledge both the poet's darkness and his hope. The betrotheds' awaiting parallels the Christian awaiting of the Holy Spirit who comes
at Pentecost not only to comfort and provide light, but also to seal the
covenant founded by Christ at the Easter triduum. The way the fourteen

---

[16] The fourteen additional sonnets contain a further small group of sonnets, *Am.* 80–
83, which reveal no relationship with the corresponding daily scripture readings for
Tuesday 7 May to Saturday 11 May. *Am.* 80 is an autobiographical sonnet; *Am.* 81 is a
translation from Tasso; *Am.* 82 is the sonnet for the Ascension and *Am.* 83 is a repetition
of *Am.* 35. That Spenser may not have had the scriptures available to him is confirmed by
a peculiar feature of *Am.* 82. The sonnet corresponds to the detail not of the ascension
account in the feast's Epistle, Acts 1.1–12, nor of the account in its Gospel, Mark 16.14–
20, but extensively to that found in the scripture's third ascension account, Luke 24.49–
53, not a reading for the day, but an account which Spenser seemingly has recalled from
memory. On such occasions, when the scriptures may not have been available to him,
Spenser seems to have felt inclined to revert to autobiography, *Am.* 33 and 80 being cases
in point.

The appended sonnets also contain one small *lacuna*. Friday 10 May and Saturday 11
May lack a corresponding sonnet. *Am.* 82 is quite clearly written for Ascension Thursday
9 May; *Am.* 84's theme of election equally corresponds to the Sunday after the Ascension,
Sunday 12 May. But the two intervening days have only *Am.* 83, a repetition of *Am.* 35.
This is the only instance in the entire sequence where a day lacks a corresponding sonnet,
and it coincides with the only occasion in the sequence when Spenser repeats a sonnet,
although what conclusions are to be drawn from the *lacuna* and duplication remain
unclear.

[17] Alastair Fowler, *Triumphal Forms. Structural Patterns in Elizabeth Poetry*, (Cambridge:
Cambridge Univ. Press, 1970) 180–83; Dunlop (1969), 24–26 and "The Unity of Spenser's
*Amoretti*," in Alastair Fowler, ed., *Silent Poetry* (London: Routledge and Kegan Paul, 1970),
153–69.

appended sonnets thus reshape the *Amoretti*, as well as prepare the way for *Epithalamion*, are explained later in the introduction.

The extensive correspondences between the sonnets and the daily scripture readings and psalms indicate that Spenser observed the widely recommended devotional practice of privately reading the *Book of Common Prayer*'s daily offices. The Prologue to the Bible exhorted that "when ye be at home in your houses, ye apply your selues from tyme to tyme to the readyng of holy scriptures," while the preface to the *Book of Common Prayer* advised "menne" without distinction to "saye Morning and Evening prayre priuatelie," but bound only priests and deacons, laying down that "al Priests and Decons shall be bounde to saye dailie the Morning and Evening prayre, either priuatelie or openlie."[18] That Spenser was familiar with daily offices is corroborated by a small piece of biographical evidence. William Ponsonby, in his preface to the 1591 edition of Spenser's *Complaints,* included an advertisement for further unpublished work of Spenser including "*The howers of the Lord.*"[19] The allusion can only refer to the popular devotional manuals, the primers, that were a feature of pre-reformation spirituality, and which continued to be published throughout the sixteenth century.[20] Ponsonby confirms that he intends such a *Book of Hours* by linking it to "*The seuen Psalmes,*" the seven penitential psalms, which were customarily

---

[18] Protestant devotional manuals went as far as they could without naming the *Book of Common Prayer* in advising its methodical approach to reading and praying. Robert Cleaver (*A Godlie Forme of Householde Gouernment* [London, 1592], 47) counsels that the duty of the householder to the members of his house lies in "acquainting them with the Scriptures, by reading them dayly in thy house, in their hearing, and directing them to marke, and make vse of those things which are plaine and easie, according to their capacitie." Such admonitions were widespread as were the prescriptions to read the scriptures in an orderly fashion; George Webb (*A Garden of spirituall Flowers* [London, 1610], sig. G3ᵛ) advises

> In reading of the Scriptures, read not heere, and there a Chapter, (except vpon some good occasion) but the Bible in order throughout, and that as oft as thou canst, that so by litle and litle, thou mayest be acquainted with the whole course and Historie of the Bible.

[19] *Poetical Works,* 470: "To which effect I vnderstand that he besides wrote sundrie others, namelie *Ecclesiastes,* and *Canticum canticorum* translated, *A senights slumber, The hell of louers, his Purgatorie,* being all dedicated to ladies; so as it may seeme he ment them al to one volume. Besides some other Pamphlets looselie scattered abroad: as *The dying Pellican, The howers of the Lord, The sacrifice of a sinner, The seuen Psalmes, &c.* which when I can either by himselfe, or otherwise attaine too, I meane likewise for your fauour sake to set foorth."

[20] While the principal *Book of Hours* was of the Blessed Virgin, there were also, "Hours of the Passion of our Lord" and "Hours of the Holy Cross," a translation of which can be found in Richard Crashaw's 1648 edition of *Steps to the Temple.*

attached to the *Horae*.[21] He thereby indicates that Spenser had, by 1591, already translated a Book of Hours, which suggests Spenser's familiarity with the liturgical practice of daily scripture readings, especially those intended for private rather than communal use.[22]

For his reading Spenser has in the first instance used a Geneva version of the Bible and in the second the psalms from the *Book of Common Prayer*.[23] Many of the Bibles available to him, whatever their provenance, would have contained the *Book of Common Prayer*'s calendar, if not the whole of the *Book of Common Prayer* itself. As often as not, as in the 1572 second folio edition of the Bishops' version, and in the 1578 first large folio edition of the Geneva version, they also contained a two-version psalter which printed in black-letter and in a parallel column, "The translation vsed in common prayer," taken from the Great Bible.[24]

Whenever Spenser has established in his sonnet a correspondence with a day's second lesson, he has used the Geneva Bible in preference to the Great Bible or Bishops' Bible. *Amoretti 4*, for example, which addresses the lady, "Then you faire flowre, in whom fresh youth doth raine," is closer to the Geneva version's "if she passe the flowre of *her* age" (1 Corinthians

---

[21] A. W. Pollard and G. R. Redgrave, *A Short-Title Catalogue of Books Printed in England, Scotland, & Ireland and of English Books Printed Abroad. 1475–1640* (London: The Bibliographical Society, 1986), 2:73: "The main components, found in all Salisbury Hours up to 1534 and most of them thereafter, are: Hours of the BVM ... Seven Penitential Psalms." See also Edgar Hoskins, *Horae Beatae Mariae Virginis or Sarum and York Primers* (London, 1906), passim, and Helen White, *The Tudor Books of Private Devotion* (Madison: Univ. of Wisconsin Press, 1951), passim.

[22] Spenser's familiarity with the *cursus* of the Latin prayers, at least seven of which were also found in the *Horae*, is evidenced by his adoption of their latinate structure in *Am.* 68, the Easter Sunday sonnet.

[23] For Spenser's use of the Bible, see Grace Warren Landrum, "Spenser's Use of the Bible and his Alleged Puritanism," *PMLA* 41 (1926): 517–44, and Naseeb Shaheen, *Biblical References in The Faerie Queene* (Memphis: Memphis State Univ. Press, 1976), whose research suggested that Spenser had generally used the Geneva version of the Bible. See also Carol V. Kaske, "Bible," in A. C. Hamilton *et al.*, eds., *The Spenser Encyclopaedia* (Toronto: Univ. of Toronto Press, 1990), 87–89.

[24] Except where stated, the Bible used throughout is the original edition of the Geneva version, *The Bible and Holy Scriptures conteyned in the Olde and Newe Testament. ... Printed by Rouland Hall* (Geneva, 1560). Its use has been supplemented whenever necessary by references from the first large folio edition of the Geneva version, *The Bible. Translated according to the Ebrew and Greeke, and conferred with the best translations in divers languages. ... Whereunto is added the Psalter of the common translation agreeing with the booke of Common prayer. ... Imprinted at London by Christopher Barker* (London, 1578) particularly for quotations from the calendar attached to its "booke of Common prayer," and from the second folio edition of the Bishops' version, *The holie Bible. ... Imprinted at London ... by Richarde Iugge* (London, 1572) for its parallel printing of the Great Bible psalter. The psalms cited throughout are taken from *The Booke of Common Prayer ... Imprinted at London by Christopher Barker ...* (London, 1582).

7.36), than the rendering "yf she passe the time of marryage," which is found in both the Great Bible version and the Bishops' version. Likewise *Amoretti* 15's opening, "Ye tradefull Merchants ... / ... make your gain," bears a closer resemblance to the Geneva version's "For we are not as manie, whiche make marchandise of the worde of God," with its marginal entry, "That is, which preache for gaine," than the version in both the Great or Bishops' Bibles, "For we are not as many are, whiche chop and change with the woorde of God" (2 Corinthians 2.17). Similarly Paul's phrase, "therefore proue I the naturalnes of your loue" (2 Corinthians 8.8), is echoed in *Amoretti* 21's opening question, "Was it the work of nature or of art," in a way that both the Bishops' version's and the Great Bible version's "unfaignednesse of your loue" are not.

As well, Spenser has frequently had recourse to the particulars of the Geneva version's marginalia — a feature absent from the other bibles. *Amoretti* 5's conceit of eyes, "rash eies," and envy, "enuide," reflects the sidenote to Matthew 20.15, which glosses "Is thine eye euil," as, "or enuious;" *Amoretti* 10's "Tyrannesse" matches the sidenote to Mark 5.7, "to mainteine his tyrannie." *Amoretti* 44's classical *topos* of Orpheus and his companions, "those renoumed noble Peres of Greece ... continuall cruell ciuill warre," reflects the sidenote to Luke 18, the second lesson at morning prayer for Thursday 7 March, with which the sonnet corresponds: Luke 18.17, an exhortation "not to waxe fainte" has attached to it the sidenote, "The Greke worde signifieth, not to shrinke backe as cowards do in warre."

Two further characteristics of the Geneva Bible and its detail are reflected in the sequence in an unmistakable way. *Amoretti* 19's third announcement of spring, "The merry Cuckow, messenger of Spring, / His trompet shrill hath thrise already sounded," observes the footnote to the calendar of the Geneva version only — it is not found in those of the Great Bible or Bishops' Bible — "As vpon this day, the Romanes began their spring, after Plinie."[25]

Another feature of the Geneva version's marginalia is peculiarly reflected in *Amoretti* 58, which bears a superscription, unique in the sequence, *By her that is most assured to her selfe*. Its existence is explained by the format of the Geneva Bible marginalia. The second lesson at evening prayer for Thursday 21 March, with which *Amoretti* 58 corresponds, 1 Timothy 5, has above it in most Geneva Bibles part of a sidenote, which is attached to the last verse of Chapter 4, but which, to avoid its extending down beyond the end of Chapter 4, has been run across the top of Chapter 5 in a one-line extension. The line appears as a short superscription above Chapter 5 in dif-

---

[25] *The booke of Common prayer* (1578), sig. aiiii.

ferent lettering, running, "*which is an assurance of thy salvation.*" Spenser's inscription visually mirrors the Geneva Bible's own apparent inscription. Where differences occur between the Geneva Bible, the Great Bible, and the Bishops' Bible, all evidence supports the contention that Spenser used the Geneva version whenever establishing correspondences with the daily lessons.

Whenever Spenser has had recourse to a day's proper psalms, however, it is clear that he has read Coverdale's Great Bible psalter, which the *Book of Common Prayer* customarily printed. *Amoretti* 1's "hands ... shall handle" is closer to the Great Bible's "They haue handes and handle not," than to the Geneva version's "Thei haue hands and touche not." The opening to *Amoretti* 12, "One day," parallels the opening to the Great Bible, Psalm 19, "One day," rather than the Geneva Bible, "Daie vnto daie," and its conclusion, the technical use of complaint, "I doo complaine," corresponds to the Great Bible's "the woordes of my complaynt," rather than the Geneva's "the wordes of my roaring." The principal conceit of *Amoretti* 14, "Gaynst such strong castles," matches the Great Bible, Psalm 31.4, "thou art my strong rocke and my castel," rather than from the Geneva translation, "thou art my rocke and my fortres." Individual words are also frequently closer to the Great Bible than the Geneva. *Amoretti* 37's concern with traps, "entrapped," reflects the Great Bible's "trappes," rather than the Geneva Bible's "grennes."[26]

When Spenser has had recourse to a psalm which is not a proper psalm of the day, however, it is apparent that he has reverted to the Geneva Bible version. *Amoretti* 86 makes use of the Geneva version of Psalm 140 and reflects its sidenotes in its terms, "plague," "false ... lies," and "kindle." Here Spenser has recalled Coverdale, but has also perused the Geneva version, both of which would have been available in most editions' parallel columns. Likewise, *Amoretti* 67, which imitates Psalm 42, has fused elements of both the Great Bible and the Geneva Bible versions. Four phrases in the sonnet directly reflect the psalm. The sonnet's opening, "Lyke as,"

---

[26] Compare also *Am.* 25, "mysery," with Great Bible, Ps. 88.15, "I am in miserie," and Geneva Bible, "I am afflicted;" *Am.* 27, "worship," with Great Bible, Ps 96.6, "Glory and woorship," and Geneva Bible, "Strength and glorie;" *Am.* 22, "seruice," with Great Bible, Ps. 72.11, "shal doo hym seruice," and Geneva Bible, "shal serue him;" *Am.* 9, "light. / Not to the Sun ... Moone ... Starres," with Great Bible, Ps. 148.3, "Prayse hym Sunne and Moone: praise him al ye starres and light," and Geneva Bible, "Praise ye him, sunne and moone: praise ye him all bright starres;" *Am.* 11, "cruell warriour," with Great Bible, Ps. 18.49, "(cruel) enimies," and Geneva Bible, "mine enemies;" *Am.* 46, "stormes," with Great Bible Ps. 42.9, "al thy ... stormes are gonne ouer me," and Geneva Bible, "All thy waues and thy floods are gone ouer me;" *Am.* 55, "compare," with Great Bible, "that shalbe compared vnto the Lorde," and Geneva Bible, "who is equal to the Lord in the heauen."

is found in the Great Bible, "Like as the hart," and not in the Geneva
Bible which has only "As the hart;" similarly the "brooke" of the sonnet
is taken from the "water brookes" of the Great Bible not the "riuers of
water" of the Geneva Bible; on the other hand the "so panteth" of the
Geneva Bible ("longeth" in the Great Bible), is adopted in the sonnet as
"panting hounds," while the sonnet's "thirst" is found in all versions: "My
soule is a thirst for God."

Finally Spenser has reverted to the Geneva version for *Epithalamion*. The
opening to Stanza 9, "Loe where she comes along with portly pace, / Lyke
Phoebe from her chamber of the East, / Arysing forth to run her mighty
race," recalls the Geneva version's Psalm 19.4–5, "The sunne. Which
commeth forthe as a bridegrome out of his chambre, and rejoyceth like a
mightie man to runne his race," rather than Coverdale's "rejoyceth as a
giant to runne his course."

The above evidence supports the conclusion that Spenser followed the
calendar and read the Great Bible psalter, both of which were commonly
found in editions of the *Book of Common Prayer*, but that for the second
lessons at morning and evening prayer he read the New Testament chapters
from the Geneva version of the Bible.

The *amoretti*'s correspondences are not limited to the English of the
Geneva Bible and the psalms of the *Book of Common Prayer*. Spenser has
also established extensive correspondences with the Latin Vulgate and, in
the case of New Testament readings, the Greek koiné. Spenser's knowledge
of classical Greek and Latin authors can readily be established from *The
Faerie Queene*. Evidence of his familiarity particularly with his favorites,
Ovid and Plato, but also with Claudian, Statius, and Catullus, his epithalamial models, is obvious throughout *Amoretti and Epithalamion*. It is equally
clear from the sonnets' correspondences that his knowledge of the Vulgate
and koiné was extensive and intricate. The correspondences with the Latin
and Greek versions of the scriptures are sometimes plainly obvious, sometimes they are jokingly simple, sometimes, after the manner of a rhetorical
poser, they extend a direct challenge to the lady to uncover the poet's
clever usage.

A detail from *Amoretti* 9's *expeditio* provides a good example of a simple
correspondence. The elements which comprise the sonnet's series of contrasts, "Not to the Sun . . . / nor to the Moone . . . / nor to the starres . . . ,"
match exactly the details of Psalm 148.3, a psalm Spenser read for 31
January with which *Amoretti* 9 corresponds,[27] "Prayse him Sunne and
Moone: prayse him all ye starres." A further element, however, "nor vnto

---

[27] See n. 9 above, for an explanation of the mistaken calendar prescription for 31
January.

Christall," has no immediately obvious correspondence—it is to be found concealed in the Vulgate version of the day's Psalm 147.17, "Mittit crystallum suum sicut buccellas."

Spenser's observing the Vulgate often extends to etymological—and homonymic—punning. A feature of morning prayer Psalm 24 for Monday 4 February, with which *Amoretti* 13 corresponds, is its repeated and highlighted verse, "Lift vp your heades, O ye gates, and be ye lift vp ye euerlasting doores" (vv. 7 & 9). The Vulgate has "Attollite portas." In opening *Amoretti* 13, "In that proud port ...." Spenser has construed the Vulgate's "portas," not as gate in the sense of entranceway, or even *port*, but as gate in the sense of gait, carriage, bearing, or *port*. The two words are associated because gait in the sixteenth century was spelled only as gate.

*Amoretti* 43 provides a more extensive parallel with the Vulgate, as well as confirming the *Amoretti* as a series of intimate jokes. The sonnet concludes by affirming the lady's ability to construe the poet's secret "loue learned letters":

> SHall I then silent be or shall I speake?
>> And if I speake, her wrath renew I shall:
>> and if I silent be, my hart will breake,
>> or choked be with ouerflowing gall.
> What tyranny is this both my hart to thrall,
>> and eke my toung with proud restraint to tie?
>> that nether I may speak nor thinke at all,
>> but like a stupid stock in silence die.
> Yet I my hart with silence secretly
>> will teach to speak, and my just cause to plead:
>> and eke mine eies with meeke humility,
>> loue learned letters to her eyes to read.
> Which her deep wit, that true harts thought can spel,
>> wil soone conceiue, and learne to construe well.

The primary meaning of the "construe" of the final line is to transliterate from one language to another by providing a word for word translation; the secondary meaning is to interpret a riddle—a sense it retains in its only other usage by Spenser, when Britomart is defeated by the riddle, "Be bold" (*FQ* III.xi.54.3–4).

Yet in asserting that the lady has such an ability and wit, the poet in fact has fashioned a construct in which the lady is considered the primary reader of the sonnet and in which a challenge is laid down to her, because the sonnet earlier contains an example of the poet's own secret construing in the dominant and concluding simile to the sonnet's octet, "I like a stupid stock in silence die." Luke 17, the second lesson at morning prayer for Wednesday 6 March, with which *Amoretti* 43 corresponds, opens with the image of the mulberry tree, "If ye ... shulde say vnto this mulbery tre, plucke thy self vp by the rootes ... " (v. 6), in the Vulgate, "dicetis huic arbori moro." Spenser has established the sonnet's correspondence with the day's parable by wittily construing the phrase not as *morus* = mulberry + *arbor* = tree, but alternatively as *morus* = stupid + *arbor* = stock, and so has provided the sonnet with its striking image. The final lines surreptitiously challenge the lady to uncover his transliteration and solve his riddle.

The Greek correspondences are generally less witty and more ponderous and serious-minded. *Amoretti* 18 and 54 both share a stage conceit deriving from the koiné and contain verbal parallelisms. *Amoretti* 18 was composed for Saturday 9 February which has as its second lesson at evening prayer, 2 Corinthians 5, which opens,

> For we knowe that if our earthlie house of this tabernacle be destroied, we haue a buylding *giuen* of God, *that is*, an house not made with hands, *but* eternal in the heauens. . . . For in dede we that are in this tabernacle, sigh and are burdened.

*Amoretti* 54 was written for the Fifth Sunday in Lent, 17 March, which has as its Epistle, Hebrews 9.11–16, which celebrates Christ as "a greater and a more perfite Tabernacle, not made with hands, that is not of this buylding" (v. 11). The theatrical motif in both sonnets corresponds with the image in both verses of "Tabernacle," in the Greek, σκηνή, a term used originally by the Greeks for a wooden stage on which actors performed.[28] Furthermore Spenser has wittily extended *Amoretti* 54's associations with the koiné through the pseudo-etymological detail provided by the Epistle's subsequent verses 12–13. Paul distinguishes the σκηνή, "not made with hands, that is not of thy buylding," from earlier σκηναι on which other performances were enacted, "by the blood of goates" (δι'αἵματος τράγων) and "the blood of bulles and of goates" (τὸ αἷμα ταύρων καὶ τράγων). *Amoretti* 54 observes this distinction in its own distinction between comedy and tragedy, "I waile and make my woes a Tragedy," where "Tragedy" ingeniously reflects the Greek's τράγων, which is its partial etymon.

A more seriously intentioned observance of the koiné can be found in *Amoretti* 45, whose *topos* of the mirror and its "ymage" (11) directly reflects the use of the term 'image' (εἰκών) in the second lesson at evening prayer for Friday 8 March, Colossians 3.9–10, with which *Amoretti* 45 corresponds, "seing that ye haue put of the olde man with his workes, And haue put on

---

[28] All references to the koiné are from *The Englishman's Greek New Testament; giving the Greek Text of Stephens 1550* (London: Samuel Bagster, 1877).

the newe, which is renewed in knowledge after the image of him that created him" (εἰς ἐπίγνωσιν κατ' εἰκόνα τοῦ κτίσαντος αὐτον). εἰκών was also used particularly of an image in a mirror by Plato in a well-known passage in *The Republic* (402B) and Spenser, in establishing a correspondence with the scriptural verse, has drawn upon the *locus classicus*: "Οὐκοῦν καὶ εἰκόνας γραμμάτων, εἴ που ἦ ἐν ὕδασιν ἦ ἐν κατόπτροις ἐμφαίνοιντο, οὐ πρότερον γνωσόμεθα πρὶν ἂν αὐτα γνῶμεν" (Is it not true that, if there are images of letters reflected in water or in mirrors, we shall not know them until we know the originals?). It is this same metaphor of the mirror which, when applied to the eyes of lovers in a passage from *Phaedrus* (255D), becomes the source of the sonneteers' mirror conceit. Plato compares the lover to one that has caught a disease of the eye from another but cannot discover its cause, not understanding that his love is like a mirror in which he beholds his true image: "ἀλλ' οἷον ἀπ' ἄλλου ὀφθαλμίας ἀπολελαυκὼς πρόφασιν εἰπεῖν οὐκ ἔχει, ὥσπερ δὲ ἐν κατόπτρῳ ἐν τῷ ἐρῶντι ἑαυτὸν ὁρῶν λέληθεν." Furthermore the context of the passage in *The Republic* clearly identifies εἰκὼν as an image associated with the original ἰδέα (Idea) which is the true image in the mind.[29] Since the Pauline phrase, "after the image of him that created him," while not Platonic, is reminiscent of Plato's ἰδέαι (ideas), the eternal and ideal forms in the (creator's) mind of which all created things are the imperfect images, Spenser clearly felt that his use of the term "Idea" (7) in a sonnet for a day whose scriptures could be construed as alluding to the Platonic ἰδέα was an appropriate correspondence.

## B. Classical and Petrarchist

*The Faerie Queene* amply demonstrates Spenser's extensive knowledge of classical incident, myth, *topoi*, and *loci amoeni*. On a smaller scale the same familiarity is manifest throughout *Amoretti and Epithalamion*. As the commentary reveals, the sequence is punctuated with references and allusions from Pliny, Horace, and Ovid, while the anacreontic verses and *Epithalamion* pay close observance to their classical antecedents. Spenser's noticing the reference to Pliny, for example, in the BCP's footnote for 10 February, with which *Amoretti* 19 corresponds ("As vpon this day, the Romanes began their spring, after Plinie"), has led to the sonnet's opening line, "The merry Cuckow, messenger of Spring," but has also caused him to adopt Pliny's classical identification of the cuckoo as the harbinger of spring (*Naturalis historia*, 10.9.11.25, "procedit vere").

---

[29] Plato, *The Republic*, trans. Paul Shorey (Cambridge: Harvard Univ. Press, 1956), 260 n.

Pliny's description of encaustic painting is also reflected in *Amoretti* 21. The conceit corresponds exactly with the striking metaphor which opens the psalms at morning prayer for Tuesday 12 February, "like as waxe melteth at the fire." Spenser's use of *inure*, however, ("with such strange termes her eyes she doth inure" [9]) is cleverly ambiguous. It carries the customary meaning of harden, but also (in a usage possibly the first in English) of burn in (from *in* + *urere*). The etymological pun thus provides the link between the psalm's metaphor and classical description of the encaustic process from Pliny, "Ceris pingere ac picturam inurere ..." (35.11.39.122), and its detail, "cerae tinguntur isdem his coloribus ad eas picturas, quae inuruntur ..." (35.11.41.149).

Spenser more frequently has recourse to Ovid during the sequence. He reflects Ovid's *Fasti* (2.79–118) in his use of the Arion myth in *Amoretti* 38, and draws on the conclusion to Ovid's description of creation in *Amoretti* 13 (*Metamorphoses* 1.75–88), and on his account of the relationship between the four substances for *Amoretti* 55 (15.237–52). The *locus classicus* of poetic immortality which concludes Ovid's *Metamorphoses* is strongly echoed in the sequence's four immortality sonnets, *Amoretti*, 25, 51, 69, and particularly 75. He has imitated Horace's "Exegi monimentum aere perennius" (*Odes*, 3.30.1) for *Amoretti* 69.10's "immortall moniment," while *Amoretti* 17.13's "greater craftesman" is in direct contrast to Horace's lesser craftsman — the "faber imus" of *Ars poetica*, 32. He draws on Plato for the mirror sonnet, *Amoretti* 45, and, in a general way, for the Platonic *Idaea* of *Amoretti* 88. He incorporates detail from Homer's accounts of Penelope in *Odyssey* 19 and 24, for the subject of *Amoretti* 23, and from *Iliad* 19, where the Furies are invoked to condemn slander and perjury, for the condemnations against false speaking which comprise *Amoretti* 86.

The clearest instances of classical imitation occur in the volume's anacreontic verses and the *Epithalamion*. The prefacing of *Epithalamion* with a series of fescennine verses is itself in imitation of a classical model, since all Renaissance editions of Claudian's *Epithalamium de nuptiis Honorii Augusti* prefaced the epithalamium with a similar series of *fescennina*. Furthermore Claudian's final *Fescenninum* has as its conceit the bee defending its honey against stealing. In choosing to imitate Theocritus' *Idyll* 19, as well as *Anacreon* 35, in his verses Spenser has followed Claudian and has also adopted the genial context which Claudian gave to Theocritus' Κηριοκλέπτης.

*Epithalamion* itself, as might be expected in a poetic form for which there was little precedent in English, draws heavily on traditional classical models but also shows an acquaintance with the continental *exempla* which came to form the Renaissance epithalamial convention and for which Scaliger laid down elaborate norms in his 1561 work, *Poetices*. Throughout his poem

Spenser shows an extensive knowledge of and indebtedness to Claudian's two epithalamia, *Epithalamium de nuptiis Honorii Augusti* and *Epithalamium dictum Palladio . . . et Celerinae*, to Statius' *Epithalamion in Stellam et Violentillam*, as well as to Catullus' epithalamial *carmina, Carmen* 61, 62, and 64.

As far as *Amoretti* is concerned, Spenser has positioned it firmly within the genre of Renaissance sonnet sequences. Earlier in this century work on *Amoretti* directed its attention towards the sonnets' continental antecedents in order to affirm their continental (and Platonic) heritage.[30] More recent endeavor has concentrated on continental precedents in order to establish *Amoretti*'s native English character.[31]

*Amoretti* owes much to Petrarchist *topoi*, conceits and mannered structures: 'fire,' 'ice,' 'plaints,' 'ships in storms,' 'eyes,' 'fayre loves,' all find some place in the sequence. Yet Spenser's debt is seldom specific, and searching Petrarch, Desportes or Tasso for equivalences is rarely helpful. Generally he recalls such precedents with a freedom and imprecision which makes their use his own, and he is scarcely so tied to them that a definite influence or culling can be cited.[32] Indeed, Spenser's use of continental

---

[30] Sidney Lee, *Elizabethan Sonnets* (Westminster, 1904), 1:92–99; L. E. Kastner, "Spenser's 'Amoretti' and Desportes," *MLR* 4 (1908–9): 65–69; Janet G. Scott, "Sources of Spenser's *Amoretti*," *MLR* 22 (1927): 189–95, and *Les Sonnet Elizabéthains* (Paris, 1929), 159–77; Veselin Kostic, *Spenser's Sources in Italian Poetry* (Belgrade: Faculté de Philologie de l'Université de Belgrade, 1969), 38–75. For a study of possible Platonic influences, see Edwin Casady, "The Neo-Platonic Ladder in Spenser's *Amoretti*," *PQ* 20 (1941): 284–95, and Mohinimohan Bhattacherje, *Platonic Ideas in Spenser* (London, 1935). Suggested Platonic elements in the *amoretti* have frequently been queried, not the least by Robert Ellrodt, *Neoplatonism in the Poetry of Spenser* (Geneva: Librairie E. Droz, 1960), 40–45.

[31] Lever, 92–138, and Reed Way Dasenbrock, "The Petrarchan Context of Spenser's 'Amoretti'" *PMLA* 100 (1985): 38–50.

[32] Attempts have been made, for example, to construe *Am.* 10 as a translation of Petrarch's "Or vedi, Amor," but the two poems are so utterly dissimilar, that no grounds of first similarity can be established upon which to base any valid comparison, and the scriptural correspondences of *Am.* 10's conceit and imagery are pronounced (Dasenbrock, 42–43). *Am.* 50, "Long languishing in double malady," has been instanced as "certainly suggested" by Sonnet 53 of Desportes' *Les Amours d'Hippolyte*, "Bien qu'une fièvre tierce en mes veines boüillonne" (L. E. Kastner," Spenser's 'Amoretti' and Desportes," *MLR* 4 [1908–9]: 63). Apart from the contrived connection betwen Desportes' "fièvre tierce" and Spenser's "double malady," however, the sonnets bear no relationship to each other. *Am.* 18's opening conceit of the wheel grinding, "The rolling wheele that runneth often round," is closer to the day's gospel image of the "milstone," than to any connection with Desportes' "L'eau tombant d'un lieu haut goute à goute a puissance," as both Kastner and Scott suggest. Desportes' sonnet is so far removed from Spenser's poem as to suggest only the faintest of echoes. *Am.* 48's opening invocation, "Innocent paper," owes a less likely debt to Desportes, "O vers que j'ai chantez en l'ardeur qui m'enflamme," as Kastner asserts, than to the complex of scriptural references for Monday 11 March. A range of other sonnets (*Am.* 42, 60, 69), for which possible allusions have been claimed, correspond

*exempla* calls attention to a problem to which any aggregative convention gives rise: in *Amoretti* an echo frequently conjures up the paratextual Petrarchist world, yet its very momentariness defeats any sustained grasp of it. Furthermore, by confining his Petrarchist debt to the shortest of glimpses and by hurrying his lines onward to create a semblance of a Petrarchist mode, Spenser continually thwarts any conventional expectation. The sonnets' brief Petrarchist allusions allow little secure indebtedness and threaten to undercut the very tradition that Spenser overtly espouses. In fact, the *amoretti* provide only five clear instances of translation, all from the later period and all from Tasso. Yet even on these occasions Spenser adapts and recasts the original and imbues his rendering with his own distinctive cadence and flow.

Spenser's most obvious use of Petrarchist conceits occurs with those sonnets which lack correspondences with a day's scripture readings. They are more conventionally correct than most in the sequence and are often undistinguished and noticeably flat. *Amoretti* 30, for which no single source has been found,[33] but the exemplum for which was Petrarch's "D'un bel, chiaro, polito e vivo ghiaccio / move la fiamma che m'incende e strugge" (*Rime*, 202), works the commonplace Petrarchist *topos* of ice and fire:

> MY loue is lyke to yse, and I to fyre;
>> how comes it then that this her cold so great
>> is not dissolu'd through my so hot desyre,
>> but harder growes the more I her intreat?

This opening quatrain is the first of three, each in the form of a question, each striving to heighten the rhetorical tension through a series of paradoxes, until the final bathetic couplet, which is made the more vulnerable by its blatant pun on "kynd":

> Such is the powre of loue in gentle mind,
>> that it can alter all the course of kynd.

The compounding of paradox with little ingenuity and to little advantage eventually reduces the poem to a run-of-the-mill Petrarchist sonnet and marks it as different from the general standard of *amoretti*.

---

more clearly to scriptural and liturgical occasions than to any Petrarchist source. (Janet G. Scott [1927], 189–95, and [1929], 159–77.)

[33] *The Works of Edmund Spenser, A Variorum Edition*, eds. E. Greenlaw, C. G. Osgood, F. M. Padelford, R. Heffner, H. G. Lotspeich, 9 vols. (Baltimore: Johns Hopkins Univ. Press, 1932–49), *The Minor Poems*, 2.429.

In these *amoretti*, furthermore, Spenser's distinctive manner of treating paradox is not evident. The Petrarchist sonneteer held the two elements of the paradox always in suspension and, by disabling any resolution, presented the contrarieties as always opposed. In such poetic endeavor paradoxes followed each other accumulatively, and keeping the edifice upright as much as anything else displayed the poet's skill. Spenser's smooth-flowing style, on the other hand, blurs the contrarieties to the extent that the distinction between the paradox's elements becomes confused and a kind of integration is suggested. His distinctive rhyme scheme also operates aggregatively, each rhyme hurrying the weft of the poem onward to the concluding couplet, which is either confirmatory or paradoxical. The thrust of the poem is towards the concluding couplet, which bears a greater weight than that which a different rhyme scheme might produce. In these specifically Petrarchist sonnets Spenser evinces none of his customary smooth handling, and the sharpness of the seriate paradoxes in *Amoretti* 30, for example, lead onward to a final couplet which is anticlimactic.

Although *Amoretti* provides frequent instances of Petrarchist *topoi* and conceits, Spenser's drawing upon them is nearly always in order to establish correspondences with a day's scriptural theme or imagery. *Amoretti* 11's Petrarchan conceit of the "Cruell warriour," *Amoretti* 14's "siege" conceit, *Amoretti* 15's blazon, *Amoretti* 17, a "portrait" sonnet, *Amoretti* 34, a "galley" sonnet, *Amoretti* 45, a "mirror" sonnet and *Amoretti* 18 and 54 with their theatrical *topos*, all find parallels in a corresponding day's scriptural readings.

Early in the sequence, however, Spenser seems less adept at fusing his sources together. Ash Wednesday's *Amoretti* 22 draws upon Desportes' "Solitaire & pensif dans un bois écarté," but the borrowings have not resulted in a happy mix and the final result is not felicitous.[34] The sonnet opens with the propriety due to a solemn feast. Yet as it moves from the Christian to the pagan, it turns from the propriety of fasting to a hyperbolic indictment of the lady. The first quatrain is full of ceremony and proper occasional intent, while the second's imagery and content are reminiscent of the Old Testament. But the influence of Desportes changes the tone of Spenser's sestet. The pagan-inspired imagery extends excessively the poem's hyperbolic mode, as it turns on the lady and establishes her as a goddess, remote and severe, who is asked to vouch a safekeeping to the poet, who now casts himself, ambiguously in the context of an altar, in the role of a "relick." This final posturing and awkward hyperbole are false to the

---

[34] Desportes, *Les Amours de Diane*, in F. de Malberbe and V. E. Graham, eds., *Les Premieres Oeuvres de Philippes Des Portes* (Genève: Librairie E. Droz, 1959), 10ᵛ, no. 39.

sonnet's opening spirit, because the intent of the Lenten fasting and praying is finally to appease a pagan goddess. It is the too forthright intrusion of the pagan into the religious that creates the concluding unease in Spenser's poem. Thus the merging of sources in *Amoretti* 22 is problematic, for the way its disparate elements have been worked together exhibits a certain edginess.

By the time of the sonnets composed for Holy Week, Spenser's use of Petrarchist sources is more assured. His reworking of the images of beast, tree and ship in *Amoretti* 56, which are found in Petrarch's "Standomi un giorno" (*Rime*, 323), and which he had already adapted for *The Visions of Petrarch*, shows growing certainty. Generally he uses a day's scripture reading to knowing advantage, but he is not averse to loosely employing a standard Petrarchist *exemplum*, when it can be accommodated to his purpose for that day. In *Amoretti* 67, written for the Saturday before Easter, for example, he has chosen to write a sonnet in imitation of the stock deer *topos*, which originated with Petrarch's "Una candida cerva," and which was developed by, among others, Tasso in his "Questa fera gentil."[35] Spenser echoes the spirit of the convention rather than the letter, because the only specific element he shares with either precedent is the "cangiato voler," the "changed will" of Tasso's gentle beast. Yet in choosing to develop the *topos* on the Saturday before Easter he is also observing a liturgical feature closely associated with the day, Psalm 42, "Like as the hart desireth the water brookes," which was traditionally sung as the catechumens proceeded to the font at the Easter Vigil. The sonnet's liturgical echoes suggest that the poet was conscious that he had finished his Lenten period of preparation and now desired to be joined with his "deare." Because the liturgical occasion has been subtly fused in the poem with traditional poetic elements, *Amoretti* 67 offers itself simultaneously as a sustained Petrarchist piece and a poem of a deeply religious cast.

In the sonnets composed for the period after Easter, Spenser has increased his direct use of Italian precedents with five sonnets closely related to sonnets of Tasso: *Amoretti* 72 draws upon "L'alma vaga di luce e di bellezza," *Amoretti* 73 upon "Donna, poichè fortuna empia mi nega," *Amoretti* 76 and 77 upon "Non son sí belli i fiori onde natura," and *Amoretti* 81 upon "Bella é la donna mia, se del bel crine."[36]

---

[35] For an extended discussion of *Am.* 67, see Prescott (1985), 33–76.

[36] *Le rime de Torquato Tasso*, ed. Paolo Solerti, 3 vols. (Bologna, 1898–1902), 2:98.67; 2:319.22; 3:133.94; 2:25.17. Echoes of Tasso can be found in earlier sonnets, the most pronounced being *Am.* 43.1–4, see Tasso, *Rime*, 2:166, "Se taccio, il duol s'avanza;" *Am.* 45.1, and Tasso, *Rime*, 2:251.169, "Qual da cristallo lampeggiar si vede Raggio;" *Am.* 56, whose structure reflects Tasso's "Voi set bella, ma ...," (*Rime*, 4:69.253); *Am.* 70, see

*Amoretti* 72's twofold direction from earth to heaven and heaven to earth is found also in Tasso's original:

> L'alma vaga di luce e di bellezza,
> Ardite spiega al Ciel l'ale amorose;
> Ma sí le fa l'umanità gravose,
> Che le dechina a quel, ch'in terra apprezza.

Yet the same twofold direction has strong ties with the second lesson at morning prayer for the Thursday in Easter Week, 4 April, Acts 1, the account of the ascension into heaven, which describes how the disciples, having "loked stedfastly towarde heauen" after the ascension, were instructed to return their eyes earthward to behold Christ's coming again: "two men stode by them in white apparel, Which also said, Ye men of Galile, why stand ye gasing into heauen? This Iesus which is taken vp from you into heauen, shal so come, as ye haue sene him go into heauen" (vv. 10–11). Similarly in *Amoretti* 72, because the beauty of heaven is manifest on earth in the lady's beauty, the poet's sight is drawn back to earth. He does not, however, pursue his use of Tasso. Where Tasso is concerned to sustain his original conceit on a metaphoric level, Spenser's sonnet adopts a tone proper to the Easter season, for its later concern is with the peace and "contentment" that has been found at Easter.

Spenser's most successful fusion of continental source and scriptural correspondence occurs with the pair of sonnets, *Amoretti* 76 and 77, which have assumed much of their imagery from Tasso's sonnet, "Non son sí belli i fiori onde natura." They are two of the most physical of the *amoretti*, yet Spenser imbues them with a quite different mood. Tasso's poem embellishes the contrast between nature and love. In *Amoretti* 76 Spenser initially takes up the elements of praise that Tasso affords: the "marvellous bosom," the "garden and nest of love," and the "earthly paradise." Yet, as Lever has pointed out,[37] he drops Tasso's contrast between nature and love and recasts his eulogy in a mode, which, for the moment, hints at an unfallen quality in "the paradice of pleasure." Where Tasso queries how he can restrain his thoughts from breaking forth to steal such heavenly fruit but contains his answer always within the framework of classical myth, Spenser adapts the question by acknowledging rather guiltily the internal urgings of physical desire, "and my frayle thoughts too rashly led astray." Furthermore,

---

Tasso, *Gerusalemme Liberata*, 16.15.5–8. David Quint, "Torquato Tasso," in *The Spenser Encyclopedia*, 679, who lists other possible correspondences with Tasso, almost entirely drawn from Kostic, *Spenser's Sources in Italian Poetry*, which I find less convincing.

[37] Lever, 110–13.

because he has dropped Tasso's contrast between nature and love, he can drop Tasso's parallel temporal contrast between April and autumn. In like manner in *Amoretti* 77, Spenser takes from Tasso the apple's mythical referents of Atalanta and Hercules, but quite changes their classical spirit. Even though in *Amoretti* 76 he had been made to feel awkward by his betrothed's physical beauty, in *Amoretti* 77 he explicitly affirms the nature of the apples to be "voyd of sinfull vice" and "brought from paradice," identical therefore to that prelapsarian gracefulness of paradise. Time, then, whose passing was an integral part of Tasso's sonnet, is absolved of any movement in Spenser's version.

These modifications have made *Amoretti* 76 correspond more closely with the account of the Annunciation, the indwelling of Christ in the womb of the Virgin Mary, in Matthew 1, which was read as the second lesson at morning prayer for Friday 3 May. As well, in the opening line to *Amoretti* 77, "Was it a dreame, or did I see it playne," Spenser has also made *Amoretti* 77 correspond more closely with the dominant, and scripturally unique, image of the "dreame," four accounts of which are found in Matthew 2, the second lesson at morning prayer for the subsequent day, Saturday 4 May. Since Tasso nowhere refers to a dream, Spenser's continuing intent to establish in the sonnets parallels with the corresponding day's readings has recast the atmosphere of Tasso's original. Just as in *Amoretti* 76 he has changed a temporal love into a love of prelapsarian origin, so his incorporation of the dream motif into *Amoretti* 77 has given his sonnet a surreal quality lacking in Tasso.

By the end of the sequence Spenser uses his Petrarchist models and *topoi* freely. In the final sonnet of the sequence, for example, his use of Tasso's "O vaga tortorella ... tu sovra il nudo ramo" is not slavishly imitative,[38] but combines liturgical correspondences with Petrarchist sources syncretically. The easy flow of these later *amoretti* suggests a confident elegance that contrasts with the tense control of Tasso. The nature of Spenser's sonnets is less exhausting than the precise juxtaposing of Tasso, and in this Spenser generally differs from poets of the Petrarchist tradition, who use paradox to tighten the reader's focus. Spenser's flow is more elastic and dissipate, enabling the reader to read smoothly, softly, and with equanimity. He has thus brought to the genre of sonnet sequences an essentially integrative disposition. His syncretism replaces the traditional Petrarchist attachment to the riches of unreconciled variances. His sequence is also distinctive because its tensions not only anticipate the outside resolution of the epithalamium, but contain within covert indicators of christic redemption, of

---

[38] Quint, *The Spenser Encyclopedia*, 679.

which the timelessness and covert incarnational references of *Amoretti* 76 and 77 are examples. Spenser's working together of allusions and attitudes from both Petrarchist sources and scriptural *loci* intimates a poetic and a personal harmony, which in *Amoretti* becomes his ultimate preoccupation and goal.

Of the two final pieces of the volume, the anacreontic verses show some indebtedness first to Tasso's madrigal, "Mentre in grembo," as Hutton has pointed out, and second to two epigrams by Marot, "Amour trouua celle qui m'est amere," and "L'Enfant Amour n'a plus fon arc estrange," as Prescott has shown.[39] *Epithalamion* owes something to Rémy Belleau's *Epithalame Sur le Mariage de Monseigneur le Duc de Lorraine et de Madame Claude Fille du Roy. Chanté par les nymphes de Seine et de Meuse*, to Joachim du Bellay's *Epithalame sur le Mariage de Prince Philibert Emanuel et Marguerite de France*, and to Marc-Claude de Buttet's *Epithalame Aux Nosses de Philibert de Savoie*. (The detail of these borrowings is shown in the commentary.)

*Epithalamion* evinces the same syncretism that marks the sonnets of *Amoretti*: Petrarchist and classical sources are woven into a rich tapestry where one allusion moves easily to the next. Spenser's handling of his sources connects their detail without hiatus or gap; all is blended together smoothly. But *Epithalamion* is more readily recognizable as an edifice than *Amoretti* and the classical and Petrarchist borrowings that go toward making up the edifice are more obvious to the eye. No doubt also, because *Epithalamion* has little or no precedent in English, the earlier sources on which the poem draws are more conspicuous. In *Epithalamion* finally the voice is more public than that of *Amoretti* and the rhetorical and learned allusions are more formal and distinguishable.

## II. Structure

The overall structure of the volume *Amoretti and Epithalamion* is clearly tripartite, its two longer works being separated by the series of short anacreontic verses. These smaller verses, because seemingly so inconsequential and improperly bawdy, have sometimes been considered non-authorial. (For the same reasons, Shakespeare's final two sonnets 153 and 154, which are concerned with the sleeping Cupid laying aside his brand which is later quenched in "a coole Well," have had their authorship challenged.) Yet recent work by Duncan-Jones, Kerrigan and Warkentin has shown that Spenser, in giving his work a tripartite shape, is observing a convention that

---

[39] James Hutton, "Cupid and the Bee," in Rita Guerlac, ed. *Essays on Renaissance Poetry* (Ithaca: Cornell Univ. Press, 1980), 106–31 and Hugh MacLean and Anne Lake Prescott, eds., *Edmund Spenser's Poetry* (New York: Norton Critical Edition, 1993), 623–24.

seems to have applied to sonnet sequences published during the 1580's and 1590's.[40] More often than not, when a sequence is followed by a longer formal or narrative piece, the two are separated by a series of short verses, often after the manner of Anacreon. Richard Barnfield separates the sonnets which comprise his sequence *Cynthia* (1595) from *The Legend of Cassandra* by an ode in iambic tetrameter beginning, "Nights were short, and daies were long." All three pieces in the volume are signed off with *Finis*. Thomas Lodge divides his sequence *Phillis* (1593) from the long narrative, *The tragicall complaynt of Elstred*, by an ode in trochaic metre — associated by the Elizabethans with Anacreon — beginning, "Nowe I find thy lookes were fained." Samuel Daniel's *Delia* (1592) is separated from *The complaint of Rosamond* by a small and seemingly inconsequential ode beginning, "nowe each creture ioyes the other." In a lesser manner Barnabe Barnes's *Parthenophil and Parthenophe* (1593), which concludes with the most formal poem of the volume, a triple sestina after the manner of an epithalamium, is preceded by a *carmen anacreontium*. Richard Lynche separates his *Diella* (1596) from *The amorous Poeme of Dom Diego and Gineura* by a last sonnet inviting a perusal of the subsequent story, "Harken awhile (*Diella*) to a storie," and Shakespeare's final two sonnets seemingly separate his sonnet sequence from *A Lover's Complaint*.

The fact that *Amoretti and Epithalamion* follows this tripartite structure suggests that Spenser's readers would have accepted it as customary and urges again that the volume be read as a single work. Within it Spenser adds the further liturgical dimension of *Amoretti*, which itself is threefold.[41] The first section comprises those sonnets written for Hilary Term and Lent leading up to Holy Week (*Amoretti* 1–57); the second those which correspond with Holy Week and the Easter season through to Low Sunday, where the direction of the sonnets is towards the serious and grave (*Amoretti* 58–75); the third section comprises the appended sonnets of expectation (*Amoretti* 76–89). The themes and preoccupations of the later sections lead towards the public celebrations and resolutions of *Epithalamion*.

## A. The Sonnets for Hilary Term and Lent
The correlations between each sonnet and its corresponding scriptural reading contribute extensively to the richness of *Amoretti* as a sonnet

---

[40] K. Duncan-Jones, "Was the 1609 *Shake-Speares Sonnets* Really Unauthorized?" *RES* n.s. 34 (1983): 168–69; William Shakespeare, *The Sonnets and A Lover's Complaint*, ed. John Kerrigan, (Harmondsworth: Penguin Books, 1986), 13–14; Germaine Warkentin, "Amoretti and Epithalamion," in *The Spenser Encyclopedia*, 31.

[41] For recent discussion of *Amoretti*'s structure, see Gibbs, 10–28, and Johnson, passim.

sequence and mark an advance in understanding the convention to which they belong. They show how Spenser constructed his sonnets and what facets of the scripture lessons he found most attractive. His choice, and the manner in which he imitates a lesson, frequently uncover readings of poems which extend beyond the purely conventional and convert the sequence's artifice into a close construct in which the varied hues of the relationship between Spenser and his betrothed are displayed.

At the beginning of the sequence, the way Spenser has neatly turned the features found in the scriptural lesson with which *Amoretti* 2 corresponds shows a hidden propriety within the sonnet, for the scriptural echoes give the sonnet an acceptability quite beyond its conventionally contrived harshness.[42] In contrasting the "Vnquiet thought" that grows from the "inward bale" in his heart with possible conduct in the presence of the lady, the sonnet imitates the inner corruption of the scribes and pharisees which is contrasted with their outward behavior in Matthew 23, the second lesson at morning prayer, which he read for January 24. The poet's calling upon the thought to "breake forth" from the "inner part," where it lurks "lyke to vipers brood," exactly reflects the gospel's condemnation of the scribes and pharisees as a "generacion of viperes" (Geneva version sidenote, "*Or, broodes*") (v. 33). The correspondences identify the poet with the scribes and pharisees and allow him to impute to himself a culpability that exceeds a courtly poet's customary worthlessness. Furthermore in the sonnet's third quatrain the poet calls the thought to humble itself, "fayrest proud / . . . fall lowly at her feet: / and with meek humblesse. . . ." The admonition is in direct response to Christ's claim that, "Whosoeuer wil exalt him self, shalbe broght low: and whosoeuer wil humble him self, shalbe exalted" (v. 12). In asking the lady to grant pardon and peace, the poet has assigned to her divinely merciful associations which are the true compliment of the sonnet. The scriptural associations thus discreetly extend the parameters of the compliment and the final couplet reflects a deft touch, by turning a rather strained and contorted pair of overlengthy lines into a compliment that betrays a restrained tenderness and a delicately extended pleading.

Such good-humored intimacies abound in this early section of the *amoretti*, as straightforward poems of praise loaded with knowing qualities. Private nuances and hints are tucked away in unlikely places, and instances where the scripture lessons unlock the private nature of a sonnet and

---

[42] Elizabeth Bieman, "'Sometimes I . . . mask in myrth lyke to a Comedy': Spenser's *Amoretti*," *SpS* 4 (1983): 134, writing of the comic coherence of the sonnet sequence, reads *Am.* 2's "Vnquiet thought" as "phallic pressure" and cites it as one example of the *amoretti*'s foreplay.

enforce a new reading are the rule rather than the exception. *Amoretti* 4, for example, which opens with a reference to January, closes with a cryptic joke, whose intent is delicately serious.

> For lusty spring now in his timely howre,
>> is ready to come forth him to receiue:
>> and warnes the Earth with diuers colord flowre,
>> to decke hir selfe, and her faire mantle weaue.
> Then you faire flowre, in whom fresh youth doth raine,
>> prepare your selfe new loue to entertaine. (8–14)

The sonnet was written for Saturday 26 February, for which the second lesson at evening prayer is 1 Corinthians 7; Paul, speaking of virginity, counsels: "if anie man thinke that it is vncomlie for his virgine, if she passe the flowre of *her* age, and nede so require, let him do what he wil, he sinneth not: let them be maried" (v. 36). Spenser has accepted the image of the virgin and the flower for the culminating admonition of the final couplet. But, given the difference in age between Spenser and Elizabeth Boyle, the fact that this verse caught Spenser's eye gives the couplet a delightful twist. It was Spenser who was the elderly one and past the flower of his age. Elizabeth Boyle, being probably in her late teens, was the younger "faire flowre," who was not affected by the strictures of the Pauline injunction. The age difference also allows him to structure the sonnet around the traditional adage, used of an older man marrying a younger woman, of "January marrying May," anticipating thereby the alignment of spring and May in *Amoretti* 70 and 76. Spenser has, therefore, turned the scriptural verse, so that it reflects disadvantageously upon himself and favorably upon his betrothed. The final Pauline admonition, "let them be married," remains unspoken, although it is clear what is implied by "prepare your selfe new loue to entertaine." The poem thus represents a clever play on the scriptural allusion and discloses a humor and tender playfulness that makes of the sonnet a private love-knot in a manner proper to *amoretti*.

Likewise the hyperbole of *Amoretti* 10 avoids becoming offensive or ridiculous through the further substance and interest it acquires from the semi-theological and scripturally based undertones of the initial quatrain.

> VNrighteous Lord of loue what law is this,
>> That me thou makest thus tormented be?
>> the whiles she lordeth in licentious blisse
>> of her freewill, scorning both thee and me.
> See how the Tyrannesse doth joy to see
>> the huge massacres which her eyes do make. (1–6)

The sonnet's opening invocation, "Vnrighteous Lord of loue," is a clear recasting of the last verse which Spenser read at morning prayer for Friday 1 February, with which *Amoretti* 10 corresponds, Psalm 11.8, "For the righteous Lorde loueth . . . ." The inverted opening also establishes a framework which will wittily set the sonnet against the propriety of the day's scripture lessons.

The sonnet's rhetorical question "what law is this" is a deliberate echo of the question in the day's second lesson at morning prayer, Mark 1, "What thing is this? what new doctrine is this? for he commandeth the foule spirits with autoritie" (v. 27), which concludes the first Marcan account of the man "tormented" by an "vncleane spirit." The spirit further exclaims, "what haue we to do with thee, . . . Iesus of Nazaret? . . . I know thee what thou art, *euen* that holie one of God" (v. 24; in Mark 5, the second account, he continues, "I charge thee by God, that thou torment me not" (v. 7), to which is attached the sidenote, "He abuseth the Name of God, to mainteine his tyrannie"). Spenser combines the interrogative, "What thing is this," the "autoritie," which he renders as "law," and the "tormented," into the sonnet's opening question. In the second quatrain he procedes to associate the lady with the powers of unrighteousness that cried out, "Art thou come to destroy us" (v. 24), by borrowing from the "tyrannie" of the gospel's later sidenote to attribute to her a similar destructive intent: "See how the Tyrannesse . . . / . . . huge massacres . . . do make." Finally Spenser has taken cognizance of the day's second lesson at evening prayer, 1 Corinthians 13, Paul's hymn of love. Where in Paul's hymn love "disdaineth not," in Spenser's sonnet the lady is guilty of "scorning both thee and me;" where love "reioyceth not in iniquitie," the lady "doth ioy to see / the huge massacres," and where love "doeth not boast it self," the lady's heart is accounted "proud."

Spenser felt it cleverly appropriate to compose a sonnet which specifically, although in an obviously hyperbolic mode, acknowledged the "Lord of loue," for an occasion when Paul's encomium to love was one of the scripture readings. As well, he has fashioned Mark's detail directly into a theological conceit. The unrighteous are those who remain reprobate and of a fallen state. Yet, although the man with the "vncleane spirit" is unrighteous and given over to lawlessness, the law of Christ is greater, "for he commandeth the foule spirits with autoritie, and they obey him." A righteousness thereby accrues to the poet, for he has turned the sonnet against the lady who remains associated with the devil's party throughout.

The sonnet's conventional hyperbole remains apparent; its adjectives are exaggerated and overstated: "huge massacres," "mightie vengeance," "humbled harts." But the scripture references further advance the sonnet's intent. That Spenser is prepared to associate his betrothed with the powers of darkness can only be construed as good-natured teasing. The scripture readings explicate an intimacy not otherwise apparent, and the intent of the concluding couplet only becomes intelligible once the humor that lies behind the text is revealed:

> That I may laugh at her in equall sort,
>> as she doth laugh at me and makes my pain her sport.
> (13–14)

On the other hand *Amoretti* 24 strikes a tone which is less proper:

> WHen I behold that beauties wonderment,
>> And rare perfection of each goodly part:
>> of natures skill the onely complement,
>> I honor and admire the makers art.
> But when I feele the bitter balefull smart,
>> which her fayre eyes vnwares doe worke in mee:
>> that death out of theyr shiny beames doe dart,
>> I thinke that I a new *Pandora* see;
> Whom all the Gods in councell did agree,
>> into this sinfull world from heauen to send:
>> that she to wicked men a scourge should bee,
>> for all their faults with which they did offend.
> But since ye are my scourge I will intreat,
>> that for my faults ye will me gently beat.

Spenser opens his sonnet by commending in his beloved the grace which complements mortal nature. His beloved becomes a new Pandora: her task is to cleanse the natural "faults" which afflict the poet. Spenser has twisted the classical source to fit his compliment, because Pandora was sent to punish with evil rather than cleanse from it. However, the reference to her as a "scourge" cannot readily be explained. A first reading suggests a sonnet which is the result of a clever working, which is technically correct, but which ends with a rather out-of-character final couplet.

But the second lesson at morning prayer for Friday 15 February, Mark 15, with which *Amoretti* 24 corresponds, throws a different light on the sonnet, for it suggests that Spenser has written a sonnet that is clearly risqué. Mark 15 recounts in detail the scourging ("when he had scourged him") and death of Christ (vv. 15–20). The gospel reading also suggests Spenser's train of thought: having read the gospel account of the scourging, he has retained the word "scourge," transferred its sense to the context of revenge, and composed a sonnet, in whose sestet "scourge" is used in both its vengeful and its physical sense.

The image of the "scourge," then, corresponds plainly with the Marcan account. But the second lesson at evening prayer, 2 Corinthians 11, suggests that Spenser had little option but to compose for the day a sonnet concerned with scourging and beating, because in it Paul refers repeatedly to his own beatings: "in stripes aboue measure," "fiue times receiued I fortie *stripes* saue one," "I was thrise beaten with roddes" (vv. 23–25).

The reasons why Spenser has chosen to identify his lady as "a new *Pandora*" are less patent. He was, at the very least, drawing upon a tradition with which he was well acquainted. He had already translated du Bellay's nineteenth sonnet, "Tout le parfait dont le ciel nous honnore," from *Antiquitez de Rome,* in which Pandora, an amalgam of good and evil, had become a symbol for Rome, the eternal city:

> All the mishap, the which our daies outweares,
> All the good hap of th'oldest times afore,
> *Rome* in the time of her great ancesters,
> Like a *Pandora,* locked long in store.[43]

The custom of associating Rome and Pandora was frequent in the 16th century. A Rome-like city, for example, constitutes the background of the well-known Renaissance *Pandora* of Jean Cousin. The painting has reclining in its foreground a sensuous nude, with a serpent curled around her arm, while the space between her and the background is bridged by an arch from which is suspended a plate bearing the inscription, "EVA PRIMA PANDORA."[44] The iconographic identification of Rome, Pandora and Eve, and the serpent (curled around Pandora/Eve's arm) was founded, in turn, on the opening verses of the day's second lesson at evening prayer, in which Paul warns against impurity infecting the true church: "But I feare lest as the serpent beguiled Eue through his subtiltie, so your mindes shoulde be corrupte from the simplicitie that is in Christ" (2 Corinthians 11.3). The Geneva Bible's sidenote to the verse identified the threat to the church as "the arrogancie of the false apostles . . . who soght nothing els, but to ouer throwe the Church." To accommodate his sonnet to the scriptural verse, Spenser has made the standard Protestant association of Eve and the serpent with Rome, and with Pandora, and has subsequently associated Pandora

---

[43] *Ruines of Rome,* 257–60.

[44] Dora and Erwin Panofsky, *Pandora's Box. The Changing Aspects of a Mythical Symbol* (London, 1956), 58–65, who see a strong correspondence between the *Eva Prima Pandora* of Cousin and the *Lutetia Nova Pandora,* which formed part of the triumphal arch marking the entry of Henry II of France into Paris in 1549, and hypothesize that the painting originally intended two figures, one personating Paris in the guise of the "new Pandora," the other Rome in the guise of the "old Pandora."

both with 2 Corinthians 11's allusions to "beating," with which he has concluded the sonnet, and with Mark 15's image of "scourge," which he has used in its twofold sense of both a whip and an instrument of divine justice.[45]

Yet more of the sonnet is indebted to Mark 15. The opening quatrain's claim that the lady's beauty is greater than the natural creation, "of natures skill the onely complement," identifies her with the new and greater creation brought about by Christ's passion and death. In the second quatrain the poet identifies himself with Christ, who was also subjected to the "bitter balefull smart" of death. In the third the roles are reversed and the lady, a new Pandora, is identified with Christ, who was sent "into this sinfull world from heauen," that he might suffer and be scourged; so the lady is "to wicked men a scourge." As Christ bore the sins and faults of all, so the lady will also drive out "all their faults with which they did offend." In the final couplet the lady is the means by which the poet's faults will be cleansed, but now the poet is identified with Christ and Paul, who both bore harsh scourgings, while he pleads for a gentle one.

The sonnet's corresponding scripture readings thereby expand a single reading of the sonnet into a poem that moves on a number of levels. The way that Spenser has manipulated the scriptural roles by shifting and reversing the christic identifications must be construed as audacious; the final couplet, especially, becomes a loaded remonstrating which involves a trusting and suggestive coyness. On an intimate level the attraction of the sonnet lies in its secret daring and the thrill that such clandestine readings might provide. Thus the private and intimate nature of the *amoretti* is revealed as ranging from straightforward compliment to the most discreet of praises: the playfulness of *Amoretti* 4 and the slightly fescennine impropriety of *Amoretti* 24 disclose their smiling good humor and hint at how Spenser has used the associations of the daily scripture lessons to create a range of voices and covertly to extend the impact of a sonnet's initial direction.

During this first section Spenser's versatility is manifest in the way in which his adopted convention sits nicely in place and its requirements are easily met. But, just when such mastery is acquired, Spenser turns upon the convention and begins subtly to parody its Petrarchism.[46] He uses the

---

[45] Spenser also refers to "the euills ... hydden in the baskette of *Pandora,*" when discussing the need for a scourge for papist Ireland in the opening exchanges of *A View of the Present State of Ireland,* 44.13–15 & 45.44, "that Allmighty god hathe not yeat Appointed the tyme of her reformacion or that he reserueth her in this vnquiet state still, for some secrete skourge, which shall by her Come vnto Englande."

[46] The parodic has often been generally noted, although seldom instanced. See Louis Martz, "The *Amoretti:* 'Most Goodly Temperature,'" in William Nelson, ed. *Form and*

scripture readings to endow his sonnets with a voice which, in being too forceful, mocks the received. He seems increasingly to have found the Petrarchist tradition an inadequate vehicle to convey the final "simple truth and mutuall good will" (*Amoretti* 65.11), which will bind the poet and his betrothed. During this first section of the sequence, however, he confines himself to extending the postured and self-absorbed nature of conceited love, only gradually discarding the capricious and whimsical in favor of a heavy and more mocking tone. The parody is paralleled by an increase in the sonnets' cautionary nature as they become more serious-minded and devotional, each movement preparing the way for the more devotional sonnets of Easter and after.

   *Amoretti* 46 is one of the few in the sequence which apparently refers to an actual incident. The poet, having visited his lady and having been bid leave, is delayed by a storm. The actuality of the occasion is reinforced by the adjective, "prefixed," which not only posits an agreed limited period of time, but also carries a sense of the prognosticatory and the ominous, as no doubt the threatening rack of clouds were. But the sonnet also profits from its accompanying day's lesson to advance its tragi-comic impact, because the poet throughout retains a propriety associated with Christ's innocence.

> WHen my abodes prefixed time is spent,
>     My cruell fayre streight bids me wend my way:
>     but then from heauen most hideous stormes are sent
>     as willing me against her will to stay.
> Whom then shall I or heauen or her obay?
>     the heauens know best what is the best for me:
>     but as she will, whose will my life doth sway,
>     my lower heauen, so it perforce must bee.
> But ye high heuens, that all this sorowe see,
>     sith all your tempests cannot hold me backe:
>     aswage your stormes, or else both you and she
>     will both together me too sorely wrack.

---

*Convention in the Poetry of Edmund Spenser* (New York: Columbia Univ. Press, 1961), 157–61; Robert Kellogg, "Thought's Astonishment and the Dark Conceits of Spenser's *Amoretti*," in J. R. Elliott, ed. *The Prince of Poets, Essays on Edmund Spenser* (New York: New York Univ. Press, 1968), 142 takes issue with Martz' argument, because he "collapses the distinction between the historical Spenser and the speaker of the sonnets." Peter M. Cummings likewise disagrees with Martz and expands Kellogg's argument in "Spenser's *Amoretti* as an Allegory of Love," *TSLL* 12 (1970–71): 164. Joseph Loewenstein ("Echo's Ring: Orpheus and Spenser's Career," *ELR* 16 [1986]: 293) has argued that "the wedding volume of 1595 engages in a critique of the degenerate Petrarchanism."

> Enough it is for one man to sustaine
>> the stormes, which she alone on me doth raine.

Spenser, having established the actual event in the opening quatrain, reshapes it in the light of the second lesson at morning prayer for Saturday 9 March, Luke 20, with which the sonnet corresponds. The chapter contains the scriptural episode in which the scribes and elders question Christ as to the source of his authority which must be obeyed. They asked: "Tell us by what autoritie thou doest these things, or who is he that hathe giuen thee this autoritie? And he answered and said vnto them, I also wil aske you one thing: tell me therefore: The baptisme of John was it from heauen, or of men?" (vv. 2–4). *Amoretti* 46 reflects the gospel's dilemma in its second quatrain, as Spenser in imitation asks whether he should obey heaven or men, "Whom then shall I or heauen or her obay?" Where the scribes subsequently debated among themselves, "If we shal say from heauen, he wil say, Why then beleued ye him not? But if we shal say, Of men, all the people wil stone vs" (vv. 5–6), so also in lines 5–8 the poet debates his dilemma. He is forced to solve his dilemma not in favor of his own interests but in favor of the lady's will, resolving to go forth into the storm and asking that the heavens withhold their fury, because he can sustain only the one storm, that which the lady rains upon him. The scribes, of course, refuse to solve their dilemma.

The sonnet's hyperbole is thus advanced by the dilemma of the scripture reading and an initial actual situation is transformed by it into an overweighty and too serious argument. The scriptural echoes also magnify the posturing of the poet, for they imply in the end a voice too redolent of pretense. Because he is forced to forsake heaven and succumb to the will of men, the poet is maneuvered into the very position the pharisees had sought to avoid. His sense of being victimized and his overly plaintive stance eventually verge on the facetious, and caricature becomes the sonnet's true direction. Otherwise, in associating the lady with a position antipathetic to Christ's intent, he is unfair to her to an improper degree. On another level, of course, the sonnet always remains a conventional one with just the proper touch or amount of hyperbole.

The scriptural key also expands the focus of *Amoretti* 47, although Spenser now drops the simple playfulness of *Amoretti* 46 and reverts to travesty:

> TRust not the treason of those smyling lookes,
>> vntill ye haue theyr guylefull traynes well tryde:
> for they are lyke but vnto golden hookes,
>> that from the foolish fish theyr bayts doe hyde:
> So she with flattring smyles weake harts doth guyde
>> vnto her loue, and tempte to theyr decay,

> whom being caught she kills with cruell pryde,
>     and feeds at pleasure on the wretched pray:
> Yet euen whylst her bloody hands them slay,
>     her eyes looke louely and vpon them smyle:
>     that they take pleasure in her cruell play,
>     and dying doe them selues of payne beguyle.
> O mighty charm which makes men loue theyr bane,
>     and thinck they dy with pleasure, liue with payne.

The thematic and verbal correspondences between the sonnet and the readings for Sunday 10 March make it clear that the poet has associated the lady with the enemies of Christ. Luke 21, the day's second lesson at morning prayer, cautions frequently against deception: "Take hede, that ye be not deceiued. ... And when ye heare of warres and seditions, be not afrayed" (vv. 8–9). Luke's theme of deception and sedition becomes *Amoretti* 47's opening conceit, "Trust not the treason of those smyling lookes." The gospel continues to repeat the warning, because "as a snare shal it come on all them" (v. 35, to which is attached the sidenote, "To catch and intangle them"). The "catch" is reflected in the sonnet's "being caught," and the "snare" is echoed in the sonnet's general theme of entrapment and in its "guylefull traynes." As well, the poet's condemnation of the lady, because "her bloody hands them slay," recalls the gospel's prophecies that "they shal lay their hands on you" (v. 12), and "some of you shal they put to death" (v. 16).

On the one hand, then, Spenser continues to allow the public poet in *Amoretti* 47 to ply his conventional conceits and metaphors. He will even allow him sufficient nuances here and there to suggest that his voice is not quite as plain-speaking as the published text might imply. The sonnet's final couplet, for example, with its plaintive vocative, its insistent paradox, and its quasi-oxymoron, verges on the histrionic, and its vocal inflections contribute to the righteousness that the conventional poet appropriates to himself. But the scriptural echoes enlarge the poem's histrionics, for they ally the lady's smile with the plottings and cunning of other persecutors. The sonnet's rancor also acquires a further edge, because the "bloody hands them slay" is similarly associated and casts the lady in an even less favorable light than the conventional indictment might suggest and excuse. Yet, because the sonnet's rancor is of the realm of artifice, and because the lady's behavior must in the end remain excusable, what the scriptural associations finally achieve is to overload the sonnet's indictment with too weighty an impact. In the final analysis the poem can only be read as travesty: only if the poet's covert voice, scripturally knowledgeable, is construed as too feigned, can escape and relief from the scriptural compounding and overstatement be found, as Spenser subtly laughs at the very convention he is employing.

A similar top-heavy effect is obtained in *Amoretti* 49. It opens with the standard Petrarchist paradox, "Fayre cruell," which it develops within the parameters of the legendary cockatrice or basilisk, the stock Petrarchist image of love and combat. The mythical reptile, born of a cock's egg and hatched by a serpent, matches exactly the striking image in Tuesday 12 March's morning prayer Psalm 58.3-4, with which *Amoretti* 49 corresponds, "The vngodly are frowarde euen from their mothers wombe. . . . They are as venemous as the poyson of a Serpent: euen like the deafe Adder that stoppeth her eares." (Spenser, in identifying the day's reference to "Serpent" and "Adder" with the cockatrice or basilisk, has accepted the traditional association of Psalm 58.3-4 with Vulgate Psalm 91.13, "Super aspidem et basilicum ambulabis, / Et conculcabis leonem et draconem.")

> FAyre cruell, why are ye so fierce and cruell?
>> Is it because your eyes haue powre to kill?
>> then know, that mercy is the mighties jewell,
>> and greater glory thinke to saue, then spill.
> But if it be your pleasure and proud will,
>> to shew the powre of your imperious eyes:
>> then not on him that neuer thought you ill,
>> but bend your force against your enemyes.
> Let them feele th'utmost of your crueltyes,
>> and kill with looks as Cockatrices doo:
>> but him that at your footstoole humbled lies,
>> with mercifull regard, giue mercy too.
> Such mercy shal you make admyred to be,
>> so shall you liue by giuing life to me.

The sonnet is replete with word-plays and etymological puns which make it a more elaborate working of the conceit than most. Its vocabulary plays extensively on an etymological pun on βασίλίσκος, which means either a basilisk or "imperious" and "mightie." He has also wittily played upon the Vulgate's adjacent *conculcabis* (from *con* + *calco*, to tread under foot) and created an etymological pleonasm, for cockatrice was thought to have derived from *calcatrix* (= she who treads under foot), the feminine form of the noun from *calco*. He has then explicated the pun in the next line, "him that at your footstoole humbled lies." The line is itself an echo of the psalm verse, "vntill I make thine enemies thy footestoole" (Psalm 110.1), which Christ's triumph over death was customarily seen as fulfilling, and which the day's second lesson at morning prayer Luke 23 recounts. Through the spilling of blood, Christ's death purchases mercy; so the poet also commends mercy: "then know, that mercy is the mighties jewell." As Luke records the jibes of Christ's enemies, "he saued others: let him saue him self" (v. 35) and "If thou be the King of the Jewes, saue thy self" (v. 37), so the lady is advised that it is a "greater glory ... to saue, then spill." As "Herode with his men or warre, despised him, and mocked him" (v. 11), so the poet calls on the lady to mock her enemies and not himself. The final couplet converts the life Christ gained into the hope that the lady, by living, will also award the poet life.

On the one hand, then, the standard conceits of *Amoretti* 49, "Fayre cruell," "imperious eyes," "mercy," "Cockatrices," all establish it initially as a piece of perfunctory artifice, while the poet's posturing is what might be expected of the thwarted lover. But the scriptural associations of the day's readings cryptically cast the lady in a role beyond the customary "Fayre cruell," for her action in killing has been covertly allied with those who caused Christ's death; only in the final couplet is she associated with the christic example of life and mercy. Moreover, the poet's voice, already strident upon first reading, now becomes impossibly so. The scriptural key, by reinforcing the voice as that of a helpless victim, affirms the poet's posturing as excessively plaintive and exposes both his courtly and poetic roles to caricature. His covert voice, revealed as exaggeratedly histrionic, finally succeeds in mocking itself and thus calls into disrepute the very vehicle with which it has chosen to express itself.

In the Elizabethan sonnet sequences of Spenser's contemporaries, particularly Sidney and Shakespeare, the lover's public voice and role are manipulated and even suborned by the author to reveal a range and variety of tones. The formal presentation and insistent proprieties of Spenser's *Amoretti*, however, initially mask any such manipulation. As well, the accented final syllables of Spenser's lines and the interlocking patterns of final sounds create a mellifluous voice which contrasts markedly with the insistent voice that juts out from the lines of many Sidneian or Shakespearean sonnets. Spenser's authorial working is thus hidden behind the *amoretti*'s fluent formality.

Spenser, however, in choosing frequently to parody the form he has adopted is not remote from his contemporaries. Indeed, like other sonnet cycles of the late sixteenth century, the rigor of *Amoretti* lies partially in his willingness to turn against his received Petrarchism, which in many ways came to be fashionable only to the degree that, once established, it could be parodied. Moreover, his parodic intent finally surpasses that of his contemporaries who turn their Petrarchism to parodic advantage without allowing it to collapse into travesty.

The scriptural key, furthermore, by unlocking other readings, shows Spenser's adroit mastery of tone to be greater than that of his contemporaries, and his use of the fashionable conceit and the sonnet structure to be free and subject to little constraint. The sonnets' language is underlaid at least once by their scriptural subsidium, and frequently more than once, either by their extensive and witty word-play or by the too high-flown hyperbole and bombast that the scripture readings show to be present. Layers of language are intermingled to create differing registers of voice and self-dialogue, so that humor, salaciousness, irony, parody, and ultimately travesty, are all revealed.

On the public level, then, the sequence observes the convention in which the poet-lover plays out his existence in "this worlds theatre in which we stay" (*Amoretti* 54.1). The scriptural subtext, however, in creating different vocal and self-dialogic registers, finally allows the poet's own voice alone to be sacrosanct and inviolate. The voice that gives birth to the irony, the mock anger, even the travesty, is the voice that profits from accepted scriptural veracity to assert itself as the ultimate register by which truth can be adjudged.

Because the ironic is hidden from the public eye, an artifice has been fashioned in which the privilege of discerning the covert voice is awarded only to the lady. The *amoretti*, then, are deeply grounded in the reality of Spenser and Elizabeth Boyle, because the poet observes the convention that the lady's "deep wit" can "construe well" (*Amoretti* 43.13–14) factors hidden in the sonnet. In challenging her to construe the detail of his wit he has fashioned a figure who is knowledgeable, conversant with languages, and striving to be, if not actually, his equal.[47] On the public level the sonnets assert always that both the poet and lady were of sufficient awareness and sophistication to see the *amoretti*'s artifices for what they were. But, because the secret of the covert voice is presented as restricted to two, natural enough to verses so closely ensconced in a betrothal period, their immensely personal nature remains hidden. Indeed the absence of an authorial dedication or introduction to *Amoretti* makes the authorial presence even more discreet and anonymous.

Yet the scripture passages reveal, in moments of extreme parody, the existence of Spenser's own voice embedded in the *amoretti*. Moreover, because it is the same voice of reason and righteousness which will speak publicly in the devotional sonnets of the second part of the sequence, the parodic *amoretti* are precursors that set the scene for the new genre of sonnets that will finally eventuate for the period around Easter. The scrip-

---

[47] For the same conclusion from a different direction, see William C. Johnson, "Gender Fashioning and the Dynamics of Mutuality in Spenser's *Amoretti*," *ES* 74.6 (1993): 503–19.

tural associations thus reveal Spenser putting his parodic sonnets to good effect. He intersperses them during the final days of the *amoretti*'s first section with sonnets of a more serious nature and establishes them as studies for what will come. The covert voice discovered behind the parody is the same voice that will speak publicly later in the sequence and in *Epithalamion*. As the *amoretti* progress they reveal their devolving nature, ultimately reaching their own unsustainability; the sequence can now either collapse upon itself or be reinvested with new found proprieties and vigor. Subsequent sonnets, and the love they portray, are no longer the fashionably conventional. That mode has been surpassed as the sonnets, with their emptied form, prepare the way for a new, personal, and particularly English Protestant resolution to the sequence.

### B. The Sonnets for the Easter Period

Spenser has established the sonnets, which correspond to the fortnight between Palm and Low Sundays, as the turning-point of *Amoretti*. The parodic, which prepared the way for the devotional, has served its purpose, while the reflective nature of the Easter sonnets demonstrates how carefully he has gone about their writing.[48] Their thoughtfulness confirms that he intends that the sequence should now have an overall design, even if it will later be modified by the addition of the Expectation sonnets. Because the scriptural allusions no longer stand out sharply, but are worked smoothly into the sonnets' texture, the poet's covert voice is also much closer to the sonnets' surface than on earlier occasions.

The sonnets of a more devotional nature are prefaced by *Amoretti* 58 and 59, in which the poet is preoccupied with the dangers of self-assurance and the flesh. These hesitancies are overcome as the poet takes stock of his life and courtship and looks forward to "this yeare ensuing" in *Amoretti* 60. *Amoretti* 61, written for Palm Sunday, 24 March 1594, makes the poet's resolve explicit. It first establishes the lady's birth as an analogue of Christ's. The feast's Epistle, Philippians 2.5–12, confirms the poet's position among the sonnet's "men of meane degree" (14), who "dare" to love. It is such men who ought not to accuse the lady of pride, "dare not hence forth aboue the bounds of dewtie, / t'accuse of pride or rashly blame for ought" (3–4). Spenser is therefore admonishing himself. The "henceforth" also gives the poem a forward direction. He affirms his intent not to subject the

---

[48] Among others, G. K. Hunter, "Spenser's *Amoretti* and the English Sonnet Tradition," in Judith M. Kennedy & James H. Reither, eds. *A Theatre for Spenserians* (Toronto: Univ. of Toronto Press, 1973), 125 confirms the sequence's change of tone, but rightly qualifies his claim: "I do not allege that what I have called a change of tone after sonnet 62 (or so) affects every sonnet on either side of this divide."

lady to accusation but qualifies his resolve by insisting that he will, if duty demands. He may so accuse or blame her, he seems to be saying, when it is his duty or when it is necessary and proper, but not on other occasions such as, for example, when poetic hyperbole might have allowed in the past. *Amoretti* 61 thus carries within it the poet's intent to resist the conventional and mannered conceits of earlier sonnets, and the subsequent poems of the Easter season generally bear out his resolve, showing Spenser to be particularly conscious of priorities that were developing in Protestant thinking on marriage.[49]

The pre-Lenten and Lenten sonnets had referred only infrequently to the poet's forthcoming marriage. *Amoretti* 6, for example, distinguishes initially between "loue" and "lusts of baser kind," both of which have their effect upon him, but sees the tension between them being resolved by marriage. The plea of the sonnet, "to knit the knot, that euer shall remaine" (14), hints, even at an very early stage in the sequence, that only in marriage will chastity and entirety be permanently accomplished. The poet's preoccupation with the inclining of his will toward evil recurs regularly throughout the sequence. *Amoretti* 8 contrasts "base affections" with "chast desires," although the poet finds comfort in the healing powers of the lady: "you calme the storme that passion did begin." As well, the period around the beginning of Lent is appropriately concerned with the the improprieties of the flesh: *Amoretti* 21, written for Shrove Tuesday, makes reference to the "looser lookes that stir up lustes impure," with which the sonnet for Ash Wednesday contrasts the "flames of pure and chast desyre" (*Amoretti* 22.12).

The sonnets corresponding to the middle period of Lent show an introspective, even melancholic tone. The poet continues to ponder his inner state and withdraws more and more into "my selfe, my inward selfe I meane" (*Amoretti* 45.3), where he inhabits his own private world. His sense of frustration is caused partly by his inability to assuage his passions. *Amoretti* 44 complains of the "ciuill warre" that plagues and tears him asunder and for which reason provides no relief, "whilest my weak powres of passions warreid arre, / no skill can stint nor reason can aslake" (7–8). Although not stated, it would have been well understood that only in marriage will the poet find the proper skill or discernment to mitigate his

---

[49] Spenser's Protestantism has been variously treated during this century, more recent discussion focussing on the relationship between nature and grace in *The Faerie Queene*, see A. S. P. Woodhouse, "Nature and Grace in *The Faerie Queene*," *ELH* 16 (1949): 194–228, and "Spenser, Nature and Grace: Mr Gang's Mode of Argument Reviewed," *ELH* 27 (1960): 1–15; Robert Hoopes, " 'God Guide Thee, Guyon': Nature and Grace Reconciled in *The Faerie Queene*, Book II," *RES* n.s. 5 (1954): 14–24, and finally Andrea Hume, *Edmund Spenser. Protestant Poet* (Cambridge: Cambridge Univ. Press, 1984).

awakened passions; only then will reason "aslake" passion, by directing the will of both spouses to the good that is mutual chastity. As yet, however, the poet can find no relief in his solitariness, and the sonnets of this period are marked by an unresolved tension, in which the passions are at war not only with each other but also with grace, and the poet's unease is reflected in his self-preoccupied complaining. Such plaintiveness fulfills the poetic requirements of Spenser's Petrarchist *exempla*, although the consistent undermining and parodying of the model during this middle section of *Amoretti* reinforce the presence of a Protestant ethos of unresolved conflict.

The sonnets subsequent to Palm Sunday indicate a resolution to these tensions, as Spenser celebrates the good will which is proper to the covenant of grace in which regeneration is sealed. *Amoretti* 65, the sonnet for Maundy Thursday, is the first to pronounce and uphold the "mutuall good will" of the betrothed and to acclaim the new freedoms that the covenant of marriage will bring, "two liberties ye gayne." *Amoretti* 65's general association of freedom and will foreshadows a similar conceit of captivity, freedom and will in *Amoretti* 67, and its phrases, "bondage earst dyd fly" and "true loue doth tye" anticipate *Amoretti* 67's "sought not to fly" and "hir fyrmely tyde." *Amoretti* 67 is a cumulative sonnet and a pivotal one; its line, "So after long pursuit and vaine assay" (5), recollects the opening line of *Amoretti* 63, "After long stormes and tempests sad assay," and introduces one of the most gentle of all the *amoretti*;[50] its culmination is full of the wonderful effects of good will, which bring the betrothed together:

> There she beholding me with mylder looke,
>> sought not to fly, but fearelesse still did bide:
>> till I in hand her yet halfe trembling tooke,
>> and with her owne goodwill hir fyrmely tyde.
> Strange thing me seemd to see a beast so wyld,
>> so goodly wonne with her owne will beguyld. (8–14)

The sonnet displays the poet's discovery of the wondrous operating, despite his or his "deare's" own endeavours. The state of good will to which the final line refers is proper to the state of regeneration. *Amoretti* 10's "licentious blisse / of her freewill" has now been surpassed; Lenten trials have ceded place to a sense of resolution, the will can now freely turn towards good, and holiness of will can occur.

The *amoretti* are shaped thus so that their direction turns on the Easter liturgical celebration.[51] Good will, being an integral part of the regenerate

---

[50] Prescott (1985), 33–76.

[51] William C. Johnson, *Spenser's Amoretti: Analogies of Love* (Lewisburg: Bucknell Univ.

state, is an accomplishment of Christ's salvific act: "the will of a Christian is renued and purified by Christ, which appeareth in that it is so farre forth freed from sinne, that it can will and choose that which is good and acceptable to God, and refuse that which is euill."[52] At Easter, Christ's loosing man from the bondage of sin and his purchasing of freedom liberate the will, which is no longer prone to captivity. The Easter *amoretti* are much concerned with the covenant, which brings grace and freedom, and the images of captivity and bondage are a dominant concern during the week.[53] But captivity is overcome by the triumph of Christ on Easter Sunday, who "led captiuitie captiue" (Ephesians 4.8), which Spenser cites in the Easter Sunday sonnet. The Easter sonnets celebrate the triumph over the old bondage of lust and passion, and acknowledge the newly founded covenant of grace, in which the will of the regenerate individual freely inclines towards good and in which the betrothed together will share.

Spenser thus finds a solution to earlier tensions in contemporary Protestant thinking on marriage, which departed from received marriage doctrine by bringing to it the theology of the covenant. For the Elizabethan divine, who espoused the traditional view of marriage, the action of grace within the partners occurred concomitantly with the marriage ceremony, because that was also the manner of grace's operating in the sacraments of baptism and the eucharist. For the Protestant, however, grace, because of election, was necessarily prior to marriage, and was even construed as the cause of the partners' decision to marry. The covenant of marriage confirmed the already existing covenant between the individuals and God and Protestant divines customarily identified marriage as a socio-political covenant under the term "league,"[54] a term Spenser employs in *Amoretti* 65.9,

---

Press, 1990), 181–201 arrives at the same conclusion from a different perspective. A. Leigh DeNeef, *Spenser and the Motives of Metaphor* (Durham: Duke Univ. Press, 1982), 73 writing of *Am.* 68, "Christ enters the textual sequence in order to force all literal narrative places into accommodating Him; but His action is itself metaphoric of the Idea of Love which He too imitates. The reformation which Christ accomplishes is thus a model rather than an end, and the poet's new task at the conclusion of the sequence is to reveal how such a model resolves all places into one, or frees all desire to love to aspire to the divine idea of Love."

[52] William Perkins, *A Treatise Tending unto a Declaration, Whether a Man Be In a Estate of Damnation, Or In the Estate of Grace*, in *The Workes of . . . M. William Perkins* (Cambridge, 1609), 1:370–71, cols. 2 & 1.

[53] Besides *Am.* 67's images of the chase and capture, with the "deare" being "so goodly wonne" and "fyrmely tyde," the Maundy Thursday sonnet also treats of bondage and reproves her "That fondly feare[s] to loose your liberty."

[54] Perkins, *A Reformed Catholike: or, A Declaration shewing how neere we may come to the present Church of Rome in sundry points of Religion: and wherein we must forever depart from them*, in *Workes*, 1:613, col. 2: "Now the marriages of Protestants with Papists are priuate

the most matrimonially directed of all the *amoretti*: "the league twixt them, that loyal loue hath bound."

*Amoretti* 65 corresponds with Maundy Thursday, which commemorated the institution of the new covenant of grace between Christ and the faithful, and Spenser has appropriately incorporated a covenantal view of marriage into his sonnet for the feast. His marriage covenant will be founded upon and will confirm the already existing covenant of grace and righteousness between each partner and God. Each partner's individual covenant with God has been absorbed into the new covenant of themselves and God.

There is, however, a further and more compelling reason for Spenser to celebrate the new covenant of grace on Maundy Thursday. In 1594, by extreme coincidence, the feast days of Maundy Thursday, 28 March, when Christ's sealing of the new covenant of love is celebrated, and St. Barnabas, 11 June, when the new covenant of grace between the spouses will be sealed, share the same reading, John 15. The chapter is the second lesson at morning prayer for 28 March, on which date Holy Thursday fell in 1594, and is also the Gospel for the feast of St. Barnabas, John 15.12–16. The gospel verses acclaim the new covenant of love, and both election to it, "Ye haue not chosen me, but I haue chosen you," and the secret nature of that election, "All things that I haue heard of my father, haue I made knowen to you." The events of Maundy Thursday thus liturgically anticipate and found the covenant whose liturgical reality the feast of St. Barnabas also celebrates. 11 June's liturgical celebration in turn underwrites the spouses' personal reality, the new covenant of grace between themselves and God, which Maundy Thursday in its anticipatory way enfolds. The elegance of Spenser's *Amoretti* 65 attests to his subtle appreciation of the coincidence, because in it, covertly, the liturgical is made to enclose the actual.

Spenser extends the parameters of the marriage "league" to accommodate within it a reflection of a further Protestant emphasis in marriage. Traditional teaching about the purposes or 'ends' of marriage had been incorporated into the 1559 *Book of Common Prayer*; it accepted the received order of the three causes of marriage: procreation and education of children, a remedy against sin, and "mutuall societie, helpe and comfort." Protestant theology placed the covenantly allied end of "mutual societie, helpe and comfort" in a more prominent position and attached to it the customary second end, "a remedie against sin," which in earlier theology was generally attached to marriage's procreative first end. Divorced from its procreative

---

leagues of amitie, betweene person and person: and therefore not to be allowed. Againe, Mal. 2.11. *Iudah hath defiled the holinesse of the Lord which he loued, and hath married the daughter of a strange God*: where is flatly condemned marriages made with the people of a false God."

function, sexual intercourse then became a way by which mutual society and comfort were furthered.

*Amoretti* 65 acclaims the "simple truth" of betrothal, innocent, therefore, and not divided, and defines the nature of the "league" as founded on "mutuall good will." Spenser thus explicitly accords the covenantly associated end of marriage, "mutuall societie," the priority his Protestant colleagues accorded it and endorses their position by appending to it the adjunctive end of the remedying of sin, "to salue each others wound":

> the league twixt them, that loyal loue hath bound:
> but simple truth and mutuall good will,
> seekes with sweet peace to salue each others wound: (10–12)

The sonnet's concluding couplet defines the covenant of love as inhabited by faith:

> There fayth doth fearlesse dwell in brasen towre,
> and spotlesse pleasure builds her sacred bowre. (13–14)

In paralleling "fayth" and "spotlesse treasure," Spenser articulates the standard association between the Easter events, faith, and a spotless and spiritual marriage. Because faith is a prerequisite of the covenant of grace, it is also a prerequisite of the marriage covenant. Through faith, the "use" of the marriage bed is "made a holy and undefiled action." According to Perkins, the word of God gives the spouses a "warrant, that they may lawfully doe this action; because whatsoeuer is not done of faith (which faith must be grounded on Gods word) is a sinne."[55] Likewise Spenser in *Amoretti* 65 affirms that faith renders the impairments of the flesh a "spotlesse pleasure," and, by remedying the lust of the flesh, absorbs its difficulties into the freedom awarded by the covenant of grace. Marriage has become the solution to the passions and the flesh, those passions that in the past reason could not "aslake" (*Amoretti* 44.8).

Spenser's debt to Protestant marriage doctrine in the *amoretti* of the Easter period lies, finally, with their baptismal allusions. Protestants disavowed any sacramental function in marriage: just as the covenant is prior to the marriage, so it is prior to the sacrament.[56] Since the events of Easter are those upon which both the covenant and the sacraments are founded, the covenant of grace confirmed in marriage is underpinned by the

---

[55] Perkins, *Christian Oeconomie*, in *Workes*, 3:689, col. 1 & 2.

[56] Perkins, *A Golden Chaine*, in *Workes*, 1:73, col. 1, explains that, "The couenant of grace is absolutely necessarie to saluation . . . but a Sacrament is not absolutely necessarie, but onely as it is a proppe and stay for faith to leane vpon."

same confirming and sealing that occurs originally in baptism. In the sonnets of Easter Spenser accepts baptism as the archetypical sign or token of the covenant of grace, of which marriage is also a sign.

There are references to baptism in *Amoretti* 67, where the deer recalls not only the "hart" of the *Sicut cervus*, the baptismal psalm, but also the Old Testament model of marriage, the marital admonition from Proverbs 5.18-19, which links baptism to marriage through the cervine association of "rejoyce with the wife of thy youth. *Let her be as* the louing hinde and pleasant roe: let her breasts satisfie thee at all times, and delite in her loue continually."[57] *Amoretti* 70 for Easter Tuesday makes reference to immersion (12), while *Amoretti* 74's division of nature, grace, and glory reflects the poet's three births, the second of which is baptism. *Amoretti* 75 further suggests that he is prepared, finally, to define his marriage in the baptismal and covenantal context of naming, which underwrites and seals the covenant of marriage. The sonnet was written for the First Sunday after Easter, 7 April, when the neophytes, having been born again through water and having received their names, are required no longer to wear their white vestments. The sonnet's fusing together of the images of water, name, the immortality that rebirth brings, and the "vaine" nature of earthly endeavor, which are all found in the day's readings, implies a baptismal context which seals the betrothed's covenant of grace.[58] It also brings to a close the sonnets of the Easter period, Spenser seemingly intending to write no further sonnets. There were appropriate religious and liturgical reasons for

---

[57] Cleaver, *A Godlie Forme of Householde Gouernment*,183 glosses the verses: "And therfore Pro. 5.19. we see that the wife should be to him, as the louing Hind: namely, delightful, and one in whom he may delight: that as the Hart delighteth in the Hind: so the wife should be a delight vnto her husband: and so in like manner, she ought to take delight in him." The increased frequency with which Spenser employs the term "delight," during this period which liturgically celebrates the foundation of marriage, is pronounced. After only 3 occurrences in the first 58 sonnets compare *Am.* 59.8: "false delight;" *Am.* 62.14: "chaunge old yeares annoy to new delight;" *Am.* 63.11: "whose least delight;" *Am.* 72.9: "There my fraile fancy fed with full delight;" *Am.* 73.11: "learne with rare delight, / to sing your name;" *Am.* 76.2: "The neast of loue, the lodging of delight."

[58] The association of naming with baptism is clearcut, as indeed is the Protestant association of "name" with the covenant of grace, see Gee, *The Ground of Christianitie* (London, 1594), 70, "What meaneth Christ, when hee saith: Baptising them into the name, or in the name of the Father, and of the Sonne, and of the Holie ghost? He dooth not simplie commaund them to baptize such as do beleue, but to consigne them in baptisme into the name, that is to say, into the possession, right, religion, and grace of the father, and of the sonne, and of the holie spirit, to be the people of God, the partakers of his couenaunt and grace. And if we doo expound into the name, that is to say, into the faith and confession of his name, or in to his possession, power, and iurisdiction, or into the strength and power, or into the couenant and grace, of the father, and the sonne, and the holie spirit, it is no matter, for all this is true, and agreeth with the nature of baptisme."

his decision to finish here. He has presented his marriage as a sign of the covenant which is sealed during the days of Easter, and the sonnets that belong to the period culminate the process of celebration in *Amoretti.* Easter Monday's sonnet acknowledges the poet's "happy purchase. ... / gotten at last with labour and long toyle," and celebrates the positive realities of "honour, loue, and chastity" (*Amoretti* 69.8). *Amoretti* 75 ends on a note of finality, with its concluding line pointing to a marriage that will persist here-after: "our loue shall liue, and later life renew." The liturgical occasion of Low Sunday has, for the moment, brought the sequence to an acceptable end, by acknowledging the sealing by grace of the everlasting covenant of marriage.

The framing of the *amoretti* thus far turns, therefore, on their distinc-tively Protestant consciousness. In the first section of *Amoretti* Spenser, having begun the sequence by meeting the requirements of Petrarchist *exem-pla,* submitted the model to parody. In the sonnets of Easter and there-abouts, his poetic vision has had recourse to a Protestant doctrine of marriage, that sees the covenant of grace as the unifying and sanctifying factor which resolves the tensions of a fallen state. In marriage God's "pre-ventyng and workyng grace" heals the individual's impaired will and, through mutuality, renders it "good wyll." The covenant of grace, to which Spenser's marriage will attest, thus provides a distinctively Protestant reso-lution to the tensions that inhabit earlier *amoretti.* Such an outcome is uniquely Spenserian: in *Amoretti* his avowal is that the physical can be ac-commodated in the mutuality of Christian love; later in *Epithalamion,* it will be seen, the physical is seen as sealing the covenant of the spouses and God. For Spenser the covenant of marriage is thus profoundly societal and mundane.

## C. The Sonnets of Expectation

Spenser's bringing the *amoretti* to a climax around the Easter season has enabled him to resolve the tension between the sonnets' artifice and their Protestant sense of reality by absorbing the artifice neatly into the weightier devotional. However the addition of *Amoretti* 76–89, the sonnets of Expec-tation—marked by the poet's lament "Thus I the time with expectation spend" (*Amoretti* 87.9)—indicates a late decision to provide the sequence with a new overall direction.

Spenser has written the subsequent *amoretti* for reasons in addition to the fact that 3 May 1594, with which *Amoretti* 76 corresponds, began a new round of gospel readings and thus occasioned him to re-engage in composing sonnets, or the fact that he must still address himself to a marriage that remains in the future, even though the marriage's liturgical reality has already been properly anticipated in the sonnet for Maundy Thursday. Protestant writers in their marriage manuals upheld the couple's election to the covenant of grace as prior to marriage. On the one hand, then, the

Easter celebrations attested to the divine workings which brought the couple together and which confirmed the election of each in the covenant of grace. On the other hand, the workings of divine grace are only final once they have overcome the couple's separateness and sealed in marriage the mutuality that will wholly embody the election of both to the covenant of grace. It is a belief in this peculiar instrumentality of God in marriage that has moved Spenser to append the fourteen extra sonnets and to give *Amoretti* at a late stage a new direction.

In so doing he has built on traces and allusions to God's providence already established in the Easter sonnets. Its workings are implicit in the opening of the Good Friday *Amoretti* 66, which alludes to a marriage made in heaven, although in a cautiously hyperbolic way:

> TO all those happy blessings which ye haue,
>> with plenteous hand by heauen vpon you thrown,
>> this one disparagement they to you gaue,
>> that ye your loue lent to so meane a one. (1–4)

The poet, by including marriage, "disparagement," among the blessings bestowed on the lady by heaven, alludes to the nature of divine instrumentality in marriage. The love of each elect for the other cannot be separated from the will of God, which instituted the covenant of marriage to relieve each individual from the burden of solitariness and it is with mutuality that Spenser concludes the sonnet. The heavenly light which shines in the darkness, having enlightened one partner, will reflect upon and enhance the light of the other:

> Yet since your light hath once enlumind me,
>> with my reflex yours shall encreased be. (13–14)

It is for this mutuality of love that Spenser prays in the Easter Sunday sonnet. Because Christ's love has dearly bought redemption, it will be weighed "worthily" by the betrothed. They will both return Christ's love to himself, "likewise loue thee for the same againe," and manifest his love to each other, "with loue . . . one another entertayne;" Christ's love is that in which their mutual love now inheres.

Spenser's voice in *Amoretti* 68 is forthrightly personal. For the moment the covert has been dropped. The sonnet's use of the common pronoun "vs," is one of only three occasions in the sequence[59] and is precise,

---

[59] The other two are also being sonnets of some import, the New Year sonnet, *Am.* 62, and the Expectation sonnet, *Am.* 87. *Am.* 62 records the movement from things past to a fresh beginning and hope, "new yeares ioy," and also includes an explicit prayer, "let

because the sonnet prays for the conjoining of love and persons that marriage will bring. Likewise, in *Amoretti* 71, the Easter Wednesday sonnet, the dominant image is of an intricate drawing, as each of the betrothed seeks to ensnare the other, until their mutuality is so interwoven that it becomes a sign of God's "eternall peace."

But immediately after the central Easter sonnets, the comfort they intimated is dispelled, as Spenser establishes a new tension between the marriage made in heaven and the present foreshadowing of the marriage on earth. Where Easter Sunday had prayed for what "ought," Easter Thursday's sonnet, *Amoretti* 72, shows traces of the new tension as the poet searches for true direction. The directions of the sonnet, from earth to heaven and then back to earth, correspond to those of the ascension account in Acts 1, the day's second lesson at morning prayer. The poet's final claim that he is comforted by the presence on earth of his heaven's bliss is a unique resolution. The lady differs generically from her Petrarchist *exempla*: although unconfined by the "burden of mortality," her presence remains firmly bound to earth. Thus Spenser, in resolving the tension between heaven and earth by incorporating heaven into earth, presents marriage as an incarnation mystically identified with the christic incarnation.

The mutuality, however, which underlies the poet's comfort and assurance, can be endangered or destroyed by two factors: either by a self-containedness on the part of one of the couple, or by separation and absence of the partners from each other. Spenser experiences and meditates upon both factors in *Amoretti*. The first is a temptation that is met and overcome in *Amoretti* 58 and 59, the sonnets which preface the mutuality and covenant of the Easter season.

Assurance was an integral part of the elect's perception of being saved, "The highest degree of faith, is πληροφορία," a full assurance,"[60] and Spenser's Protestant colleagues warned continuously against the false assurance that the flesh might provide.[61] In accusing the lady of self-assurance in *Amoretti* 58, Spenser is also accusing her of being false to the mutuality upon which their marriage covenant will be founded. Indeed, the opening quatrain of *Amoretti* 59, by paralleling "for better" and "with worse," contains a covert allusion to the marriage vows. A self-reliance on

---

vs. . . . / chaunge eeke our mynds and former lives amend," while *Am.* 87 ponders upon the "ioyous houres" of the betrothal.

[60] Perkins, *A Golden Chaine*, in *Workes*, 1:81, col. 2.

[61] Perkins, *Gods free Grace, and Mans Free-Will*, in *Workes*, 1:714, col. 2. Spenser reflects this standard Protestant position elsewhere in his writings, not the least in the stanza which introduces the House of Holinesse in *FQ* I.x.1, which links assurance, flesh and good will in one; see also Hume, 68.

the part of one necessarily obscures the other's perception of election. It imperils not only Spenser's forthcoming marriage but also his happiness and comfort, and he asks plaintively in the final couplet, "Why then doe ye proud fayre, misdeeme so farre, / that to your selfe ye most assured arre." The misjudgement, which is the final temptation prior to the approaching liturgical celebration of the covenant's being sealed, is only to be overcome in the opening lines of the Maundy Thursday sonnet, in which the partners' mutuality is celebrated: "The doubt which ye misdeeme, fayre loue, is vaine." *Amoretti* 65's "fayre loue" has now prevailed over *Amoretti* 58's "proud fayre."

But the factor that most imperilled the covenantal assurance of the betrothed was absence, which is the preoccupation of the Expectation sonnets. Yet even in the first of the appended *amoretti*, *Amoretti* 76 and 77, Spenser proposes a peculiarly Protestant way to turn absence to advantage, by construing it as a sign of God's grace working mundanely within himself, and the possibility of so accommodating absence becomes the theme of subsequent sonnets. The Expectation sonnets, then, look to the future and not to the past. Despite the separation which underpins them and the brooding with which they are occasionally imbued, they affect a security and a hope proper to the season.

Lever has demonstrated how in *Amoretti* 76 Spenser has recast the spirit of Tasso's "Non son sì belli i fiori onde natura," to obtain an unfallen quality, reminiscent of prelapsarian goodness, for the lady's breast is now "the bowre of blisse, the paradice of pleasure."[62] Yet the poet remains unsettled by the physical absence of his beloved, for it threatens the part-ners' mutuality and weakens the poet's belief in the supernatural blessedness of his marriage. In *Amoretti* 77, however, Spenser proposes a solution to the incompleteness that has beset him. Firstly, he gives to Tasso's mythic apples a prelapsarian origin, for they are "brought from paradice" and "voyd of sinfull vice." Secondly, by adopting the repeated image of "dreame" from the second lesson at morning prayer for Saturday 4 May, Matthew 2, he transforms the nature of the original physical separation and elevates his experience to a level beyond the physical. He can take comfort in the supernatural origin and prelapsarian nature of his love, even if absence threatens his equilibrium and blessedness, undermines the perception of his assurance, and drives him to seek internal solace. Only within himself can he discover the supernal nature of mutual love. There is a sense of expecta-tion here: the poet's continuous desire for "harbour" and "rest" looks forward to future solace and comfort rather than recalls past trials.

---

[62] Lever, 110–13.

The physical separation is made explicit in the opening line of the next sonnet, *Amoretti* 78, written for the 5th Sunday after Easter, 5 May; its first quatrain is openly concerned with absence, and physical searching proves futile, "I seek ... / nor ... can fynd," thus disproving the day's Gospel's instruction, "aske, and ye shal receiue" (John 16.24, to which the other gospels, Luke 11.9 and Matthew 7.7, append, "seke, and ye shal finde"). The poet is driven to direct his eyes inwardly; only there can his thoughts contemplate their "trew obiect." Despite his inward focusing and self-preoccupation, however, the poet remains unalarmed at the absence of his lady, resolving not to engage in vain or frenetic activity, but rather to rest quietly within the self. The absence of his betrothed may have muted somewhat his perception of the security found at Easter, but its existence is in no way threatened. Rather it has been turned to advantage, because, paradoxically, only through absence can the physical be transcended and proper assurance found. Absence directs the poet away from the physical to the spiritual nature of his troth, named in *Amoretti* 78 as his "trew obiect," and recast, in *Amoretti* 79, in a platonic vein, as "diuine and borne of heavenly seed."

Absence thus assists in its own overthrow, because by heightening the poet's awareness of his inner state it makes him secure in his knowledge of the grace that his covenant bestows upon him. The operation of grace also confirms his election and it is to the thought of election that Spenser turns in *Amoretti* 82, which he opens, "I blesse my lot, that was so lucky placed," and in *Amoretti* 84, written for the Sunday after the Ascension, 12 May, which he concludes with an explicit reference to election:

> LEt not one sparke of filthy lustfull fyre
> > breake out, that may her sacred peace molest:
> > ne one light glance of sensuall desyre
> > Attempt to work her gentle mindes vnrest.
> But pure affections bred in spotlesse brest,
> > and modest thoughts breathd from wel tempred sprites,
> > goe visit her in her chast bowre of rest,
> > accompanyde with angelick delightes.
> There fill your selfe with those most joyous sights,
> > the which my selfe could neuer yet attayne:
> > but speake no word to her of these sad plights,
> > which her too constant stiffenesse doth constrayn.
> Onely behold her rare perfection,
> > and blesse your fortunes fayre election.

Here absence is construed delicately to advance the sense of comfort to be found in election.[63] In the sonnet the poet is addressing his two selves: in the first instance his carnal self, which he calls upon to suppress itself, and secondly his other spiritual self, addressed in the vocative, "pure affections" and "modest thoughts," and in the imperative, "goe visit." It is the "pure" self, which is finally enjoined to behold the lady's "rare perfection" and to bless its "fayre election," because election operates only in the realm of grace.

The sonnet thus observes the Pauline doctrine of election, expounded in the day's second lesson at evening prayer, Romans 11. Paul firstly claims that election is of the realm of grace, not the flesh, "if it be of grace, it is no more of workes: or els were grace no more grace" (v. 6), and further explains that the election found in the covenant is linked with love and seen as a gift and calling of God: "this is my couenant to them ... as touching the election, they are beloued for the fathers sakes. For the giftes and calling of GOD are without repentance" (vv. 27-29). In *Amoretti* 84 Spenser acknowledges the inner perfection that such election confers on him and takes comfort from it. Yet the election, which according to Paul is "secret" (v. 25), remains firmly ensconced in the poet's breast, and, in *Amoretti* 85, is shown to be hidden from the the wider world:

> Deepe in the closet of my parts entyre,
> her worth is written with a golden quill. (9-10)

*Amoretti* 85 supplements the nature of the betrothed's election, whose existence had been affirmed in the preceding sonnet. Its distinction between "The world that cannot deeme of worthy things," and the poet's inner world, where alone truth resides, is accepted directly from the readings for the Monday of Expectation Week 13 May, Matthew 11 and Romans 12, both of which are concerned with the extent of God's revelation and its discernment. In Matthew, Christ praises God for the restricted nature of heavenly revelation, distinguishing between those to whom true judgement

---

[63] The sonnet sequence has finally reached a stage where it identifies marriage and covenant. William Perkins, for example, uses the image of marriage to define election and covenantal donation (*A Golden Chaine*, in *Workes*, 1:78, col. 1): "The first degree, is an effectuall calling, whereby a sinner beeing seuered from the world, is entertained into Gods familie.... Of this there be two parts. The first is *Election*, which is a separation of a sinner from the cursed estate of all mankind.... The second, is the reciprocall donation or free gift of God the Father, whereby he bestoweth the sinfull man to bee saued vpon Christ, and Christ againe actually & most effectually vpon that sinfull man: so that he may boldly say this thing, namely Christ, both God and man, is mine, and I for my benefit & vse enjoy the same. The like we see in wedlock: The husband saith, this woman is my wife, whome her parents haue given vnto me, so that, shee beeing fully mine, I may both haue her, and gouerne her: Againe, the woman may say, this man is mine husband, who hath bestowed himselfe vpon me, and doth cherish me as his wife."

is given, and those who are worldly wise: "I giue thee thankes, ô Father, Lord of heauen and earth, because thou hast hid these things from the wise and men of vnderstanding, and hast opened them vnto babes" (v. 25). The gospel's subsequent observation about knowing the secrets of the world, "no man knoweth the Sonne, but the Father: nether knoweth any man the Father, but the Sonne" (v. 27), is reflected in the sonnet's further defining those of the world, as those "that skill not," and who "know not."

Paul, in Romans, further explains the nature of election. He calls on the Romans to forgo the ways of this world and revert to deeper truth: "facion not your selues like vnto this worlde, but be ye changed by the renuing of your minde" (v. 2). Spenser observes the Pauline instruction to disregard the world and shape his thought inwardly, while his advice to others, not to aspire to "deeme of her desert," corresponds to Paul's admonition to the elect not to allow their judgement to overreach itself: part of being elected to grace is "that no man presume to understand aboue that which is mete to vnderstand" (v. 3).

Properly, the world's awareness of the election of Spenser and his betrothed in *Amoretti* 85 is restricted. Their covenant, furthermore, will prevail until the last day, because the sonnet's "her shrill trump shal thunder" is obliquely apocalyptic and recalls the gospel's repeated reference to the "day of judgement" (vv. 22 & 24; v. 25's "hast opened" is also apocalyptic, the koiné being απεκάλυψας). In the interim, the world may "chose to enuy or to wonder," because discernment of the secrets of the poet's love, and its expression, will remain concealed from the unelected, who witlessly consider the sonnets' intent merely to "flatter," and who can see their words as only "clatter."

In the concluding sonnets of the sequence Spenser thereby shapes an artifice in which the *amoretti*'s covert nature is aligned with the hidden, apocalyptic nature of scriptural truths. The secret of the *amoretti*, *Amoretti* 6's "not" or "knot," darkness or marriage, is that to which the *amoretti* lead, and which they anticipate, although their truth is hidden from the "wise and men of vnderstanding," and their depths lie beyond the comprehension of the elect, and ultimately in the realm of the in-fans, Matthew's "babes." To the world is given some syntactical discernment, but the true mysteries lie in the realm of preterlingual innocency.

The *amoretti* are, therefore, informed by a range of paradoxical and perspectival possibilities to be unravelled, so that their poetic secret, which is replicated in the intimacy of the betrotheds' election, can be discerned. Only she, whose election opens the hidden of the scriptures, can be privy to the sonnets' hidden artifice. In this lies the paradox which comprises the sequence itself. To be privy to the secret is also to know the knitted "not," to be part of an essential negative darkness. The mystery will always be brought to light, but never in its entirety, and Paul, in Romans 12, counsels against the presumption that it might be. Scriptures and sonnets are wed-ded, for both embody truths for the initiate, the word to be comprehended only in part and only by them. But they must remain, as well, unknowing of the dark conceit, so that the truth, of scriptures and sonnets, can be further revealed. In the final analysis, *Amoretti* 85's "worth" defies compre-hension and can only instill wonder, and it is with wonder that Spenser concludes the sonnet: "let the world choose to enuy or to wonder."

As well, *Amoretti* 85's "Deepe in the closet of my parts entyre" echoes *Amoretti* 1's "in harts close bleeding book." The poet's first orison, that the lady throw light on the poems and that her "lamping eyes" and "starry light" open their secrets to her alone, reveals, even at the outset, *Amoretti*'s enclosed intent. *Amoretti* 1 becomes a post-conceit of the whole work, whose final result is not internal to itself, but lies outside the sequence in *Epithalamion*, which seals the christic covenant encrypted in the sequence. Furthermore, because of *Amoretti*'s elective potentiality, the sequence can only end for the elected poet in darkness and expectation, as the betrothed await another light. The final sonnets of expectation and darkness are thus integral to the sequence, because the pentecost of both the poetic and liturgical secret will assuredly become for the elect the pentecost in which all will be sealed physically and spiritually.

The involvement of the *amoretti* with the daily scripture readings thus operates beyond mere verbal or topical imitation and enters the realm of the euchological. The New Testament, because of its discontinuities, abounds in phrases describing astonishment, marvel, and amazement, and its wonder is caused partly by the writers' continual thwarting of the reader's expecta-tions by breaking the narrative continuum. Spenser has exploited the New Testament's episodic nature and its juxtaposing of the random to display in *Amoretti* the discontinuities experienced in his betrothal.[64] As well, be-cause the evangelical subtext ends archetypically by awaiting from outside the Spirit's consolation, so must the *amoretti* end in expectation. *Amoretti* is, therefore, unique among Renaissance artifacts, because any rhetorical *concordia* ultimately remains foreign to it, to be sealed later from beyond its bounds. The sequence's fractured nature, by imitating its evangelical

---

[64] Because the sequence presents a range of experiences perceived as various and dissembled, any other ascribed totality or set of correspondences must break under the pressure of contrarieties. Here lies the major difficulty with any numerological and Neo-Platonic reconstructions of *Amoretti*. They presume either a residual harmony underlying the sequence, or the sequence's rounded and complete nature. But such presumptions run contrary to the *amoretti*'s liturgical and scriptural artifice, and constrain it in a formalistic straitjacket that is conclusive and given to the enclosed.

subsidium, inhibits any final settlement from within itself. The *amoretti* continue unencompassed to the end, their nature allowing no telos.

*Amoretti and Epithalamion* also contravenes customary Petrarchan and Petrarchist resolutions to sonnet sequences.[65] Although in the final *Amoretti* 76–89 the lady is absent just as Laura is absent, Laura's death brings about her angelification—thus raising Petrarch (and his successors) from darkness to light and from earth to heaven. In Petrarch the opposites remain always at variance: only the absence of the flesh—the death of Laura—allows the presence of the spiritual. The circumstances surrounding *Amoretti*, however, differ from those of *Il Canzoniere*: Spenser's beloved remains alive and the marriage, which will eventually dissolve the tensions of the *amoretti*, will be, first and foremost, an earthly, not a heavenly, marriage. *Amoretti*, as a piece of poetic artifice, thereby avoids the traditional Petrarchist resolution of sublimatory angelification. Because the post-poetic factor that closes the sequence is external to it, *Amoretti* does not arrive at an anagogical reality, but remains anchored to the darkness of the world, which *Epithalamion* will creatively make sacrosanct.

The sequence's final sonnets also reveal that the sequence is intimately attached to and mimics the courtship between Spenser and Elizabeth Boyle. Courtships of their nature don't end (unless broken off), but are ended from outside with the celebration of marriage. *Amoretti* thus reveals three aspects of incompletion, the personal, the poetic and the liturgical, all of which are interwoven and all of which are resolved by the ritualistic and public forces that inhabit *Epithalamion*. They anticipate the future enactment of a physical reality that will seal the grace and beauty of which they sing.

The final sonnets, *Amoretti* 87–89, conclude the sequence on a note of absence and lack of comfort. Yet each of them holds out a cryptic assurance. *Amoretti* 87, which makes the expectation of the poet explicitly liturgical, anticipates the arrival of the Comforter at Pentecost. Spenser awaits the lady's coming, just as the disciples awaited the Spirit's coming, and identifies the comfort that the lady will bring with that which the Holy Spirit will

---

[65] Lisa M. Klein, " 'Let us love, deare love lyke as we ought': Protestant Marriage and the Revision of Petrarchan Loving in Spenser's *Amoretti*," *SpS* 10 (1989): 109–137 has recently argued that Spenser continually moves towards reshaping both Petrarchist and sexual poetics by repudiating the exaggerations of Petrarchism and replacing them with "a poetics expressive of the mutuality and concord which ought to characterize a loving marriage" (112). The lady of the sequence then "emerges into representation" through the repudiation of the proud Petrarchist mistress whose characteristics contravene the model of a Christian wife: "A humble companion of a wife is formed from and supplants a proud tyrant of a mistress, and the concord of marriage is ensured only after the possibility of discord is eliminated" (118). Klein concludes that "the process of fashioning identity in the *Amoretti* contradicts the recent new historicist paradigm" (129).

bring.[66] *Amoretti* 88's opening, "Since I have lackt the comfort of that light," which couples it to *Amoretti* 87's theme of night and day, defines the lady as, "th'onely image of that heavenly ray," and the "Idea playne." While plainly Platonic in character, the ascriptions also suggest the imminent coming of the Holy Spirit, the comforter. As the Spirit's brightness filled the disciples, so the poet will draw upon the brightness of the lady to sustain his inner self. Spenser has fused together the comfort that Pentecost will bring and the comfort of the second lesson at morning prayer for Thursday 16 May, Matthew 14, with which *Amoretti* 88 corresponds, "Be of good comfort. It is I: be not afraied" (v. 27), to underscore a personal reassurance, which operates despite the overt darkness of the sonnet. The reassurance runs counter to the sonnet's opening mood of physical separation and reinforces the sense of light, which the poet knows will finally be a source of grace and consolation.

*Amoretti* 89 concludes *Amoretti* by employing as its principal image the dove associated with the Holy Spirit. The poet remains smitten by the darkness which absence induces in him, and is preoccupied with his lack of comfort. Yet the sonnet also contains a coded and intimate message for the future, from which only the elect could take comfort:

> So I alone now left disconsolate,
>> mourne to my selfe the absence of my loue:
>> and wandring here and there all desolate,
>> seek with my playnts to match that mournful doue. (5–8)

The thought is a proper liturgical one for the season. But Spenser would have taken heart from the biblical associations of "disconsolate" with the name, Barnabas, which is explicated in Acts 4.36, "Barnabas (that is by interpretation the sonne of consolation)."[67] The word thus carries with it a cryptic reference to his forthcoming marriage on the feast of St. Barnabas, 11 June, when such consolation will occur and he will be united with his betrothed. His "disconsolate" mood will be overcome on the very day when

---

[66] Spenser thus reflects a common identification in Protestant treatises on marriage. Cleaver (*A Godlie Forme of Householde Gouernment*, 158–59), for example, deals extensively with the duties of the wife as a "comforter," for which role he claims the authority of the "holy Ghost, who saith, that she was ordeined as a *Helper*."

[67] Henry Smith ("The Ladder of Peace" in *The Sermons of Maister Henrie Smith* [London, 1593], 854): "It is not vaine that the holy Ghost when he named *Barnabas*, interpreted his name too, because it signifieth *the sonne of consolation*: as though he delighted in such men as were *the sonnes of consolation. Comfort one another* saith *Paule*: How shal we comfort one another without comfort? Therefore *Paule* saith, GOD *comforteth vs, that we may be able to comfort other by the comfort whereby we ourselues are comforted of God*: shewing, that wee cannot comfort other, unlesse wee be comfortable our selues: and therefore that we may performe this dutie, we are bound to nourish comfort in our selues."

the feast of "the sonne of consolation" is celebrated. Then, each of the betrothed will be able to comfort the other, because each will find in their covenant with each other assurance of their covenant with God and of their election and grace.

The appended sonnets of Expectation are, then, an integral part of the sequence's ultimate design and provide *Amoretti* with a final euchological direction. Spenser has been moved to conclude the work with expectation because it is of the nature of covenantal election that the betrothed await its conferment patiently. As well, the feasts of Pentecost and St. Barnabas are conjoined through their common function in sealing covenantal comfort and consolation, and the interval between them surmounted.

## D. Epithalamion

Spenser's *Epithalamion* celebrates, with ritualistic and public force, that which was privately avowed in *Amoretti*. The two works are linked thematically. *Amoretti* 89 concludes on a note of solitariness and lack of comfort, as it sends forth an unrequited song:

> LYke as the Culuer on the bared bough,
>> Sits mourning for the absence of her mate:
>> and in her songs sends many a wishfull vow,
>> for his returne that seemes to linger late.
> So I alone now left disconsolate,
>> mourne to my selfe the absence of my loue. (1–6)

*Epithalamion*'s opening stanza insists on the same realities, as the poet resolves to sing to himself, "So Orpheus did for his owne bride, / So I vnto my selfe alone will sing," and the lack of reply to his song is reflected in the singular personal pronoun of the opening stanza's refrain, "The woods shall to me answer and my Eccho ring."

Where the *amoretti* were directed to the beloved, *Epithalamion*'s audience is a wider one. It brings into the open that which in *Amoretti* was not societal or given to the world, by affording public voice and mythic proportions to, first, a public and, later, a private enactment. *Epithalamion* presents the public reconciliation of *Amoretti*'s personal tensions and the public consummation of its private separateness, because in it, physically and spiritually, the covenant is sealed.

*Epithalamion*'s most apparent structure is of twenty-three stanzas and a short envoy. Each stanza is comprised of a series of long and short lines; the short lines, which occur without strict pattern, generally divide the stanza into quarters. Each stanza, in turn, narrates a segment of the wedding day, and each is concluded with an individualized variant of the refrain which concludes Stanza 1.

The wedding day is identified as 11 June, the feast of St. Barnabas, "This day the sunne is in his cheifest hight, / With Barnaby the bright" (265–66), and A. Kent Hieatt has demonstrated the 'polyoramic' structure embodied in the poem.[68] Temporal and calendrical structures are discernible, not only in the number of stanzas, twenty four, representing both the number of hours in the day and, through its short lines, the quarter-hours, but also in the number of long lines, three hundred and sixty five, representing the number of days in the year, and even in the number of short lines, sixty eight, representing, Hieatt suggests, fifty-two weeks + four seasons + twelve months. If the six long lines of the envoy are excluded, the number of resulting long lines is 359, the number of degrees through which the sun travels, while the celestial sphere is completing its full revolution of 360° around the earth. On 11 June, furthermore, the period of time between the sun's rising and falling corresponds to the hours of daylight in the poem, and the arrival of night in the seventeenth stanza accords with the moment when the sun set in southern Ireland on 11 June 1594. In its simplest form Hieatt's thesis convincingly demonstrates the manner in which Spenser has both located his epithalamium in southern Ireland and yet, by advancing and absorbing the local into the cosmographical, has extended the poem's temporal bounds beyond the span of a single day to that of a whole year.

---

[68] A. Kent Hieatt, *Short Time's Endless Monument. The symbolism of the numbers in Edmund Spenser's Epithalamion* (New York, 1960), passim. Carol Kaske, "Spenser's *Amoretti* and *Epithalamion* of 1595: Structure, Genre, Numerology," *ELR* 8 (1978): 271–95, J. C. Eade, "The Pattern in the Astronomy of Spenser's *Epithalamion*," *Review of English Studies*, n.s. 23 (1972): 173–78 and Shohachi Fukuda, "The Numerological Patterning of *Amoretti and Epithalamion*," *SpS* 8 (1988): 33–48, argue for further astronomical complexities in the poem. Max A. Wickert in "Structure and Ceremony in Spenser's *Epithalamion*," *ELH* 35 (1968): 137 has argued that Hieatt's attempts to interpret his mathematical discoveries by pairing Stanzas 1 and 13, Stanzas 2 and 14 and so forth places considerable strain on reading the poem integrally. He proposed that "the imaginative order of the poem's second half is not a *da capo* repetition but a mirror-inversion of the imaginative order of the first half" and that Stanza 1 matches Stanza 24, Stanza 2 matches Stanza 23 and so on. If such correspondences are accepted, Wickert argued, the eternizing function of *Epithalamion* is not subordinate to the poem's formal design and its "literal" meaning—its movement through the marriage rite. He finally claimed that *Epithalamion*'s action peaks "at the mathematically exact center of the poem" at lines 216–17, "The sacred ceremonies there partake, / The which do endlesse matrimony make." Recently David Chinitz ("*Epithalamion* and the Golden Section," *JMRS* 21 [1991]: 251–68) elaborated upon Wickert's claims by pointing out that lines 263–64 constitute the mathematical (and architectural) golden section or mean of the poem: "The golden section divides the 359 long lines preceding the envoy at 221.87, and long lines 221–22 turn out to be precisely those same claimactic lines, ll. 263–64 of the poem as a whole." Chinitz argued that such a golden mean comprises a Vergilian shaping of *Epithalamion*.

Spenser, however, departs from received epithalamial standards. In the first place he is forced by circumstances to annul the customary epithalamial distinction between the epithalamium's poet/presenter and its bridegroom. The customary epithalamial presenter arranges events only to the threshold of the bridal chamber, and remains outside the innermost chamber, orchestrating further festivities after the couple's entry. The voice of Spenser's epithalamium, however, because it is the bridegroom's, introduces the audience to the intimacy of the bridal chamber itself. A private act is thus publicly celebrated, and gathers to itself a social cast both within and without the poem. In *Epithalamion* the masque's presenter and principal consciousness is at the one time public voice and private player, simultaneously an invoker of the cosmographical harmonies and forces, yet subject to them; a suppliant before the poem's priest, yet directing him also; a controller of time, yet subordinate to it; conceded the one day sought, yet encompassed by the year.

> Doe not thy seruants simple boone refuse,
> But let this day let this one day be myne,
> Let all the rest be thine. (124–26)

*Epithalamion*'s presenter also departs from the manner in which conventional presenters customarily advanced an epithalamium's ceremonial quality by distancing its events from the audience. The conventional presenter was prominent to the degree to which his voice gained authority through a variety of tones, through his frequent imperatives and commands, and through his arranging and directing the players, both subordinate and principal. His fescennine and bawdy asides also added character to his voice and asserted his mediating presence within the masque. Much of this is not allowed Spenser. His syncretic genius always enables him to capture moments of genial fun, and by directing the action and adjusting its pace manipulate responses to effect a quick-moving tableau. But because the public voice must enter a private place, a fine balance must be struck between public and private, which the indecorous or improper would jeopardize.[69] In Spenser's epithalamium the voice always remains a caring and reserved one, attributes of the bridegroom rather than the customary Catullan presenter, and Spenser has chosen to remove from his epithalamium the customary *carmina fescennina* of ribaldry and bawdiness, and to erect

---

[69] To maintain decorum Spenser is prepared to discard customary epithalamial practices. Puttenham, *The Arte of English Poesie* (London, 1589), 41, advises that noise and merriment are necessary after the couple's entry into the bridal chamber to disguise any ensuing noise: "the tunes of the songs were very loude and shrill, to the intent there might no noise be hard out of the bed chamber by the skreeking & outcry of the young damosell feeling the first forces of her stiffe & rigorous young man."

them as a series of irreverent anacreontic verses, separate from *Epithalamion* and dividing it from *Amoretti*.

Like the *amoretti*, the anacreontic verses, being less a recapitulation of past endeavors than an anticipatory extraction of the *carmina fescennina*, also look forward to the epithalamium.[70] The manner in which they play with the physical, although tactful, is opposed to the skillful parodies or the well-intentioned aspirations of the preceding *amoretti*. Their mythical surrounds,[71] which themselves are part of a tradition and make more acceptable that which they celebrate, also anticipate the epithalamium, while the allusive nature of the verses insinuates a sense of physical threshold, similar to the *limen*, celebrated in epithalamia.[72] The lines

> And then she bath'd him in a dainty well
> the well of deare delight.
> Who would not oft be stung as this,
> to be so bath'd in Venus blis? (69–72)

anticipate a sexual consummation rather than recall something past.

*Epithalamion*, in contrast, is marked by great propriety and reserve. It is not initially concerned with the physical, and only introduces it slowly and by degrees. The bride does not appear until Stanza 9, where her features are described emblematically and her bearing as one of chaste modesty. Only in Stanza 13, in the wedding ceremony, is the actual physical first acknowledged: the physical closeness of the priest's benedictory imposition of hands, a form of blessing also common to the coronation and to all ordination rites, causes the bride to blush, "And blesseth her with his two happy hands, / How the red roses flush vp in her cheekes" (225–26). Likewise the joining of hands later in the Stanza 13, in accordance with the Marriage Service's instruction, "And the Minister . . . shall cause the man to take the woman by the right hande,"[73] reveals the bride to be particularly sensitive to the touch: "Why blush ye loue to giue to me your hand, / The pledge of all our band?" (238–39). Although the physical is now sanctioned, ceremo-

---

[70] Robert S. Miola, "Spenser's Anacreontics: A Mythological Metaphor," *SPh* 77 (1980): 50–66, argues that the anacreontic verses "recapitulate the *Amoretti's* spiritual conflict and anticipate its epithalamial resolution," although the greater part of his argument enquires into their recapitulatory nature. G. K. Hunter, 124 sees them as an interpolation which should be ignored, while J. C. Nohrnberg, *The Analogy of The Faerie Queene* (Princeton: Princeton Univ. Press, 1976), views them as a short interlude. See J. L. Smarr, "Anacreontics," in *The Spenser Encyclopedia*, 39.

[71] For further mythical and continental antecedents of the "Anacreontics," see Hutton, 119–123.

[72] Statius, *Epith. in Stellam*, 34–35 in J. H. Mozley, trans., *Works* (London: William Heinemann, 1928), "licet expositum per limen aperto / Ire redire gradu."

[73] *The booke of Common prayer* (1578), sig. dvi*ᵛ*.

nial decorum prevails for another six stanzas, until Stanza 13's delicate intimations are silently consummated in Stanza 20.

Although Spenser has deliberately imbued his poem with a bourgeois and mercantile cast,[74] and localized it in rural Ireland (Stanza 4's locale is particularly Irish and folklorist, while the rural nature of Stanza 19's lengthy exorcism extends even to the croaking of the frogs in the Irish bog), it is the cosmographical which gives the piece coherent forward movement. The poem's occasional style and variable lines allow of little narrative continuity and project a series of individual tableaux. It is the architectonic progression of the hours which provides the poem with cohesion and structure.[75] The dominance of the cosmographical also obscures any liturgical or biblical subsidium,[76] although Spenser's ability to transform material drawn from classical and continental antecedents, so that no single source is apparent, is equally true of his scriptural sources. Biblical allusions are limited: the Song of Solomon is evoked in Stanza 2, while the opening to Stanza 9,

---

[74] In singing his own epithalamion Spenser need not direct it to higher patrons, the nobility to whom epithalamies had customarily been directed. (Thomas M. Greene, "Spenser and the Epithalamic Convention," *Comparative Literature* 9 [1957]: 218.) He obviously felt a bourgeois and mercantile cast befitted his position more closely. The images of small business abound, from the orison, "That shall for al the paynes and sorrowes past, / Pay to her vsury of long delight" (32–33), to the opening of Stanza 10, "Tell me ye merchants daughters did ye see / So fayre a creature in your towne before," which explicitly echoes the opening to *Am.* 15, "Ye tradeful Merchants," and repeats its comparisons of eyes as "Saphyres," and "forhead" as "yuory." Stanza 14 acclaims "the glory of her gaine" (244), and in Stanza 15 the young men are called vpon to "leaue your wonted labors for this day" (262). Stanza 18 takes up the earlier reference to "vsury" and speaks of repayment and recompense for past costs in its welcome to night, "That long daies labour doest at last defray, / And all my cares, which cruell loue collected, / Hast sumd in one, and cancelled for aye" (316–18). Stanza 23's "posterity," "possesse," and "inherit," and finally Stanza 24's "recompens," are all in keeping with the mercantile surrounds of the poem. Loewenstein, 289 reads the economic image not only as the long debt of courtship paid off in a single night, but as applying to *Epithalamion* itself, which both substitutes for material gifts and is in lieu of many other (poetic) ornaments.

[75] Spenser has also been prepared to disregard, for the sake of the wider cosmographical proportions, the customary divisions of an epithalamion. For example, George Puttenham, *The Arte of English Poesie* (London 1589; facsimile, Amsterdam: Theatrum Orbis Terrarum Ltd., 1971), 41–42, advises a threefold division, 1. "the first parte of the night when the spouse and her husband were brought to their bed." 2. "About midnight or one of the clocke." 3. "In the morning when it was faire broad day."

[76] John N. Wall, *Transformations of the Word: Spenser, Herbert, Vaughan* (Athens: Univ. of Georgia Press, 1988), 127–65, on the other hand, has argued for further scriptural and liturgical echoes in *Epithalamion*, which he considers are employed to "overgo" the classical conventions that Spenser observed. William C. Johnson, " 'Sacred Rites' and Prayer Book Echoes in Spenser's 'Epithalamion,' " *Ren. & Ref.* 12 (1976): 53 also sees a parallel structure between the *Book of Common Prayer*'s marriage service and *Epithalamion*, although the verbal correspondences he cites between the two are less strong. *Epithalamion*'s "Poure out your blessing on us plentiously," for example, need not be particularly tied to the service's "powre vpon you the riches."

"Loe where she comes along with portly pace / Lyke Phoebe from her chamber of the East, / Arysing forth to run her mighty race," recalls the Geneva version's Psalm 19.4–5, "the sunne. Which commeth forthe as a bridegrome out of his chambre, *and* rejoyceth like a mightie man to runne *his* race." The allusions in Stanza 12, "Open the temple gates," "with girlands trim," "ye virgins," and "with honour dew," which conjure up possible precedents in both Catullus and de Buttet, also suggest the apocalyptic parable of the virgins awaiting the bridegroom with its verbal echoes of "bridegrome," "virgins . . . trimmed their lampes," and "Lord, open [the gate] to us." The opening to Stanza 14, "Now al is done," recalls the marriage of the Lamb in John's triumphant apocalyptic vision. John sees the "holie citie," which the Geneva Bible glosses as, "The holie companie of the elect," descending, "Prepared as a bride trimmed for her housband," and hears the great voice exclaim: "It is done. I am α and ω, the beginning and the end" (Revelations 21.2 & 6).[77] The scriptural echoes attach an apocalyptic surround to the marriage service and reinforce its ultramundane dimensions, but since classical epithalamia lacked a corresponding service, Spenser's reverting to the scriptures for this section of his epithalamium would not be unusual.[78] Spenser has, however, generally avoided any unifying scriptural imagery in favor of the cosmographical and mythopoeic.

The most pertinent feature of *Epithalamion,* however, is its recapitulating, in mythic and cosmogonic terms, that which had been liturgically anticipated in Maundy Thursday's *Amoretti* 65 and in the surrounding Easter sonnets and is now to be ratified on the feast of St. Barnabas. It gives public recognition to the liturgical realities of both days, each of which discretely underscore and empower the sealing of the spouses' own covenant of grace in wedlock. The feast of St. Barnabas, then, stabilizes the vagaries and contrarieties of courtship and passion, and sees eros and the realm of nature as fundamental to the realm of grace. The physical, having been sanctified by faith, consummates the covenant of marriage with fecund intent, and thereby attests to the spouses' covenant of grace. *Epithalamion*'s structure, then, asserts not merely that the physical is now sanctioned, but that it seals the spiritual. The gulf between the beloved, so variously experienced and so unsuccessfully bridged in the *amoretti*, is late in *Epithalamion* sealed by the physical, whose culminating touch is shrouded in silence.

---

[77] Douglas Anderson argues cogently and at length for the apocalyptic overtones in *Epithalamion* in " 'Vnto My Selfe Alone': Spenser's Plenary Epithalamion," *SpS* 5 (1985): 149–66.

[78] The *Book of Common Prayer*'s marriage service also laid down the apocalyptic injunction, "I Require and charge you (as you will answere at the dreadful day of judgement, when the secretes of all hearts shalbe disclosed)," when inquirying about impediments; see *The booke of Common prayer* (1578), sig. dvi[v].

*Epithalamion*'s celebration of flesh-made-one is thus a public sign of an existent covenant, sealed mutually between the spouses, and by both spouses with God. Where in *Amoretti* Spenser came finally to lay great stress on the covenant of grace, because in it could be solved the tensions between fallen flesh and grace, in the volume's concluding poem flesh and spirit are reconciled through the flesh's becoming a comfortable sign of election to the covenant of grace. The need to transcend the flesh is avoided by accepting the necessity of fleshly reality to witness to the covenant of grace. In *Epithalamion* is publicly sealed, with propriety and without the fescennine, the covenant whose conferment was formerly acknowledged liturgically and whose pentecost was awaited in the final sonnets. Pentecost is the primary liturgical force, in which triumph over absence is celebrated and comfort afforded, and pentecostal light occurs, appropriately, on the longest day of the year.

*Epithalamion*'s envoy asserts forcefully, that the principal characters of *Epithalamion*, although surrounded by literary *typoi* and mythographic figures, are not fictional figures. By intimating that the epithalamium was written to recompense the lack of "many ornaments," which should have decked his love, but which, if Spenser here intended poems,[79] were not written because of "hasty accidents," the envoy intrudes an apologetic note. It also argues for a connection between the earlier sonnets and *Epithalamion*. Its syntactically-contorted line, "Ye would not stay your dew time to expect," affirms the hope of physical fecundity, because Spenser only uses "due time" in connection with childbirth.[80] It also recalls the Expectation sonnets, for they conclude with the poet in solitariness and darkness which, while his beloved remains absent, lack the necessary mutuality to be creative. *Epithalamion* begins in solitude and darkness, but more and more figures are called forth, as it becomes progressively populated and moves from initial darkness to the daylight hours, in which the public revelries are celebrated. Only once the social cast is assembled and the mythopoeic cosmography established, can the covenant be sealed. Then from "the secret darke" ensues creativity.[81] Because creation is summoned only out of darkness, Spenser prefaces the introduction of night with primeval mythogonies:

---

[79] Most commentators favor the view that Spenser here intended poems: see Cortlandt Van Winkle, *Epithalamion* (New York, 1926), 34; Enid Welsford, *Spenser: Fowre Hymnes Epithalamion: A Study of Edmund Spenser's Doctrine of Love* (Oxford: Basil Blackwell, 1967), 81–83; Richard Neuse, "The Triumph Over Hasty Accidents," *MLR* 61 (1966): 163–64.

[80] *FQ* I.vii.9.6 & VI.xii.6.5.

[81] Neuse (1966), passim, argues at length for the creative function of darkness in the poem.

> Lyke as when Joue with fayre Alcmena lay,
> When he begot the great Tirynthian groome:
> Or lyke as when he with thy selfe did lie,
> And begot Majesty. (328–31)

*Epithalamion* thus affirms that covenantal love requires the realm of nature as essential to its endless transforming power. Furthermore, by associating the apocalyptic suggestions, whose covert presence in the final *amoretti* was shown to be pertinent to the nature of election, with the apocalyptic overtones of the epithalamium, Spenser cryptically avers an "endlesse" and ultramundane dimension to both his marriage and his poetry. And, by identifying the primordial element of Revelation's "The beginning and the end" with the mythogonic, he also subtly reinforces the cosmographical dimensions of the poem, and makes all three structures coexistent.

In the final *amoretti* the poet's silence was sterile, as he lamented his mate's lack of reply. He begins *Epithalamion* on the same singular note. Only from mutuality and presence can the Word or words come forth. The "Idaea playne" of *Amoretti* 88 may provide him with some solace, but it is insufficient to console the whole person, and in the sonnet's final couplet the poet, curtly and rather sharply, dismisses its ability to comfort:

> But with such brightnesse whylest I fill my mind,
> I starue my body and mine eyes doe blynd. (13–14)

For the moment, the "Idaea" is not that in whose image something may be valorized, because, as yet, there is no accommodation of the physical through whose mutuality the truth of the poet's words will be sealed. In *Epithalamion* words gradually flow forth and the stanzaic refrain reverberates with sound. At the moment when the spouse is introduced to bed, however, the damsels are called to "leave my loue alone, / And leaue likewise your former lay to sing" (312–13). The refrain changes into the negative and silence is invoked, "The woods no more shall answere, nor your echo ring" (314); "stil Silence" and "trew night watches" are identified (353). In the moments of mutual silence, after the sounds of the night have been exorcised in Stanza 19, Spenser's song is sealed. Thus in the covenant are identified physical, religious, and poetic fecundity.[82] Poetic valorizing is underwritten by physical fecundity conceived in silence; out of the silent darkness of physical mutuality the poetic comes forth, and a "Song made in lieu of many ornaments" is sung.

---

[82] Eileen Jorge Allman, "Epithalamion's Bridegroom: Orpheus-Adam-Christ," *Renascence* 32 (1979–80): 240–47, similarly finds a threefold dimension to the poem, although she arrives at it by a different route.

# Amoretti

## To the right worshipfull
## Sir Robart Needham Knight.

Sir, to gratulate your safe return from Ireland, I had nothing so readie, nor thought any thing so meete, as these sweete conceited Sonets, the deede of that weldeseruing gentleman, maister Edmond Spenser: whose name sufficiently warranting the worthinesse of the work: I do more confidently presume to publish it in his absence, vnder your name to whom (in my poore opinion) the patronage therof, doth in some respectes properly appertaine. For, besides your iudgement and delighte in learned poesie: This gentle Muse for her former perfection long wished for in Englande, nowe at the length crossing the Seas in your happy companye, (though to your selfe vnknowne) seemeth to make choyse of you, as meetest to giue her deserued countenaunce, after her retourne: entertaine her, then, (Right worshipfull) in sorte best beseeming your gentle minde, and her merite, and take in worth my good will herein, who seeke no more, but to shew my selfe yours in all dutifull affection.

W. P.

## G: W. *senior to the Author*

DArke is the day, when *Phoebus* face is shrowded,
    and weaker sights may wander soone astray:
    but when they see his glorious raies vnclowded,
    with steddy steps they keepe the perfect way,
So while this Muse in forraine landes doth stay,
    inuention weepes, and pens are cast aside,
    the time like night, depriud of chearefull day,
    and few do write, but (ah) too soone may slide.
Then, hie thee home, that art our perfect guide,
    and with thy wit illustrate Englands fame,
    dawnting thereby our neighboures auncient pride,
    that do for poesie, challendge cheefest name.
So we that liue and ages that succeede,
    With great applause thy learned works shall reede.


Ah Colin, *whether on the lowly plaine,*
    *pyping to shepherds thy sweet roundelaies:*
    *or whether singing in some lofty vaine*
    *heroick deedes, of past, or present daies:*
*Or whether in thy louely mistris praise,*
    *thou list to exercise thy learned quill,*
    *thy muse hath got such grace, and power to please,*
    *with rare inuention bewtified by skill,*
*As who therein can euer ioy their fill.*
    *O therefore let that happy muse proceede*
    *to clime the height of vertues sacred hill,*
    *where endles honor shall be made thy meede.*
*Because no malice of succeeding daies,*
    *can rase those records of thy lasting praise.*

G. W. I.

### SONNET. I.

HAppy ye leaues when as those lilly hands,
    which hold my life in their dead doing might
    shall handle you and hold in loues soft bands,
    lyke captiues trembling at the victors sight.
And happy lines, on which with starry light,
    those lamping eyes will deigne sometimes to look
    and reade the sorrowes of my dying spright,
    written with teares in harts close bleeding book.
And happy rymes bath'd in the sacred brooke
    of *Helicon* whence she deriued is,
    when ye behold that Angels blessed looke,
    my soules long lacked foode, my heauens blis.
Leaues, lines, and rymes, seeke her to please alone,
    whom if ye please, I care for other none.

### SONNET. II.

VNquiet thought, whom at the first I bred,
    Of th'inward bale of my loue pined hart:
    and sithens haue with sighes and sorrowes fed,
    till greater then my wombe thou woxen art.
Breake forth at length out of the inner part,
    in which thou lurkest lyke to vipers brood:
    and seeke some succour both to ease my smart
    and also to sustayne thy selfe with food.
But if in presence of that fayrest proud
    thou chance to come, fall lowly at her feet:
    and with meeke humblesse and afflicted mood,
    pardon for thee, and grace for me intreat.
Which if she graunt, then liue and my loue cherish,
    if not, die soone, and I with thee will perish.

### SONNET. III.

THe souerayne beauty which I doo admyre,
    witnesse the world how worthy to be prayzed:
    the light wherof hath kindled heauenly fyre,
    in my fraile spirit by her from basenesse raysed.
That being now with her huge brightnesse dazed,
    base thing I can no more endure to view:

but looking still on her I stand amazed,
    at wondrous sight of so celestiall hew.
So when my toung would speak her praises dew,
    it stopped is with thoughts astonishment:
    and when my pen would write her titles true,
    it rauisht is with fancies wonderment:
Yet in my hart I then both speake and write
    the wonder that my wit cannot endite.

## SONNET. IIII.

NEw yeare forth looking out of Ianus gate,
    Doth seeme to promise hope of new delight:
    and bidding th'old Adieu, his passed date
    bids all old thoughts to die in dumpish spright.
And calling forth out of sad Winters night,
    fresh loue, that long hath slept in cheerlesse bower:
    wils him awake, and soone about him dight
    his wanton wings and darts of deadly power.
For lusty spring now in his timely howre,
    is ready to come forth him to receiue:
    and warnes the Earth with diuers colord flowre,
    to decke hir selfe, and her faire mantle weaue.
Then you faire flowre, in whom fresh youth doth raine,
    prepare your selfe new loue to entertaine.

## SONNET. V.

RVdely thou wrongest my deare harts desire,
    In finding fault with her too portly pride:
    the thing which I doo most in her admire,
    is of the world vnworthy most enuide.
For in those lofty lookes is close implide,
    scorn of base things, and sdeigne of foule dishonor:
    thretning rash eies which gaze on her so wide,
    that loosely they ne dare to looke vpon her.
Such pride is praise, such portlinesse is honor,
    that boldned innocence beares in hir eies:
    and her faire countenance like a goodly banner,
    spreds in defiaunce of all enemies.
Was neuer in this world ought worthy tride,
    without some spark of such self-pleasing pride?

### SONNET. VI.

BE nought dismayd that her vnmoued mind
    doth still persist in her rebellious pride:
    such loue not lyke to lusts of baser kynd,
    the harder wonne, the firmer will abide.
The durefull Oake, whose sap is not yet dride,
    is long ere it conceiue the kindling fyre:
    but when it once doth burne, it doth diuide
    great heat, and makes his flames to heauen aspire.
So hard it is to kindle new desire
    in gentle brest that shall endure for euer:
    deepe is the wound, that dints the parts entire
    with chast affects, that naught but death can seuer.
Then thinke not long in taking litle paine,
    to knit the knot, that euer shall remaine.

### SONNET. VII.

FAyre eyes, the myrrour of my mazed hart,
    what wondrous vertue is contaynd in you
    the which both lyfe and death forth from you dart
    into the obiect of your mighty view?
For when ye mildly looke with louely hew,
    then is my soule with life and loue inspired:
    but when ye lowre, or looke on me askew,
    then doe I die, as one with lightning fyred.
But since that lyfe is more then death desyred,
    looke euer louely, as becomes you best,
    that your bright beams of my weak eies admyred,
    may kindle liuing fire within my brest.
Such life should be the honor of your light,
    such death the sad ensample of your might.

### SONNET. VIII.

MOre then most faire, full of the liuing fire,
    Kindled aboue vnto the maker neere:
    no eies but ioyes, in which al powers conspire,
    that to the world naught else be counted deare.
Thrugh your bright beams doth not the blinded guest
    shoot out his darts to base affections wound?
    but Angels come to lead fraile mindes to rest

in chast desires on heauenly beauty bound.
You frame my thoughts and fashion me within,
   you stop my toung, and teach my hart to speake,
   you calme the storme that passion did begin,
   strong thrugh your cause, but by your vertue weak.
Dark is the world, where your light shined neuer;
   well is he borne, that may behold you euer.

## SONNET. IX.

LOng-while I sought to what I might compare
   those powrefull eies, which lighten my dark spright,
   yet find I nought on earth to which I dare
   resemble th' ymage of their goodly light.
Not to the Sun: for they doo shine by night;
   nor to the Moone: for they are changed neuer;
   nor to the Starres: for they haue purer sight;
   nor to the fire: for they consume not euer;
Nor to the lightning: for they still perseuer;
   nor to the Diamond: for they are more tender;
   nor vnto Christall: for nought may them seuer;
   nor vnto glasse: such basenesse mought offend her;
Then to the Maker selfe they likest be,
   whose light doth lighten all that here we see.

## SONNET. X.

VNrighteous Lord of loue what law is this,
   That me thou makest thus tormented be?
   the whiles she lordeth in licentious blisse
   of her freewill, scorning both thee and me.
See how the Tyrannesse doth ioy to see
   the huge massacres which her eyes do make:
   and humbled harts brings captiues vnto thee,
   that thou of them mayst mightie vengeance take.
But her proud hart doe thou a little shake
   and that high look, with which she doth comptroll
   all this worlds pride bow to a baser make,
   and al her faults in thy black booke enroll.
That I may laugh at her in equall sort,
   as she doth laugh at me and makes my pain her sport.

### SONNET. XI.

DAyly when I do seeke and sew for peace,
    And hostages doe offer for my truth:
        she cruell warriour doth her selfe addresse
        to battell, and the weary war renew'th.
Ne wilbe moou'd with reason or with rewth,
        to graunt small respit to my restlesse toile:
        but greedily her fell intent poursewth,
        Of my poore life to make vnpittied spoile.
Yet my poore life, all sorrowes to assoyle,
        I would her yield, her wrath to pacify:
        but then she seekes with torment and turmoyle,
        to force me liue and will not let me dy.
All paine hath end and euery war hath peace,
        but mine no price nor prayer may surcease.

### SONNET. XII.

ONe day I sought with her hart-thrilling eies,
        to make a truce and termes to entertaine:
        all fearelesse then of so false enimies,
        which sought me to entrap in treasons traine.
So as I then disarmed did remaine,
        a wicked ambush which lay hidden long
        in the close couert of her guilefull eyen,
        thence breaking forth did thick about me throng.
Too feeble I t' abide the brunt so strong,
        was forst to yeeld my selfe into their hands:
        who me captiuing streight with rigorous wrong,
        haue euer since me kept in cruell bands.
So Ladie now to you I doo complaine,
        against your eies that iustice I may gaine.

### SONNET. XIII.

IN that proud port, which her so goodly graceth,
        whiles her faire face she reares vp to the skie:
        and to the ground her eie lids low embaseth,
        most goodly temperature ye may descry,
Myld humblesse mixt with awfull maiesty.
        for looking on the earth whence she was borne,

her minde remembreth her mortalitie,
what so is fayrest shall to earth returne.
But that same lofty countenance seemes to scorne
base thing, and thinke how she to heauen my clime:
treading downe earth as lothsome and forlorne,
that hinders heauenly thoughts with drossy slime.
Yet lowly still vouchsafe to looke on me,
such lowlinesse shall make you lofty be.

### SONNET. XIIII.

REtourne agayne my forces late dismayd,
Vnto the siege by you abandon'd quite,
great shame it is to leaue like one afrayd,
so fayre a peece for one repulse so light.
Gaynst such strong castles needeth greater might,
then those small forts which ye were wont belay,
such haughty mynds enur'd to hardy fight,
disdayne to yeild vnto the first assay.
Bring therefore all the forces that ye may,
and lay incessant battery to her heart,
playnts, prayers, vowes, ruth, sorrow, and dismay,
those engins can the proudest loue conuert.
And if those fayle fall downe and dy before her,
so dying liue, and liuing do adore her.

### SONNET. XV.

YE tradefull Merchants that with weary toyle
do seeke most pretious things to make your gain:
and both the Indias of their treasures spoile,
what needeth you to seeke so farre in vaine?
For loe my loue doth in her selfe containe
all this worlds riches that may farre be found,
if Saphyres, loe her eies be Saphyres plaine,
if Rubies, loe hir lips be Rubies sound:
If Pearles, hir teeth be pearles both pure and round;
if Yuorie, her forhead yuory weene;
if Gold, her locks are finest gold on ground;
if siluer, her faire hands are siluer sheene:
But that which fairest is, but few behold,
her mind adornd with vertues manifold.

### SONNET. XVI.

ONe day as I vnwarily did gaze
    on those fayre eyes my loues immortall light:
    the whiles my stonisht hart stood in amaze,
    through sweet illusion of her lookes delight,
I mote perceiue how in her glauncing sight,
    legions of loues with little wings did fly:
    darting their deadly arrowes fyry bright,
    at euery rash beholder passing by.
One of those archers closely I did spy,
    ayming his arrow at my very hart:
    when suddenly with twincle of her eye,
    the Damzell broke his misintended dart.
Had she not so doon, sure I had bene slayne,
    yet as it was, I hardly scap't with paine.

### SONNET. XVII.

THe glorious pourtraict of that Angels face,
    Made to amaze weake mens confused skil:
    and this worlds worthlesse glory to embase,
    what pen, what pencill can expresse her fill?
For though he colours could deuize at will,
    and eke his learned hand at pleasure guide,
    least trembling it his workmanship should spill,
    yet many wondrous things there are beside.
The sweet eye-glaunces, that like arrowes glide,
    the charming smiles, that rob sence from the hart:
    the louely pleasance and the lofty pride,
    cannot expressed be by any art.
A greater craftesmans hand thereto doth neede,
    that can expresse the life of things indeed.

### SONNET. XVIII.

THe rolling wheele that runneth often round,
    The hardest steele in tract of time doth teare:
    and drizling drops that often doe redound,
    the firmest flint doth in continuance weare.
Yet cannot I with many a dropping teare,
    and long intreaty soften her hard hart:

that she will once vouchsafe my plaint to heare,
     or looke with pitty on my payneful smart.
But when I pleade, she bids me play my part,
     and when I weep, she sayes teares are but water:
     and when I sigh, she sayes I know the art,
     and when I waile, she turnes hir selfe to laughter.
So doe I weepe, and wayle, and pleade in vaine,
     whiles she as steele and flint doth still remayne.

## SONNET. XIX.

THe merry Cuckow, messenger of Spring,
     His trompet shrill hath thrise already sounded:
     that warnes al louers wayt vpon their king,
     who now is comming forth with girland crouned.
With noyse whereof the quyre of Byrds resounded
     their anthemes sweet devized of loues prayse,
     that all the woods theyr ecchoes back rebounded,
     as if they knew the meaning of their layes.
But mongst them all, which did Loues honor rayse
     no word was heard of her that most it ought,
     but she his precept proudly disobayes,
     and doth his ydle message set at nought.
Therefore O loue, vnlesse she turne to thee
     ere Cuckow end, let her a rebell be.

## SONNET. XX.

IN vaine I seeke and sew to her for grace,
     and doe myne humbled hart before her poure:
     the whiles her foot she in my necke doth place,
     and tread my life downe in the lowly floure.
And yet the Lyon that is Lord of power,
     and reigneth ouer euery beast in field:
     in his most pride disdeigneth to deuoure
     the silly lambe that to his might doth yield.
But she more cruell and more saluage wylde,
     then either Lyon or the Lyonesse:
     shames not to be with guiltlesse bloud defylde,
     but taketh glory in her cruelnesse.
Fayrer then fayrest let none euer say,
     that ye were blooded in a yeelded pray.

### SONNET. XXI.

WAs it the worke of nature or of Art,
    which tempred so the feature of her face,
    that pride and meeknesse mixt by equall part,
    doe both appeare t' adorne her beauties grace?
For with mild pleasance, which doth pride displace,
    she to her loue doth lookers eyes allure:
    and with sterne countenance back again doth chace
    their looser lookes that stir vp lustes impure.
With such strange termes her eyes she doth inure,
    that with one looke she doth my life dismay:
    and with another doth it streight recure,
    her smile me drawes, her frowne me driues away.
Thus doth she traine and teach me with her lookes,
    such art of eyes I neuer read in bookes.

### SONNET. XXII.

THis holy season fit to fast and pray,
    Men to deuotion ought to be inclynd:
    therefore, I lykewise on so holy day,
    for my sweet Saynt some seruice fit will find.
Her temple fayre is built within my mind,
    in which her glorious ymage placed is,
    on which my thoughts doo day and night attend
    lyke sacred priests that neuer thinke amisse.
There I to her as th'author of my blisse,
    will builde an altar to appease her yre:
    and on the same my hart will sacrifise,
    burning in flames of pure and chast desyre:
The which vouchsafe O goddesse to accept,
    amongst thy deerest relicks to be kept.

### SONNET. XXIII.

*PEnelope* for her *Vlisses* sake,
    Deuiz'd a Web her wooers to deceaue:
    in which the worke that she all day did make
    the same at night she did againe vnreaue:
Such subtile craft my Damzell doth conceaue,
    th'importune suit of my desire to shonne:
    for all that I in many dayes doo weaue,

in one short houre I find by her vndonne.
So when I thinke to end that I begonne,
    I must begin and neuer bring to end:
    for with one looke she spils that long I sponne,
    and with one word my whole years work doth rend.
Such labour like the Spyders web I fynd,
    whose fruitlesse worke is broken with least wynd.

## SONNET. XXIIII.

WHen I behold that beauties wonderment,
    And rare perfection of each goodly part:
    of natures skill the onely complement,
    I honor and admire the makers art.
But when I feele the bitter balefull smart,
    which her fayre eyes vnwares doe worke in mee:
    that death out of theyr shiny beames doe dart,
    I thinke that I a new *Pandora* see,
Whom all the Gods in councell did agree,
    into this sinfull world from heauen to send:
    that she to wicked men a scourge should bee,
    for all their faults with which they did offend.
But since ye are my scourge I will intreat,
    that for my faults ye will me gently beat.

## SONNET. XXV.

HOw long shall this lyke dying lyfe endure,
    And know no end of her owne mysery?
    but wast and weare away in terms vnsure,
    twixt feare and hope depending doubtfully.
Yet better were attonce to let me die,
    and shew the last ensample of your pride:
    then to torment me thus with cruelty,
    to proue your powre, which I too wel haue tride.
But yet if in your hardned brest ye hide
    a close intent at last to shew me grace:
    then all the woes and wrecks which I abide,
    as meanes of blisse I gladly wil embrace.
And wish that more and greater they might be,
    that greater meede at last may turne to mee.

### SONNET. XXVI.

SWeet is the Rose, but growes vpon a brere;
    Sweet is the Iunipere, but sharpe his bough;
    sweet is the Eglantine, but pricketh nere;
    sweet is the firbloome, but his braunches rough.
Sweet is the Cypresse, but his rynd is tough,
    sweet is the nut, but bitter is his pill;
    sweet is the broome-flowre, but yet sowre enough;
    and sweet is Moly, but his root is ill.
So euery sweet with soure is tempred still,
    that maketh it be coueted the more:
    for easie things that may be got at will,
    most sorts of men doe set but little store.
Why then should I accoumpt of little paine,
    that endlesse pleasure shall vnto me gaine?

### SONNET. XXVII.

FAire proud now tell me why should faire be proud,
    Sith all worlds glorie is but drosse vncleane:
    and in the shade of death it selfe shall shroud,
    how euer now thereof ye little weene.
That goodly Idoll now so gay beseene,
    shall doffe her fleshes borowd fayre attyre:
    and be forgot as it had neuer beene,
    that many now much worship and admire.
Ne any then shall after it inquire,
    ne any mention shall thereof remaine:
    but what this verse, that neuer shall expyre,
    shall to you purchas with her thankles paine.
Faire be no lenger proud of that shall perish,
    but that which shal you make immortall, cherish.

### SONNET. XXVIII.

THe laurell leafe, which you this day doe weare,
    giues me great hope of your relenting mynd:
    for since it is the badg which I doe beare,
    ye bearing it doe seeme to me inclind:
The powre thereof, which ofte in me I find,
    let it lykewise your gentle brest inspire

with sweet infusion, and put you in mind
of that proud mayd, whom now those leaues attyre.
Proud *Daphne* scorning Phaebus louely fyre,
on the Thessalian shore from him did flee:
for which the gods in theyr reuengefull yre
did her transforme into a laurell tree.
Then fly no more fayre loue from Phebus chace,
but in your brest his leafe and loue embrace.

### SONNET. XXIX.

SEe how the stubborne damzell doth depraue
my simple meaning with disdaynfull scorne:
and by the bay which I vnto her gaue,
accoumpts my selfe her captiue quite forlorne.
The bay (quoth she) is of the victours borne,
yielded them by the vanquisht as theyr meeds,
and they therewith doe poetes heads adorne,
to sing the glory of their famous deedes.
But sith she will the conquest challeng needs,
let her accept me as her faithfull thrall,
that her great triumph which my skill exceeds,
I may in trump of fame blaze ouer all.
Then would I decke her head with glorious bayes,
and fill the world with her victorious prayse.

### SONNET. XXX.

MY loue is lyke to yse, and I to fyre;
how comes it then that this her cold so great
is not dissolu'd through my so hot desyre,
but harder growes the more I her intreat?
Or how comes it that my exceeding heat
is not delayd by her hart frosen cold:
but that I burne much more in boyling sweat,
and feele my flames augmented manifold?
What more miraculous thing may be told
that fire which all thing melts, should harden yse:
and yse which is congeald with sencelesse cold,
should kindle fyre by wonderfull deuyse?
Such is the powre of loue in gentle mind,
that it can alter all the course of kynd.

### SONNET. XXXI.

AH why hath nature to so hard a hart,
    giuen so goodly giftes of beauties grace?
      whose pryde depraues each other better part,
      and all those pretious ornaments deface.
Sith to all other beastes of bloody race,
    a dreadfull countenaunce she giuen hath:
      that with theyr terrour al the rest may chace,
      and warne to shun the daunger of theyr wrath.
But my proud one doth worke the greater scath,
    through sweet allurement of her louely hew:
      that she the better may in bloody bath
      of such poore thralls her cruell hands embrew.
But did she know how ill these two accord,
    such cruelty she would haue soone abhord.

### SONNET. XXXII.

THe paynefull smith with force of feruent heat,
    the hardest yron soone doth mollify:
      that with his heauy sledge he can it beat,
      and fashion to what he it list apply.
Yet cannot all these flames in which I fry,
    her hart more harde then yron soft awhit:
      ne all the playnts and prayers with which I
      doe beat on th'anduyle of her stubberne wit:
But still the more she feruent sees my fit,
    the more she frieseth in her wilfull pryde:
      and harder growes the harder she is smit,
      with all the playnts which to her be applyde.
What then remaines but I to ashes burne,
    and she to stones at length all frosen turne?

### SONNET. XXXIII.

GReat wrong I doe, I can it not deny,
    to that most sacred Empresse my dear dred,
      not finishing her Queene of faëry,
      that mote enlarge her liuing prayses dead:
But lodwick, this of grace to me aread:
    doe ye not thinck th'accomplishment of it

sufficient worke for one mans simple head,
    all were it as the rest but rudely writ.
How then should I without another wit
    thinck euer to endure so taedious toyle?
    sins that this one is tost with troublous fit
    of a proud loue, that doth my spirite spoyle.
Ceasse then, till she vouchsafe to grawnt me rest,
    or lend you me another liuing brest.

### SONNET. XXXIIII.

LYke as a ship that through the Ocean wyde
    by conduct of some star doth make her way,
    whenas a storme hath dimd her trusty guyde,
    out of her course doth wander far astray:
So I whose star, that wont with her bright ray
    me to direct, with cloudes is ouercast,
    doe wander now in darknesse and dismay,
    through hidden perils round about me plast.
Yet hope I well, that when this storme is past
    my *Helice* the lodestar of my lyfe
    will shine again, and looke on me at last,
    with louely light to cleare my cloudy grief.
Till then I wander carefull comfortlesse,
    in secret sorow and sad pensiuenesse.

### SONNET. XXXV.

MY hungry eyes through greedy couetize,
    still to behold the obiect of their paine:
    with no contentment can themselues suffize,
    but hauing pine and hauing not complaine.
For lacking it they cannot lyfe sustayne,
    and hauing it they gaze on it the more:
    in their amazement lyke *Narcissus* vaine
    whose eyes him staru'd: so plenty makes me poore.
Yet are mine eyes so filled with the store
    of that faire sight, that nothing else they brooke,
    but lothe the things which they did like before,
    and can no more endure on them to looke.
All this worlds glory seemeth vayne to me,
    and all their showes but shadowes sauing she.

## SONNET. XXXVI.

TEll me when shall these wearie woes haue end,
    Or shall their ruthlesse torment neuer cease:
    but al my dayes in pining languor spend,
    without hope of aswagement or release?
Is there no meanes for me to purchace peace,
    or make agreement with her thrilling eyes:
    but that their cruelty doth still increace,
    and dayly more augment my miseryes?
But when ye haue shewed all extremityes,
    then thinke how litle glory ye haue gayned
    by slaying him, whose lyfe though ye despyse,
    mote haue your life in honour long maintayned.
But by his death which some perhaps will mone,
    ye shall condemned be of many a one.

## SONNET. XXXVII.

WHat guyle is this, that those her golden tresses
    She doth attyre vnder a net of gold:
    and with sly skill so cunningly them dresses,
    that which is gold or heare, may scarse be told?
Is it that mens frayle eyes, which gaze too bold,
    she may entangle in that golden snare:
    and being caught may craftily enfold
    theyr weaker harts, which are not wel aware?
Take heed therefore, myne eyes, how ye doe stare
    henceforth too rashly on that guilefull net,
    in which if euer ye entrapped are,
    out of her bands ye by no meanes shall get.
Fondnesse it were for any being free,
    to couet fetters, though they golden bee.

## SONNET. XXXVIII.

ARion, when through tempests cruel wracke,
    He forth was thrown into the greedy seas:
    through the sweet musick which his harp did make
    allur'd a Dolphin him from death to ease.
But my rude musick, which was wont to please
    some dainty eares, cannot with any skill

the dreadfull tempest of her wrath appease,
    nor moue the Dolphin from her stubborne will,
But in her pride she dooth perseuer still,
    all carelesse how my life for her decayse:
    yet with one word she can it saue or spill,
    to spill were pitty, but to saue were prayse.
Chose rather to be praysd for dooing good,
    then to be blam'd for spilling guiltlesse blood.

## SONNET. XXXIX.

SWeet smile, the daughter of the Queene of loue,
    Expressing all thy mothers powrefull art:
    with which she wonts to temper angry Ioue,
    when all the gods he threats with thundring dart.
Sweet is thy vertue as thy selfe sweet art,
    for when on me thou shinedst late in sadnesse,
    a melting pleasance ran through euery part,
    and me reuiued with hart robbing gladnesse.
Whylest rapt with ioy resembling heauenly madnes,
    my soule was rauisht quite as in a traunce:
    and feeling thence no more her sorowes sadnesse,
    fed on the fulnesse of that chearefull glaunce.
More sweet than Nectar or Ambrosiall meat
    seemd euery bit, which thenceforth I did eat.

## SONNET. XL.

MArk when she smiles with amiable cheare,
    And tell me whereto can ye lyken it:
    when on each eyelid sweetly doe appeare
    an hundred Graces as in shade to sit.
Lykest it seemeth in my simple wit
    vnto the fayre sunshine in somers day:
    that when a dreadfull storme away is flit,
    thrugh the broad world doth spred his goodly ray:
At sight whereof each bird that sits on spray,
    and euery beast that to his den was fled,
    comes forth afresh out of their late dismay,
    and to the light lift vp theyr drouping hed.
So my storme beaten hart likewise is cheared
    with that sunshine when cloudy looks are cleared.

### SONNET. XLI.

IS it her nature or is it her will,
    to be so cruell to an humbled foe?
    if nature, then she may it mend with skill,
    if will, then she at will may will forgoe.
But if her nature and her wil be so,
    that she will plague the man that loues her most:
    and take delight t'encrease a wretches woe,
    then all her natures goodly guifts are lost.
And that same glorious beauties ydle boast
    is but a bayt such wretches to beguile:
    as being long in her loues tempest tost,
    she meanes at last to make her piteous spoyle.
O fayrest fayre let neuer it be named,
    that so fayre beauty was so fowly shamed.

### SONNET. XLII.

THe loue which me so cruelly tormenteth,
    So pleasing is in my extreamest paine:
    that all the more my sorrow it augmenteth,
    the more I loue and doe embrace my bane.
Ne doe I wish (for wishing were but vaine)
    to be acquit fro my continuall smart:
    but ioy her thrall for euer to remayne,
    and yield for pledge my poore captyued hart;
The which that it from her may neuer start,
    let her, yf please her, bynd with adamant chayne:
    and from all wandring loues which mote peruart
    his safe assurance strongly it restrayne.
Onely let her abstaine from cruelty,
    and doe me not before my time to dy.

### SONNET. XLIII.

SHall I then silent be or shall I speake?
    And if I speake, her wrath renew I shall:
    and if I silent be, my hart will breake,
    or choked be with ouerflowing gall.
What tyranny is this both my hart to thrall,
    and eke my toung with proud restraint to tie?

that nether I may speak nor thinke at all,
but like a stupid stock in silence die.
Yet I my hart with silence secretly
will teach to speak, and my iust cause to plead:
and eke mine eies with meeke humility,
loue learned letters to her eyes to read.
Which her deep wit, that true harts thought can spel,
wil soone conceiue, and learne to construe well.

## SONNET. XLIIII.

WHen those renoumed noble Peres of Greece,
thrugh stubborn pride amongst themselues did iar
forgetfull of the famous golden fleece,
then Orpheus with his harp theyr strife did bar.
But this continuall cruell ciuill warre,
the which my selfe against my selfe doe make:
whilest my weak powres of passions warreid arre,
no skill can stint nor reason can aslake.
But when in hand my tunelesse harp I take,
then doe I more augment my foes despight:
and griefe renew, and passions doe awake
to battaile fresh against my selfe to fight.
Mongst whome the more I seeke to settle peace,
the more I fynd their malice to increace.

## SONNET. XLV.

LEaue lady in your glasse of christall clene,
Your goodly selfe for euermore to vew:
and in my selfe, my inward selfe I meane,
most liuely lyke behold your semblant trew.
Within my hart, though hardly it can shew
thing so diuine to vew of earthly eye:
the fayre Idea of your celestiall hew,
and euery part remaines immortally:
And were it not that through your cruelty,
with sorrow dimmed and deformd it were:
the goodly ymage of your visnomy,
clearer then christall would therein appere.
But if your selfe in me ye playne will see,
remoue the cause by which your fayre beames darkned be.

### SONNET. XLVI.

WHen my abodes prefixed time is spent,
    My cruell fayre streight bids me wend my way:
    but then from heauen most hideous stormes are sent
    as willing me against her will to stay.
Whom then shall I or heauen or her obay?
    the heauens know best what is the best for me:
    but as she will, whose will my life doth sway,
    my lower heauen, so it perforce must bee.
But ye high heuens, that all this sorowe see,
    sith all your tempests cannot hold me backe:
    aswage your stormes, or else both you and she
    will both together me too sorely wrack.
Enough it is for one man to sustaine
    the stormes, which she alone on me doth raine.

### SONNET. XLVII.

TRust not the treason of those smyling lookes,
    vntill ye haue theyr guylefull traynes well tryde:
    for they are lyke but vnto golden hookes,
    that from the foolish fish theyr bayts doe hyde:
So she with flattring smyles weake harts doth guyde
    vnto her loue and tempte to theyr decay,
    whom being caught she kills with cruell pryde,
    and feeds at pleasure on the wretched pray:
Yet euen whylst her bloody hands them slay,
    her eyes looke louely and vpon them smyle:
    that they take pleasure in her cruell play,
    and dying doe them selues of payne beguyle.
O mighty charm which makes men loue theyr bane,
    and thinck they dy with pleasure, liue with payne.

### SONNET. XLVIII.

INnocent paper whom too cruell hand
    Did make the matter to auenge her yre:
    and ere she could thy cause wel vnderstand,
    did sacrifize vnto the greedy fyre.
Well worthy thou to haue found better hyre,
    then so bad end for hereticks ordayned:
    yet heresy nor treason didst conspire,

but plead thy maisters cause vniustly payned.
Whom she all carelesse of his griefe constrayned
    to vtter forth the anguish of his hart:
    and would not heare, when he to her complayned,
    the piteous passion of his dying smart.
Yet liue for euer, though against her will,
    and speake her good, though she requite it ill.

### SONNET. XLIX.

FAyre cruell, why are ye so fierce and cruell?
    Is it because your eyes haue powre to kill?
    then know, that mercy is the mighties iewell,
    and greater glory thinke to saue, then spill.
But if it be your pleasure and proud will,
    to shew the powre of your imperious eyes:
    then not on him that neuer thought you ill,
    but bend your force against your enemyes.
Let them feele th'utmost of your crueltyes,
    and kill with looks as Cockatrices doo:
    but him that at your footstoole humbled lies,
    with mercifull regard, giue mercy too.
Such mercy shal you make admyred to be,
    so shall you liue by giuing life to me.

### SONNET. L.

LOng languishing in double malady,
    of my harts wound and of my bodies griefe:
    there came to me a leach that would apply
    fit medicines for my bodies best reliefe.
Vayne man (quod I) that has but little priefe
    in deep discouery of the mynds disease,
    is not the hart of all the body chiefe?
    and rules the members as it selfe doth please?
Then with some cordialls seeke first to appease
    the inward languour of my wounded hart,
    and then my body shall haue shortly ease:
    but such sweet cordialls passe Physitions art.
Then my lyfes Leach doe you your skill reueale,
    and with one salue both hart and body heale.

### SONNET. LI.

DOe I not see that fayrest ymages
    Of hardest Marble are of purpose made?
    for that they should endure through many ages,
    ne let theyr famous moniments to fade.
Why then doe I, vntrainde in louers trade,
    her hardnes blame which I should more commend?
    sith neuer ought was excellent assayde,
    which was not hard t'atchiue and bring to end.
Ne ought so hard, but he that would attend,
    mote soften it and to his will allure:
    so doe I hope her stubborne hart to bend,
    and that it then more stedfast will endure.
Onely my paines wil be the more to get her,
    but hauing her, my ioy wil be the greater.

### SONNET. LII.

SO oft as homeward I from her depart,
    I goe lyke one that hauing lost the field,
    is prisoner led away with heauy hart,
    despoyld of warlike armes and knowen shield.
So doe I now my selfe a prisoner yeeld,
    to sorrow and to solitary paine:
    from presence of my dearest deare exylde,
    longwhile alone in languor to remaine.
There let no thought of ioy or pleasure vaine
    dare to approch, that may my solace breed:
    but sudden dumps and drery sad disdayne
    of all worlds gladnesse more my torment feed.
So I her absens will my penaunce make,
    that of her presens I my meed may take.

### SONNET. LIII.

THe Panther knowing that his spotted hyde
    Doth please all beasts but that his looks them fray:
    within a bush his dreadfull head doth hide,
    to let them gaze whylest he on them may pray.
Right so my cruell fayre with me doth play,
    for with the goodly semblant of her hew,

she doth allure me to mine owne decay,
and then no mercy will vnto me shew.
Great shame it is, thing so diuine in view,
made for to be the worlds most ornament:
to make the bayte her gazers to embrew,
good shames to be to ill an instrument.
But mercy doth with beautie best agree,
as in theyr maker ye them best may see.

### SONNET. LIIII.

OF this worlds Theatre in which we stay,
My loue lyke the Spectator ydly sits
beholding me that all the pageants play,
disguysing diuersly my troubled wits.
Sometimes I ioy when glad occasion fits,
and mask in myrth lyke to a Comedy:
soone after when my ioy to sorrow flits,
I waile and make my woes a Tragedy.
Yet she beholding me with constant eye,
delights not in my merth nor rues my smart:
but when I laugh she mocks, and when I cry
she laughes, and hardens euermore her hart.
What then can moue her? if nor merth nor mone,
she is no woman, but a sencelesse stone.

### SONNET. LV.

SO oft as I her beauty doe behold,
And therewith doe her cruelty compare:
I maruaile of what substance was the mould
the which her made attonce so cruell faire.
Not earth; for her high thoghts more heauenly are,
not water; for her loue doth burne like fyre:
not ayre; for she is not so light or rare,
not fyre; for she doth friese with faint desire.
Then needs another Element inquire
whereof she mote be made; that is the skye.
for to the heauen her haughty lookes aspire:
and eke her mind is pure immortall hye.
Then sith to heauen ye lykened are the best,
be lyke in mercy as in all the rest.

### SONNET. LVI

FAyre ye be sure, but cruell and vnkind,
    As is a Tygre that with greedinesse
    hunts after bloud, when he by chance doth find
    a feeble beast, doth felly him oppresse.
Fayre be ye sure but proud and pittilesse,
    as is a storme, that all things doth prostrate:
    finding a tree alone all comfortlesse,
    beats on it strongly it to ruinate.
Fayre be ye sure, but hard and obstinate,
    as is a rocke amidst the raging floods:
    gaynst which a ship of succour desolate,
    doth suffer wreck both of her selfe and goods.
That ship, that tree, and that same beast am I,
    whom ye doe wreck, doe ruine, and destroy.

### SONNET. LVII.

SWeet warriour when shall I haue peace with you?
    High time it is, this warre now ended were:
    which I no lenger can endure to sue,
    ne your incessant battry more to beare:
So weake my powres, so sore my wounds appeare,
    that wonder is how I should liue a iot,
    seeing my hart through launched euery where
    with thousand arrowes, which your eies haue shot:
Yet shoot ye sharpely still, and spare me not,
    but glory thinke to make these cruel stoures.
    ye cruell one, what glory can be got,
    in slaying him that would liue gladly yours?
Make peace therefore, and graunt me timely grace,
    that al my wounds wil heale in little space.

### SONNET. LVIII.

*By her that is most assured to her selfe.*

WEake is th'assurance that weake flesh reposeth
    In her owne powre and scorneth others ayde:
    that soonest fals when as she most supposeth
    her selfe assurd, and is of nought affrayd.
All flesh is frayle, and all her strength vnstayd,
    like a vaine bubble blowen vp with ayre:

deuouring tyme and changeful chance haue prayd
   her glories pride that none may it repayre.
Ne none so rich or wise, so strong or fayre,
   but fayleth trusting on his owne assurance:
   and he that standeth on the hyghest stayre
   fals lowest: for on earth nought hath enduraunce.
Why then doe ye proud fayre, misdeeme so farre,
   that to your selfe ye most assured arre?

## SONNET. LIX.

THrise happie she, that is so well assured
   Vnto her selfe and setled so in hart:
   that nether will for better be allured,
   ne feard with worse to any chaunce to start,
But like a steddy ship, doth strongly part
   the raging waues and keepes her course aright:
   ne ought for tempest doth from it depart,
   ne ought for fayrer weathers false delight.
Such selfe assurance need not feare the spight
   of grudging foes, ne fauour seek of friends:
   but in the stay of her owne stedfast might,
   nether to one her selfe nor other bends.
Most happy she that most assured doth rest,
   but he most happy who such one loues best.

## SONNET. LX.

THey that in course of heauenly spheares are skild,
   To euery planet point his sundry yeare:
   in which her circles voyage is fulfild,
   as Mars in three score yeares doth run his spheare.
So since the winged God his planet cleare,
   began in me to moue, one yeare is spent:
   the which doth longer vnto me appeare,
   then al those fourty which my life outwent.
Then by that count, which louers books inuent,
   the spheare of Cupid fourty yeares containes:
   which I haue wasted in long languishment,
   that seemd the longer for my greater paines.
But let my loues fayre Planet short her wayes
   this yeare ensuing, or else short my dayes.

### SONNET. LXI.

THe glorious image of the makers beautie,
    My souerayne saynt, the Idoll of my thought,
    dare not henceforth aboue the bounds of dewtie
    t'accuse of pride, or rashly blame for ought.
For being as she is diuinely wrought,
    and of the brood of Angels heuenly borne:
    and with the crew of blessed Saynts vpbrought,
    each of which did her with theyr guifts adorne;
The bud of ioy, the blossome of the morne,
    the beame of light, whom mortal eyes admyre:
    what reason is it then but she should scorne
    base things that to her loue too bold aspire?
Such heauenly formes ought rather worshipt be,
    then dare be lou'd by men of meane degree.

### SONNET. LXII.

THe weary yeare his race now hauing run,
    The new begins his compast course anew:
    with shew of morning mylde he hath begun,
    betokening peace and plenty to ensew,
So let vs, which this chaunge of weather vew,
    chaunge eeke our mynds and former liues amend:
    the old yeares sinnes forepast let vs eschew,
    and fly the faults with which we did offend.
Then shall the new yeares ioy forth freshly send
    into the glooming world his gladsome ray:
    and all these stormes which now his beauty blend,
    shall turne to caulmes and tymely cleare away.
So likewise loue cheare you your heauy spright,
    and chaunge old yeares annoy to new delight.

### SONNET. LXIII.

AFter long stormes and tempests sad assay,
    Which hardly I endured heretofore:
    in dread of death and daungerous dismay,
    with which my silly barke was tossed sore:
I doe at length descry the happy shore,
    in which I hope ere long for to arryue:
    fayre soyle it seemes from far and fraught with store

of all that deare and daynty is alyue.
Most happy he that can at last atchyue
    the ioyous safety of so sweet a rest:
    whose least delight sufficeth to depriue
    remembrance of all paines which him opprest.
All paines are nothing in respect of this,
    all sorrowes short that gaine eternall blisse.

### SONNET. LXIIII.

COmming to kisse her lyps, (such grace I found)
    Me seemd I smelt a gardin of sweet flowres:
    that dainty odours from them threw around
    for damzels fit to decke their louers bowres.
Her lips did smell lyke vnto Gillyflowers,
    her ruddy cheekes lyke vnto Roses red:
    her snowy browes lyke budded Bellamoures,
    her louely eyes lyke Pincks but newly spred,
Her goodly bosome lyke a Strawberry bed,
    her neck lyke to a bounch of Cullambynes:
    her brest lyke lillyes, ere theyr leaues be shed,
    her nipples lyke yong blossomd Iessemynes:
Such fragrant flowres doe giue most odorous smell,
    but her sweet odour did them all excell.

### SONNET. LXV.

THe doubt which ye misdeeme, fayre loue, is vaine,
    That fondly feare to loose your liberty,
    when loosing one, two liberties ye gayne,
    and make him bond that bondage earst dyd fly.
Sweet be the bands, the which true loue doth tye,
    without constraynt or dread of any ill:
    the gentle birde feeles no captiuity
    within her cage, but singes and feeds her fill.
There pride dare not approch, nor discord spill
    the league twixt them, that loyal loue hath bound:
    but simple truth and mutuall good will,
    seekes with sweet peace to salue each others wound:
There fayth doth fearlesse dwell in brasen towre,
    and spotlesse pleasure builds her sacred bowre.

### SONNET. LXVI.

TO all those happy blessings which ye haue,
    with plenteous hand by heauen vpon you thrown,
    this one disparagement they to you gaue,
    that ye your loue lent to so meane a one.
Yee whose high worths surpassing paragon,
    could not on earth haue found one fit for mate,
    ne but in heauen matchable to none,
    why did ye stoup vnto so lowly state?
But ye thereby much greater glory gate,
    then had ye sorted with a princes pere:
    for now your light doth more it selfe dilate,
    and in my darknesse greater doth appeare.
Yet since your light hath once enlumind me,
    with my reflex yours shall encreased be.

### SONNET. LXVII.

LYke as a huntsman after weary chace,
    Seeing the game from him escapt away,
    sits downe to rest him in some shady place,
    with panting hounds beguiled of their pray,
So after long pursuit and vaine assay,
    when I all weary had the chace forsooke,
    the gentle deare returnd the selfe-same way,
    thinking to quench her thirst at the next brooke.
There she beholding me with mylder looke,
    sought not to fly, but fearelesse still did bide:
    till I in hand her yet halfe trembling tooke,
    and with her owne goodwill hir fyrmely tyde.
Strange thing me seemd to see a beast so wyld,
    so goodly wonne with her owne will beguyld.

### SONNET. LXVIII.

MOst glorious Lord of lyfe that on this day
    Didst make thy triumph ouer death and sin:
    and hauing harowd hell didst bring away
    captiuity thence captiue vs to win:
This ioyous day, deare Lord, with ioy begin,
    and grant that we for whom thou diddest dye

being with thy deare blood clene washt from sin,
        may liue for euer in felicity:
And that thy loue we weighing worthily,
        may likewise loue thee for the same againe:
        and for thy sake that all lyke deare didst buy,
        with loue may one another entertayne.
So let vs loue, deare loue, lyke as we ought,
        loue is the lesson which the Lord vs taught.

### SONNET. LXIX.

THe famous warriors of the anticke world,
        Vsed Trophees to erect in stately wize:
        in which they would the records haue enrold,
        of theyr great deeds and valarous emprize.
What trophee then shall I most fit deuize,
        in which I may record the memory
        of my loues conquest, peerelesse beauties prise,
        adorn'd with honour, loue, and chastity?
Euen this verse vowd to eternity,
        shall be thereof immortall moniment:
        and tell her prayse to all posterity,
        that may admire such worlds rare wonderment.
The happy purchase of my glorious spoile,
        gotten at last with labour and long toyle.

### SONNET. LXX.

FResh spring the herald of loues mighty king,
        In whose cote armour richly are displayd
        all sorts of flowers the which on earth do spring
        in goodly colours gloriously arrayd:
Goe to my loue, where she is careless layd,
        yet in her winters bowre not well awake:
        tell her the ioyous time wil not be staid
        vnlesse she doe him by the forelock take.
Bid her therefore her selfe soone ready make,
        to wayt on loue amongst his louely crew:
        where euery one that misseth then her make
        shall be by him amearst with penance dew.
Make hast therefore sweet loue, whilest it is prime,
        for none can call againe the passed time.

### SONNET. LXXI.

I Ioy to see how in your drawen work,
    Your selfe vnto the Bee ye doe compare;
    and me vnto the Spyder that doth lurke
    in close awayt to catch her vnaware.
Right so your selfe were caught in cunning snare
    of a deare foe, and thralled to his loue:
    in whose streight bands ye now captiued are
    so firmely, that ye neuer may remoue.
But as your worke is wouen all aboue,
    with woodbynd flowers and fragrant Eglantine:
    so sweet your prison you in time shall proue,
    with many deare delights bedecked fyne.
And all thensforth eternall peace shall see,
    betweene the Spyder and the gentle Bee.

### SONNET. LXXII.

OFt when my spirit doth spred her bolder winges,
    In mind to mount vp to the purest sky:
    it down is weighd with thoght of earthly things
    and clogd with burden of mortality,
Where when that souerayne beauty it doth spy,
    resembling heauens glory in her light:
    drawne with sweet pleasures bayt, it back doth fly,
    and vnto heauen forgets her former flight.
There my fraile fancy fed with full delight,
    doth bath in blisse and mantleth most at ease:
    ne things of other heauen, but how it might
    her harts desire with most contentment please.
Hart need not wish none other happinesse,
    but here on earth to haue such heuens blisse.

### SONNET. LXXIII.

BEing my selfe captyued here in care,
    My hart, whom none with seruile bands can tye,
    but the fayre tresses of your golden hayre,
    breaking his prison forth to you doth fly.
Lyke as a byrd that in ones hand doth spy
    desired food, to it doth make his flight:
    euen so my hart, that wont on your fayre eye

to feed his fill, flyes backe vnto your sight.
Doe you him take, and in your bosome bright,
    gently encage, that he may be your thrall:
    perhaps he there may learne with rare delight,
    to sing your name and prayses ouer all.
That it hereafter may you not repent,
    him loding in your bosome to haue lent.

## SONNET. LXXIIII.

MOst happy letters fram'd by skilfull trade,
    with which that happy name was first desynd:
    the which three times thrise happy hath me made,
    with guifts of body, fortune and of mind.
The first my being to me gaue by kind,
    from mothers womb deriu'd by dew descent,
    the second is my souereigne Queene most kind,
    that honour and large richesse to me lent.
The third my loue, my liues last ornament,
    by whom my spirit out of dust was raysed:
    to speake her prayse and glory excellent,
    of all aliue most worthy to be praysed.
Ye three Elizabeths for euer liue,
    that three such graces did vnto me giue.

## SONNET. LXXV.

ONe day I wrote her name vpon the strand,
    but came the waues and washed it away:
    agayne I wrote it with a second hand,
    but came the tyde, and made my paynes his pray.
Vayne man, sayd she, that doest in vaine assay,
    a mortall thing so to immortalize,
    for I my selue shall lyke to this decay,
    and eek my name bee wyped out lykewise.
Not so, (quod I) let baser things deuize
    to dy in dust, but you shall liue by fame:
    my verse your vertues rare shall eternize,
    and in the heuens wryte your glorious name,
Where whenas death shall all the world subdew,
    our loue shall liue, and later life renew.

### SONNET. LXXVI.

FAyre bosome fraught with vertues richest tresure,
 The neast of loue, the lodging of delight:
 the bowre of blisse, the paradice of pleasure,
 the sacred harbour of that heuenly spright:
How was I rauisht with your louely sight,
 and my frayle thoughts too rashly led astray?
 whiles diuing deepe through amorous insight,
 on the sweet spoyle of beautie they did pray.
And twixt her paps like early fruit in May,
 whose haruest seemd to hasten now apace:
 they loosely did theyr wanton winges display,
 and there to rest themselues did boldly place.
Sweet thoughts I enuy your so happy rest,
 which oft I wisht, yet neuer was so blest.

### SONNET. LXXVII.

WAs it a dreame, or did I see it playne,
 a goodly table of pure yvory:
 all spred with iuncats, fit to entertayne
 the greatest Prince with pompous roialty?
Mongst which there in a siluer dish did ly
 twoo golden apples of vnualewd price:
 far passing those which Hercules came by,
 or those which Atalanta did entice.
Exceeding sweet, yet voyd of sinfull vice,
 That many sought yet none could euer taste,
 sweet fruit of pleasure brought from paradice
 by loue himselfe and in his garden plaste.
Her brest that table was so richly spredd,
 my thoughts the guests, which would thereon haue fedd.

### SONNET. LXXVIII.

LAckyng my loue I go from place to place,
 lyke a young fawne that late hath lost the hynd:
 and seeke each where, where last I sawe her face,
 whose ymage yet I carry fresh in mynd.
I seeke the fields with her late footing synd,
 I seeke her bowre with her late presence deckt,

yet nor in field nor bowre I her can fynd:
yet field and bowre are full of her aspect.
But when myne eyes I thereunto direct,
    they ydly back returne to me agayne,
    and when I hope to see theyr trew obiect,
    I fynd my selfe but fed with fancies vayne.
Ceasse then myne eyes, to seeke her selfe to see,
    and let my thoughts behold her selfe in mee.

## SONNET. LXXIX.

MEn call you fayre, and you doe credit it,
    For that your selfe ye dayly such doe see:
    but the trew fayre, that is the gentle wit,
    and vertuous mind is much more praysd of me.
For all the rest, how euer fayre it be,
    shall turne to nought and loose that glorious hew:
    but onely that is permanent and free
    from frayle corruption, that doth flesh ensew.
That is true beautie: that doth argue you
    to be diuine and borne of heauenly seed:
    deriu'd from that fayre Spirit, from whom al true
    and perfect beauty did at first proceed.
He onely fayre, and what he fayre hath made,
    all other fayre lyke flowres vntymely fade.

## SONNET. LXXX.

AFter so long a race as I haue run
    Through Faery land, which those six books compile,
    giue leaue to rest me being halfe fordonne,
    and gather to my selfe new breath awhile.
Then as a steed refreshed after toyle,
    out of my prison I will breake anew:
    and stoutly will that second worke assoyle,
    with strong endeuour and attention dew.
Till then giue leaue to me in pleasant mew,
    to sport my muse and sing my loues sweet praise:
    the contemplation of whose heauenly hew,
    my spirit to an higher pitch will rayse.
But let her prayses yet be low and meane,
    fit for the handmayd of the Faery Queene.

### SONNET. LXXXI.

FAyre is my loue, when her fayre golden heares,
    with the loose wynd ye wauing chance to marke:
    fayre when the rose in her red cheekes appeares,
    or in her eyes the fyre of loue does sparke.
Fayre when her brest lyke a rich laden barke,
    with pretious merchandize she forth doth lay:
    fayre when that cloud of pryde, which oft doth dark
    her goodly light with smiles she driues away.
But fayrest she, when so she doth display
    the gate with pearles and rubyes richly dight:
    throgh which her words so wise do make their way
    to beare the message of her gentle spright:
The rest be works of natures wonderment,
    but this the worke of harts astonishment.

### SONNET. LXXXII.

IOy of my life, full oft for louing you
    I blesse my lot, that was so lucky placed:
    but then the more your owne mishap I rew,
    that are so much by so meane loue embased.
For had the equall heuens so much you graced
    in this as in the rest, ye mote inuent
    som heuenly wit, whose verse could haue enchased
    your glorious name in golden moniment.
But since ye deignd so goodly to relent
    to me your thrall, in whom is little worth,
    that little that I am, shall all be spent
    in setting your immortall prayses forth.
Whose lofty argument vplifting me,
    shall lift you vp vnto an high degree.

### SONNET. LXXXIII.

MY hungry eyes, through greedy couetize
    Still to behold the obiect of theyr payne:
    with no contentment can themselues suffize,
    but hauing pine, and hauing not complayne.
For lacking it, they cannot lyfe sustayne,
    and seeing it, they gaze on it the more:

in theyr amazement lyke Narcissus vayne
    whose eyes him staru'd: so plenty makes me pore.
Yet are myne eyes so filled with the store
    of that fayre sight, that nothing else they brooke:
    but loath the things which they did like before,
    and can no more endure on them to looke.
All this worlds glory seemeth vayne to me,
    and all theyr shewes but shadowes sauing she.

### SONNET. LXXXIIII.

LEt not one sparke of filthy lustfull fyre
    breake out, that may her sacred peace molest:
    ne one light glance of sensuall desyre
    Attempt to work her gentle mindes vnrest.
But pure affections bred in spotlesse brest,
    and modest thoughts breathd from wel tempred sprites,
    goe visit her in her chast bowre of rest,
    accompanyde with angelick delightes.
There fill your selfe with those most ioyous sights,
    the which my selfe could neuer yet attayne:
    but speake no word to her of these sad plights,
    which her too constant stiffenesse doth constrayn.
Onely behold her rare perfection,
    and blesse your fortunes fayre election.

### SONNET. LXXXV.

THe world that cannot deeme of worthy things,
    when I doe praise her, say I doe but flatter:
    so does the Cuckow, when the Mauis sings,
    begin his witlesse note apace to clatter.
But they that skill not of so heauenly matter,
    all that they know not, enuy or admyre,
    rather then enuy let them wonder at her,
    but not to deeme of her desert aspyre.
Deepe in the closet of my parts entyre,
    her worth is written with a golden quill:
    that me with heauenly fury doth inspire,
    and my glad mouth with her sweet prayses fill.
Which when as fame in her shrill trump shal thunder,
    let the world chose to enuy or to wonder.

### SONNET. LXXXVI.

VEnemous toung tipt with vile adders sting,
 Of that selfe kynd with which the Furies fell
 theyr snaky heads doe combe, from which a spring
 of poysoned words and spitefull speeches well,
Let all the plagues and horrid paines of hell,
 vpon thee fall for thine accursed hyre:
 that with false forged lyes, which thou didst tel,
 in my true loue did stirre vp coles of yre,
The sparkes whereof let kindle thine own fyre,
 and catching hold on thine owne wicked hed
 consume thee quite, that didst with guile conspire
 in my sweet peace such breaches to haue bred.
Shame be thy meed, and mischiefe thy reward,
 dew to thy selfe that it for me prepard.

### SONNET. LXXXVII.

SInce I did leaue the presence of my loue,
 Many long weary dayes I haue outworne:
 and many nights, that slowly seemd to moue
 theyr sad protract from euening vntill morne.
For when as day the heauen doth adorne,
 I wish that night the noyous day would end:
 and when as night hath vs of light forlorne,
 I wish that day would shortly reascend.
Thus I the time with expectation spend,
 and faine my griefe with chaunges to beguile,
 that further seemes his terme still to extend,
 and maketh euery minute seeme a myle.
So sorrow still doth seeme too long to last,
 but ioyous houres doo fly away too fast.

### SONNET. LXXXVIII.

SInce I haue lackt the comfort of that light,
 The which was wont to lead my thoughts astray:
 I wander as in darknesse of the night,
 affrayd of euery dangers least dismay.
Ne ought I see, though in the clearest day,
 when others gaze vpon theyr shadowes vayne:

but th'onely image of that heauenly ray,
    whereof some glance doth in mine eie remayne.
Of which beholding the Idaea playne,
    through contemplation of my purest part:
    with light thereof I doe my selfe sustayne,
    and thereon feed my loue-affamisht hart.
But with such  brightnesse whylest I fill my mind,
    I starue my body and mine eyes doe blynd.

## SONNET. LXXXIX.

LYke as the Culuer on the bared bough
    Sits mourning for the absence of her mate:
    and in her songs sends many a wishfull vow,
    for his returne that seemes to linger late,
So I alone now left disconsolate,
    mourne to my selfe the absence of my loue:
    and wandring here and there all desolate,
    seek with my playnts to match that mournful doue:
Ne ioy of ought that vnder heauen doth houe
    can comfort me, but her owne ioyous sight:
    whose sweet aspect both God and man can moue,
    in her vnspotted pleasauns to delight.
Dark is my day, whyles her fayre light I mis,
    and dead my life that wants such liuely blis.

# [Anacreontics]

IN youth before I waxed old,
The blynd boy Venus baby,
For want of cunning made me bold,
    In bitter hyue to grope for honny.
        But when he saw me stung and cry,
        He tooke his wings and away did fly.

AS Diane hunted on a day,
        She chaunst to come where Cupid lay,
    his quiuer by his head:
One of his shafts she stole away,          10
And one of hers did close conuay,
    into the others stead:
        With that loue wounded my loues hart,
        but Diane beasts with Cupids dart.

I Saw in secret to my Dame,
        How little Cupid humbly came:
    and sayd to her All hayle my mother.
But when he saw me laugh, for shame
His face with bashfull blood did flame,
    not knowing Venus from the other.        20
Then neuer blush Cupid (quoth I)
    for many haue err'd in this beauty.

Vpon a day as loue lay sweetly slumbring,
        all in his mothers lap:
A gentle Bee with his loud trumpet murm'ring,
        about him flew by hap.
Whereof when he was wakened with the noyse,
        and saw the beast so small:

Whats this (quoth he) that giues so great a voyce,
        that wakens men withall?           30
In angry wize he flyes about,
        and threatens all with corage stout.

To whom his mother closely smiling sayd,
        twixt earnest and twixt game:
See thou thy selfe likewise art lyttle made,
        if thou regard the same.
And yet thou suffrest neyther gods in sky,
        nor men in earth to rest:
But when thou art disposed cruelly,
        theyr sleepe thou doost molest.         40
Then eyther change thy cruelty,
        or giue lyke leaue vnto the fly.

Nathlesse the cruell boy not so content,
        would needs the fly pursue:
And in his hand with heedlesse hardiment,
        him caught for to subdue.
But when on it he hasty hand did lay,
        the Bee him stung therefore:
Now out alasse (he cryde) and welaway,
        I wounded am full sore:         50
The fly that I so much did scorne,
        hath hurt me with his little horne.

Vnto his mother straight he weeping came,
        and of his griefe complayned:
Who could not chose but laugh at his fond game,
        though sad to see him pained.
Think now (quod she) my sonne how great the smart
        of those whom thou dost wound:
Full many thou has pricked to the hart,
        that pitty neuer found:         60
Therefore henceforth some pitty take,
        when thou doest spoyle of louers make.

She tooke him streight full pitiously lamenting,
        and wrapt him in her smock:
She wrapt him softly, all the while repenting,
        that he the fly did mock.

She drest his wound and it embaulmed wel
   with salue of soueraigne might:
And then she bath'd him in a dainty well
   the well of deare delight.    70
Who would not oft be stung as this,
   to be so bath'd in Venus blis?

The wanton boy was shortly wel recured
   of that his malady:
But he soone after fresh againe enured
   his former cruelty.
And since that time he wounded hath my selfe
   with his sharpe dart of loue:
And now forgets the cruell carelesse elfe,
   his mothers heast to proue.    80
So now I languish till he please
   my pining anguish to appease.

FINIS.

# Epithalamion

[1]
YE learned sisters which haue oftentimes
    beene to me ayding, others to adorne:
Whom ye thought worthy of your gracefull rymes,
That euen the greatest did not greatly scorne
To heare theyr names sung in your simple layes,
But ioyed in theyr prayse,
And when ye list your owne mishaps to mourne,
Which death, or loue, or fortunes wreck did rayse,
Your string could soone to sadder tenor turne,
And teach the woods and waters to lament          10
Your dolefull dreriment,
Now lay those sorrowfull complaints aside,
And hauing all your heads with girland crownd,
Helpe me mine owne loues prayses to resound,
Ne let the same of any be enuide,
So Orpheus did for his owne bride,
So I vnto my selfe alone will sing,
The woods shall to me answer and my Eccho ring.

[2]
EArly before the worlds light giuing lampe
    His golden beame vpon the hils doth spred,        20
Hauing disperst the nights vnchearefull dampe,
Doe ye awake and with fresh lusty hed,
Go to the bowre of my beloued loue,
My truest turtle doue,
Bid her awake; for Hymen is awake,
And long since ready forth his maske to moue,
With his bright Tead that flames with many a flake,
And many a bachelor to waite on him,
In theyr fresh garments trim.

Bid her awake therefore and soone her dight,                    30
For lo the wished day is come at last,
That shall for al the paynes and sorrowes past,
Pay to her vsury of long delight,
And whylest she doth her dight,
Doe ye to her of ioy and solace sing,
That all the woods may answer and your eccho ring.

[3]
BRing with you all the Nymphes that you can heare
        both of the riuers and the forrests greene:
And of the sea that neighbours to her neare,
Al with gay girlands goodly wel beseene.                    40
And let them also with them bring in hand
Another gay girland
For my fayre loue of lillyes and of roses,
Bound trueloue wize with a blew silke riband.
And let them make great store of bridale poses,
And let them eeke bring store of other flowers
To deck the bridale bowers.
And let the ground whereas her foot shall tread,
For feare the stones her tender foot should wrong,
Be strewed with fragrant flowers all along,                    50
And diapred lyke the discolored mead.
Which done, doe at her chamber dore awayt,
For she will waken strayt,
The whiles doe ye this song vnto her sing,
The woods shall to you answer and your Eccho ring.

[4]
YE Nymphes of Mulla which with carefull heed,
        The siluer scaly trouts doe tend full well,
and greedy pikes which vse therein to feed,
(Those trouts and pikes all others doo excell)
And ye likewise which keepe the rushy lake,                    60
Where none doo fishes take,
Bynd vp the locks the which hang scatterd light,
And in his waters which your mirror make,
Behold your faces as the christall bright,
That when you come whereas my loue doth lie,
No blemish she may spie.
And eke ye lightfoot mayds which keepe the dere,

That on the hoary mountayne vse to towre,
And the wylde wolues which seeke them to deuoure,
With your steele darts doo chace from comming neer,                    70
Be also present heere,
To helpe to decke her and to help to sing,
That all the woods may answer and your eccho ring.

[5]
WAke, now my loue, awake; for it is time,
        The Rosy Morne long since left Tithones bed,
All ready to her siluer coche to clyme,
And Phoebus gins to shew his glorious hed.
Hark how the cheerefull birds do chaunt theyr laies
And carroll of loues praise.
The merry Larke hir mattins sings aloft,                    80
The thrush replyes, the Mauis descant playes,
The Ouzell shrills, the Ruddock warbles soft,
So goodly all agree with sweet consent,
To this dayes merriment.
Ah my deere loue why doe ye sleepe thus long,
When meeter were that ye should now awake,
T'awayt the comming of your ioyous make,
And hearken to the birds louelearned song,
The deawy leaues among?
For they of ioy and pleasance to you sing,                    90
That all the woods them answer and theyr eccho ring.

[6]
MY loue is now awake out of her dreames,
        and her fayre eyes like stars that dimmed were
With darksome cloud, now shew theyr goodly beams
More bright then Hesperus his head doth rere.
Come now ye damzels, daughters of delight,
Helpe quickly her to dight,
But first come ye fayre houres which were begot
In Ioues sweet paradice, of Day and Night,
Which doe the seasons of the yeare allot,                    100
And al that euer in this world is fayre
Doe make and still repayre.
And ye three handmayds of the Cyprian Queene,
The which doe still adorne her beauties pride,
Helpe to addorne my beautifullest bride

And as ye her array, still throw betweene
Some graces to be seene,
And as ye vse to Venus, to her sing,
The whiles the woods shal answer and your eccho ring.

[7]
NOw is my loue all ready forth to come,                    110
    Let all the virgins therefore well awayt,
And ye fresh boyes that tend vpon her groome
Prepare your selues; for he is comming strayt.
Set all your things in seemely good aray
Fit for so ioyfull day,
The ioyfulst day that euer sunne did see.
Faire Sun, shew forth thy fauourable ray,
And let thy lifull heat not feruent be
For feare of burning her sunshyny face,
Her beauty to disgrace.                                    120
O fayrest Phoebus, father of the Muse,
If euer I did honour thee aright,
Or sing the thing, that mote thy mind delight,
Doe not thy seruants simple boone refuse,
But let this day let this one day be myne,
Let all the rest be thine.
Then I thy souerayne prayses loud wil sing,
That all the woods shal answer and theyr eccho ring.

[8]
HArke how the Minstrels gin to shrill aloud
    Their merry Musick that resounds from far,    130
The pipe, the tabor, and the trembling Croud,
That well agree withouten breach or iar.
But most of all the Damzels doe delite,
Whey they their tymbrels smyte,
And thereunto doe daunce and carrol sweet,
That all the sences they doe rauish quite,
The whyles the boyes run vp and downe the street,
Crying aloud with strong confused noyce,
As if it were one voyce.
Hymen io Hymen, Hymen they do shout,                       140
That euen to the heauens theyr shouting shrill
Doth reach, and all the firmament doth fill,
To which the people standing all about,

As in approuance doe thereto applaud
And loud aduaunce her laud,
And euermore they Hymen Hymen sing,
that al the woods them answer and theyr eccho ring.

[9]
LOe where she comes along with portly pace,
    Lyke Phoebe from her chamber of the East,
Arysing forth to run her mighty race,                           150
Clad all in white, that seemes a virgin best.
So well it her beseemes that ye would weene
Some angell she had beene.
Her long loose yellow locks lyke golden wyre,
Sprinckled with perle, and perling flowres a tweene,
Doe lyke a golden mantle her attyre,
And being crowned with a girland greene,
Seeme lyke some mayden Queene.
Her modest eyes abashed to behold
So many gazers, as on her do stare,                            160
Vpon the lowly ground affixed are.
Ne dare lift vp her countenance too bold,
But blush to heare her prayses sung so loud,
So farre from being proud.
Nathlesse doe ye still loud her prayses sing,
That all the woods may answer and your eccho ring.

[10]
TEll me ye merchants daughters did ye see
    So fayre a creature in your towne before?
So sweet, so louely, and so mild as she,
Adornd with beautyes grace and vertues store,                  170
Her goodly eyes lyke Saphyres shining bright,
Her forehead yuory white,
Her cheekes lyke apples which the sun hath rudded,
Her lips lyke cherryes charming men to byte,
Her brest like to a bowle of creame vncrudded,
Her paps lyke lyllies budded,
Her snowie necke lyke to a marble towre,
And all her body like a pallace fayre,
Ascending vppe with many a stately stayre,
To honors seat and chastities sweet bowre.                     180
Why stand ye still ye virgins in amaze,

Vpon her so to gaze,
Whiles ye forget your former lay to sing,
To which the woods did answer and your eccho ring?

[11]
BVt if ye saw that which no eyes can see,
    The inward beauty of her liuely spright,
Garnisht with heauenly guifts of high degree,
Much more then would ye wonder at that sight,
And stand astonisht lyke to those which red
Medusaes mazeful hed.                 190
There dwels sweet loue and constant chastity,
Vnspotted fayth and comely womanhed,
Regard of honour and mild modesty,
There vertue raynes as Queene in royal throne,
And giueth lawes alone.
The which the base affections doe obay,
And yeeld theyr seruices vnto her will,
Ne thought of thing vncomely euer may
Thereto approch to tempt her mind to ill.
Had ye once seene these her celestial threasures,    200
And vnreuealed pleasures,
Then would ye wonder and her prayses sing,
That al the woods should answer and your echo ring.

[12]
OPen the temple gates vnto my loue,
    Open them wide that she may enter in,
And all the postes adorne as doth behoue,
And all the pillours deck with girlands trim,
For to recyue this Saynt with honour dew,
That commeth in to you.
With trembling steps and humble reuerence,      210
She commeth in, before th'almighties vew:
Of her ye virgins learne obedience,
When so ye come into those holy places,
To humble your proud faces;
Bring her vp to th'high altar that she may
The sacred ceremonies there partake,
The which do endlesse matrimony make,
And let the roring Organs loudly play
The praises of the Lord in liuely notes,

The whiles with hollow throates                                    220
The Choristers the ioyous Antheme sing,
That al the woods may answere and their eccho ring.

[13]
Behold whiles she before the altar stands
        Hearing the holy priest that to her speakes
And blesseth her with his two happy hands,
How the red roses flush vp in her cheekes,
And the pure snow with goodly vermill stayne,
Like crimsin dyde in grayne,
That euen th'Angels which continually,
About the sacred Altare doe remaine,                               230
Forget their seruice and about her fly,
Ofte peeping in her face that seemes more fayre,
The more they on it stare.
But her sad eyes still fastened on the ground,
Are gouerned with goodly modesty,
That suffers not one looke to glaunce awry,
Which may let in a little thought vnsownd.
Why blush ye loue to giue to me your hand,
The pledge of all our band?
Sing ye sweet Angels, Alleluya sing,                               240
That all the woods may answere and your eccho ring.

[14]
NOw al is done; bring home the bride againe,
        bring home the triumph of our victory,
Bring home with you the glory of her gaine,
With ioyance bring her and with iollity.
Neuer had man more ioyfull day then this,
Whom heauen would heape with blis.
Make feast therefore now all this liue long day,
This day for euer to me holy is.
Poure out the wine without restraint or stay,                      250
Poure not by cups, but by the belly full,
Poure out to all that wull,
And sprinkle all the postes and wals with wine,
That they may sweat, and drunken be withall.
Crowne ye God Bacchus with a coronall,
And Hymen also crowne with wreathes of vine,
And let the Graces daunce vnto the rest;

For they can doo it best:
The whiles the maydens doe theyr carroll sing,
To which the woods shal answer and theyr eccho ring. 260

[15]
RIng ye the bels, ye yong men of the towne,
    And leaue your wonted labors for this day:
This day is holy; doe ye write it downe,
that ye for euer it remember may.
This day the sunne is in his chiefest hight,
With Barnaby the bright,
From whence declining daily by degrees,
He somewhat loseth of his heat and light,
When once the Crab behind his back he sees.
But for this time it ill ordained was, 270
To chose the longest day in all the yeare,
And shortest night, when longest fitter weare:
Yet neuer day so long, but late would passe.
Ring ye the bels, to make it weare away,
And bonefiers make all day,
And daunce about them, and about them sing:
that all the woods may answer, and your eccho ring.

[16]
AH when will this long weary day haue end,
    and lende me leaue to come vnto my loue?
How slowly do the houres theyr numbers spend? 280
How slowly does sad Time his feathers moue?
Hast thee O fayrest Planet to thy home
Within the Westerne fome:
Thy tyred steedes long since haue need of rest.
Long though it be, at last I see it gloome,
And the bright euening star with golden creast
Appeare out of the East.
Fayre childe of beauty, glorious lampe of loue
That all the host of heauen in rankes doost lead,
And guydest louers through the nights sad dread, 290
How chearefully thou lookest from aboue,
And seemst to laugh atweene thy twinkling light
As ioying in the sight
Of these glad many which for ioy doe sing,
That all the woods them answer and their echo ring.

[17]
Now ceasse ye damsels your delights forepast;
    Enough is it, that all the day was youres:
Now day is doen, and night is nighing fast:
Now bring the Bryde into the brydall boures.
Now night is come, now soone her disaray,                    300
And in her bed her lay;
Lay her in lillies and in violets,
And silken courteins ouer her display,
And odourd sheetes, and Arras couerlets.
Behold how goodly my faire loue does ly
In proud humility;
Like vnto Maia, when as Ioue her tooke,
In Tempe, lying on the flowry gras,
Twixt sleepe and wake, after she weary was,
With bathing in the Acidalian brooke.                        310
Now it is night, ye damsels may be gon,
And leaue my loue alone,
And leaue likewise your former lay to sing:
The woods no more shal answere, nor your echo ring.

[18]
NOw welcome night, thou night so long expected,
    that long daies labour doest at last defray,
And all my cares, which cruel loue collected,
Hast sumd in one, and cancelled for aye:
Spread thy broad wing ouer my loue and me,
that no man may vs see,                                       320
And in thy sable mantle vs enwrap,
From feare of perrill and foule horror free.
Let no false treason seeke vs to entrap,
Nor any dread disquiet once annoy
the safety of our ioy:
But let the night be calme and quietsome,
Without tempestuous storms or sad afray:
Lyke as when Ioue with fayre Alcmena lay,
When he begot the great Tirynthian groome:
Or lyke as when he with thy selfe did lie,                   330
And begot Maiesty.
And let the mayds and yongmen cease to sing:
Ne let the woods them answer, nor theyr eccho ring.

[19]
LEt no lamenting cryes, nor dolefull teares,
    Be heard all night within nor yet without:
Ne let false whispers breeding hidden feares,
Breake gentle sleepe with misconceiued dout.
Let no deluding dreames, nor dreadful sights
Make sudden sad affrights;
Ne let housefyres, nor lightnings helpelesse harmes,          340
Ne let the Pouke, nor other euill sprights,
Ne let mischiuous witches with theyr charmes,
Ne let hob Goblins, names whose sence we see not,
Fray vs with things that be not.
Let not the shriech Oule, nor the Storke be heard:
Nor the night Rauen that still deadly yels,
Nor damned ghosts cald vp with mighty spels,
Nor griesly vultures make vs once affeard:
Ne let th'unpleasant Quyre of Frogs still croking
Make vs to wish theyr choking.                               350
Let none of these theyr drery accents sing;
Ne let the woods them answer, nor theyr eccho ring.

[20]
BVt let stil Silence trew night watches keepe,
    That sacred peace may in assurance rayne,
And tymely sleep, when it is tyme to sleepe,
May poure his limbs forth on your pleasant playne,
The whiles an hundred little winged loues,
Like diuers fethered doues,
Shall fly and flutter round about your bed,
And in the secret darke, that none reproues,                360
Their prety stealthes shal worke, and snares shal spread
To filch away sweet snatches of delight,
Conceald through couert night.
Ye sonnes of Venus, play your sports at will,
For greedy pleasure, carelesse of your toyes,
Thinks more vpon her paradise of ioyes,
Then what ye do, albe it good or ill.
All night therefore attend your merry play,
For it will soone be day:
Now none doth hinder you, that say or sing,                 370
Ne will the woods now answer, nor your Eccho ring.

[21]
WHo is the same, which at my window peepes?
    Or whose is that faire face, that shines so bright?
Is it not Cinthia, she that neuer sleepes,
But walkes about high heauen al the night?
O fayrest goddesse, do thou not enuy
My loue with me to spy:
For thou likewise didst loue, thought now vnthought,
And for a fleece of woll, which priuily,
The Latmian shephard once vnto thee brought,                    380
His pleasures with thee wrought.
Therefore to vs be fauorable now;
And sith of wemens labours thou hast charge,
And generation goodly dost enlarge,
Encline thy will t'effect our wishfull vow,
And the chast wombe informe with timely seed,
That may our comfort breed:
Till which we cease our hopefull hap to sing,
Ne let the woods vs answere, nor our Eccho ring.

[22]
ANd thou great Iuno, which with awful might            390
    the lawes of wedlock still dost patronize,
And the religion of the faith first plight
With sacred rites hast taught to solemnize:
and eeke for comfort often called art
Of women in their smart,
Eternally bind thou this louely band,
And all thy blessings vnto vs impart.
And thou glad Genius, in whose gentle hand,
The bridale bowre and geniall bed remaine
Without blemish or staine,                                      400
And the sweet pleasures of theyr loues delight
With secret ayde doest succour and supply,
Till they bring forth the fruitfull progeny,
Send vs the timely fruit of this same night.
And thou fayre Hebe, and thou Hymen free,
Grant that it may so be.
Til which we cease your further prayse to sing,
Ne any woods shal answer, nor your Eccho ring.

[23]
ANd ye high heauens, the temple of the gods,
    In which a thousand torches flaming bright          410
Doe burne, that to vs wretched earthly clods,
In dreadful darknesse lend desired light;
And all ye powers which in the same remayne,
More then we men can fayne,
Poure out your blessing on vs plentiously,
And happy influence vpon vs raine,
That we may raise a large posterity,
Which from the earth, which they may long possesse,
With lasting happinesse,
Vp to your haughty pallaces may mount,                 420
And for the guerdon of theyr glorious merit
May heauenly tabernacles there inherit,
Of blessed Saints for to increase the count.
So let vs rest, sweet loue, in hope of this,
And cease till then our tymely ioyes to sing,
The woods no more vs answer, nor our eccho ring.

[24]
SOng made in lieu of many ornaments,
    With which my loue should duly haue bene dect,
Which cutting off through hasty accidents,
Ye would not stay your dew time to expect,             430
But promist both to recompens,
Be vnto her a goodly ornament,
And for short time an endlesse moniment.

FINIS.

*Imprinted by P. S. for Wil-*
liam Ponsonby.

# Commentary

The abbreviations used in the commentary follow the author and are standard: Shakespeare, *AYLI: As You Like It*; Sidney, *AS: Astrophil and Stella*. The exception is Spenser, where no author is given and only the standard abbreviation for a work occurs: *FQ: The Faerie Queene; Am: Amoretti; Ana: Anacreontics; Epith: Epithalamion; SC: The Shepheardes Calender; TM: The Teares of the Muses; RT: The Ruines of Time; Col: Colin Clouts Come Home Againe; Gn: Virgils Gnat; Pet: The Visions of Petrarch; Ro: Ruines of Rome; Hub: Mother Hubberds Tale; Van: Visions of the Worlds Vanitie; HL: An Hymne in Honour of Love; HB: An Hymne in Honour of Beautie; HHL; An Hymne of Heavenly Love; HHB: An Hymne of Heavenly Beautie; Proth: Prothalamion; View: A View of the Present State of Ireland.* The text throughout, apart from *Amoretti and Epithalamion*, is Spenser, *Poetical Works*, eds. J. C. Smith and E. de Selincourt (Oxford: Oxford Univ. Press, 1969).

## The Device.

The framed device occurs before both *Amoretti* and *Epithalamion*. Its motto, "ET VSQVE AD NVBES VERITAS TVA," is taken from Ps. 57.11 and replicates Ps. 36.5, "Et veritas tua usque ad nubes," which both Coverdale and the Geneva version translate as, "*and* thy faithfulnes [ô Lord, *reacheth*] vnto the cloudes." The device suggests a scriptural context for the volume. The emblem's bell, the hand reaching down from the clouds which upholds the dove, which in turn trails from its beak bands from which hang an opened book surrounded by the sun's rays, find an exact precedent in Whitney's *A Choice of Emblemes*, 166, "Veritas invicta"; Whitney's device has an identical top half also with a hand reaching through the clouds, upholding a dove's wings, which in turn hold a book surrounded by the sun's rays, on which is inscribed "Et Vsque Ad Nubes Veritas Tua." His accompanying verses " . . . the Lorde doth giue such lighte, / That . . . those, that are so happie for to looke, / Saluation finde, within that blessed booke," together with the dove, scriptures, and the psalm reference, imply scriptural inspiration and the light of the Holy Spirit. Peter Short, the master printer, had already used the design in *Amoretti and Epithalamion* in 1592 for Thomas Tymme's, *A plaine discoverie of ten English lepers, verie noisome to the church and common wealth. [i.e., schismatics, church robbers, etc.].* That he has chosen a device whose principal significance was scriptural inspiration and truth for Spenser's volume may indicate that he was aware of *Amoretti*'s own scriptural inspiration.

Short's design for the volume, by devoting a separate page to each sonnet and to each stanza of *Epithalamion*, and by decorating each sonnet and stanza above and below with an ornamental band, depicts the volume as a record of self-contained yet consecutive units. Since the volume lacks Spenser's customary preface, Short's device, besides reinforcing the volume's authorial anonymity, also creates visual and emblematic expectations.

### The Epistle Dedicatory.

*Sir Robart Needham:* a cavalry captain of Shropshire who was knighted for service in Ireland on 1 September 1594; he departed for England on 25 September 1594 and resided there until April 1595. Ponsonbys' observation that "This gentle Muse [is] . . . nowe at length crossing the Seas in your happy companye," suggests that the manuscript of *Amoretti and Epithalamion* may have accompanied him. Nothing is known of the relationship between Needham and Spenser or Ponsonby.

### Dedicatory Sonnet I.

*G: W. senior:* possibly Geoffrey Whitney Senior.

### Dedicatory Sonnet II.

1. *Colin:* Colin Clout, a Spenser pseudonym.
2. *roundelaies:* simple songs, such as the "laies of sweet loue" to which Colin, "The Shepheards boy," alludes at the beginning of *Colin Clouts come home againe.*
3-4. A reference presumably to *The Faerie Queene.*
5-6. A possible reference to the lady of *Amoretti and Epithalamion.*
15. G. W. I.: the italics of the *I* in the 1595 octavo edition suggest the signature is a contraction of G. W. Iunior, possibly Geoffrey Whitney Junior. Gottfried 544–5 established a link between the Spenser circle and that of Geoffrey Whitney, author of *A Choice of Emblemes* ("in the catalogue of students at the University of Leyden . . . he was listed as *Godfridus Whitneus, Junior*"). Later in 1600 Whitney bequeathed his best ring to Lady Needham, wife of Sir Robert Needham, mentioned in The Epistle Dedicatory above. The fact that Whitney's emblem "Veritas invicta" has been adapted for *Amoretti*'s device supports the identification of the initials as belonging to him.

## *Amoretti*

### Sonnet 1

The sonnet corresponds with the beginning of Hilary Term, 23 January 1594. Spenser, who sat in the County of Cork as a Justice of the Queen in 1594, would have been familiar with the dates of the terms. The poem's threefold division reflects the trinitarian treatise for which St. Hilary was famous, while its triple *Happy* reflects his name (*Hilaris* = happy). Its allusions to the three faculties, soul (*soules* [12]), spirit (*spright* [7]), and *hart* (8), observe the standard Neo-Platonic distinction between soul, spirit, and body – see Ficino, *Commentary on Plato's Symposium*, 6.6, "three things seem to be in us: the soul, the spirit and the body."

Gollancz reported a copy of *The Faerie Queene* (first edition) towards the end of which, "on the blank left-hand page facing Spenser's letter to Sir Walter Raleigh," another version of *Am.* 1 had been inscribed, which Gollancz claimed to be autographical.

> *A sa mistresse*
> Happy ye leaues when as those lilly Hands
> That houlds my life in hir deaddoing might

Shall handle yo$^u$ and hold in Loues swete bandes
Like captiues trembling at y$^e$ victors sight.
　　Happy ye lines when as w$^{ith}$ starry light
Those lamping eies shall deigne on yo$^u$ to looke
And reade the sorowes of my dieng spright
written w$^{ith}$ tears in harts close bleeding book.
　　Happy ye rymes bathde in y$^e$ sacred brook
of Helicon whence shee deriued is
when as you shall beholde y$^t$ angells looke
my soules longe lacked foode my heauens blisse.
　　Leaues, lines & rymes seeke her to please alone
Whome if yo$^u$ please I care for others none / .

Judson ("*Amoretti*, Sonnet I") compared the version with specimens of Spenser's handwriting and concluded that it is not autographical. The variants suggest it is more likely to be a slightly misremembered version of the printed *Am.* 1.

1. *Happy*: See headnote, Hilary. The term ran from 23 January until 12 February, which in 1594 dovetailed with the beginning of Lent, Wednesday 13 February; see *The booke of Common prayer*, 1578, sig. a iii: "Hillarie Terme beginneth the .xxiii. or .xxiv. day of Ianuari [sic], and endeth the .xii. or .xiii. day of Februarie."

　　*leaues*: 1. leaves of a book; 2. the suggestion of tree leaves is found again in *trembling* (4); see "the trembling leaues" of the *locus amoenus*, *FQ* I.vii.3.3; for their association with *lilly hands* see Shakespeare, *TA* II.iv.44-45, "lily hands / Tremble like aspen leaues."

　　*lilly hands*: 1. white and tender; 2. chaste; heroines in *FQ* often have innocent hands, notably Astraea who is lead forth "by the lilly hand" (VII.vii.37.3-9); 3. Spenser also associates *lilly hands* with the arts of curing and bestowing life (see *FQ* III.iv.41.1, "the lilly handed Liagore"), an allusion brought out immediately in line 2.

1-3. *hands ... shall handle*: In direct contradiction to the day's evening prayer Ps. 115.7, "They haue handes, and handle not."

2. *dead doing*: killing, doing to death.

3. *bands*: 1. chains, shackles such as hold *captiues* (4); the motif in various guises, traps, webs, bonds, will become a familiar one during the Lenten section of the sequence; 2. the cords, which in book-binding cross the back of the book to bind the gatherings together; 3. as in *Am.* 65.5, "Sweet be the bands," an engagement or betrothal is also implied.

6. *lamping eyes*: clear, beaming, resplendent (possibly from Italian *lampante* = shining as a lamp). Spenser uses the word only once elsewhere; here it corresponds with morning prayer Ps. 112.4, "there ariseth vp light in the darkenesse" (Vulgate, *Exortum est in tenebris lumen*). *Lumen*, 1. specifically meant a lamp, 2. was occasionally used of the stars, and 3. very particularly of the eye and its pupil. Spenser has worked all three meanings into *starry light, / those lamping eyes*.

8. *close*: secretly, internally; *close* was associated with the heart because closet was used of the pericardium, see *Am.* 85.9 note.

　　*bleeding*: 1. suffused with blood; 2. figuratively, full of anguish. The hypallage — it is the heart not the book that is secretly bleeding — reinforces the reading, 'book of the heart's secret bleeding.'

> *book:* although used also of an unbound sheaf of manuscript poems, *bands* (3) suggests an intended bound volume.

9. *rymes:* Spenser, like Shakespeare in his sonnets, generally intends poems (in imitation of Petrarch's *rime*) not rhymes.

10. *Helicon:* See the opening to *TM* 1–5, and *SC* April 42. Properly Helicon was the mountain only, but such earlier authors as Chaucer and Lydgate had already identified *Helicon* as a spring or well.

11–12. *that Angels blessed looke . . . my heauens blis:* morning prayer Ps. 110.3, "The deawe of thy birth is the wombe of the morning," was traditionally considered an Old Testament analogue of the virginal conception in the Blessed Virgin, announced by an angel. That *that Angels blessed looke* is intended to echo the analogue is confirmed later by the verse's echo in *Am.* 61.6–7, "of the brood of Angels heuenly borne" (see *Am.* 61.6–7, note). The lady's heavenly origin and her being a source of poetic inspiration and knowledge will persist throughout the sequence.

> *blessed:* see morning prayer Ps. 112.1, "Blessed is the man" (Vulgate, *Beatus vir; blessed* was synonymous with *happy;* e.g., the Bishops' and Geneva Bibles give "blessed" at James 1.25, Tyndale and Cranmer, "happy").

14. *care for other none:* 1. pay attention to none other than her; 2. hold only her dear (with a spurious etymological pun on *carus* = dear — see *Am.* 34.13); 3. watch over, look upon only her. But, given that *other none* could also imply no other *Leaues, lines, and rymes,* then all the above three meanings of the verb with these objects also.

**Wednesday 23 January:** *Morning Prayer:* Pss. 110–13, Matt. 21. *Evening Prayer:* Pss. 114–15, 1 Cor. 5.

## Sonnet 2

The conceit of poetic childbirth was commonplace from classical times onward. Sonnet 2, however, gives the *topos* a particular twist by identifying the poet's conceit and its delivery with the self-delivery by which the young viper gave birth to itself by eating its way out of its mother's side. As a consequence the mother died. See Bart. Angl. 386ʳ, citing Isidore 12, "that Vipera hath that name, for she bringeth forth broode by strength; for when hir wombe draweth to the time of whelping, the whelpes abideth not couenable time nor kinde passing, but gnaweth and fretteth the sides of their dam, and they come so into this world with strength, and with the death of the breeder." The conceit of the viper directly corresponds to the maledictive epithet, "generacion of viperes," of Matt. 23.33, the gospel chapter which Spenser seems to have read for the second lesson at morning prayer for Thursday 24 January. (The day's correct second lesson at morning prayer was Matt. 22, with which *Am.* 2 bears no resemblance. Spenser seemingly read a mistaken chapter, Matt. 23, for the day, having been confused by one of the few mistakes in the *Book of Common Prayer* calendar, for the entry which should have read Matt. 23 was in frequent editions mistakenly replaced by Matt. 13.)

1. *Vnquiet thought:* anxious thought. In *FQ* IV.v.35.9 Spenser identifies "vnquiet thoughts, that carefull minds inuade" as the wedges that *Care* makes. *Cura,* meant 1. anxious, but also 2. *thought,* and 3. occasionally a written work (see Tacitus, *Annales,* 4.11), which obliquely identifies the poet's *thought* as his poem.

2. *inward . . . hart:* Compare evening prayer Ps. 119.11, "Thy words haue I hid within my heart."

*inward bale:* the poet's contrasting his *inner part* with possible outward conduct in the presence of the lady, matches Matt. 23.27–28, which contrasts the inner corruption and outward conduct of the scribes and pharisees who "appeare beautiful outwarde, but are within ful . . . of all filthines . . . for outwarde ye appeare righteous vnto men, but within ye are ful of hypocrisie and iniquitie."

  *bale:* 1. misery; 2. the physical injury or death associated with the viper's birth through eating.

3. *sithens:* since that time.

4. *woxen:* waxen; 1. grown; 2. earlier used either as i) to be born or ii) specifically, to be created, e.g., Langland, writing of God, *Piers P.* (A text), 10.33, "For with word that he warp woxen forth beestes."

6. *vipers brood:* The Geneva Bible in all parallel passages to Matt. 23.33, "generacion of viperes," appends the sidenote, "Or [vipers] broodes" (see Matt. 3.7 & 12.34, Luke 3.7). Spenser's only use of the phrase (although compare *Am.* 86, whose curses reflect the verse when Matt. 23 was read for Tuesday 14 May).

7. *thought . . . bred . . . smart:* See *FQ* III.iv.6.1–5, where such thoughts also afflict Britomart in a passage employing a like metaphor.

8. *sustayne thy self with food:* The viper, when hibernating, was thought able to sustain itself with food, Bart. Angl. explaining that the viper "sustaineth and may beare hunger long time."

10. *fall . . . at her feet:* Similar to morning prayer Ps. 116.8, "my feete from falling."

10–11. *fall lowly . . . / . . . meeke humblesse:* Reflects precisely the paradoxical judgement of Matt. 23.12, "whosoeuer wil exalt him self, shalbe broght low: and whosoeuer wil humble him self, shalbe exalted."

11. *afflicted mood:* Matches the particulars of morning prayer Ps. 116.10 (Bishops' Bible Version), "I was greatly afflicted." 1. dejected state of mind; 2. the phrase also contains a Spenserian pun: *mood* (from *modus*, a rendering of the Greek τρόπος = syllogism) also means argument; since *afflicted* is used by Spenser also to mean *humble*, the phrase carries the allied meaning of 'humble argument.' Spenser plays with the same pun in the Proem to *FQ* I, "The argument of mine afflicted stile" (4.8), where *afflicted* intends both *humble* and also that which his thrown-down ("afflicted" = *ad* + *fligere [flictus]* = thrown down) pen ("stile" = *stilus* = pen) had previously put to paper. Here, at the beginning of the sequence, the 'humble argument' presents itself to his betrothed.

13–14. *liue . . . / . . . die soone . . . perish:* Compare the detail of Matt. 23.24, "them ye shal kil and crucifie" and evening prayer Ps. 118.17, "I will not die, but liue."

**Thursday 24 January:** *Morning Prayer:* Pss. 116–18, Matt. 22/23; *Evening Prayer:* Ps 119.1–32, 1 Cor. 6.

## Sonnet 3

Sonnet 3's motif of light, of Neo-Platonic cast and heavenly origin, matches the principal feature of the conversion of St. Paul, the feast celebrated on Friday 25 January, the heavenly light which struck him down on the road to Damascus. For the feast all three conversion accounts were read, Acts 9.1–23 (Epistle), Acts 22.1–21 (special second lesson at morning prayer) and Acts 26 (special second lesson at evening prayer).

1. *souerayne beauty:* See *HHB* 295–97, which celebrate the "soueraine light, / From

whose pure beams al perfect beauty springs, / That kindleth loue in euery godly spright."

    *admyre:* the sense of wonder (*ad* + *miror* = wonder) is continued through the dispersed polyptoton, *wondrous* (8), *wonderment* (12), *wonder* (14).

2. *witnesse the world:* directly imitating the purpose of Paul's conversion, "For thou shalt be his witnes vnto all men of the things, which thou hast sene and heard" (Acts 22.15), and "to appoint thee a minster and a witnesse" (Acts 26.16; see also 26.18 & 22). A second extended polyptoton, *witnesse, wit* (14).

3. *light . . . heauenly fyre:* a feature of all three accounts of Paul's conversion, "suddenly there shone from heauen a great light rounde about me" (Acts 22.6), and "light from heauen" (Acts 9.3 & Acts 26.13).

    *kindled:* 1. lit; 2. given birth to. The pun is repeated in *Am.* 6.6, 7.12 & 8.2.

5. *being now:* in contrast to *looking still* (7).

    *huge:* Paul identifies the light as "a great (Vulgate, *copiosa* = *huge*) light rounde about me" (Acts 22.6).

    *brightnesse:* Likewise the light's surpassing brightness so dazzled Paul, that he could see nothing, "I sawe in the way a light from heauen, passing the brightnes of the sunne" (Acts 26.13).

6. *can no more endure to view:* The light affects Paul and the poet identically: as the poet, because of the brightness of the heavenly light, is blind to earthly things, so also Paul "colde not se for the glorie of that light" (Acts 22.11). Such purifying, so better to contemplate the lady's spiritual beauty, is a standard Neo-Platonic (and Petrarchist) assertion.

    *endure:* See evening prayer Ps. 119.89, "O Lorde, thy woorde: endureth for euer in heauen"; *Am.* 33.10, "to endure so taedious toyle," and *Am.* 63.2, "Which hardly I endured heretofore," match the verse when it was read again on 24 February and 24 March.

7. *looking still:* 1. continuing to look on her; 2. looking on her silently (see *toung . . . stopped* [9–10]); 3. the sense of looking on her secretly is also implied.

    *I stand amazed:* Compare the day's Epistle, Acts 9.7, "The men . . . stode amased"; see also Acts 9.21, "amased."

    *amazed:* 1. bewildered, dazed; 2. a synonym for infatuated, see *Am.* 7.1 note.

8. *celestiall hew:* 1. heavenly form or shape, used by Spenser frequently as a Neo-Platonic indicator — see *Am.* 7.5; 21.10; 45.7; 53.6; 79.6; 80.11; 2. heavenly complexion or even color; 3. heavenly vision — directly imitating Paul's "heauenlie vision" (Acts 26.19; Vulgate, *visioni caelesti* = *celestiall hew*).

9–12. The four lines are a *compar* or *isocolon* (a rhetorical construction when the number of syllables "bee almoste of a iuste number . . . but yet the equalitye of the partes of members, must not be measured vppon our Fyngers, but be tryed by a secreate sence of the eare"; see Rix 32). The comparison is evident between *toung, speak, stopped* and *thoughts astonishment,* and *pen, write, rauisht* and *fancies wonderment.*

9–14. *So when my toung would speak . . . / and when my pen would write . . . / Yet in my hart . . . / . . . endite:* The final sestet reflects the vocabulary and structure of Ps. 45.1–2, an epithalamial psalm; "My heart is inditing of a good matter: I speake of the things which I haue made vnto the king. My tongue is the penne: of a ready writer."

10. *stopped:* 1. obstructed, bottled up; 2. of the voice, hoarse or choked up; see *Am.* 8.9, "you stop my toung."

    *astonishment:* Compare Acts 9.6, where the "light from heauen" causes Paul to stand "astonied."

11. *write her titles true:* both 1. write 'her titles truly'; and 2. write 'her true titles.'

    *titles:* 1. descriptive headings or features; 2. the right accorded a *souerayne* (1).

12. *fancies:* 1. Neo-Platonically, the faculty, distinguished from the imagination, which forms mental representations of things not present to the senses; 2. occasionally a deluded or delusive imagination — in contrast to the *titles true* (11); 3. as a contraction of fantasy, the allusion to an apparition or vision (see line 8 note, *hew*) cannot be discounted.

13. *hart . . . write:* See Sidney, *AS* 1.14.

    *hart:* Johnson, " 'Sacred Rites,' " 380 argues for a homonym between heart and hart = art.

14. *wit:* Reflects Paul's resolution to continue "witnessing bothe to small and to great . . . to *wit* that Christ . . . shulde shew light vnto the people" (Acts 26.22-23).

    *endite:* 1. (from *indictus* = *in* + *dicere* = speak) put into words (in contrast to the poet's attempts to *speak* [9]), especially give a literary form to words; 2. even more specifically, write words down with a pen (in contrast to his attempts to *write* [13]); the poet's difficulty, in both senses, corresponds to that of the Red Cross Knight, "O soueraigne Queene, whose prayse I would endite" (*FQ* III.ii.3.4); 3. since *indictus* alternatively carried the meaning of unsaid or even ineffable, Spenser may also have intended an echo of the word's paradoxical etymology as a continuance of *toung . . . stopped* (9–10).

**Friday 25 January, Conversion of St. Paul:** *Epistle:* Acts 9.1–23. *Gospel:* Matt. 19.27–30. *Morning Prayer:* Ps. 119.33–72, Acts 22.1–21. *Evening Prayer:* Ps. 119.73–104, Acts 26.

### Sonnet 4

The approach of the new year and/or spring is a popular occasional topic of the Petrarchist and Spenser celebrates the coming of the new in a similar vein four times in the sequence (*Am.* 19, 60, 62, 70).

1. *New Yeare:* For Spenser's use of January as the beginning of the year, see Introduction, 4–5.

    *Ianus gate:* a conventional etymological pleonasm; Janus (*ianua* = gate), besides presiding over the beginning of things, was represented with a face on the front and the back of the head and, with the motto "Respice et Prospice," was considered to look both backwards and forwards. (See Whitney 108.) The two-directional becomes the basis of the sonnet's argument. Line 1 apparently celebrates the month of January as the beginning of the year rather than the beginning of January as the start of the year. See also Du Bellay, "Du Premier Jour De L'An," (*Vers Lyriques,* 6.26),

    Voicy le Pere au double front,
    Le bon Janus, qui renouvelle
    Le cours de l'an, qui en un rond
    Ameine la saison nouvelle.
        Renouvelons aussi

> Toute vieille pensée,
> Et tuons le soucy
> De fortune insensée.

Spenser is also playing with the adage, "January marrying May," used to describe an older man marrying a young woman (*OED*, May sb³ 1 d, which cites Chaucer, *Merch. T.* 448, and Thomas Howell, *Devises* [1581], I.ii, "In fayth doth frozen Ianus double face, / Such favour finde, to match with pleasant Maye"). The adage corresponds with the Pauline injunction about age and marriage in 1 Cor. 7, the second lesson at evening prayer for Saturday 26 January (see line 13 note).

3. *his passed date:* if *his* (its) refers back to *New yeare* (1), then a temporal referent looking back to 1 January.

4. *all old thoughts:* See Du Bellay, "Toute vieille pensée."

   *dumpish:* 1. sad, melancholic; 2. spiritless; *dumpish spright* is effectively a paradox.

6. *fresh loue:* identified in line 8 as Cupid.

8. *wanton:* 1. naughty, cruel, pampered, particularly of children (and hence allusively of Cupid); 2. amorous, lascivious.

   *darts:* Cupid and his arrows are everywhere present among the *amoretti:* e.g., Am. 8.5-6, 16.4-8, 17.9, 24.7, 39.1-4, 57.8.

9. *For lusty spring now in his timely howre:* Compare *FQ* IV.X.45.4, the Temple of Venus, where "The spring breake forth out of his lusty bowres."

   *lusty:* vigorous, youthful.

   *timely:* 1. temporal or seasonal; 2. opportune; a favorite late word employed variously in *Epith.* (355, 386, 404, 425). Paul intimates a similar urgency in 1 Cor. 7.29, "because the time is short."

12. *mantle:* Venus' instrument of cheer in the Temple of Venus (*FQ* IV.x.44.7). 1. A conventional metaphor for the covering of the earth; 2. used symbolically when a widow or widower took a vow of chastity (*OED* sb 1d; 1 Cor. 7 contains advice for widows). Because Elizabeth was not a widow, the symbolism rebounds onto Spenser the widower, implying, albeit obliquely, a chaste resolve on his part.

13. *faire flowre, in whome fresh youth doth raine:* Compare 1 Cor. 7.36, containing Paul's admonitions about marriage and virginity: "if anie man thinke that is is vncomlie for his virgine, if she passe the flowre of her age, and nede so require, let him do what he wil, he sinneth not: let them be maried." Given the difference in age between Spenser and Elizabeth Boyle, the appellation *faire flowre* is particularly apposite and intimate. It was, of course, Spenser who was the elderly one and past the flower of his age (*flos aetatis* = youth). Elizabeth Boyle, as the younger *faire flowre*, was not affected by the strictures of the Pauline injunction.

14. *entertaine:* (*inter* = between + *tenere* = hold); 1. engage, accept; 2. the mutuality of betrothal and the period of preparation before marriage is also implied. Spenser later uses the word of marriage in the orational sonnet for Easter Sunday, "with loue may one another entertayne" (*Am.* 68.12). He thus covertly observes Paul's admonition, "let them be maried."

Saturday 26 January: *Morning Prayer:* Ps. 119.105-44, Matt. 23. *Evening Prayer:* Ps. 119.145-76, 1 Cor. 7.

## Sonnet 5

1. *Rvdely thou wrongest:* The sonnet's accusations of wrong judgement correspond to the conclusions of the coincidentally successive readings, 1 Cor. 8 and 9 (vv. 24–27), respectively the second lesson at evening prayer and the Epistle for Septuagesima Sunday 27 January, the first of the Sundays leading to Lent. Each ends with Paul attempting to avoid giving scandal and being wrongly judged, "that I may not offend my brother" (8.13), and "lest ... I my self shulde be reproued" (9.27). As well, morning prayer Ps. 120.2, "Deliuer my soule, O Lorde, from lying lippes: and from a deceitfull tongue," is a celebrated prayer against slander. The phrase is the first of 9 alliterations or semi-alliterations which punctuate the sonnet.

   *Rvdely:* 1. ignorantly; 2. offensively or roughly.

   *thou:* evidently an outsider to the sequence (if not read as part of the poet himself), and matched only by *Am.* 86's condemnation of the slanderer. Otherwise Spenser only uses *thou / thee* within the parameters of the sequence.
2. *portly:* dignified. The sonnet's argument divides it uniformly between pride and portliness.
4. *enuide:* Compare the day's Gospel, Matt. 20.15, Geneva version sidenote, "Or enuious."
5. *lofty lookes:* In exact correspondence with evening prayer Ps. 131.1, "Lorde, I am not high minded: I haue no proude lookes" (Geneva Bible "nether are mine eies loftie").

   *close:* secretly, hiddenly.

   *implide:* 1. physically enfolded (*in* + *plicare* = in + folded) − Spenser uses the word of the coils of a snake (*FQ* I.iv.31.5); 2. contained, exists (*FQ* V.vii.12.8).
6. *scorn of base things:* The phrase (*Fuge Turpia*) was proverbial, see *Am.* 13.9–10 & 61.11–12. The poet's complaints about pride and scorn are the focus also of morning prayer Ps. 123.3–4, "we are vtterly despised. Our soule is filled with the scornefull reproofe of the wealthy and with the despitefulnes (Vulgate, *despectio* = the looking down upon) of the proude."

   *sdeigne:* disdain; etymologically (*dis* + *dignus* = un + worthy) it compounds the *vnworthy* motif of the sonnet: *world vnworthy* (4) and *neuer in this world ought worthy* (13).
7. *rash eies ... loosely ... looke:* Such eyes resemble the question concluding the day's Gospel parable, Matt. 20.1–15, "Is thine eye euil." See also the morning prayer Ps. 121.1, "I will lift vp mine eyes vnto the hilles," and Ps. 123.1, "Vnto thee lift I vp mine eyes." The "hungry eyes" of *Am.* 35 correspond with the same verses when they were read on Tuesday 26 February.
9. *portlinesse:* (from *port* = a carrying, gait) dignified, applied generally to manner of walking and echoing Ps. 131.2 (Geneva version), "nether haue I walked in great matters."
10. *boldned:* See 1 Cor. 8.10, "boldened," a distinctive verbal parallel; it is the only occasion when the Geneva Bible uses the word and its only usage in *Amoretti.*
11. *countenance:* disyllabic by syncopation.
13. *tride:* 1. attempted; 2. proven; 3. purified (as metal is purified by fire), an allusion picked up in *spark* (14).
14. *spark:* 1. the spark of fire that refines; 2. a small something.

> *self-pleasing pride:* Spenser only uses the adjective reprehensibly, see Crud-
> or's "selfe pleasing mynd" (*FQ* VI.i.15.1–2).

**Septuagesima Sunday 27 January:** *Epistle:* 1 Cor. 9.24–27. *Gospel:* Matt. 20.1–17. *Morning Prayer:* Pss. 120–25, Matt. 24. *Evening Prayer:* Pss. 126–31, 1 Cor. 8.

## Sonnet 6

Sonnets 5 and 6 constitute a pair of sonnets linked by a common theme and bridged by the one's concluding "self-pleasing pride" and the other's opening *rebellious pride*. The purifying function of Sonnet 5's "ought worthy tride, / without some spark" becomes also one of Sonnet 6's motifs. By coincidence in 1594 the second lesson at evening prayer for Monday 28 January, 1 Cor. 9, was also read as the prior day's Epistle, 1 Cor. 9.24–27.

1. *nought:* The sonnet is the most labyrinthical of the sequence, particularly in its virtuoso upholding of the long *traductio*, *nought . . . not . . . not . . . naught . . . not . . . knot.* (See Johnson, "Amoretti 6," 38 and "Punning," 384, and A. Fowler, *Conceitful Thought*, 89–91.)

   *nought dismayd:* the beginning of a fescennine subtext to the sonnet, *nought* bawdily implying the vagina (see Shakespeare, Sonnet 136.11–12 and *Rich. III* I.i.99–100), and *dismayd* obliquely suggesting un-maided, a pun used earlier of the "Maide," Britomart (*FQ* V.vii.16.9).

3–4. The contrast of the carnal, *lusts of baser kynd,* with spiritual love, that *the harder wonne, the firmer will abide,* observes the distinction made in 1 Cor. 9.11, "If we haue sowen vnto you spiritual things, *is it* a great thing if we reape your carnal things?"

   *kynd:* 1. nature; 2. birth; the word's etymological verb form in Old English is reflected in the secondary sense of *kindling* (6), to give birth to.

4. *wonne:* 1. achieve; 2. homonymically, undivided (compare *diuide* (7) and *entire* [11]). Compare the dominant image of 1 Cor. 9, Paul seeking to "winne the mo." In contrast to the poem's *harder* and *firmer*, Paul will become weak to win: "To the weake I become as weake, that I may winne the weake" (v. 22).

   *abide:* 1. remain — taken up in *endure* (10); 2. by association, bide its time — developed in *thinke not long* (13); and 3. suffer — alluded to in *taking little paine* (13).

5. *durefull Oake:* A forced pleonasm: *durefull* is identified with *Oake* through an etymological homonym, Spenser associating the *durus* (= hard) of *durefull* with δουρός, genetive of δρῦς = oak. The two are earlier identified in the name of Druon, who, in contrast to the sonnet's invoked mutuality, is opposed to love because enamored of a single life (See *FQ* IV.ix.21.1–2). Here by contrast the poet, the oak, will espouse a married life. Ovid, *Met.* 13.799–800, likewise describes the oak (and the willow), "durior (= harder) annosa quercu . . . lentior (= firmer) et salicis virgis" (Golding, 13.874–75, "more hard than warryed Oke too twyne, / More tough than willow twiggs"). If Ovid was in Spenser's mind, his memory may have been prompted by the day's associative evening prayer Ps. 137.2, "As for our harpes wee hanged them vp: vpon the trees (Vulgate, *salicibus* = willows, Geneva version, willowes) that are therein."

6. *kindling fyre:* 1. fire bursting into flame; 2. figuratively, inflaming passion; 3. *fyre* (or passion) that gives birth to something, as in *kynd* (3) and *kindle* (9), a word play reinforced by *conceiue.* Lines 5–6 continue the series of *double entrendres* beginning with *harder* and *firmer* (4); *sap, long, conceiue,* and the pun on *kindling*

can all be construed to give *Oake* a suggestively potent meaning, which becomes a covert metaphor for the fecundity that the future marriage will bring. The oak is associated with lust in the description of the wodwo in *FQ* IV.vii.7.4.

6–7. *fyre: / but when it once doth burne:* See the first lesson at evening prayer (a lesson for which Spenser seldom finds a correspondence), Exod. 3.2, "Then the Angel of the Lord appeared vnto him in a flame of fyre, out of the middes of a bushe: and he loked, and beholde, the bushe burned with fyre, and the bushe was not consumed."

7. *diuide:* 1. split apart; 2. share; 3. spread about.

8. *aspire:* 1. through its association with 'spire,' mount up as fire or smoke (see *Am.* 55.11 note); 2. the sense of 'expire' is captured later in *naught but death can seuer* (12).

10. *gentle:* 1. noble, opposed to those of *baser* (3) birth; 2. generous or courteous; 3. soft, not rough or hard; 4. when applied to trees, a domestic variety — in contrast to the oak (*OED* 4a).

  *shall endure for euer:* the puns and running word-play on *endure* and *durefull* (5; and *harder* [4]) imitate exactly the unique running refrain to evening prayer Ps. 136, "for his mercie endureth for euer," which is repeated in each of its twenty-seven verses. The half-verse is mirrored explicitly here.

11. *dints:* strikes, affects.

  *entire:* 1. primarily the interior or inward parts; 2. intact, undivided (see *Am.* 84.9).

13–14. *paine . . . euer shall remaine:* Compare the day's second lesson at morning prayer, Matt. 25.46, "And these shal go into euerlasting paine."

14. *to knit the knot:* A commonplace image for the poet's forthcoming marriage, used also for the marriage of the Red Cross Knight and Una (*FQ* I.xii.37.1–4). The sonnet bears some resemblance to the account:

  His owne two hands the holy knots did knit,
    That none but death for euer can deuide.
  His owne two hands, for such a turne most fit,
    The housling fire did kindle and prouide.

  *Knot:* 1. recalls the earlier oak; 2. carries the undertone of a 'virgin knot' or maidenhead (see Shakespeare, *Per* IV.ii.150 and *Temp* IV.i.15).

**Monday 28 January:** *Morning Prayer:* Pss. 132–35, Exod. 2, Matt. 25. *Evening Prayer:* Pss. 136–38, Exod. 3, 1 Cor. 9.

## Sonnet 7

The eyes of their ladies were of frequent concern to sonneteers; this is the first of many occasions among the *amoretti* (see *Am.* 12, 16, 21, 24–26, 37, 43, 47, 49, 57, 61, and 81). The sonnet conceals within it an implied metaphor of the basilisk, the fabulous creature from whose eyes death darts forth (see *Am.* 49).

1. *Fayre eyes:* See *Am.* 49.1, "Fayre cruell."

  *mazed:* 1. bewildered, dazed; 2. synonymically, infatuated, see *Am.* 35.7; 3. confused, interwoven like a maze — see *Epith.* 190, "Medusaes mazeful hed," recalling the serpents coiled in a maze about Medusa's head, the sight of which brought death.

2. *vertue:* power, strength.

3. *lyfe and death forth from you dart:* Spenser elsewhere likens death-issuing eyes to those of the basilisk, e.g., Corflambo's eyes: "Like as the Basiliske of serpents

seede, / From powrefull eyes close venim doth conuay / Into the lookers hart, and killeth farre away" (*FQ* IV.viii.39.7–9). The conceit here corresponds to Tuesday 29 January's morning prayer Ps. 140.3: "They haue sharpened their tongues like a serpent: Adders poyson is vnder their lips." Just as Spenser has drawn upon the parallell references to serpent's poison in Ps. 58.3 (and the basilisk in Ps. 91.13) for the conceit of the cockatrice in *Am.* 49.10, so he has chosen to construe the present verse as a reference to the basilisk. (The image of the serpent also occurs in the day's first lesson at morning prayer, Exod. 4.2–3, where Moses' rod "was *turned* into a serpent.")

5–8. An example of the rhetorical device, *compar* or *isocolon*.

5. *hew:* 1. appearance; 2. complexion, color (in contrast to *lowre* [7]).

6. *inspired: inspired, fyred,* and *desyred* recall Sonnet 6's rhymes, "aspire," "fyre," and "desire."

7. *askew:* not directly, sideways; see the gloss to *SC* March, "Ascaunce) askew or asquint." It generally suggests disdain, e.g., *FQ* VI.vii.42.3.

10. *louely:* 1. loving; 2. lovingly — Spenser nearly always uses the word to mean both.

11. *bright beams:* See *FQ* IV.viii.39.1 where Corflambo's eyes (see line 3 note) are described as "two fierie beames," and *FQ* II.iii.23.3 where from Belphoebe's eyes "darted fyrie beames" (*FQ* II.iii.23.3).

12. *kindle liuing fire:* The second of three successive sonnets to use the punning phrase, see *Am.* 6.6 & 8.1.

14. *ensample:* See the day's second lesson at evening prayer, 1 Cor. 10, in which Paul lists a series of occasions, given as "ensamples," when God was dishonored, "Now these are ensamples to vs" (v. 6). These include being killed by serpents: "some of them . . . were destroyed of serpents. . . . Now all these things came vnto them for ensamples" (vv. 10–11). The archaic "ensample" was infrequently used in the Geneva Bible.

**Tuesday 29 January**: *Morning Prayer:* Pss. 139–41, Exod. 4, Matt. 26; *Evening Prayer:* Pss. 142–43, Exod. 5, 1 Cor. 10.

## Sonnet 8

Sonnet 8 differs from all other sonnets in the sequence because of its Surreyan form and secondly because it exists in other manuscript versions, see L. Cummings 125–35 who conducted a detailed examination and comparison of the manuscripts' minor textual variants, from which he constructs "an hypothesis of serial change." He concluded on historical evidence that the versions probably date from a period prior to the sonnet's published form and that "the dating of the first version of *Amoretti* viii would be before fall 1580," the poem in its manuscript forms bearing a strong resemblance in its opening three lines to the opening three of Fulke Greville's *Caelica* 3, which apparently dates from around that year:

> More than most faire, full of that heauenly fire,
> Kindled aboue to shew the makers glory,
> Beauties first-born, in whom all powers conspire.

The sonnet's differing Surreyan form and its other recensions tend to confirm that Spenser wrote the original version in friendly rivalry with Fulke Greville, and probably with Sidney. He has accepted the sonnet, although in another revised form, as the sonnet for Wednesday 30th January.

The manuscript versions are found in Bodleian, MS. Rawlinson Poetry 85 (f. 7ᵛ), Cambridge University Library, MS. Dd 5.75 (f. 37ᵛ), British Library, MS. Sloane 1446 (f. 43) and British Library, MS. Harley 7392 (f. 28), which contains the first four lines of the sonnet only:

*Bodleian, MS. Rawlinson Poetry 85 (f. 7ᵛ):*

> O more than moste fayre full of the liuinge fyre,
> Kindled aboue the hyghe creator neere
> No eyes but ioyes wᵗʰ whome the fates conspyre
> That to the worlde noughte else be counted deere
> Throughe theire cleere beames dothe not the blinded guest
> Shote forthe his darte to blase affectinge woundes
> But aungells com to leade fraylle myndes to reste.
> In chaste desyres ohe heauenlye bewtye bownde
> The mor my thoughtes you fashione me wᵗʰin
> You staye my songe yet force myne harte to speake
> You calme the storme that passione did beginn.
> Stronge throughe your looks but by your vertwe weak
> Loue is not knowne wher your lyghte shined neuer
> Thrise happy he that may beholde you euer.

*Cambridge University Library, MS. Dd 5.75 (f. 37ᵛ):*

> More fayr then most fair full of the lyuing fyre
> kyndled aboue the highe creatour neer
> not eyes but ioyes wᵗʰ whom all powers (*thoughts deleted*) conspire
> that to the world nought els be counted deer
> Throughe your deer beames doth not the blinded guest
> Shoote forth his darts to bare affections wound
> but angels com to lead frail mynds to rest
> in chast desires on heauenly bewtye bound.
> You rule my thoughts you fashion me wᵗʰin
> you stay my tongue & moue my hart to speake
> you calme the stormes yᵗ passion dothe begin
> strong throughe your looke but through your bewties weake
> Loue is not knowen wher your loue shineth neuer
> blessed are they wᶜʰ may behold you euer. .

*British Library, MS. Sloane 1446 (f. 43):*

> More then most faire full of that liueinge fire
> Kindled aboue the highe Creatoᵘʳ neere
> no eyes but ioyes, wᵗʰ whome all powers Conspire (y *deleted after* no)
> that in this world may else bee counted deare
> Throughe yoᵘʳ cleere beames doth not the blinded guest
> shoote out his darts to base affections wound
> But Angells come to leade fraile mindes to rest
> in chast desires on heauenlie beauties bounde
> Yoᵘ hold my thoughtes yoᵘ fashion mee wᵗʰin
> Yoᵘ tie my tongue and force my hart to speake
> Yoᵘ calme the stormes when passions doe begin
> Strong throughe yoᵘʳ power but through yoᵘʳ vertue weake
> Loue is not knowne where yoᵘʳ light shineth euᵉʳ
> well is hee borne that may behold yoᵘ euᵉʳ.

British Library, MS. Harley 7392 (f. 28):
> More then most faire full of the liuing fyre,
> Kindled aboue vnto the maker neere,
> Not Eies, but Ioies, wherw$^{th}$ y$^e$ heuuens conspire,
> That to y$^e$ would not els be counted deere

1–14. Heavenly birth, with its Neo-Platonic associations, occurs explicitly at least 35 times in Spenser's total *corpus*. A similar description of womanly eyes is found in the *blason* of Belphoebe, FQ II.iii.23:
> In her faire eyes two liuing lamps did flame,
> Kindled aboue at th' heauenly makers light,
> And darted fyrie beames out of the same,
> So passing persant, and so wondrous bright,
> That quite bereau'd the rash beholders sight:
> In them the blinded god his lustfull fire
> To kindle oft assayd, but had no might;
> For with dredd Maiestie, and awfull ire,
> She broke his wanton darts, and quenched base desire.

Sonnet 8 embodies the standard Neo-Platonic divisions between heavenly, human, and bestial love (*base affections* [6]), as well as its doctrines that love aspires after beauty (*on heauenly beauty bound* [8]) and that virtue overwhelms passion (*by your vertue weak* [12]). (See Quitsland 256–76 for an extended study of the Platonic and Petrarchan influences on *Am.* 8.) Spenser incorporates the divisions and doctrines in the address which begins *FQ* III.iii.1, whose detail *Am.* 8 resembles:
> Most sacred fire, that burnest mightily
> In liuing brests, ykindled first aboue,
> Emongst th'eternall spheres and lamping sky,
> And thence pourd into men, which men call Loue;
> Not that same, which doth base affections moue
> In brutish minds, and filthy lust inflame,
> But that sweet fit, that doth true beautie loue,
> And choseth vertue for his dearest Dame

2. *kindled aboue:* 1. having taken fire from above; 2. having been given birth to from above. (For the final of three uses of *kindled*, see *Am.* 6.6 & 7.12) The reasons for Spenser's choosing the sonnet and inserting it into the sequence for 30 January lie with the corresponding day's scripture readings. The opening of its earlier versions, where the lady's fairness is cast in terms of a divine birth, "Kindled aboue vnto the maker (highe creatour) neere" (Cambridge and Harley MSS.), corresponds to the principal theme of heavenly birth found in the day's second lesson at evening prayer, 1 Cor. 11.9 & 12, where Paul extols man as "the image and glorie of God," claiming that all things are born of God: "the man was not created for the womans sake: but the woman for the mans sake .. as the woman is of the man, so is the man also by the woman: but all things are of God."

3. *powers:* 1. an allusion to the powers which are identified with the classical *virtus* of the gods; 2. Neo-Platonically the *powers* or *Angels* (7) which exist beyond human sight, inhabiting the highest sphere and governing human destinies, the sixth order of *Angels* being Powers — see *HHB* 50–105 & *Epith.* 413 note.

5-6. The eyes as Cupid's arrows are a frequent image in *Amoretti* (see *Am.* 4.8; 12.1-8; 16.4-8; 17.9; 24.7; 39.1-4; 57.8) and a Petrarchan commonplace, e.g., Petrarch, *Rime*, 151.5-9. The convention generally drew on Ovid, *Ars Am.* 2.708, "In quibus occulte spicula figit Amor." A coincidence of phrase occurs between the earlier versions' "shoote out his darts," and the day's morning prayer Ps. 144.6, "shoote out thine arrowes."

5. *bright:* A substantive authorial change for publication which brings it into line with the above description of Belphoebe; the other changes are: *You frame my thoughts* (9); *stop* (10); *Dark is the world* (13).

   *blinded guest:* Cupid.

7. *Angels come to lead fraile mindes to rest:* A detail of the manuscript version which finds a match in the account of Christ's passion and death, read in the day's second lesson at morning prayer, Matt. 27 (in Luke's parallel account, 22.43), "there appeared an Angel vnto him from heauen, comforting him," as well as Paul's instructions about womanly beauty, "Therefore oght the woman to haue power on *her* head, because of the Angels" (1 Cor. 11.10; men will then be able to avoid lusts that might arise in them [v. 16]). Although there is a difference of *locus* between women's hair and the lady's eyes, the Pauline "power" and "Angels" also recall the manuscript versions of the sonnet, "in whome all powers Conspire" (Cambridge and Sloane MSS. and also Greville). The sonnet, as does Paul, sees a connection between angels and the triumphing over *base affections wounds.*

8. *bound:* 1. destined, prepared for; 2. *bound* also carries the transferred association of pregnant (*OED* 1b).

9. *You frame my thoughts and fashion me within:* an alternative revision for publication, strengthening the poem's childbirth imagery (lacking in the MSS. versions).

   *frame:* 1. direct; 2. give shape to.

   *fashion:* mould, give shape to. The line carries a strong suggestion of a fetal shaping, because both terms, *fashion* and *frame*, were used specifically of the foetus — e.g., La Primaudaye 2.393, "*Of the fashion of a childe in the wombe, and how the members are framed.*"

10. *you stop my toung:* put a gag or block on; see *Am.* 3.9-10.

13. *Dark is the world:* A final example of Spenser's modifying the manuscript versions to accord with the day's readings. The manuscript variants show that the sonnet's final couplet had always been problematic. Spenser has solved its unsatisfactory nature by echoing Matt. 27.45, where on the death of Christ "there [was] darkenes ouer all the land."

14. *well is he borne:* 1. born; 2. carried, taking up the thought of *Angels come to lead* (7).

**Wednesday 30 January:** *Morning Prayer:* Pss. 144-46, Matt. 27. *Evening Prayer:* Pss. 147-50, 1 Cor. 11.

## Sonnet 9

The first of three occasions, the others being *Am.* 26 and 55, when Spenser uses a rhetorical *expeditio*, a recognized sonneteer's device, where a list of juxtaposed contrasts which are consecutively excluded until the series of proposals is exhausted. Its shape mirrors Paul's argument in the second lesson at evening prayer for Thursday 31 January, 1 Cor. 12. The elements of the *expeditio* correspond to elements of the day's psalms, particularly Ps. 148, "O Praise the Lorde of heauen." (The calendar of the *Book of Common Prayer* sometimes erroneously prescribed for 31 January a repetition of the psalms for Day 30 [Pss. 144–46, 147–50] and apparently Spenser followed a mistaken calendar.)

3–4. *yet find I nought on earth to which I dare / resemble:* In direct contrast to the judgement of morning prayer Ps. 144.4, "Man is like a thing of nought."
> *resemble:* (re + *similis* = like) liken to another, as in the Vulgate Ps. 144.4, *Homo vanitati similis factus est.*

4–12. Compare the *expeditio* with the argument of 1 Cor. 12.16–17 & 21, in which Paul juxtaposes a series of paradoxes: "if the eare wolde say, Because I am not the eye, I am not of the bodie, is it therefore not of the bodie? If the whole bodie *were* an eye, where *were* the hearing? If the whole *were* hearing, where *were* the smelling? . . . And the eye can not say vnto the hand, I haue no nede of thee: nor the head againe to the fete, I haue no nede of you."

5–7. *Not to the Sun . . . / nor to the Moone . . . / nor to the Starres:* Corresponding exactly with the detail provided by evening prayer Ps. 148.3, "Prayse him Sunne and Moone: prayse him all ye starres."

8. *fire:* Corresponding to the further detail of Ps. 148.8, "Fire and haile."

9. *lightning:* See the feature of morning prayer Ps. 144.6, "Cast foorth thy lightning, and teare them." The day's second lesson at morning prayer, Matt. 28.3, describes the angel at the tomb whose "countenance was like lightning."
> *still:* 1. continue to; 2. unmovingly.
> *perseuer:* remain, not passing in a flash.

8 & 11. *consume . . . seuer:* See Ps. 144.6, "teare them . . . consume them."

11. *Christall:* 1. ice; see evening prayer Ps. 147.17. "He casteth foorth his yce like morsels," (Vulgate, *Mittit crystallum suum sicut buccellas;* crystal was used in earlier translations of the verse, e.g., Richard Rolle of Hampole's 1340 version, "He sendis his kristall as morcels"); 2. secondarily, rock-crystal or precious stone, associated with the *Diamond* (10); 3. crystal-glass, an association developed in *glasse* (12).

12. *glasse:* there is a possible homophonic play on Vulgate Ps. 148.8, *glacies* = 1. ice; 2. in a transferred sense, hardness.
> *mought:* might.

13. *Then to the Maker selfe they likest be:* The *expeditio*'s conclusion coincides with Paul's conclusion that, despite diverse gifts, there is but one maker, "there are diuersities of operations, but God is the same, which worketh all in all" (1 Cor. 12.6).

14. *light doth lighten:* Prescott, *Spenser's Poetry*, 590, points out the echo of Luke 2.32, said each day after the second lesson at evening prayer, "a light to lighten the Gentiles." If so, then Spenser may have cited the phrase because of its associatons with the mandatum of Matt. 28.19, "Go therefore, and teach all nacions."

**Thursday 31 January:** *Morning Prayer:* Pss. 144–46 or 1–5, Matt. 28. *Evening Prayer:* Pss. 147–50 or 6–8, 1 Cor. 12.

## Sonnet 10

The sonnet comprises, in the first instance, a loose rendering of Petrarch's madrigal, "Or vedi, Amor" (*Rime*, 121), in which Cupid, the Lord of love, is called to wage vendetta with bow and arrow:

> Or vedi, Amor, che giovenetta donna
> tuo regno sprezza e del mio mal non cura,
> e tra duo ta' nemici è sì secura.
> Tu se' armato, et ella in treccie e 'n gonna
> si siede e scalza in mezzo i fiori e l' erba,
> ver me spietata e 'n contr' a te superba.
> I' son pregion, ma se pietà ancor serba
> l' arco tuo saldo e qualcuna saetta,
> fa di te e di me, Signor, vendetta.

Petrarch's closing reference to Cupid's bow and arrow finds a parallel in the action of the ungodly in Ps. 11.2 at morning prayer for Friday 1 February: "For loe, the vngodly bende their bowe, and make readie their arrowes within the quiver: that they may privily shoote at them which are true (Geneva version, vpright) of heart."

1. *Vnrighteous Lord of loue:* A direct adaptation of morning prayer Ps. 11.8, "For the righteous Lord loueth righteousnes." See headnote, Petrarch, "Amor / Signor." (Renwick 197 and Dasenbrock 38-50 provide a detailed comparison with Petrarch's madrigal.) Addressing Cupid as the *Lord of loue* was common (e.g., Sidney, AS 50.6, "my Lord *Loue's* owne behest") and Spenser's recasting the sacred as profane becomes a growing tendency through the sequence.

    *Vnrighteous:* not conforming to the moral law, not upright (see headnote, Ps. 11.2, Geneva version). The word anticipates the sustained legal conceit (*Lord* [1], *law* [1], *licent(ious)* [1], *comptroll* [10]), culminating with the wordplay on *pain* (14).

    *What law is this:* Compare the day's second lesson at morning prayer, Mark 1.27, with its response to Christ's casting out the "vncleane spirit" from the "tormented" man, "What thing is this? what new doctrine is this? for he commandeth the foule spirits with autoritie."

2. *tormented:* In the Marcan account, the spirit, once cast out, exclaims, "what have we to do with thee . . . Iesus of Nazaret? Art thou come to destroy vs?" (v. 24, to which Mark 5.7 [and the other evangelists] add, "I charge thee by God, that thou torment me not"). Spenser has played with the etymology of *tormented* = *tormentum*, a military engine for throwing missiles, an allusion made explicit with Cupid's darts in lines 5-6.

3. *lordeth:* rule tyrannically; the only occasion Spenser uses the word — see evening prayer Ps. 12.4, "Who is Lord ouer vs?"

    *licentious:* trisyllabic by syncopation; from *licentia*, 1. unrestrained by law or decorum; 2. overly free; 3. lustful — see morning prayer Ps. 110.2, "The vngodly for his owne lust doeth persecute the poore," (see Mark 1.26 & 27, "vncleane spirit," and "foule spirits").

4. *freewill:* an unusual word in Spenser, carrying here a sense of reprehensible abandon.

    *scoming both thee and me:* see headnote, Petrarch, "sprezza" and "di te e di me." Spenser has also used the day's second lesson at evening prayer, 1 Cor. 13, Paul's celebrated hymn of love, to make a series of unfavorable comparisons: where, here, the lady is guilty of *scoming both thee and me*, in Paul's hymn love "disdaineth not" (v. 5).

5. *Tyrannesse:* Cupid is described similarly in SC Oct., 108. See the Geneva version sidenote to Mark 5.7, "He abuseth the Name of God, to mainteine his tyrannie."

   *doth ioy to see:* in contrast to the Pauline claim, 1 Cor. 13.6, that love
"reioyceth not in iniquitie."
6. *massacres:* massàcres; See *F. Q,* III.iii.35.6.
   *vengeance take:* See headnote Petrarch, "fa . . . vendetta."
7. *humbled harts:* clearly 1. hearts; but possibly 2. a witty allusion to *harts* = deer and
   *humbled* = umbled, umbles being the innards of a deer (*OED* 1; see Johnson,
   *Analogies,* 89).
9. *hart:* 1. heart; possibly 2. hart — continued in *shake* with its allusive connotation
   of 'shaking an animal' and in the secondary meaning of *bow* (see line 11 note).
   *shake:* 1. move; 2. weaken; 3. of an animal, to worry its prey.
10. *comptroll:* used by Spenser only here; 1. regulate, hold in check; 2. call to
    account; Spenser is playing with the word's etymology, the Anglo-French
    *contreroller,* "to record in an account, to enroll (specifically faults) in a book,"
    a meaning explicated precisely in *al her faults in thy black booke enroll* (12).
11. *bow:* 1. bend, submit; 2. homonymically, the hunting bow is recalled. The day's
    morning prayer Ps. 11.2, "bende their bowe" underwrites both meanings.
    *baser:* 1. lower; 2. not gentle; 3. opposite of *free.*
    *make:* mate; see *Am.* 70.11.
12. *black booke:* in which the names of people liable to punishment are inscribed,
    see *Zepheria,* Canzon. 38.8, "Be they recogniz'd in black book of shame."
    *enroll:* the same root as *comptroll.*
13. *in equall sort:* to an equal degree or extent.
14. An alexandrine — so also *Am.* 45.14.
    *sport:* 1. entertainment, diversion, often associated with Cupid, e.g., *FQ*
    II.ix.34.6–7; 2. amorous dalliance; 3. blood-sport, a possible reference to the
    earlier deer-hunting.
    *pain:* 1. *torment,* suffering; 2. from *poena* it gains the association of a legal
    penalty (see *Am.* 11.13–14 note) — *poena captivitatis* was a common idiom from
    Justinian onwards; 3. *Poena* was also the God of vengeance (see *vengeance* [8]).

**Friday 1 February:** *Morning Prayer:* Pss. 9–11, Mark 1. *Evening Prayer:* Pss. 12–14, 1 Cor. 13.


## Sonnet 11

The sonnet's conceit of the *cruell warriour* belongs to the tradition of Petrarch's
"dolce mia guerrera" (*Rime,* 21) and "dolce mia nemica" (*Rime,* 202), although
Spenser has here associated the martial imagery with that of courtship (*sew* [1], *offer
for my truth* [2], *addresse* [3]), so that the conceit is underwritten by a discreet
compliment proper to a betrothal. The *cruell warriour* image replicates the warfare
epithet, "cruel enemies," in evening prayer Ps. 18.49 for the feast of the Purification, Saturday 2 February.
1. *seeke and sew:* a common yoking, e.g., *Am.* 20.1.
   *sew:* 1. petition; 2. in an implied sense, woo (see *FQ* VI.viii.20.6). The
   bridegroom and marriage chamber occur as a metaphor in the day's second
   lesson at morning prayer, Mark 2.19–20.
   *peace:* Repeatedly seeking peace recalls Simeon's presence in the day's
   Gospel's account of the Purification, Luke 2.22–27, whose prayer, the *Nunc
   Dimittis,* opens, "Lord, now lettest thou thy seruant departe in peace." The
   poet's prayer will find no such resolution.

2. *hostages:* 1. persons handed to the enemy as a security; 2. a pledge, often associated with host (see Daniel, *Civil Wars*, 2. 23, "The ost of Christ, an ostage for his troth"). Spenser is playing with the Pauline metaphor of combat (Vulgate, *agone*) in the day's Epistle, 1 Cor. 9.24–27, and has accepted the ancient association of *agon* with host ("Hostiam enim antiqui agoniam vocabant" [Paul. ex Fest. 10]). See Luke 2.24, where Mary and Joseph visit the Temple "to giue an oblation" (Vulgate, *ut darem hostiam*). The poet's offering his life as a victim becomes the matter of the sonnet's sestet; 3. *hostage* was also ironically associated with marriage, e.g., Bacon, *Essay on Marriage*, "He that hath *Wife* and *Children*, hath giuen Hostages to Fortune."

   *offer for my truth:* identifiable as the troth which the poet offers his betrothed.
3. *cruell warriour:* Compare the warfare conceit in *Am.* 57.1.

   *cruell:* disyllabic.

   *warriour:* disyllabic by syncopation.
3–4. *doth her selfe addresse / to battell:* 1. prepare for battle, in direct imitation of the warfare metaphor in the day's second lesson at evening prayer, 1 Cor. 14.8, "who shal prepare him self to battel"; 2. by implication, courtship of a lady (*OED* v.8c); the poet has already addressed himself to the lady, while the lady can only *address* herself to war.
5. *rewth:* pity, compassion.
6. *respit:* 1. an interval of rest; 2. a temporary cessation of war (*OED* sb 2).

   *toile:* 1. labor; 2. war.
7. *greedily:* Compare morning prayer Ps. 17.12, "Like as a Lyon that is griedy of his pray."

   *fell:* cruel, savage.
9–10. The parallelisms make the syntax contorted; the primary sense is not of an intransitive verb, 'I would that she would desist,' but of a transitive whose object is *life*, 'I would yield to her my poor life.'

   *life . . . I would her yield:* 1. expire; 'to yield up life' was equivalent to 'to give up the ghost'; 2. militarily, surrender; 3. offer to her (*OED* v 10), continuing the image of sacrifice.
9. *assoyle:* dissolve, remove, dispel.
12–13. *to force me liue, and will not let me dy. / . . . peace:* The lady's actions are in contrast to the promise made to Simeon (Luke 2.27), "that he shulde not se death, before he had sene the Lords Christ."
13–14. *paine:* 1. suffering; 2. legally, when associated with *poena*, its etymon, punishment or fine, a sense explicated in, "*no price . . . may surcease.*"

   *price:* Compare the nature of the Pauline combat, 1 Cor. 9.24, in which "one receiueth the price" (= prize).

   *war . . . surcease:* Proverbial, See Smith, *Proverb Lore*, 602. The poet's complaint bears comparison with the actions of Blandina (*FQ* VI.vi.43.4–9).
14. *surcease:* stop, bring to an end.

**Saturday 2 February, Purification:** *Epistle:* 1 Cor. 9.24–27. *Gospel:* Luke 2.22–27. *Morning Prayer:* Pss. 15–17, Mark 2. *Evening Prayer:* Ps. 18, 1 Cor. 14.

## Sonnet 12

1. *One day:* Directly imitating the opening to morning prayer Ps. 19 for Sexagesima Sunday, 3 February in 1634, "One day."

_sought:_ continues the conceit of _Am._ 11 and recapitulates its opening.

_hart-thrilling:_ 1. heart-piercing; see the prophetic echo of the Sunday's evening prayer Ps. 22.17, "They pearced my handes, and my feete"; 2. militarily, a hurled dart (or weapon) which pierces; 3. a heart that is moved by emotion; 4. since _thrill_ was a substitute for thrall (_OED_ v 2), heart-capturing, a sense taken up in _captiuing_ (11).

_eies:_ forces which lie in ambush and dart forth as weapons to strike the lover's heart was a common device among Petrarchist poets. Castiglione, _The Courtier,_ 3 (Everyman, 247), makes the same point: "The eyes therefore lye lurking like souldiers in war, lying in waite in bushment, and if the forme of all the bodie be well favoured and of good proportion, it draweth uñto it and allureth who so beholdeth it a farre off: untill he come nigh: and as soone as he is at hand, the eyes shoote, and like sorcerers bewitch, and especially when by a right line they send their glistering beames into the eyes of the wight beloved."

2. _termes to entertaine:_ accept (mutually) the conditions of the truce.
3. _false enimies:_ Compare "the fetches of false apostles," and the "false brethren" of the day's Epistle, 2 Cor. 11.26.
4. _to entrap in treasons traine:_ a pleonasm, a _traine_ meaning an _entrap_ment. Such entrapment reproduces that of Ps. 22.16's complaint, "the counsell of the wicked layde siege against me," and the pharisees' plottings in the day's second lesson at morning prayer, Mark 3.6, who "straight waye gathered a councel with the Herodians against him, that they might destroye him."
5. _disarmed:_ 1. without weapons, having been defeated; 2. lacking hostility, harmless.
7. _close couert:_ a second pleonasm, _close_ = hidden, _couert_ = hiding place. Identifying the recesses of the eyes as secret is proper to the feast's second lesson at evening prayer, 1 Cor. 15.51–52, "Behold, I shew you a secret thing . . . in the twinkling of an eye. . . ."
8. _throng:_ the only occasion when the verb occurs in the sequence and imitating Mark 3.9, "lest they shulde throng him" (one of only two Geneva version's uses of the verb).
9. _t'abide the brunt:_ to bear the assault; a colloquial expression (_OED_ 2).
10. _yeeld my selfe into their hands:_ See _Am._ 11.9–10, note. The poet's submission contrasts with the escape of Paul, in the day's Epistle, 2 Cor. 11.33, who thwarted the governor of Damascus and "escaped his hands."
11. _streight:_ 1. of imprisonment (_captiuing_), rigorous, strict; 2. of _bands,_ tightly drawn together — see _Am._ 71.6–7 (and its note for the line's covert military allusion); 3. immediately.

_rigorous:_ extremely strict, unyielding (particularly of laws and justice).
13. _complaine:_ lodge a complaint, make a formal statement of grievance. The legal conceit imitates Ps. 22.1, "My God, my God (looke upon me) why . . . art [thou] so farre . . . from the words of my complaint?"

**Sunday 3 February, Sexagesima Sunday**: _Epistle:_ 2 Cor. 11.19–33. _Gospel:_ Luke 8.4–16. _Morning Prayer:_ Pss. 19–21, Mark 3. _Evening Prayer:_ Pss. 22–23, 1 Cor. 15.

## Sonnet 13

1. _port:_ gait, carriage, mode of walking — an etymological, scriptural and homonymic pun. A feature of morning prayer Ps. 24 for Monday 4 February is its repeated

verse, "Lift vp your heades, O ye gates, and be ye lift vp ye euerlasting doores" (vv. 7 & 9; Vulgate, *Attollite portas*). Spenser has construed *portas* not as gate = gate, but as gate = port or gait, in the 16th century spelled only as gate (see *Hub* 600; *FQ* V.v.4.1-2 contains a clearer instance of the etymological pun).

(Ps. 24.7-9 are also reflected in the final couplet of the sonnet for the Ascension, *Am.* 82, "Whose lofty argument vplifting me, / shall lift you vp vnto an high degree." As well, *Am.* 13's matter [and vocabulary], the lifting of the eyes to the heavens and the scorning of earth, is found in *Am.* 72, which also corresponds to an Ascension account.)

    *goodly graceth*: imitating the Geneva Bible introduction to Ps. 24, "gracious goodnes."

2. *rears vp to the skie*: 1. directs upwards, echoing *Attollite* (= "lift vp"). Compare Ovid's description of creation, echoes of which persist throughout the sonnet, *Met.* 1.86, "erectos ad sidera tollere vultus (= reared their faces upwards to the skie)"; 2. secondarily, nourishes — sustained in the pun on *born* (6).

3 & 5. *ground & earth*: Mark 4, the day's second lesson at morning prayer, mostly consists of the parable of the sower sowing in various types of *ground* and *earth*, "stonie ground" (vv. 5 & 16), "good grounde" (v. 8) and "earth" (vv. 5, 28, 31). References to *ground* and *earth* are later overlaid with Ovid's creation account and that of Genesis.

3. *low*: The sonnet is marked by progressions and repetitions: the progressive polyptoton, *low, lowly* (13), *lowlinesse* (14), and the repetitions of *goodly* (1 & 4) and *lofty* (9 & 14).

    *embaseth*: 1. direct themselves downwards; 2. humble themselves. (The biblical analogue for such humbling is Isa. 7.10-11.)

4. *temperature*: 1. combination or blending of physical attributes; 2. disposition or bent of mind, temperament — compare Belphoebe, whose face is "withouten blame or blot, / Through goodly mixture of complexions dew" (*FQ* II.iii.22.3-7).

    *descry*: discover.

5. *maiesty*: the distinguishing characteristic of the human person in Ovid's account of creation: "He gaue to man a stately looke replete with maiestie." (*Met.* 1.84-85 [Golding 1.97-99]).

6. *borne*: 1. from which she was carried — reversed in *returne* (6); 2. from which she was born, given birth. The pun was a frequent Elizabethan one, e.g., *Am.* 8.14 & 61.6.

7. *mind . . . mortalitie*: *Am.* 72.1-3 shows the same twofold direction.

8. *shall to earth returne*: Axiomatic and an adaptation of Gen. 3.19, "til thou returne to the earth: for out of it wast thou taken, because thou art dust, and to dust shalt thou returne."

9. *lofty countenance*: disyllabic by syncopation; see Ovid, *Met.* 1.86 (Golding, 1.99), "wyth countnance cast on hie."

9-10. *scorne / base thing*: The phrase (*Fuge turpia*) was proverbial — see *Am.* 5.6 & 61.11-12.

11-12. See the Geneva Bible introduction to Ps. 24, "*purged from the sinful filth of this worlde*," and Ovid's creation, *Met.* 1.68, "quicquam terrenae faecis habentem" (Golding (1.78), "all dregs of earthly filth or grossenesse").

    *drossy*: impure, the surface scum detracting from or hiding the purity of *heauenly thoughts*, see *Am.* 27.2. The word was an apposite Neo-Platonic term and was used particularly by Spenser in his Neo-Platonic hymns, see *HL* 184, *HB* 48, *HHL* 276, & *HHB* 279.

> *slime:* the human body as a mixture of earth and water (compare Ovid, *Met.* 1.80 ff.). In Gen. 2.7 *de limo terrae* was normally translated as "the dust of the grounde," even though *limus* was thought to be the stem of *slime.*

11. *forlorne:* abandoned, destined for nothing (as in "to dust shalt thou returne").

13-14. Women's sovereignty is a frequent theme in the sequence, see *Am.* 25, 31, 38, 41, 47, 49, 55 & 57; *FQ* VI.viii.1–2.

**Monday 4 February**: *Morning Prayer: Pss.* 24–26, Mark 4. *Evening Prayer: Pss.* 27–29, 1 Cor. 16.

## Sonnet 14

The siege conceit is stock among Petrarchist sonneteers. Here it corresponds with the dominant image of the morning prayer Psalm for Tuesday 5 February, Ps. 31.3–4, "be thou my strong rocke, and the house of defence. . . . For thou art my strong rocke, and my castell." The sonnet brings to a close a series of preceding sonnets, whose pleadings become the *engins* of the present siege. The siege metaphor easily carried a range of obliquely sexual puns.

1. *forces:* 1. primarily physical strength; 2. military might.

> *late:* recently, see line 11 note.

> *dismayd:* used only once elsewhere — with bawdy associations, *Am.* 6.1.

2. *siege:* The siege *topos* can be found, *inter alia*, in the opening lines to Sidney, *AS* 36, "Stella, whence doth this new assault arise"; Lynche, *Diella*, Sonnet 7, "When Loue had first besieg'd my harts strong wall," and Percy below, *Coelia*, Sonnet 10.

4. *peece:* 1. castle, stronghold (*OED* 10 b); 2. by implication, a piece of artillery; 3. of a person, either male (often a soldier) or female (*OED* 9); 4. in conjunction with *fayre*, a fine structure, masterpiece — see *FQ* II.xi.14.9.

> *for:* because of.

> *repulse:* 1. the repelling of a military assault; 2. the refusal or rebuff of a suit or approach.

5. *Gaynst such strong castles:* See headnote, Ps. 31.3–4. *needeth* = it needeth.

6. *fort:* a polyptoton of *forces*, identified through its root (*fortis* = strong) with *strong* and echoing morning prayer Ps. 31.27, "Be strong, and he shall stablish (Vulgate = *confortetur*) your heart."

> *wont:* accustomed to.

> *belay:* (= to lay beside) besiege with the sense of encircling (hence a remotely bawdy touch). The only occasion Spenser uses the word which has the same sense and root as beleaguer.

7. *haughty:* 1. proud, disdainful; 2. highly courageous, thus ironically the same as *hardy*, courageous.

> *enur'd:* 1. accustomed, as in *wont* above; 2. of the military, hardened through training and endurance.

> *hardy:* 1. courageous; 2. in keeping with *enur'd*, capable of enduring hardship (normally a quality of the mind rather than a *fight*).

8. *assay:* 1. assault (but with sexual associations, e.g., Shakespeare, *VA* 607, and Percy, *Coelia*, Sonnet 10, "To winne the Fort how oft haue I assayd"); it is connected with *battery* through the phrase, "assault and battery"; 2. secondarily, tried or tested.

10–12. *heart . . . conuert:* a correct sixteenth century rhyme, see *FQ* V.v.28.2–7 &
     *Am.* 42.8–11.
10. *lay . . . battery to:* 1. apply a series of artillery blows against a castle; 2. a *battery*
     was also a combined group of separate artillery pieces (which are individually
     named in the next line); 3. the sounds of beating drums during a siege (such as
     the poet's *playnts, prayers, vowes,* etc.).
       *incessant:* 1. without pausing; 2. unending.
       *to her heart:* Compare Artegal's properly gentle advances towards Britomart,
     *FQ* IV.vi.40.3–4, "with meeke seruice and much suit did lay / Continuall siege
     vnto her gentle hart."
11–12. *playnts . . . conuert: conuert* is an unusual word for Spenser and a playful
     rendering of the Vulgate's version of morning prayer Ps. 30.12, *convertisti
     planctum meum,* where *convertisti* has been rendered as *conuert,* and *planctum* as
     *playnt,* whose etymon *planctum* is.
11. *playnts, prayers, vowes, ruth, sorrow, and dismay:* recapitulating the *engins* of the
     preceding sonnets: *playnts: Am.* 12.13; *prayers* (and *vowes*): *Am.* 11.14; *ruth: Am.*
     11.5; *sorrow: Am.* 11.11; *dismay: Am.* 14.1.
       *vowes:* prayers or supplications rather than a solemn promise.
12. *engins:* 1. machines used in warfare; 2. ingenious devices (from the word's root,
     *ingenium*).
13. *fall downe:* In direct imitation of two episodes in Mark 5, the day's second lesson
     at morning prayer, that of the woman cured of a flow of blood, who "fel downe
     before him" (v. 33), and that of Jairus, who, when he saw Christ, also "fel
     downe at his fete" (v. 22).
13–14. *dy before her, / so dying liue, and liuing do adore her:* The paradoxical juxtaposi-
     tion recalls Jairus who besought Christ, "My litle daughter lieth at point of
     death . . . come and laye thine hands on her, that she may be healed, and liue"
     (Mark 5.22).
14. *adore her:* Compare Mark 5.6, "ranne, and worshipped (Vulgate, *adoravit*) him."
**Tuesday 5 February:** *Morning Prayer:* Pss. 30–31, Mark 5. *Evening Prayer:* Pss. 32–24, 2 Cor. 1.

## Sonnet 15
The sonnet is a fine example of the traditional *blason,* whose conventions Geoffrey
de Vinsauf had laid down in the thirteenth century. In 1536 an anthology of French
blasons, *Les Blasons anatomiques du corps feminin, ensemble les contreblasons,* was
published and frequently reprinted. The convention extolled the lady's beauty,
describing her every part emblematically (often by biblical analogues from the Song
of Solomon (e.g., 5.10–16) or Prov. 31.10–31) and concluding with a reference to
her inner perfection.
1–2. *tradefull Merchants . . . to make your gaine:* The conceit corresponds to the
     second lesson at evening prayer for Wednesday 6 February, 2 Cor. 2.17, "For we
     are not as manie, which make marchandise of the worde of God," with its
     Geneva version gloss, "That is, which preache for gaine, and corrupt it to serue
     mens affections." The Geneva Bible generally construed such 'merchants' as the
     Pope and his priests (see 1 Pet. 2.3, "they with faigned words make marchandize
     of you," with its sidenote, "This is euidently sene in the Pope and his priests").
     Such glosses took their force from the condemnation of the merchants of
     Babylon in Rev. 18.11–19, identified in that chapter's marginal entries as

"Romish prelates and marchants of soules." Spenser has had recourse to the details of Revelation for the sonnet's *divisio*: "And the marchants of the earth shal wepe and waile ouer her: for no man byeth their ware any more. The ware of golde and siluer, and of precious stone, and of pearles . . . and of all vessels of yuorie. . . . The marchants of these things which were waxed riche, shal stand a farre from her. . . . Alas, alas, the great citie, that was . . . guilded with golde, and precious stone, and pearles." Spenser adopts many of the passage's details for the parallel *blason* in *Epith*. 167–80.

Most Elizabethan sonneteers included at least one *blason* in their sequence, e.g., Sidney's extended and frequently revised *blason* in *OA* 62 and the riposte in *AS* 32.10–12. See also Lynche, *Diella*, Sonnets 3, 16, 31, & *The Love of Dom Diego and Gyneura*, 69–78; Barnfield, *Cynthia with certaine Sonnets*, 17; and Shakespeare's parody, Sonnet 130.

3–4. *spoile . . . needeth:* Spenser has drawn on the *blason*'s further Old Testament source, the virtuous woman, defined by Solomon in Prov. 31.10–31: "Who shal finde a vertuous woman? for her price *is* farre aboue the pearles. The heart of her housband trusteth in her, and he shal haue no nede of spoile. . . . She is like the shippes of marchants: she bringeth her fode from a farre. . . . She feleth that her marchandise is good. . . . Manie daughters haue done vertuously: but thou surmountest them all."

7. *Saphyres:* Bart. Angl. 266[r-v], describes the sapphire as "cheife of precious stones," and associates it with the eyes, "His vertue keepeth and saueth the sight, and cleanseth eien of filth without any greefe." It also "loueth chastity."

7–8. *Rubies . . . Pearles:* Belphoebe's mouth is similarly described (*FQ* II.iii.24.8–9).

9. *Rubies:* Compare *Am*. 81.9–10, "the gate with pearls and rubies richly dight." (A translation of Tasso's "Porta de' bei rubin." The biblical analogue is Rev. 21.21.)

   *sound:* unflawed, but *sound* is associated with the lips. The ruby was considered to temper fleshly urges. (See *FQ* IV.viii.6.7.)

10. *Yuorie:* Compare Belphoebe's "iuorie forhead" (*FQ* II.iii.24.1). The yoking was frequent, e.g., Ariosto, *Orl. Fur.*, VII.11.7, "di terso avorio era la fronte lieta."

   *weene:* either 1. consider; or 2. possibly beautiful, the only such usage by Spenser but in keeping with the parallel syntax of lines 7–12.

13–14. *That which fairest is . . . vertues manifold:* Prov. 31.29 concludes its definition of a virtuous woman, "Manie daughters haue done vertuously: but thou surmountest them all."

**Wednesday 6 February:** *Morning Prayer:* Pss. 35–36, Mark 6; *Evening Prayer:* Ps. 37, 2 Cor. 2.


### Sonnet 16

1. *One day:* a favorite Spenserian opening, see *Am*. 12. Cupid and his arrows occurs frequently among the *amoretti* (e.g., *Am*. 4.8, 8.5–6, 17.9, 24.7, 39.1–4, 57.8) and was stock-in-trade among Petrarchists. Compare Petrarch, *Rime*, 2.1–6, with which this sonnet bears some resemblance:

   Per fare una leggiadra sua vendetta
   e punire in un dì ben mille offese,
   celatamente Amore l'arco riprese,
   come uom ch'a nocer luogo e tempo aspetta;

era la mia virtute al cor ristretta
per far ivi e negli occhi sue difese....

*vnwarily:* incautiously, imprudently; see *Am.* 24.6.

2. *eyes ... light:* The physical nature of the lady's looks matches the detail of the second lesson at morning prayer for Thursday 7 February, Mark 7.21-22, "*euen out of the heart of men, procede euil thoghts ... a wicked eye,*" which the Geneva Bible glosses as "wantonnes." Compare morning prayer Ps. 38.10, "the sight (Vulgate, *lumen oculorum meorum* = light) of mine eies is gone from me."

*immortall:* not subject to death, in contrast to the fleshly eyes from which Cupid darts his *deadly arrowes* (7).

3. *stonisht hart:* Mark 7.37 likewise reports that, because of Christ's miracles, the multitudes "were beyonde measure astonied."

*amaze:* 1. confusion (see *Am.* 17.2); 2. infatuation, see *Am.* 35.7, "in their amazement lyke *Narcissus* vaine."

4. *illusion:* 1. deception — used elsewhere by Spenser only as magical or false; 2. scorning or mockery.

5. *glauncing:* 1. of the eyes, looking momentarily; 2. of light, flashing; 3. Spenser also uses the word of a dart (see *F. Q,* I.vi.17.5-6).

6. *legions:* used twice elsewhere by Spenser as "a whole legione / Of wicked Sprightes" (*FQ* III.ix.2.7-8); either an "infinit nomber" or "aboue 6000" in the Geneva glosses to Matt. 26.53 and Mark 5.9, where the devil cast out by Christ responds "My name *is* Legion." Mark 7.24-30 contains an account of the casting out of devils. (In *Am.* 57.7-8 the darts number only 1000.)

*loues:* 1. little cupids (little devils?); 2. *amoretti.*

7. *deadly arrowes:* The sagittal *topos* imitates directly morning prayer Ps. 38.2, "For thine arrowes sticke fast in me: and thy hand presseth me sore." Compare Belphoebe's eyes, *FQ* II.iii.23.3.

9. *closely:* 1. secretly, hence 'I did spy the archer secretly aiming'; 2. privately, hence 'I privately did spy the archer aiming.'

10. *hart:* The object of the *fyry arrowes,* the poet's heart, reflects the psalmist's cry in morning prayer Ps. 39.4, "My heart was hot (Vulgate, *concaluit* = to glow warmly or with love) within me, and while I was thus musing, the fire kindled."

11. *twincle:* 1. blink; 2. an instant of time.

12. *misintended dart:* the only Spenserian usage and a Spenserian coinage (*OED* cites only this instance giving the sense of "maliciously purposed"); 1. of an arrow, misdirected (*intendere* = to aim an arrow, e.g., Vergil, *Aen.* 9.590, "intendisse sagittam"; Spenser renders Ps. 58.6, *Intendit arcum suum* as "bend your force" in *Am.* 49.8). See *FQ* II.iii.23.9, where Belphoebe also "broke his [Cupid's] wanton darts"; 2. of eye-glances (which constitute the darts), 'intend the eyes' was a Latinism deriving from *intendere oculos;* 3. if Spenser is playing on 'in' and the surgical term 'tent,' (to pierce or probe [*OED* v 4]), a dart that wrongly pierced the poet.

14. *hardly:* 1. with difficulty or barely; 2. painfully — hence the pleonasm, 'painfully *scap't with paine*'; 3. secretly, echoing *closely* (9).

**Thursday 7 February**: *Morning Prayer:* Pss. 38-40, Mark 7. *Evening Prayer:* Pss. 41-43, 2 Cor. 3.

## Sonnet 17

This example of the familiar portrait sonnet closely resembles in its opening line the descriptions of Belphoebe, whose "face so faire as flesh it seemed not, / But heauenly pourtraict of bright Angels hew" (*FQ* II.iii.22.1–2), and Amoret, "Whose face discoured, plainely did expresse / The heauenly pourtraict of Angels hew" (*FQ* IV.v.13.3–4). The sonnet imitates closely morning prayer Ps. 45 for Friday 8 February, an epithalamial psalm which the Geneva version describes as a song, "Of that perfite loue that ought to be betwene the housband and the wife."

1–2. *The glorious pourtraict of that Angels face ... confused skil:* The terms, *glorious, Angels, face* and *confused* find coincident parallels in three of the day's scriptural passages. The detail firstly imitates the second lesson at morning prayer, Mark 8.38, "whosoeuer shalbe ashamed (Vulgate, *confusus*) of me ... of him shal the Sonne of man be ashamed (Vulgate, *confundetur*) also, when he cometh in the glorie of his Father with the holie Angels." Similarly the second lesson at evening prayer, 2 Cor. 4.4 & 6, celebrate, "the light of the glorious Gospel of Christ, which is the image of God," and a God who is "he which hathe shined in our hearts, to giue the light of the knowledge of the glorie of God in the face of Iesus Christ." Morning prayer Ps. 44.16 confirms the detail, "My confusion is dayly before me: and the shame of my face hath couered me." To match the correspondences Spenser has recalled the earlier descriptions of Belphoebe and Amoret.

1. *glorious:* See Ps. 45.14, "The kings daughter is all glorious within."

3. *this worlds worthlesse glory:* Reflecting Christ's maxim in Mark 8.36, "For what shal it profite a man, thogh he shulde winne the whole worlde, if he lose his soule." (The like thought in *Am.* 35.13, "All this worlds glory seemeth vayne to me," reflects the parallel biblical verse, Luke 9.25, "What auantageth it a man, if he winne the whole worlde.")
    *embase:* degrade.

4. *what pen, what pencill can expresse her fill?:* Matching the psalmist's exclamation, Ps. 45.2, "My tongue is the penne of a ready writer," even if the poet disparages his pen while the psalmist acclaims his. Compare *FQ* II.iii.25.8, "How shall fraile pen descriue her [Belphoebe's] heauenly face."
    *pencill:* an artist's brush, often of sable, used for delicate work. The comparison was commonplace, e.g., Shakespeare, Sonnet 101.6–7 & *Zepheria*, Canzon 2.1–4.

5–6. *he/his:* it/its, that is the pen, which implies a subsequent series of actions by the pen that are autonomous of the poet and which depict a still-born portrait, not something lively.

5. *colours:* Imitating Ps. 45.10, "wrought about with diuers colours."

6. *pleasure:* Matches the pleasure of the king, Ps. 45.12, "So shal the king haue pleasure in thy beautie."

7. *spill:* destroy.

9. *The sweet eye-glaunces, that like arrowes glide: oeillades:* amorous glances by which the lady captures the poet's heart without intending to satisfy him; see Ps. 45.6 for the metaphor of eyes that, like *arrowes*, afflict the heart, "Thy arrowes are very sharpe" (Vulgate, *Sagittae tuae acutae ... in corda* (Geneva version, "Thine arrowes *are* sharpe *to perce* the heart").

10–11. *The charming smiles, that rob sence from the hart: / the louely pleasance:* For a detailed account of the φιλομμειδής Ἀφροδίτη, see *Am.* 39.

13–14. *A greater craftesmans hand thereto doth neede, / that can expresse the life of things indeed:* A divine hand capable of giving life to the portrait. In *FQ* III. Pr.2.1–2 & 3.6–8 the hands of painter and poet are compared and each found inadequate to express the beauty of Elizabeth.

*greater craftesmans hand:* The poet is associating his lowly endeavors with those of the lesser craftsman ("faber imus") of Horace, *Ars Poet.* 32–25, whose art can express ("exprimet") detail, but who cannot portrait the figure as a whole, "faber imus et ungues / exprimet et molles imitabitur aere capillos, / infelix operis summa, quia ponere totum / nesciet."

*hand:* In Mark 8.23 & 25 sight is given by Christ's hand: "he toke the blind by the hand," and, "he put his hands againe upon his eyes."

Friday 8 February: *Morning Prayer:* Pss. 44–46, Mark 8. *Evening Prayer:* Ps. 47–49, 2 Cor. 4.

## Sonnet 18

Of the sonnet's two parts, the first is built upon the much-used proverb of the wheel, the second is a fresh treatment of a favorite Spenserian conceit, the stage.

1. *rolling wheele:* The image of the turning wheel corresponds to the image in the second lesson at morning prayer for Saturday 9 February, Mark 9.42, the well-known admonition involving the millstone, "better for him rather, that a milstone were hanged about his necke, and that he were cast into the sea."

2. *tract of time:* 1. the course of time — a commonplace (*tractus temporum*); 2. secondarily, the course of a dramatic action, thus identifying the sonnet's two parts, see Sidney, *Apologie* K2ᵛ, "the whole tract of a Comedy, shoulde be full of delight."

   *teare:* compare the word's unusual use, Mark 9.18 & 20, "he teareth him," and, "he tare him." (See also morning prayer Ps. 50.22 [Geneva Version], "lest I teare you in pieces.")

3–4. *drops . . . flint . . . weare:* Proverbial from classical times; see Lucretius, *De rerum Natura,* 1.313, "Stillicidi lapsus lapidem cavat," and Ovid, *Ex Ponto,* 4.10.5, "Gutta cavat lapidem"; see also Fletcher, *Licia,* 28.5, & Lynche, *Diella,* 9.11–14.

3. *drizzling:* of rain, but poetically associated with tears. *redound:* overflow.

4. *in continuance:* in the course of time, see Ovid, *Met.* 15.235 (Golding, 15.259), "And when [tyme] that long continuance hath them bit."

5. *soften her hard hart:* See morning prayer Ps. 55.22, "The words of his mouth were softer then butter" (Vulgate, *Molliti sunt sermones eius*). The sonnet's phrase is more complex than the customary trite usage: Mark's stone, in the Vulgate, is *mola,* a grinding stone, not *lapis.* Spenser has identified the Latin semi-homophones *molliti* and *mola* to produce the contrasting *soften . . . hard.* (See Varro, *De re rustica,* 1.55, "molae oleariae duro et aspero lapide.")

9–14. As in Sonnet 54 the theatrical conceit corresponds with the biblical image of the tabernacle and, through the koiné, the stage, see the day's second lesson at evening prayer, 2 Cor. 5.1–4, "For we knowe that if our earthlie house of this tabernacle be destroied, we haue a buylding *giuen* of God, *that is,* an house not made with hands, *but* eternal in the heauens. . . . For in dede we that are in this tabernacle, sigh and are burdened"; "tabernacle" renders the koiné σκήνους, which was both a tabernacle and the technical term for a wooden stage on which actors performed. (Am. 54, "Of this worlds Theatre . . . pageants play" corresponds with Heb. 9.11 of "a greater and more perfite Tabernacle [koiné, σκηνῆς], not made with hands, that is, not of this buylding.") See also Mark 9.5, "let vs make also thre tabernacles (koiné, σκηνὰς τρεῖς)."

The etymology was well established in the sixteenth century, see Scaliger, *Poetices,* 16, "Nomen [scenae] invenit ex eo, quod alia atque alia facies subinde appareret ex aediculis, quae olim quum e ramis ac frondibus conficerentur, ita sunt ab umbris et tabernaculis appellatae. Et sane verbum militare σκηνοῶ. Et apud Timeum Locum σκανός, haud longe abest ab ea significatione." The sixteenth century also associated tabernacle with pageant (*OED* sb 4a).

9–14. The dramatic is reinforced by the sestet's ambiguous punctuation: by placing commas after *sayes* in lines 10 and 11 and by the spelling of *Teares*, the 1611 and 1617 folios suggest that their editors understood the words to belong in the lady's mouth as rebuttals of direct discourse.

9–12. *when I . . . when I:* Replicating the rhetorical structure of the Geneva version's sidenote q to 2 Cor. 5.16, "When I praise my ministerie, I commende the power of God: when I commende our worthie factes, I praise the mightie power of God."

9. *play my part:* Compare Mark 9.40, "Whosoeuer is not against vs, is on our part."

10. *teares are but water:* so also with Blandina: "all her teares but water" (*FQ* VI.vi.42.9). Compare the father in Mark 9.24, who "crying with teares, said, Lord, I beleue."

11. *sigh:* Compare Paul's sighing, 2 Cor. 5.2 & 4, "therefore we sigh," and, "we that are in this tabernacle, sigh and are burdened."

12. *turnes hir selfe to laughter:* See morning prayer Ps. 52.7, "shall laugh him to scorne." Compare *Am.* 54.11–12, "but when I laugh she mocks, and when I cry / she laughes, and hardens euermore her hart" (corresponding with Ps. 80.6, "laugh vs to scorne").

14. *steele and flint:* also an apparatus used to produce fire.
     *still:* 1. yet; 2. quietly, not responding.

**Saturday 9 February:** *Morning Prayer:* Pss. 50–52, Mark 9. *Evening Prayer:* Pss. 53–55, 2 Cor. 5.

## Sonnet 19

Sonnet 19's covert allusions to the betrothal period are reminiscent of the intimacy of Sonnet 4. It is the first of two sonnets celebrating the arrival of spring, the other being Sonnet 70. Its celebrating spring agrees with a footnote attached to most sixteenth century editions of the *BCP*'s calendar and belonging to February 8: "As vpon this day, the Romanes began their spring, after Plinie." Sonnet 19, which corresponds to Quinquagesima Sunday 10 February, observes the calendar's instruction and for the subsequent third day celebrates the third announcement of the cuckoo's trumpet.

1. *Cuckow . . . messenger of Spring:* Spenser refers to the cuckoo again in *Am.* 85.3. Two lines of allusive thought converge here: 1. from ancient times the cuckoo was identified as the harbinger of spring (see Pliny, *Nat. Hist.*, 10.9.11.25, "procedit vere") and Spenser has accepted the standard association; 2. a more oblique vein of allusion begins with the second lesson at morning prayer, Mark 10, with its *precept:* "For the hardnes of your heart he wrote this precept vnto you." The precept warns against adultery because of marriage's indissoluble nature, "what God hathe coupled to gether, let not man separate. . . . Whosoeuer shal put away his wife and marie another, comitteth adulterie against her. And if a woman put away her housband, and be maried to another, she committeth adulterie" (Mark 10.5–12 passim. That Spenser intended the echo is confirmed by his unusual use of *precept* [11] – it occurs only twice elsewhere in the Spenser canon and not in *Amoretti* – and its unusual use in the Geneva Bible –

which normally uses 'commandment'). That the lady should not be separated from her betrothed is a stricture of the sonnet. From classical times adulterers and cuckoldry were associated with the cuckoo because of its habit of laying eggs in another's nest (see Pliny, *Nat. Hist.*, 10.9.11.27, "educat ergo subditum adulterato feta nido," and Plautus, *Asinaria*, 5.3, "Te cuculum uxor ex lustris rapit"). Spenser has thus used the biblical injunctions against separation and adultery to condemn his betrothed's absence as the cuckoo announces spring.

2. *trompet shrill:* the cacophonous mating call of the cuckoo — in contrast to the *anthemes sweet deuized* (6) of the other birds.

*thrise:* See headnote and Pliny, *Nat. Hist.*, 2.47.47.122, "Ver ergo aperit ... dies sextus Februarias ante idus." Spenser's use of the subsequent third day to celebrate the third announcement of the cuckoo's trumpet is confirmed by both Mark 10 and Luke 18.31–42, the day's Gospel, which contain, in identical words, Christ's third prediction of his rising again on the third day: "the third day he shal rise againe." Only in 1594 was Quinquagesima Sunday the third day after the beginning of the Roman spring.

4. *girland:* 1. garland; 2. figuratively, glory, see *Col* 498–99.

6. *anthemes:* from *antiphona,* a composition sung responsively by a divided choir.

*deuized:* trisyllabic; 1. invented; 2. etymologically, divided (from *dividere*), as in two-part antiphonal singing.

*anthemes . . . loues prayse:* the sonnet's secondary motif of love matches the day's Epistle, 1 Cor. 13, Paul's celebrated hymn in praise of love.

7. *that all the woods theyr ecchoes back rebounded:* Looks forward to the refrain in *Epith.;* see *FQ* VI.x.10.5 and passim: "That through the woods their Eccho did rebound." The stanza introduces the episode of the Graces dancing to Colin Clout's melody to which Sonnet 19 bears some resemblance, although Colin Clout pipes to a fourth grace, Elizabeth, who is present (16.6–8).

8. *as if they knew the meaning of their layes:* 1. as if the woods knew the meaning of the choirs' lays; 2. as if the woods knew the meaning of the woods' echoes.

10. *no word was heard:* Compare the presence and response of the second lesson at evening prayer, 2 Cor. 6.2, "I haue heard thee in a time accepted ... beholde now the accepted time, beholde now the daye of saluation." The Geneva Bible glosses Mark 10.6's precept about marrriage by stating that the only true test is "to returne to the institution of thinges, to trie them by Gods worde." The lady's silence is thus opposed to God's word.

11. *precept:* 1. a moral commandment particularly a biblical one; 2. legally an order or proclamation issued by a legal authority, such as a king, requiring the attendance of someone at a court (OED 4), a meaning sustained in the legal use of *rebell* (14).

*proudly:* 1. vaingloriously; 2. possibly lustfully, particularly following the phrase *Loues honor rayse.* The Geneva sidenote to Mark 10.15 explains that, "we must be ... voide of all pride and concupiscence."

12. *ydle:* vain.

*set at nought:* Compare the second lesson at morning prayer for the prior day, Mark 9.12, "the Sonne of man must ... be set at noght."

13. *turne to thee:* See evening prayer Ps. 60.1, "O turne thee vnto vs againe."

14. *ere Cuckow end:* A covert allusion to the time of the poet's marriage on 11 June 1594. Pliny recounts that the cuckoo appears in spring, changes its voice, and has disappeared by the rising of the dog-star (*Nat. Hist.*, 10.9.11.26, "occultatur

caniculae ortu"). The Glosse to *SC* 23 July identifies the reign of the dog-star with the middle of summer. (In the calendar to the 1561 *BCP* its beginning is indicated as 7 July, although it was sometimes calculated as early as 20 June.) The poet's separation from his betrothed should then be overcome by his marriage on 11 June before the disappearance of the cuckoo.

*rebell:* one who disobeys a legal summons or *precept;* as *re-bell* chosen possibly as a verbal continuance of *resounded* and *ecchoes back rebounded.*

Quinquagesima Sunday 10 February: *Epistle:* 1 Cor. 13.1–13. *Gospel:* Luke 18.31–43. *Morning Prayer:* Pss. 56–58, Mark 10. *Evening Prayer:* Pss. 59–61, 2 Cor. 6.

### Sonnet 20

The sonnet's conceit plays upon the common belief that the lion yields before the innocent (and indeed the prostrate). Spenser had developed the emblem in *FQ* I.iii.5–7, where Una's beauty and truth cause the lion to submit to her. Here the lady is impervious to the poet's suit and is revealed not as innocence which calms the lion but as cruelty beyond that of the lion.

1. *In vaine I seeke:* An exact rendering of the Vulgate version of morning prayer Ps. 63.10 (for Monday 11 February), *Ipsi vero in vanum quaesierunt* = In vain they did seek. Coverdale renders the verse, "These also that seeke the hurt of my soule: they shall go under the earth."
2. *myne humbled hart before her poure:* In direct imitation of morning prayer Ps. 62.8, "powre out your hearts before him."
3. *her foot she in my necke doth place:* Compare *FQ* V.iv.40.2–3. The phrase's biblical analogue is Josh. 10.24.
4. *floure:* the earth; see Ps. 63.10, "they shall go under the earth."
4–5. *tread my life downe in the lowly floure. / ... the Lyon that is Lord of power:* That the lion alone spares the suppliant was proverbial. see Pliny, *Nat. Hist.*, 8.19.48, "Leoni tantum ex feris clementia in supplices." That it spares the prostrate, see Ovid, *Tristia*, 3.5.33: "Corpora magnanimo satis est prostrasse leoni"; Erasmus, *Similia*, 611B, "Leo ... simplicibus ac prostratis parcit"; & Lynche, *Diella*, 21.9–12. The phrase's biblical analogue was Ps. 17.2 & 45.
5–7. *Lyon ... deuoure:* See Ps. 63.11, Geneva Bible, sidenote f, "shal ... be de-uoured with wilde beastes."
8. *silly lambe:* innocent — see *FQ* I.vi.10.
13–14. See *Am.* 41.13–14 for a similar concluding couplet.
14. *blooded:* bloodied or smeared with blood — perhaps as a first scent given to a hunting dog.

Monday 11 February: *Morning Prayer:* Pss. 62–64, Mark 11. *Evening Prayer:* Pss. 65–67, 2 Cor. 7.

### Sonnet 21

The sonnet's concern with *lustes impure* (8) is appropriate for a sonnet written for Shrove Tuesday 12 February.

1–4. The painting *topos* of the opening quatrain is identified more precisely as encaustic painting, an ancient technique whereby colors are dissolved in wax and then set by fire, by the terms *tempred* (2), technically the process of soften-ing wax by fire, and *inure* (9), artistically the burning of colors dissolved in wax into a surface by fire. The *topos* and its method correspond exactly to the striking metaphor which opens morning prayer Ps. 68.2 for Tuesday 12 February, "like as waxe melteth at the fire."

1. *worke of nature or of Art:* The question focuses on the contemporary debate concerning the place of art and nature in the artistic process. It matches the concern of the second lesson at evening prayer, 2 Cor. 8, which questions and proves the naturalness of the Corinthians' grace and love, "Therefore proue I the naturalnes of your loue" (v. 8. The Vulgate version, *vestrae charitatis ingenium bonum comprobans*, underscores the sonnet's question, because *ingenium* can mean both 1. *nature* [1] and 2. disposition or *temper* [2]).

2. *tempred:* contains a variety of general and technical significances: 1. in a predominantly Neo-Platonic context, mix elements together with one another in proper proportion — a sense taken up in *mixt by equall part* (3); 2. moisten or mix elements into a paste; 3. specifically, soften wax by heating (OED 13) ; 4. technically and artistically, prepare colors for use in painting by mixing with wax dissolved in fire; 5. bring to health, cure, a meaning taken up in *recure* (11).

   *feature:* 1. the shape or proportions of the face; 2. etymologically, that which *nature* creates, a creature (= *factura*), and, through its association with the Greek ποίησις, an artistic creation.

   *face:* corresponding to the third element of Ps. 68.2, Vulgate version, *Sicut fluit cera a facie ignis ... a facie Dei* = As wax melts before the face of the fire ... before the face of God."

5. *pleasance:* Contrast Am. 17.11–12, "the louely pleasance and the lofty pride, / cannot expressed be by any art."

6–14. Proverbial; see Smith, *Proverb Lore*, 485. See Petrarch, *Rime*, 154, "Le stelle, il cielo e gli elementi a prova."

6. *allure:* 1. entice, charm; 2. draw towards, as in *her smile me draws* (12).

7. *countenance:* disyllabic by syncopation.

9. *inure:* Spenser elsewhere uses the word (= in + ure = use) only to mean 1. put into operation, exercise; or 2. harden through use or discipline (see Am. 14.7 note). The hardening of the lady's eyes has the effect in line 10, the first of two contrasting effects, of setting the poet's life in *dismay*.

   Here Spenser has also used the word with a different etymology (= *in* + *urere* = to burn in) in its specific artistic context of encaustic painting. Pliny recounts (*Nat. Hist.*, 35.11.39.122), "Ceris pingere ac picturam inurere quis primus excogitaverit, non constat ... sed aliquanto vetustiores encaustae picturae exstitere ... quod profecto non fecisset nisi encaustica inventa." (In Holland's translation [1601], "As touching the feat of setting colours with waxe, and enamelling with fire, who first began and deuised the same, it is not knowne. ...") He also briefly describes the process (35.7.31.49), "cerae tinguntur (= *tempred* in its sense of moisten — see line 2 note) isdem his coloribus ad eas picturas, quae inuruntur. ..."(See 35.11.41.149.)

   Since the effect of the eyes of neo-Platonist ladies was to burn out the poet's *lusts impure*, the parallel and contrasting effect of the lady's looks is to *cure* the poet in line 11.

11. *recure:* 1. from *re-curare*, repair, restore to health — a sense introduced by *tempred* (2); 2. from *re-cour* = re-cover, possess again, save.

12. *me driues away:* In direct imitation of Ps. 68.2, "Like as the smoke vanisheth, so shalt thou driue them away." Compare the comfort of Am. 81.7–8, "that cloud of pride ... with smiles she driues away."

13. *train*: 1. from *trahere* = draw, draw by art or inducement, *allure*; 2. instruct, discipline, as in *inure* above.

14. *I neuer read in bookes*: Contrast the riposte in the day's second lesson at morning prayer, Mark 12.26, "haue ye not red in the boke of Moses." Compare Lynche, *Diella*, 4.4. "Such eloquence was neuer read in bookes." The sonnet thus concludes that the lady's eyes neither belong properly to the realm of *art*, nor, by implication, are they to be read of in the *book* (of *nature*). His working of the contemporary discussion is not dissimilar to Sidney, *AS* 71.1–5.

**Tuesday 12 February**: *Morning Prayer*: Ps. 68, Mark 12. *Evening Prayer*: Pss. 69–70, 2 Cor. 8.

### Sonnet 22

The sonnet, written to celebrate Ash Wednesday, the beginning of Lent (in 1594, Wednesday 13 February), is a loose paraphrase of Desportes' *Les Amours de Diane*, 39, "Solitaire et pensif dans un bois écarté" (see Kastner 67 and Lever 105 ff. for detailed comparisons):

> Solitaire et pensif dans un bois écarté,
> Bien loing du populaire et de la tourbe épesse
> Ie veux bastir un temple à ma seule Déesse,
> Pour appendre mes voeux à sa divinité.
>
> Là de jour et de nuict par moy sera chanté
> Le pouvoir de ses yeux, sa gloire et sa hautesse;
> Et, devôt, son beau nom i'invoqueray sans cesse,
> Quand ie seray pressé de quelque adversité.
>
> Mon oeil sera la lampe et la flamme immortelle,
> Qui me va consumant, servira de chandelle:
> Mon corps sera l'autel, et mes souspirs les voeux.
>
> Par mille et mille vers ie chanteray l'office:
> Puis épanchant mes pleurs, et coupant mes cheveux,
> I'y feray tous les iours de mon coeur sacrifice.

Lever quotes this version of Desportes' sonnet from the editions of 1573–89; Kastner quotes a version which derives from 1611 Rouen edition. The differences are minimal: 3 seule: fiere; 9 et la flamme immortelle: ardant continuelle; 10 Qui me va consumant, servira de chandelle: Devant l'image saint d'une dame si belle. Certainly Spenser's *sweet Saynt* (4) and *glorious ymage* (6) are closer to the 1611 Rouen "l'image saint." The paraphrase has been made to reflect not only the tenor and imagery of the special readings for Ash Wednesday, but also the *BCP*'s "Commination against Sinners" (which included Ps. 51), appointed for the first day of Lent (see Prescott, *Spenser's Poetry*, 596).

1. Spenser has substituted for Desportes' opening the occasional reference to Ash Wednesday.

*fit*: 1. made, fashioned (with associations of Latin, *fit* = it is made); 2. appropriate, as in *fit* (4).

*fast*: Besides acknowledging the start of the Lenten period, the sonnet's opening reflects the day's Epistle, Joel 2.12–18, with its instruction, "Turne you vnto me with all your heart, and with fasting" (v. 12), and its call to "sanctifie a fast."

2. *ought*: the verb opens and closes the Lenten section of the sequence, see *Am.* 68.13, "So let vs loue, deare loue, lyke as we ought."

*inclynd*: disposed, in the 16th century a synonym for *fit* (*OED* 5b).

4. *Saynt some seruice fit will find:* The liturgical resolve conforms to the intent of the day's second lesson at evening prayer, 2 Cor. 9, in which Paul addresses the necessity of "ministring to the Saintes" and concludes, "this seruice . . . supplieth the necessities of the Saintes" (v. 12; see also morning prayer Ps. 72.11, "all nations shall doe him seruice").

    *Saynt:* Spenser similarly addresses his betrothed in *Am.* 61.2 for Palm Sunday, "My souerayne saynt," and in *Epith.* 208, "For to receyue this Saynt with honour dew." He normally uses the address with a Neo-Platonic flavor, e.g., *Daph.* 379–82. (For a fuller discussion, see Bhattacherje 187–88.)

5. *Her temple fayre is built:* See headnote, Desportes, *Diane*, 39.3, "bastir un temple." The poet's temple contrasts with the physical temple of stones in the day's second lesson at morning prayer, Mark 13.1, "And as he went out of the Temple, one of his disciples said vnto him, Master, se what stones, and what buyldings *are here.* . . . Seest thou these great buyldings?" The intermingling of profane and religious was not uncommon – see Tasso, *Rime*, 2.18.10.7–10:

> Io per me vo' ch' anzi l'altar d'Amore
> Le sia in vittima il cor sacrato ed arso.
> Ed or dentro la mente un tempio l'ergo
> Ove sua forma il mio pensier figura. . . .

    By omitting to translate the opening two lines of Desportes' sonnet Spenser has discarded its motif of solitariness, for which the *locus classicus* was Dante's "selva oscura." (See Petrarch, *Rime*, 35, "Solo e pensoso i più deserti campi," and 176, "Per mezz' i boschi inospiti e selvaggi.")

6. *ymage:* See headnote, Desportes, *Diane* (Rouen, 1611), 39.10, "l'image saint," and its infrequent psalmic use in evening prayer Ps. 73.19, "image."

7. *day and night:* See headnote, Desportes, *Diane*, 39.5. See also evening prayer Ps. 74.17, "The day is thine, and the night is thine."

8. *lyke sacred priests that neuer thinke amisse:* The poet's thoughts will attend the lady's image with proper devotion, not like the priests condemned in the day's Gospel who bear only outward signs of repentance (Matt. 6.16–22).

10–11 *build an altar / . . . hart will sacrifise:* See headnote, Desportes, *Diane*, 39.11 &14.

10. *altar to appease her yre:* Joel 2.17 calls upon the Old Testament "Priests" to "wepe betwene the porche and the altar." As the Israelites were called to offer a sacrifice because God is "slowe to angre" (v. 13), so the poet will build an altar *to appease her yre* and, like them, offer a burnt holocaust.

11–12. *my hart will sacrifise, / burning in flames of pure and chast desyre:* The poet thus acknowledges the "Commination against Sinners," Ps. 51.16–17, "For thou desirest no sacrifice, els would I giue it thee: but thou delightest not in burnt offeringes. The sacrifice of God is a troubled spirit: a broken and contrite heart . . . ," as well as the instruction of the Geneva version's sidenote to Joel 2.13, "serue God with purenes of heart and not with ceremonies."

13. *O goddesse:* See headnote, Desportes, *Diane*, 39.3, "Déesse." The appellation was frequent among the French, see Du Bellay, *Olive*, 7, 14, 19, 41 & 114.

Ash Wednesday 13 February: *Epistle:* Joel 2.12–18. *Gospel:* Matt. 6.16–22. *Morning Prayer:* Pss. 71–72, Mark 13. *Evening Prayer:* Pss. 73–74, 2 Cor. 9. *Commination against Sinners:* Ps. 51.

## Sonnet 23

1. *Penelope:* The legend of Ulysses and Penelope is not one of Spenser's favorites; Ulysses is mentioned by name only in *Virgils Gnat*, while Penelope's wonder at

his return is commended only in *FQ* V.vii.39.2. The account of Penelope's web is found in *Od.* 19.137–51 & 24.120–41.

2. *Deuiz'd a Web*: Imitating *Od.* 24.128, "δόλον ... μερμήριξε" (*Deuiz'd a Web* or a deceit).

    *Deuiz'd*: 1. fashion, arrange; 2. since *Deuiz'd* derives from *dividere*, divide, take apart (*vnreaue* [4] (see *Am.* 19.6).

    *web*: 1. a woven fabric; the web of Penelope (from Πήνη = woof or web) was a work proverbially, 'never ending, always beginning.' Penelope, while waiting twenty years for the return of Ulysses, wove a winding sheet for her father-in-law Laertes by day and unwove it by night to thwart the importunate suitors whose offers she had promised to entertain when the web was complete. She became the emblem of a chaste wife, see *FQ* V.vii.39.2; 2. possibly a winding sheet such as Penelope wove for her father-in-law — as in *wynd* (14); 3. when associated with *Spyder* (13) , a subtly woven snare or entanglement.

    *deceaue*: 1. ensnare; 2. deceive — see Penelope's intent, *Od.* 19.137, "ἐγὼ δὲ δόλους τολυπεύω" (I wind a web of deceits). Spenser has accepted the Homeric pun on τολυπεύω: 1. *wind* off the corded wool for spinning; 2. accomplish, *bring to end* (10).

4. *vnreaue*: unravel; the only use by Spenser.
5. *subtile*: 1. finely woven (*sub* = under + *texla, tela* = woven stuff, *web* [2]); 2. ingenious, cleverly devised.
6. *th' importune suit*: 1. untimely; 2. pressing — like those urged on Penelope, see Horace, *Odes*, 3.10.11, "Penelope difficilis procis," and Claudian, *Carm. Min.* 30.31, "Penelope trahat arte procos fallatque."
7 & 12. *in many dayes ... whole years work*: Seemingly less an autobiographical detail than an allusion to the references to days and years in morning prayer and evening prayer Psalms for Thursday 14 February, Ps. 77.5, "I haue considered the dayes of olde: and the yeeres that are past," and Ps. 78.33, "their dayes did he consume in vanitie: and their yeeres in trouble." Penelope labored for three years.
7. *weaue*: Homer's ὑφαίνω could mean both to *weaue* and to *deceaue*.
9–10. *So when I thinke to end that I begonne, / I must begin and neuer bring to end*: In exact imitation of Homer, *Od.* 24.126, " οὔτ' ἐτελεύτα" (*neuer bring to end*). The phrase was proverbial, see Smith, *Proverb Lore*, 605. Compare Scudamour's account of the conquest of Amoret, which the "harder may be ended, then begonne" (*FQ* IV.x.3.4). The account of Scudamour and his "twenty valiant Knights" (8.6) seems to allude to the number of years that Ulysses struggled to reach Penelope (see Hamilton, *Faerie Queene*, 497).
11. *spils*: 1. wastes or spends time or labor fruitlessly (*OED* 6b); 2. kills, destroys — e.g., *Am.* 49.4.
13–14. *Such labour like the Spyders web I fynd, / whose fruitlesse worke is broken with least wynd*: contrasts with Penelope's false assurances, *Od.* 24.133, "μή μοι μεταμώνια νήματ' ὄληται" (I would not that my web should prove fruitless). νήμα was used specifically of a spider's web.
13. *Spyders*: In *Am.* 72 the lady, in her weaving, associates the poet with the spider (and herself with the bee), apparently because the letters B and S(P) are the initial letters to Boyle and Spenser.
14. *wynd*: a homonymic pun; 1. wind, breeze; see evening prayer Ps. 78.40, "they were euen a wind that passeth away"; 2. a winding, weaving (*OED.* sb. 2.2), as

in Penelope's winding sheet; 3. breath or words — the poet's suit is thus greeted with least words or silence.

Thursday 14 February: *Morning Prayer*: Pss. 75–77, Mark 14. *Evening Prayer*: Ps. 78, 2 Cor. 10.

## Sonnet 24

Pandora was sent by Zeus into the world to punish Prometheus for giving fire to humans (Hesiod, *Theogony*, 507–616). Zeus provided her with a box containing evils. Spenser has adapted the classical story, because the lady's task is to cleanse the poet's natural faults. Thus she is a new Pandora, sent as a scourge to cleanse from evil rather than punish with it. Her function as a scourge associates the sonnet with a range of incident in the readings for Friday 15 February; their detail suggests that Spenser felt little option but to compose for the day a sonnet concerned with scourging and beating.

1. *beauties wonderment*: wonderful beauty; *wonderment* is a favorite late word of Spenser occurring four times among the *amoretti* (*Am*. 3, 24, 69, 81).
2. *rare perfection*: See *Am*. 84.13; compare the "rare perfection" of Elizabeth I (*FQ* II.ii.41.7), who is also identified as Pandora in *TM* 578.
   *rare*: 1. uncommon; 2. splendid, fine.
5. *bitter balefull smart*: A common Spenserian alliterative pleonasm, e.g., *FQ* I.vii.25.8.
6. *vnwares*: 1. without warning; 2. unknowingly, either on the part of the lady or the poet.
7. *dart*: Cupid's arrows are everywhere in the sequence (e.g., *Am*. 4.8; 8.5–6; 16.4–8; 17.9; 24.7; 39.1–4; 57.8).
8 & 11. *new Pandora . . . scourge*: Compare the day's second lesson at morning prayer, Mark 15.15–20, which recounts in detail the scourging, "when he had scourged him," and death of Christ, and the second lesson at evening prayer, 2 Cor. 11, in which Paul refers repeatedly to his own beatings: "in stripes aboue measure" (v. 23), "fiue times receiued I fortie *stripes* saue one" (v. 24), "I was thrise beaten with roddes" (v. 25).
   *scourge*: 1. whip; 2. person regarded as an instrument of divine vengeance, see morning prayer Ps. 79.11, "O let the vengeance of thy seruants blood that is shed: be openly shewed upon the heathen in our sight." For the link between Pandora as a scourge and the day's readings, see Introduction, 33–35.
9. *Whom all the gods in councell*: In imitation of Mark 15.1, where the *councell* agrees to Christ's scourging, "the hie Priests helde a counsel with the Elders, and the Scribes, and the whole Council."
10–11. Compare the mission of the Blattant Beast (*FQ* VI.i.8.6–8), "Into this wicked world he forth was sent, / To be the plague and scourge of wretched men."
14. *gently beat*: See 2 Cor. 11.25, "I was thrise beaten with roddes." A somewhat risqué conclusion.

Friday 15 February: *Morning Prayer*: Pss. 79–81, Mark 15. *Evening Prayer*: Pss. 82–85, 2 Cor. 11.

## Sonnet 25

Sonnet 25 contains more twists of meaning than any other in the sequence, apart from Sonnet 6 with which it is associated. The cohesion of both sonnets is enhanced by their sustained punning and by words etymologically akin.

1–2. *Lyke dying lyfe endure, / . . . mysery:* The poet's question is in direct imitation of the psalmist's complaint in morning prayer Ps. 88.15 for Saturday 16 February, "I am in miserie, and like vnto him that is at the point to dye . . . thy terrours haue I suffered with a troubled minde."

> *endure:* As in *Am.* 6 Spenser is playing with the etymology of *endure* (*in* + *durus* = hard) meaning both 1. harden and 2. be sustained continuously.

3. *in terms vnsure:* 1. in an unsure state, condition or relationship with another; the phrase has a legal flavor; 2. possibly a reference to the poet's language (and poems) which remain unsure.

4. *depending:* hanging.

8. *to proue your powre:* Contrast Paul's comfort received in the second lesson at 'evening prayer, 2 Cor. 12.9, because his "power is made perfite through weakenes."

> *tride:* 1. tested, particularly in a legal sense; 2. endured.

9. *hardned brest:* The poet's reproving the lady accords with Christ's reproof of the apostles in the second lesson at morning prayer, Mark 16.14, "he reproued them of their vnbelief and hardnes (= *duritiam*) of heart."

10. *a close intent:* 1. a secret purpose; 2. but since *close* was associated with the heart because closet was used of the pericardium (see *Am.* 16.12 & 85.9 notes), Spenser may have intended a surgical echo, *in* + *tent* = to probe or open up; hence a secret opening up or disclosing of the lady's *hardned* heart.

> *shew me grace:* Contrasts with the assurance given Paul that "My grace is sufficient for thee" (2 Cor. 12.1).

11–14. Such consolation is commonplace in the volume, e.g., *Am.* 26, 51, 63, 69 & *Epith.* 32–33.

11. *abide:* as in *Am.* 6, *abide* reflects a variety of meanings all of which are earlier facets of the poem: 1. accept; 2. remain with continuously (*endure* (1), *tride* [8]); 3. suffer (*mysery* (2), *torment* [7]).

14. *meede:* reward, recompense.

**Saturday 16 February:** *Morning Prayer:* Pss. 86–88, Mark 16. *Evening Prayer:* Ps. 89, 2 Cor. 12.

## Sonnet 26

The definition of love as sweet-bitter originates with Sappho's ἔρος γλυκύπικρος (= sweet-bitter). Petrarch (*Trionfo del Amore*, 3.67–68) renders the phrase, "Vuoi veder in un cor diletto e tedio / dolce ed amaro." Spenser often plays with the paradox, beginning with Thomalin's Emblem, SC March, "Of Hony and of Gaule in loue there is store: / The Honye is much, but the Gaule is more." Yale 616 notes that "This is the first of two floral catalogues, symmetrically placed fourth after the Ash Wednesday sonnet and fourth before the Easter sonnet."

The sonnet's paradoxes contrasting the natural (but not emblematic) sweetness and bitterness of various trees and flowers mirror the structure of Paul's argument in 2 Cor. 6.1–11, the Epistle for the First Sunday in Lent, 17 February. Paul lists his afflictions in similarly pithy paradoxes linked by "yet": "as deceiuers, and yet true: As unknowen, and yet knowen: as dying, and beholde, we liue: as chastened, and yet not killed: As sorowing, and yet alway reioycing: as poore, and yet make manie riche: as hauing nothing, and yet possessing all things" (vv. 8–10).

The sonnet contains a series of *double entendres* on *Rose* (1), *Eglantine / pricketh* (3), *rynd* (5), *nut / pill* (6), and *root* (8). The sestet can also be construed bawdily. The suggestive assocations of the bitter/sweet paradox were standard; Whitney's emblem 165, "*Post amara dulcia,*" for example, reestablishes the paradox's former fescennine context in its opening line, "Sharpe prickes preserue the Rose," which is taken from Claudian's fescennine preamble to *Epith. Honorii,* which identifies the rose's pricks with the scratches a new bride might in defense inflict on the face of the bridegroom: "Non quisquam ... / Hyblaeos latebris nec spoliat favos / si fronti caveat, si timeat rubos; / Armat spina rosas, mella tegunt apes." (4.7–10). Whitney thus adds a genial context to his adage, "None merites sweete, who tasted not the sower," a translation of "Dulcia non meruit qui non gustavit amara."

1. *Sweet:* Paul also boasts of his *suavitate* (2 Cor. 6.6; Geneva, "kindnes").

    *Rose:* used bawdily of maidenhead, see Shakespeare, *AYLI* III.ii.112–3, "He that sweetest Rose will find, / Must find loue's prick and Rosalind."

2. *Iunipere, but sharpe his bough:* See Bart. Angl. 298ᵛ, describing the Juniper, "a rough tree with prickes, and many small leaues and sharpe."

3. *sweet is the Eglantine, but pricketh nere:* See Turner, *Herball,* 1. N.vi.a, "The eglentine is much like the common brere but the leues are swete and pleasant to smel to."

    *Eglantine:* (from *acus* = needle, *aculeus* = prickle) the needlework of *Am.*71 is woven about with "fragrant Eglantine"; see *SC* May 13 & *FQ* II.v.29.4–5, "fragrant Eglantine did spred / His pricking armes."

    *pricketh:* bawdily, copulate. Spenser's etymological play on *Eglantine* as prickle or needle compounds the sexual suggestiveness.

4. *Firbloome:* the bloom or exudation of the fir — its "sweet smelling Rosen" (Bart. Angl. 276ʳ) — frankincense; see *FQ* I.i.9.2.

5. *Cypresse:* Bart. Angl. 281ᵛ recounts that the Cypress is "most sweetest smelling," but that its "stocke and leaues ... be sowre."

    *rynd:* 1. bark; 2. bawdily, see line 6 note, *nut* & *pill.*

6. *nut, but bitter is his pill:* Compare Bart. Angl. 305 ʳ/ᵛ, "The fruit thereof hath a harde / rinde without and bitter, and a sweete kernell within."

    *pill:* peel; *nut* and *pill* can be read as references to the testicles — see Shakespeare, *AYLI* III.ii.110–11.

7. *broome-flowre, but yet sowre enough:* See Maplet 34, "Brome ... of some is called Mirica for the bitternesse of his taste."

8. *Moly, but his root is ill:* a fabulous herb having a white flower and black root. In *Od.* 10.304, Hermes gives it to Odysseus to protect him from Circe's charms. See Ovid, *Met.* 14.292, "moly vocant superi, nigra radice tenetur." See also Davies, *Epigrammes,* 36.1–2, "Homer of Moly, and Nepenthe sings, / Moly, the Gods most soueraigne hearbe diuine."

    *root:* a possible distant sense of copulation — see Shakespeare, *MWW* IV.i.46, "And that's a good root."

9–10. See headnote, Thomalin's Embleme, from Plautus, *Cistellaria,* 1.1.70–71, "Namque ecastor Amor et melle et felle est fecundissmus; / Gustui dat dulce, amarum ad satietatem usque oggerit." See *FQ* IV.x.1.2 & VI.xi.1.8–9. Chaucer has a similar phrase (*Rom. R.* 2295–6) "For euir of loue the sickernesse / Is meint with swete and bittirnesse." It became proverbial, see Wilson, *The Arte of Rhetorike,* 30, "The sweete hath his sower ioned with him."

11–12. *Easie things ... little store:* Proverbial, see Smith, *Proverb Lore,* 363. Compare the counsel of *HL* 167–68, "And hauing got it, may it more esteeme. / For things hard gotten, men more dearely deeme." A sense of unrelieved — but rationalized — physical (and sexual) hardship cannot be discounted.

13–14. *little paine, / that endlesse pleasure shall vnto me gaine:* Whitney 165 similarly concludes, "So after paines, our pleasures make vs glad, / But without sower, the sweete is hardlie had."

**First Sunday in Lent 17 February:** *Epistle:* 2 Cor. 6.1–11. *Gospel:* Matt. 4.1–12. *Morning Prayer:* Pss. 90–92, Luke 1.1–39. *Evening Prayer:* Pss. 93–94, 2 Cor. 13.

### Sonnet 27

The conceit of poetic immortality occurs four times in *Amoretti* (*Am.* 69.9–14, 75.11–14, 82.11–14). Its chief sources include Horace, *Odes*, 3.30 and 4.8–9, as well as Ovid, *Amores*, 1.15, and the conclusion to *Met.* 15.871–79. Its biblical analogue was the Blessed Virgin's claim in the *Magnificat* that she would be remembered forever after as blessed, "for beholde, from hence forthe shal all ages call me blessed." (Luke 1.48, with its Geneva version gloss, "This fauour that God hathe shewed me, shalbe spoken of for euer."). The *Magnificat* was a feature of the second lesson at morning prayer for Monday 18 February, Luke 1.40–80.

1. *proud:* In the *Magnificat* the proud are punished, God having "scattered the proude in the imagination of their hearts" (Luke 1.51).
2. *drosse vncleane:* the surface scum which covers the pure — a popular late word of Spenser used particularly in a Neo-Platonic context when contrasted with heavenly thoughts (see *Am.* 13.12, "that hinders heauenly thoughts with drossy slime") and "pure-sighted" eyes (see *HHL* 275–76).
3. *in the shade of death:* In direct imitation of Zacharias' prophecy in the *Benedictus,* Luke 1.79, "giue light to them that sit in darkenes, and in the shadowe of death" (v. 79).
        *shroud:* 1. cover, clothe; 2. prepare for burial with a winding sheet; 3. as a pleonasm with *shade,* screen or shade (*OED* 5).
4. *how euer now thereof ye little weene:* however inconsequential you now think death to be.
5/8. *Idoll / worship:* the terms mirror directly morning prayer Ps. 96.5–6, "As for the goddes of the heathen, they be but idoles: but it is the Lorde that made the heauens. Glorie and worship are before him," and Ps. 97.7, "Confounded bee all they that worship carued images, and that delight in vaine gods (Geneva version, "that glorie in idoles"): worship him all ye gods" (see Ps. 96.7 & 9).
        *gay beseene:* finely dressed, adorned.
9–11. See Ovid, *Met.* 15.878–79, "perque omnia saecula fama, siquid habent veri vatum praesagia, vivam." The contrast of the fleshly with the immortal echoes Ovid's earlier juxtaposition of his "brittle flesh" with his "better part" which "assured bee too clyme / Aloft aboue the starry skye. And all the world shall neuer / Be able for too quench my name" (Golding, 15.989–91).
10. *mention:* the action of commemorating particularly a name by speech or writing, e.g., *FQ* VI.x.28.9, where Spenser celebrates a fourth grace, Elizabeth, "To future age of her this mention may be made."

**Monday 18 February:** *Morning Prayer:* Pss. 95–97, Luke 1.40–80. *Evening Prayer:* Pss. 98–101, Gal. 1.

## Sonnets 28–33

Sonnets 28–33 bear no resemblance to the coincident scripture readings for the days, Tuesday 19 February to Sunday 24 February. Spenser has written a series of five sonnets which are broadly reminiscent of continental *exempla*, beginning with "My loue is lyke to yse," including a "laurell," "bay," and "smith" sonnet, and concluding in Sonnet 33 with an apology to Lodowick Bryskett for not having completed *The Faerie Queene*. This last sonnet suggests the companionship and hospitality of Bryskett and might infer Spenser's temporary absence from home and books.

## Sonnet 28

Daphne (δάφνη = laurel or bay tree), daughter of the river Peneus, which runs through Thessaly, was beloved by Phoebus. She resolved to spend her life a virgin and fled from him. Pursued, she sought the protection of the gods and was changed into a laurel tree. The legend is recounted by Ovid (*Met.* 1.452–567), where her transformation causes her to escape Phoebus. From Petrarch onwards a tradition developed in which Daphne is transformed because she refuses to submit. Petrarch identifies Laura and the laurel, see *Rime*, 34.12–14,

> Si vedrem poi per meraviglia inseme
> seder la Donna nostra sopra l'erba
> e far de le sue braccia a se stessa ombra.

3. *badg*: an emblem distinguishing the retainers of a noble person. Spenser also bears the badge because he is a poet (see *Am.* 29.7–8).
4. *inclind*: When Phoebus embraced the laurel tree, it inclined towards him, see Ovid, *Met.* 1.566–67.
7. *sweet infusion*: 1. inpouring, often of a Neo-Platonic tenor, of divine life and grace into the heart, see *HHB* 50; 2. poetic inspiration, e.g., *FQ* IV.ii.34.6, "infusion sweete of [Dan Chaucer's] spirit."
10. *on the Thessalian shore*: See Petrarch, *Rime*, 34.2, "a le tesaliche onde."
11. *in theyr reuengefull yre*: a Spenserian addition to the myth.
12. *transform*: an echo of Ovid, *Met.* 1.547, "mutando . . . figuram."
14. *leaf*: 1. laurel leaf; 2. homonymically, life, beloved, as in the phrase "lief and love" (*OED* 4b; see *Col* 16);
       *embrace*: as Apollo embraced the tree: "complexusque suis ramos" (Ovid, *Met.* 1.555; Golding 1.681, "in his armes embracing fast"). Ovid also uses the laurel as an emblem of sexual conquest, e.g., *Amores*, 2.12.1–2.

Tuesday 19 February: *Morning Prayer*: Pss. 102–3, Luke 2. *Evening Prayer*: Ps. 104, Gal. 2.

## Sonnet 29

The sonnet continues the laurel conceit of the preceding sonnet by contrasting its double function of crowning both victor and poet.

1. *depraue*: (de + pravus = crooked) 1. distort, make crooked my simple (= straightforward) meaning; 2. corrupt my simple (=honest) meaning.
2. *simple*: 1. unadorned; 2. without guile, honest; 3. poor.
       *disdaynfull scorne*: a typical Spenserian pleonasm.
5. *of the victours borne*: The Roman general in triumphal processions wore a laurel crown.
9. *conquest*: 1. spoils of war; 2. the gaining of a lady's affections or hand.

11. *triumph:* suggesting the Roman triumph in which the victorious general led in procession the spoils of war — see *Epith.* 243.

> *which my skill exceeds:* 1. which is greater than my skill; 2. which my skill is greater than.

12. *trump of fame:* see *Am.* 85.13, "Fame in her shrill trump shall thunder."

> *blaze:* 1. proclaim with a trumpet; 2. blazon, describe heraldically; 3. publish. The bay was impervious to the lightning's blaze.

14. *her victorious prayse:* 1. praise of the victorious lady; 2. the poet's victorious praise of the lady.

**Wednesday 20 February**: *Morning Prayer:* Ps. 105, Luke 3. *Evening Prayer:* Ps. 106, Gal. 3.

## Sonnet 30

Spenser has written for Thursday 21 February a more mannered sonnet than many in the sequence. It is a good specimen of the source problem that *Amoretti* poses. The contraries of ice and fire were a common *topos* among sonneteers and searching Petrarch or his heirs for exact antecedents to Sonnet 30 produces no satisfactory outcome. In any case Spenser makes of the conceit his own piece of artifice.

1. *ice . . . fire:* Renwick 199 cites Cazza, *Rime Scelte di Diversi Autori* (1587) 517, Scott, *Sonnets Elizabéthains*, 170 cites Watson, *Hecatompathia*, 43 and Séraphin, whom Watson himself cites, as possible sources of the sonnet. The original *exemplum* was Petrarch, *Rime*, 202, "D'un bel, chiaro, polito e vivo ghiaccio / move la fiamma che m'incende e strugge," but the conceit is frequent in Petrarch, e.g., *Rime*, 182 & 153.1, "Ite, caldi sospiri, al freddo core, / rompete il ghiaccio. . . ."

6. *delayd:* tempered, assuaged.

7. *boyling:* Yale 618 suggests a pun here on Elizabeth Boyle's name, *ling* being a diminutive.

> *sweat:* 1. perspiration; 2. homonymically and for rhyme, sweet; 3. life-blood (*OED* 1), opposed to *sencelesse cold* (11) and *course* (14 see note).

12–14. *kindle . . . kynd:* an etymological word-game, through the secondary meaning of *kindle*, to give birth to (see *Am.* 6.3 & 6 notes); the word-game is compounded by *gentle* (13), from *gens* = race, *kynd*.

14. *course of kynd:* 1. course of nature, the altering of which constitutes a *miraculous thing* (9); 2. homonymically, *corse* = corpse, dead body, as in *senceless cold* (10).

**Thursday 21 February**: *Morning Prayer:* Ps. 107, Luke 4. *Evening Prayer:* Pss. 108–9, Gal. 4.

## Sonnet 31

Spenser's advice in *FQ* VI.viii.2.1–6 to "gentle Ladies," which contrasts their natural tenderness with the results of proud hardheartedness, is relevant to the sonnet:

> And as ye soft and tender are by kynde,
>> Adornd with goodly gifts of beauties grace,
>> So be ye soft and tender eeke in mynde;
>> But cruelty and hardnesse from you chace,
>> That all your other praises will deface,
>> And from you turne the loue of men to hate.

1. *hard a hart: Am.* 18, 20, 32, 51, 54 are further variations on the lady's hardness of heart. The *locus classicus* was Petrarch, *Rime*, 265.1–4:

Aspro core e selvaggio cruda voglia
in dolce, umile, angelica figura,
se l'impreso rigor gran tempo dura,
avran di me poco onorata spoglia.

Petrarch's "selvaggio" (= savage, wild) and "cruda" (= not gentle, but also, as a substitute for *crudele*, = cruel, and through its associative *cruento*, = bloody) establish the contrast with Laura's "angelica figura." In *Rime*, 152 her "forma d'angel" is contrasted with a "cor di tigre o d'orsa." Spenser's working the conceit is scarcely new.

2. *goodly gifts of beauties grace:* See headnote, FQ VI.viii.2.2.

3. *depraues:* 1. etymologically, makes crooked (*de* + *pravus* = crooked); 2. perverts, corrupts (see *Am.* 29.1–2). The word is seldom used by Spenser and occurs here in two sonnets close together.

4. *ornaments:* see *Am.* 53.10, "the worlds most ornament"; the sonnet shares the image of bloody beasts with *Am.* 53.

   *deface:* doth deface; Spenser often deletes the expletive, e.g., FQ I.iii.5.5. See headnote, FQ VI.viii.2.5. 1. ravage, destroy (*de-facere* = unmake); 2. mar the face (*de-facies* = unface); 3. outface, outshine (*OED* v.5), as do the countenances of bloody beasts (see *Am.* 53).

6. *dreadfull countenaunce:* See *Am.* 53.3.

9. *her louely hew:* See *Am.* 53.6. *louely;* both beautiful and loving.

   *hew:* 1. form, figure, particularly of a Neo-Platonic variety; 2. complexion or color; see *Am.* 3.8 note.

10. *through sweet allurement:* See *Am.* 53.7.

12. *embrew:* stain; see *Am.* 53.11.

**Friday 22 February**: *Morning Prayer:* Pss. 110–13, Luke 5. *Evening Prayer:* Pss. 114–115, Gal. 5.

## Sonnet 32

The sonnet bears some resemblance to the battle, with its sexual undertones, between Artegall and Radigund in FQ V.v.7.6–8.2:

Like as a Smith that to his cunning feat
The stubborne mettall seeketh to subdew,
Soone as he feeles it mollifide with heat,
With his great yron sledge doth strongly on it beat.

So did Sir *Artegall* vpon her lay,
As if she had an yron anduile beene.

1. *paynefull:* 1. painstaking, careful; 2. since Spenser is the smith, full of suffering.

   *smith:* see FQ IV.v.35.6, where Care is a blacksmith.

   *feruent:* glowing.

2. *hardest yron:* through its association with adamant (ἀδάμας = hardest iron) it retains the sense of inflexible, unyielding (even, figuratively, in love; see *Am.* 42.10 note).

   *mollify:* 1. of iron, make soft; the smith and the artist who mollifies metal are linked by Horace, *Ars Poet.* 32–33, "faber imus ... molles imitabitur aere capillos" (see *Am.* 17.13 note); 2. of hearts, make tender; see headnote, FQ V.v.7.8 & FQ V.viii.1.8–9, "with melting pleasaunce mollifye / Their hardned hearts."

*yron:* Compare the first lesson at morning prayer for Saturday 23 February, Deut. 4.20, "But the Lord hathe taken you and broght you out of the yron fornace" — one of only a few occasions in the sequence when a sonnet shows some correspondence with a first lesson at morning prayer, see *Am.* 66.

4. *apply:* 1. etymologically (Lat. *plicare*), twist or shape; 2. accompanying use; in line 12 only the sense of attached is retained.

5–6. *cannot . . . soft awhit:* cannot soften at all.

7. *playnts:* 1. laments; 2. the sense of a complaint or poem, which the lady spurns, is also present.

9. *fit:* 1. a frenzy, particularly a (painful) feverish trance anticipating death (see *RT* 598); 2. a section of a poem or song as in *playnts* (7); see *Am.* 33.11 note.

11. *smit:* recalls the *smith* (1); compare the second lesson at morning prayer, Luke 6.29, "that smiteth thee. . . ."

13–14. *ashes . . . frosen:* The *ashes* suggest the floor of the now-cold forge, while *frosen* suggests the hardening again of the iron after its hot forging.

14. *stones:* See *Am.* 54.14. Compare morning prayer Ps. 119.25 (Vulgate), *Adhaesit pavimento (anima mea)*, where *pavimentum* primarily connotes a floor of "beaten stones."

**Saturday 23 February:** *Morning Prayer:* Pss. 116–18, Luke 6. *Evening Prayer:* Ps. 119.1–32, Gal. 6.

## Sonnet 33

The sonnet's reference to the yet-to-be-completed *The Faerie Queene* has been variously used to throw light on Spenser's overall intent and plan for the work. The date for which the sonnet was written, Sunday 24 February 1594, when combined with the reference in Sonnet 80 (for Tuesday 7 May) to the work's "six books," confirms Spenser's on-going intention to advance the work towards further completion.

1. *Great wrong:* Compare morning prayer Ps. 119.67 for 24 February, "Before I was troubled, I went wrong."

2. *my dear dred:* the object of awe and reverence; in *FQ* Elizabeth I is thus addressed in four out of six Proems.

3. *faëry:* trisyllabic.

4. *enlarge:* 1. magnify; 2. set at large, discharge (the sense Spenser normally attributes to the word, see *FQ* II.v.18.3).

5. *ludwick:* Lodowick Bryskett, an intimate of Spenser and his superior when Spenser was Clerk of the Council of Munster. Bryskett presents Spenser as a respected friend in his *A Discourse of Ciuill Life* and attributes to Spenser's mouth an apology for his unfinished "Faerie Queene" together with his intention to complete the work. ("Which work, as I haue already well entred into, if God shall please to spare me life that I may finish it according to my mind, your wish [M. Bryskett] will be in some sort accomplished, though perhaps not so effectually as you could desire" [Bryskett, *A Discourse of Ciuill Life* (1606) 27].) Bryskett had accompanied Philip Sidney in his travels and is identified as Thestylis by his elegy, *The Mourning Muse of Thestylis*, in the Astrophel collection. See *Col* 156.

   *to me aread:* 1. counsel or instruct, "learne of me" (see line 10 note, *taedious toyle*). In *FQ* I. Pr.1.7 the Muse similarly counsels Spenser: "Me, all too meane, the sacred Muse areeds"; 2. divine the meaning of obscure words, solve a riddle (*OED* 5) — looking forward to the challenge of the personal pun involved in *rudely writ* (8).

8. *rudely writ*: a pun on Bryskett's pseudonym: Thestylis = θής = rustic, rude + στύλος = writing. Bryskett, in his "Pastorall Aeglogue vpon the death of Sir Phillip Sidney" in the Astrophel collection, refers to his own verses as "rude rymes" (35).

10. *taedious toyle*: Spenser has made his sonnet reflect the readings, not for the 2nd Sunday in Lent, which in 1594 fell on 24 February, but for the feast of St. Matthias, whose date 24 February was. (Normally the feast would have been transferred to the closest following open day, the subsequent Monday.) The weariness his laboring on *FQ* has caused him, and his final prayer *to grawnt me rest* (13), acknowledge the relief promised in the Gospel for St. Matthias, Matt. 11.28–30: "Come vnto me, all ye that are wearie and laden, and I will ease you. Take my yoke on you, and learne of me . . . and ye shal finde rest vnto your soules."

11. *troublous fit*: See line 1 note, Ps. 119.67, "Before I was troubled."

   *fit*: as in *Am.* 32: 1. troubled feverishness; 2. a poem or section of a poem, e.g., *FQ* VII.vii.3.3; see Puttenham, *The Arte of English Poesie* 41: "This *Epithalamie* was deuided by breaches into three partes to serue for three seuerall fits or in times to be song"; hence this poem, which is troubling and preventing me from dedicating myself to a further section (*fit*) of *FQ*.

13. *Ceasse then*: Compare the second lesson at evening prayer, Eph. 1.16, "I cease not to giue thanks for you." See *Am.* 78.13.

   *grawnt me rest*: see Matt. 11.29, "ye shal finde rest vnto your soules."

**Sunday 24 February, Second Sunday in Lent**: *Epistle*: 1 Thess. 4.1–5. *Gospel*: Matt. 15.21–28. **St. Matthias**: *Epistle*: Acts 1.15–26. *Gospel*: Matt. 11.25–30. *Morning Prayer*: Ps. 119.33–72, Luke 7. *Evening Prayer*: Ps. 119.73–104, Eph. 1.

## Sonnet 34

A favorite Spenserian conceit, the *locus classicus* being Petrarch's "Passa la nave mia" (*Rime*, 189). Spenser's sonnet is his own and not a 'galley' sonnet such as Wyatt's translation, "My galley charged with forgetfulness." He employs the opening simile in various forms 6 times; see TM 141 & FQ I.vi.1.1, III.iv.53.3–4, V.ii.50.1, VI.iv.1.1, VI.xi.1.1 (for an identical line).

1–3. *Lyke as a ship . . . storme*: the *topos* exactly matches the episode, recounted in the second lesson at morning prayer for Monday 25 February, Luke 8.22–23, "And it came to passe on a certeine day, that he went into a ship with his disciples. and there came downe a storme . . . and they . . . were in ieopardie."

2. *conduct*: guidance.

4/10. *guyde / the lodestar of my lyfe*: A possible echo of morning prayer Ps. 119.105, "Thy worde is a lanterne (Vulgate, *lucerna* = lantern, guide or lodestar) vnto my feete: and a light vnto my pathes"; see lodestar (*OED* 2), which cites Douglas, *The xiii bukes of Enneados* (1513) Prologue, 8, "Lanterne, leid sterne, mirrour."

4. *course*: Compare the second lesson at evening prayer, Eph. 2.2, "in time past ye walked, according to the course of this worlde." Whitney 137 associates the endangered ship with the constant man and storms with the world.

   *astray*: Similiar to evening prayer Ps. 119.176, "I haue gone astray."

6. *direct*: 1. guide; 2. etymologically, make a course straight (*di* + *regere*) and hence contrasting with *wander* (4 & 7).

9. *Yet hope I well:* The poet's hope is for a calm similar to that wrought by Christ, who "rebuked the winde, and the waues of water: and they ceased, and it was calme" (Luke 8.24).

10. *Helice:* 1. the Greater Bear, see Ovid, *Fasti* 3.107–8: "Esse duas Arctos ... Helicen Graia carina notet." Ovid (*Met.* 13.293) notes that the constellation — in the northern hemisphere — never sets; 2. a possible play on Elizabeth Boyle's name, if *Helice* is read as Elis. The constellation was popular with Petrarch, see *Rime*, 33.2.

   *lodestar:* Spenser elsewhere associates *lodestar* with heavenly knowledge, e.g., TM 495, while Amoret is described as the "Lodestarre of all chaste affectione" (*FQ* III.vi.52.5).

11–12. *looke on me at last, / with louely light:* In imitation of morning prayer Ps. 119.135, "Shewe the light of thy countenance vpon thy seruant."

13. *carefull:* 1. full of care, worry; 2. full of love — with a pseudo-etymological play on *carus* = dear, beloved (see *Am.* 1.14 note).

   *comfortlesse:* The poet's state persists despite the counsel of Luke 8.48, "Be of good comfort."

14. *secret:* Relief from the poet's burden is intimated by Christ's maxim, Luke 8.17, "For nothing is secret, that shal not be euident; nether any thing hid, that shal not be knowen, and come to light."

**Monday 25 February**: *Morning Prayer:* Ps. 119.105–144, Luke 8. *Evening Prayer:* Ps. 119.145–176, Eph. 2.

### Sonnet 35

Sonnet 35 is repeated later in the sequence as Sonnet 83 with a single verbal change (6, hauing it (*Am.* 35): seeing it (*Am.* 83).

The sonnet is a fine example of Spenser's syncretic ability to encapsulate and reshape a wide variety of coinciding biblical and classical sources into a poem. Firstly the sonnet corresponds with the detail in the second lesson at morning prayer for Thursday 26 February, Luke 9, which contains the accounts of Christ's feeding the hungry multitude and the transfiguration. As well, Spenser has recalled the classical *topos* of Narcissus, drawing on Golding's translation of Ovid, *Met.* 13.339–510, especially Narcissus' exclamation, "inopem me copia fecit." (For Spenser's use of the Narcissus myth, see Edwards 63ff.) Finally, the later part of the sonnet, with its lowly estimation of the world, owes much to the judgement that Spenser provides Meliboe in his discourse on the quiet life (*FQ* VI.ix.20–30). The relevant lines and phrases of the conversation between Meliboe and Calidore are: "That hauing small, yet doe I not complaine / Of want, ne wish for more it to augment, / But doe my self, with that I haue, content (20.3–5) ... drinke of euery brooke (23.9) ... youth in vaine (25.4) ... the knight with greedy eare ... was rapt with double rauishment, / Both of his speach that wrought him great content, / And also of the obiect of his vew, / On which his hungry eye was alwayes bent (26.4–7).... That all this worlds gay showes, which we admire, Be but vaine shadowes (27.4–5) ... behold / The glorie of the great (28.1–2) ... in greatest store" (30.4).

1–2. *My hungry eyes through greedy couetize / still to behold the obiect of their paine:* An adaptation of Golding's rendering, 3.546, "With greedie eyes he gazeth still vppon the falced face," of Ovid, *Met.* 3.439, "spectat inexpleto mendacem lumine formam"; Spenser has even copied Golding's gratuitous *still*, included by both poets for metrical purposes. See also headnote, *FQ* VI.ix.26.7 and 26.1.

Spenser has also transferred the "hunger" of Luke 9 to the *eyes; eyes* then finds a correspondence in the parallel openings of morning prayer Ps. 121, "I will lift vp mine eyes vnto the hilles," and Ps. 123, "Vnto thee lift I vp mine eyes."

2. *behold:* See headnote, *FQ* VI.ix.30.4.

> *obiect of their paine:* See headnote, *FQ* VI.ix.26.6. The cause of the poet's pain, as for Narcissus, is the face of the lady.

> *paine:* 1. suffering; 2. punishment.

3. *contentment:* See headnote, *FQ* VI.ix.20.5.

> *suffize:* found neither in Golding's translation nor Meliboe's speech, but a clear echo of Luke 9.17, where the crowd "did all eat, and were satisfied" (Vulgate, *saturati sunt*, in the parallel synoptic passages, "suffized" [see Matt. 14.20 & Mark 8.8]).

4. *but hauing pine:* imitating Golding, 3.554, "That hath so pinde (Ovid, "tabuerit") away as I."

> *hauing not complaine:* See headnote, *FQ* VI.ix.20.3.

5. *gaze on it the more:* See headnote, *FQ* VI.ix.20.4.

7. *Narcissus:* Rather than the substance which cast the shadow, Narcissus loved the shadow itself and thus starved. Spenser alludes to the fact in *FQ* III.ii.44.4–6, where Britomart compares herself to "*Cephisus* foolish child" and explains that she does "feed on shadowes, whiles I die for food."

> *vaine:* imitating Ovid's epithet, "credule" (*Met.* 3.432); 1. idle; 2. foolish. See headnote, *FQ* VI.ix.25.4. Spenser elsewhere describes Narcissus as "foolish Narcisse" (*FQ* III.vi.45.5; see Golding, 3.535, "foolish elfe").

> *amazement:* 1. confusion; 2. infatuation (see *Am.* 16.3 note). Like the "amazement" of Narcissus the disciples "were all amased" (Luke 9.43; Vulgate, *Stupebant*) at Christ's curing of the possessed man. See Golding, 3.516–17. The descriptions of the *amazement* in the Vulgate and Ovid coincide: Vulgate, "Stupebant autem omnes . . . omnibusque mirantibus in omnibus quae faciebat"; Ovid, *Met.* 3.418–24, "Adstupet . . . cunctaque miratur, quibus est mirabilis ipse."

8. *so plenty makes me poore:* a translation of Ovid's, "inopem me copia fecit" (*Met.* 3.466), which Golding renders "my plentie makes me poore" (3.582). It became proverbial (see Smith, *Proverb Lore*, 619) and was a favorite adage of Spenser's, who made it the emblem to *SC* Sept., 261, with its gloss,

> This is the saying of Narcissus in Ouid. For when the foolishe boye by beholding hys face in the brooke, fell in loue with his owne likenesse: and not hable to content him selfe with much looking thereon, he cryed out, that plentye made him poore, meaning that much gazing had bereft him of sence.

> The proverb is also used to describe the fourth deadly sin, greed or covetousness, in *FQ* I.iv.29.3–4.

10. *brooke:* See headnote, *FQ* VI.ix.23.9; 1. they enjoy nothing else; 2. particularly of food, they can find nourishment in nothing else; 3. figuratively, *endure* (12), as in the saying, 'they could stomach nothing else.'

12. *can no more endure on them to looke:* During Christ's transfiguration the disciples could not bear to look upon his glory. The effect is used in *FQ* to illustrate the splendor of Dame Nature's face: the disciples, "When they their glorious Lord in strange disguise / Transfigur'd sawe; his garments so did daze their eyes." The glory was such "That eye of wight could not indure to view." (VII.vii.6.5 and 7.8–9).

13–14. *All this worlds glory seemth vayne to me, / and al their showes but shadowes:* See headnote, *FQ* VI.ix.27.4–5. In direct imitation of Christ's maxim in the second lesson at morning prayer about the vainness of the world, "what auantageth it a man, if he winne the whole worlde, and destroye him self" (Luke 9.25; *Am.* 17.3, "this worlds worthlesse glory," finds an identical correspondence with the parallel verse, Mark 8.36).

14. *shadowes:* At the transfiguration the true glory of Christ was covered by shadow ("there came a cloude and ouershadowed them" [Luke 9.34; Vulgate, *obumbravit eos*]). By contrast Narcissus saw the shadow and thought it the true substance (Ovid, *Met.* 3.434, "quam cernis, imaginis umbra est").

**Tuesday 26 February**: *Morning Prayer*: Pss. 120–125, Luke 9. *Evening Prayer*: Pss. 126–131, Eph. 3.

## Sonnet 36

1. *Tell me . . . woes:* The lament corresponds directly with Christ's condemnation of various cities that rejected him in the second lesson at morning prayer for Wednesday 27 February, Luke 10.12–13, "I say to you . . . Wo *be* to thee, Chorazin: wo *be* to thee, Beth-saida."

3. *pining:* See *Ana.* 59–60, "So now I languish, till he please / my pining anguish to appease."

   *languor:* 1. woeful plight or imprisonment; 2. sickness.

   *spend:* 1. wear out; 2. pay out for a *purchace* (3), see the payment provided by the Good Samaritan in Luke 10.35, "spendest."

4. *aswagement:* 1. mitigation, softening; 2. an assuaging medicine, a lenitive (for the preceding *languor* — such as the Good Samaritan poured into the wounds of the thieves' victim in Luke 10.34; the other occasion when Spenser uses the word also intends medicine [*FQ* VI.v.40.4].)

5–8. A Petrarchist commonplace, e.g., Petrarch, *Rime*, 150.1–4:

   "Che fai alma? che pensi? avrem mai pace?

   avrem mai tregua? od avrem guerra eterna?"

   "Che fia di noi, non so, ma in quel ch 'io scerna

   a' suoi begli occhi il mal nostro non piace."

5. *peace:* The poet's inability to obtain peace contrasts with the Lucan greeting, "Peace be to this house," and its approval of "the sonne of peace," upon whom "your peace shal rest" (Luke 10.5–6).

6. *make agreement with her thrilling eyes:* An identical trucial thought to *Am.* 12.1–2. Contrast the eyes' happiness in Luke 10.23, "Blessed *are* the eyes, which se that ye se."

   *thrilling:* 1. eyes that pierce; 2. as a substitute for 'thralling,' eyes that capture or enthrall.

9. *shewed:* disyllabic.

   *all extremityes:* 1. utmost severities; 2. extremes which exclude the mean or, by transference, moderation.

11. *whose lyfe . . . ye despyse:* The complaint imitates Christ's in Luke 10.16, "he that despiseth you, despiseth me: and he that despiseth me, despiseth him that sent me."

**Wednesday 27 February**: *Morning Prayer*: Pss. 132–135, Luke 10. *Evening Prayer*: Pss. 136–138, Ephes. 4.

## Sonnet 37

1 & 14. *golden tresses & fetters, though they golden bee:* Proverbial, see Smith, *Proverb Lore,* 258, and a Petrarchist commonplace. Compare *FQ* V.viii.1.7, "wrapt in fetters of a golden tresse," in a passage from which *Am.* 39 also draws (see *Am.* 39.7–8 note).

 *golden tresses:* 1. locks of golden hair; 2. because the suns rays were termed *tresses,* particularly *golden tresses,* the notion of the sun's rays dazzling the looker persists throughout the poem.

1. *guyle:* Through the saying, 'Fickle under her lock' — to have guile in her head — hair and guile were commonly associated.

2. *net:* 1. a fine mesh used confining the hair; 2. a *snare* or *trap.*

4. *heare:* Spenser evidently intends that its homonym 'hear' be suggested by *told.*

5–8. The second quatrain imitates exactly the dominant feature of Pss. 140, 141 & 142 at both morning and evening prayer for Thursday 28 February, the casting of the eyes as "snares," "trappes" and "nettes." The final verses to Ps. 141.9–11 associate all three images with the eyes: "But mine eyes looke vnto thee. ... Keepe me from the snare which they haue layde for mee: and from the trappes of the wicked doers. Let the vngodly fall into their owne nettes together: and let me euer escape them." (See Ps. 140.5, "The proude haue layed a snare for me, and spred a net abroade with cordes: yea, and set trappes in my way," and Ps. 142.3, "in the way wherein I walked, haue they priuily laid a snare for me.") The general theme of guile and ambush matches the wider motif of entrapment of the day's second lesson at morning prayer, Luke 11, as the scribes and pharisees were "laying wait for him [Christ]" (v. 54).

7. *being caught may craftily enfold:* See *FQ* II.i.4.1–5.

 *enfold:* 1. capture; 2. plait (as in the Geneva version's stricture not "to folde" the hair, 1 Tim. 2.9, sidenote).

9. *Take heed therefore, myne eyes:* The caution directly imitates Christ's admonition in Luke 11.34–35: "The light of the bodie is the eye.... Take hede therefore, that the light which is in thee, be not darkenes." The formula is repeated in the day's second lesson at evening prayer, Eph. 5.15, "Take hede therefore, that ye walke ... not as fooles."

12. *bands:* 1. chains, fetters; 2. fillets which confine the hair.

13. *Fondnesse:* 1. foolishness (see line 9 note, Eph. 5.15, "fooles"); 2. affection; 3. the implied sense of beguilement towards an ambush (*OED* v 4b) is probably also intended (see *FQ* III.i.10.8 & IV.x.24.8).

**Thursday 28 February**: *Morning Prayer:* Pss. 139–141, Luke 11. *Evening Prayer:* Pss. 142–143, Ephes. 5.

## Sonnet 38

1. *Arion:* The sonnet is constructed around Ovid's account of the myth of Arion (*Fasti,* 2.79–118), who, having jumped into the sea to deliver himself from the hands of a crew of merciless pirates, charmed a dolphin with his harp, and was carried to safety. Spenser alludes to the myth in the epithalamial passage recounting the marriage of the Thames and Medway (*FQ* IV.xi.23). His use of the myth here matches the harp (lute) and its association with deliverance from water in morning prayer Ps. 144 for Friday 1 March, "deliuer me, and take me out of the great waters, from the hand of strange children.... I will sing ... prayses vnto thee vpon a ten stringed Lute" (vv. 7–9).

*wracke:* 1. wreck; 2. ruin, as in "rack and ruin"; 3. *wracke*, through its homonym rack, suggests the storm clouds which the tempest racks up (see *Am.* 46.12 note).

2. *greedy:* in Ovid's account it is the pirate crew who are greedy.

3. *harp:* see the recurrent image of the stringed instrument in evening prayer Ps. 147.7, "Sing praises vpon the harpe"; Ps. 149.3, "with Tarbret and Harpe"; Ps. 150.3, "vpon the Lute and Harpe." Coverdale uses 'harp' and 'lute' interchangeably for *psalterium* and *cithara: psalterium* becoming "Lute" in Ps. 144.9 and "Harpe" in Ps. 149.3, while *cithara* becomes "Harpe" in Ps. 147.7 & Ps. 150.3; in Ovid Arion's instrument is the *cithara*, "ille sedens citharamque tenet" (*Fasti*, 2.115).

4. *from death to ease:* Contrast the rich man's resolve in the second lesson at morning prayer, Luke 12.19, to "liue at ease."

5–6. *musick ... / ... dainty eares:* See *FQ* IV.xi.23.2 & 5, "dainty musicke ... eares."

    *dainty:* 1. delicate — in contrast to the poet's *rude musick* (5); 2. the sense of worthy (the etymon of *dainty* is *dignitatem* = worth) cannot be discounted.

5. *skill:* expertise in music (Ovid's *arte* [*Fasti*, 2.96]) — used also of Orpheus' music in *Am.* 44.8.

7. *the dreadfull tempest ... appease:* See *Fasti*, 2.116, "aequoreas carmine mulcet (= *appease*) aquas."

8. *Dolphin:* here, seemingly, a device betokening pride or anger; the dolphin customarily indicated guile.

10. *decayse:* loses strength, dies (see *FQ* I.vi.48.7); see Ps. 144.14, "That there be no decay" — an infrequent biblical term and confined here to Coverdale's translation.

11. *can it saue or spill, / to spill were pitty, but to saue were prayse:* The phrase was proverbial — see Smith, *Proverb Lore*, 265 and Spenser's definition of Mercy, "As it is greater prayse to saue, then spill" (*FQ* V.x.2.8; see *Am.* 49.4).

    *spill:* kill, destroy.

**Friday 1 March:** *Morning Prayer:* Pss. 144–46, Luke 12. *Evening Prayer:* Pss. 147–50, Ephes. 6.

## Sonnet 39

1–2. *Sweet smile ... mothers:* Spenser's favorite Homeric epithet, φιλομμειδής Ἀφροδίτη (loving-to-smile Venus; see Homer *Od.* 8.362, *Il.* 3.424, and *Hymn*, 5.65 & 155); see *FQ* IV.x.47.8, "Mother of laughter," *Ana.* 33, "his mother closely smiling" and *Am.* 17.10. In *FQ* IV. Pr.5.5–8 Venus, the "sweete smyling Mother," prompted by her son, bestows from heaven "drops of melting loue / Deawd with ambrosiall kisses."

    The epithet likely corresponds to the uncommon concluding verse (a direct translation of the Hebrew and not in the Vulgate) of morning prayer Psalm for Saturday 2 March, Ps. 2.12, "Kisse the sonne least he be angrie." In the sonnet the smiles of Venus are used *to temper angry loue* (3). See also v. 4: "He that dwelleth in heauen shal laugh them to scorne (Vulgate, *irridebit*): the Lord shal haue them in derision."

4. *thundring dart:* thundering Jove ('Jove tonans' or Ζεὺς βροντιαῖος), the traditional epithet from Homer onwards.

7–8. *melting plesance ... hart robbing gladnesse:* Contrast the emasculating effect that "beauties louely baite" can have on mighty warriors (*FQ* V.viii.1.6–9):

> Drawne with the powre of an heart-robbing eye,
> And wrapt in fetters of a golden tresse,
> That can with melting pleasaunce mollifye
> Their hardned hearts . . .

7–10. The trance recalls the heavenly rapture, to which Paul alludes in the second
lesson at evening prayer, Phil. 1.22–23, "what to chose I know not. For I am
greatly in doute on bothe sides, desiring to be losed (Vulgate, *desiderium habens
dissolvi* = melting) and to be with Christ, which is beste of all." See Petrarch,
*Rime*, 193.1–8, lines also indebted to Paul's vision in Phil. 1.22 (& 2 Cor. 12.2),
particularly "ratto per man d'amor, né so ben dove" (the equivalent of Paul's "I
know not").

> Pasco la mente d'un sì nobil cibo
> ch' ambrosia e nettar non invidio a Giove;
> ché, sol mirando, oblio ne l' alma piove
> d'ogni altro dolce, e Lete al fondo bibo.
>
> Talor ch' odo dir cose e 'in cor describo
> per che da sospirar sempre ritrove,
> ratto per man d'Amor, né so ben dove,
> doppia dolcezza in un volto delibo;

7. *melting:* See line 1 note, *FQ* IV. Pr.5.5.
8. *hart robbing gladnesse:* F12, *hart-robbing*.
9. *rapt:* See lines 7–10 note, Petrarch, *Rime*, 193.7, "ratto."
   *ioy:* See Phil. 1.18, "and I therein ioye; yea, and with ioye. . . ."
   *heauenly madnes:* different from the poetic "heauenly fury" of *Am.* 85.11.
13. *Nectar or Ambrosiall meat:* See lines 7–10 note, Petrarch, *Rime*, 193.2, "ambrosia
   e nettar."
14. *I did eat:* Luke 13, the day's second lesson at morning prayer, concludes a series
   of metaphors by asserting that, although some may search for the kingdom of
   God claiming "we haue eaten and drunke in thy presence" (v. 26), it will be
   others who "shal sit at table in the kingdome of God" (v. 29).

Saturday 2 March: *Morning Prayer: Pss.* 1–5, Luke 13. *Evening Prayer: Pss.* 6–8, Phil. 1.

## Sonnet 40

Sonnet 40 continues to concern itself with the lady's smile but shifts the principal
*locus* of its mythical comparison from Venus to Hero.

1. *Mark:* observe. Compare the word's infrequent biblical use in the second lesson
   at morning prayer for Sunday 3 March, the Third Sunday in Lent, Luke 14.7,
   "he marked how they chose out the chief roumes."
   *amiable:* 1. friendly (French, *amiable*); 2. or worthy to be loved (French,
   *aimable*).
2. *lyken:* The *comparatio* is a stock Spenserian device; *lyken* introduces a dispersed
   polyptoton, *Lykest* (5), *likewise* (13).
3–4. *each eyelid . . . / an hundred Graces:* The *topos* of the *eyelid* corresponds exactly
   to the striking feature of morning prayer Ps. 11.5, "his eye lids tryeth the
   children of men." E. K.'s gloss to *SC* June, 25, explains "that in Heroes eyther
   eye there satte a hundred graces. And by that authoritye, thys same Poete in his
   Pageaunts sayth. An hundred Graces on her eyeledde satte." (Upton 1.414 cites

Musaeus [*Hero & Leander*, 63–65], "οἱ δὲ παλαιοὶ / Τρεῖς Κάριτας ψεύσαντο πεφυκέναι. εἰς δέ τις ᾿Ηροῦς / Ὀφθαλμὸς γελόων ἑκατὸν Χαρίτεσσι τεθήλει.") Belphoebe is similarly described, *FQ* II.iii.25.1 (see *HB* 253–56).

5. *simple wit:* not the "deep wit" needed to unravel the riddle of *Am.* 43.13 — see *Am.* 43.13 & 14 notes.

6–7. *fayre sunshine in somers day . . . dreadfull storme:* See *FQ* IV.x.44. passim, where Spenser expands the image of the smiling-Venus: "Great *Venus* . . . Does fayrest shine . . . That with thy smyling looke . . . makst the stormes to flie . . . And heauens laugh, and al the world shew ioyous cheare."

6–8. *fayre sunshine . . . thrugh the broad world doth spred his goodly ray:* Johnson, in "*Amoretti* and the Art of the Liturgy" 54, suggests the elements of the poet's *comparatio* accord with the contrast between light and dark in the Sunday's Epistle, Eph. 5.1–15, "For ye were once darkenes, but are now light in the Lord: walke as children of light" (v. 8; see v. 13). See Paul's upholding the Philippians as lights to the world in the second lesson at evening prayer, Phil. 2.15–16: "among whome ye shine as lights in the worlde, Holding forthe the worde of life, that I may reioyce in the day of Christ."

9. *bird:* Compare the opening detail of morning prayer Ps. 11.1, "that she should flee as a bird vnto the hill."

   *spray:* a new slender shoot or branch — following Musaeus' τεθήλει (= bloom freshly).

10. *euery beast that to his den was fled:* Reflects the detail and simile of morning prayer Ps. 10.8–9, "priuily in his lurking dennes . . . euen as a Lion lurketh he in his denne."

11. *comes forth afresh:* corresponding to Musaeus' πεφυκέναι (= came forth afresh; translated by Upton 1.414 as *pullulabat* = come forth as a young bird or plant).

**Sunday 3 March, Third Sunday in Lent:** *Epistle:* Ephes. 5.1–15. *Gospel:* Luke 11.14–29. *Morning Prayer:* Pss. 9–11, Luke 14. *Evening Prayer:* Pss. 12–14, Phil. 2.

## Sonnet 41

1–4. A rhetorical *divisio* — the first of three occasions when the device is used for days within the same week (see *Am.* 43 & 46).

4. *skill:* reason: right reason can partly restore fallen will.

8. *lost:* The sonnet reflects — in a limited manner — the celebrated aphorism which concludes all three parables in the second lesson at morning prayer for Monday 4 March, Luke 15, the hundred sheep of which one is lost, the woman who loses one piece of silver, and the prodigal son — "that which is lost" is found (vv. 4, 6, 8, 9, 24, 31; see the second lesson at evening prayer Phil. 3.8, "Yea doubtles I thinke all things but losse for the excellent knowledge sake of Christ Iesus my Lord, for whome I haue counted all things losse.")

13–14. *O fayrest fayre:* See *Am.* 20.13–14 for a like final couplet.

13. *neuer it be named:* See morning prayer Ps. 16.5, "neither make mention of their names within my lippes."

9 & 14. *glorious . . . shame:* Phil. 3.19 extends a similar caution by condemning those "*whose* glory *is* to their shame, which minde earthlie things." (The prodigal son's return is glossed by the Geneva version, "therefore was ashamed thereof" [sidenote h].)

**Monday 4 March:** *Morning Prayer:* Pss. 15–17, Luke 15. *Evening Prayer:* Ps. 18, Phil. 3.

## Sonnet 42

1–2. *tormenteth ... pleasing ... extreamest paine:* The *pleasing* nature of the poet's *torment* and *paine* contrasts with that of the rich man in the parable of Lazarus in the second lesson at morning prayer for Tuesday 5 March, Luke 16, who is "in hel in torments" (v. 23) and "tormented in this flame" (v. 24); he is advised by Abraham, "Sonne, remember that thou in thy life time receiuedst thy plea- sures, and likewise Lazarus paines; now therefore is he comforted, and thou art tormented" (v. 25; see v. 28, "this place of torment").

4. *loue ... my bane:* See *Am.* 47.13.

   *bane:* 1. destruction, murder; 2. poison — as in *Am.* 47.13; 3. the first in- stance in the sonnet intimating betrothal, *bane* (and its plural *banes*) being the public proclamations of the forthcoming marriage, whose intent the poet will gladly *embrace.*

6. *ioy ... to remayne:* For the same construction, see *Am.* 71, "I Ioy to see...." Compare the second lesson at evening prayer, Phil. 4.7, "my ... beloued and longed for, my ioy and my crowne."

8–11. Compare Petrarch, *Rime,* 76.9–12:

> e come vero prigioniero afflitto
>
> de le catene mie gran parte porto,
>
> e'l cor negli occhi e ne la fronte ò scritto.

8. *for pledge:* 1. for a surety; 2. in its figurative sense, for a token of mutual love in marriage — see *FQ* IV.x.55.7–8. "The pledge of faith, her hand engaged held, / Like warie Hynd ... ," and *Epith.* 239, "your hand, / The pledge of all our band."

   *hart:* 1. heart; 2. the sense of a hart with its emblematic ties to marriage (as in the preceding "Hynd") is also implied.

9. *start:* 1. depart, desert; 2. of a hart, leave its hiding place (*OED* 17).

10. *adamant:* disyllabic by syncopation: 1. unbreakable (ἀδάμας) used of steel, iron and the diamond, and betokening constancy in faith — in earlier literature it also carried the sense of "unwedded"; 2. intensely loving (*ad* + *amans* = loving deeply).

   *adamant chayne:* a commonplace, see Seneca, *Hercules Furens,* 807, "Ada- mante texto vincire."

11. *wandring loues:* 1. restless; 2. wanton — e.g., *FQ* II.v.34.2.

   *peruart:* 1. turn from the right direction — as in *wandring;* 2. subvert, ruin.

12. *his:* its, heart's. 1611 changes *his* to *in.*

   *safe assurance:* 1. confidence, steadiness; 2. by implication, betrothal; in *FQ* I.ii.27.1 the words "safe assurance" constitute the plighting of a troth (See *FQ* IV.i.15.9, IV.ix.16.4, & *Epith.* 354).

14. *doe me not before my time to die:* Compare the answered prayer in morning prayer Ps. 21.4, "He asked life of thee, and thou gauest hym a long lyfe." The phrase was proverbial — e.g., Erasmus, *Adagia,* 104C, "Qui mori nolit ante tempus."

Tuesday 5 March: *Morning Prayer:* Pss. 19–21, Luke 16. *Evening Prayer:* Pss. 22–23, Phil. 4.

## Sonnet 43

The sonnet's conclusion, which affirms the lady's ability to construe the poet's secret love-learned letters, throws down a secret challenge to her, because the poem contains an example of the poet's own secret construing of the Vulgate's phrase in

Luke 17.6, *dicetis huic arbori moro.* The conclusion also intimately contrasts the
poet's present silence with the lady's soon-to-be-uttered marriage vows.

1. *Shall I then silent be or shall I speake:* Proverbial (Smith, *Proverb Lore*, 714), e.g.,
   Erasmus, *Encomium*, 429 D, "Eloquarne, an sileam." The rhetorical *divisio* (Rix
   50) between silence or speech mirrors the division in the second lesson at
   morning prayer for Wednesday 6 March, Luke 17, which records Christ's
   observation that the secret of God's kingdom can be discerned only within:
   "The kingdome of God cometh not with obseruacion. Nether shal men say, Lo
   here, or lo there: for beholde the kingdome of God is within you" (vv. 20–21),
   to which the Geneva Bible adds a sidenote, "It can not be discerned by anie
   outward shew."
1–4. The *divisio*'s subsequent argument finds a precedent in Tasso, *Rime*, 2, 166:
   > Se taccio, il duol s'avanza;
   >> Se parlo, accresco l'ira,
   >> Donna bella e crudel, che mi martira.
   >> Ma prendo al fin speranza
   >> Che l'umiltà vi pieghi,
   >> Ché nel silenzio ancor son voci e preghi.
   >> E prego Amor che spieghi
   >> Nel mio doglioso aspetto
   >> Con lettre di pietà l'occulto affetto.
4. *gall:* 1. bile; 2. bitterness of spirit.
5. *tyranny:* See morning prayer Ps. 25.18, "they beare a tyrannous hate against me"
   (a usage unique to Coverdale and not found in the Geneva version).
6. *toung . . . tie:* strike dumb.
8. *stupid stock:* Luke 17 opens with the parable of the mulberry tree, "If ye . . .
   shulde say vnto this mulbery tre (Vulgate, *dicetis huic arbori moro*) plucke thy self
   vp by the rootes" (v. 6). Spenser has otherwise construed the phrase, *morus* =
   mulberry + *arbor* = tree, and rendered it as *morus* = stupid + *arbor* = stock.
   See *FQ* I.ix.34.1 (and III.xii.45/49.9), "like two senceles stocks in long embrace-
   ment dwelt," a translation of Ovid, *Met.* 4.375, "conducat cortice ramos."
9. *Yet I my hart . . . / will teach to speak:* A common resolve among the *amoretti*, e.g.,
   *Am.* 3.13–14 & 8.9.
9–10. *secretly / will teach:* Corresponding exactly to the repeated elements of morning prayer Ps. 25.3, 7 & 11 "and teache me," Ps. 25.4 & 8 "and learne me,"
   Ps. 25.13 "The secret of the Lorde is among them that feare him," and evening
   prayer Ps. 27.5, "in the secret place of his dwelling shal he hide me."
12. *loue learned:* (F12 *loue-learned*) 1. learned in love; 2. learned through love.
13. *deep wit:* the wit needed to unravel a riddle − so profound as to be known only
   to the elect; not "commune wit" (see line 14 note).
   *deep:* deep silence was proverbial (OED 12.4).
   *spel:* concerned nearly always with combinations of letters (as distinct from
   *construe*): 1. pronounce or read letter by letter; 2. form words by letters; 3.
   discover by close study; 4. the sense of a protective prayer or verse is probably
   also present, see E. K.'s note to *SC* March 54, "a kinde of verse or charme"
   This last sense gives confirmation to the *true* nature of the heart's thought.
14. *conceiue:* 1. comprehend; 2. after the manner of *concipere aliquid verbis*, express
   in words or give voice to, especially an oath or vow.
   *soone:* since *concipere* was specifically used of a woman marrying (e.g., Ovid,

*Met.* 11.222, " 'dea' dixerat 'undae,' / concipe"), an intimation that the lady will soon give voice to her marriage vows.

*learne:* See lines 9–10 note, Ps. 25.4 & 8.

*construe:* 1. analyze a grammatical construction especially in a classical language, adding a word for word translation (*OED* 3) — as Spenser has done with *stupid stock;* 2. combine words into a speech — in contrast to the poet's silence; 3. interpret a riddle (*OED* 4); *construe* is used only once elsewhere by Spenser — when Britomart is defeated by the riddle *Be bold,* "yet could not construe it / By any ridling skill, or commune wit" (*FQ* III.xi.54.3–4).

Wednesday 6 March: *Morning Prayer:* Pss. 24–26, Luke 17. *Evening Prayer:* Pss. 27–29, Col. 1.

### Sonnet 44

1–4. The opening *topos,* the Greek myth of Orpheus, matches the marginal note "The Greke worde signifieth, not to shrinke backe as cowards do in warre" attached to the phrase "not to waxe fainte" of the second lesson at morning prayer for Thursday 7 March, Luke 18.1. Spenser has amplified "Greke" into *Peres of Greece,* and accepted "warre" in *cruell ciuill warre* (5). He has also identifed the psalmist David's song in evening prayer Ps. 33.2, "Praise the Lorde with Harpe," with the harp with which Orpheus quelled the strife, thus recalling the patristic typological association of *FQ* IV.ii.1.7–2.4 between the psalmist and Orpheus.

Such as was *Orpheus,* that when strife was growen
Amongst those famous ympes of Greece, did take
His siluer Harpe in hand, and shortly friends them make.

Or such as that celestiall Psalmist was,
That when the wicked feend his Lord tormented,
With heauenly notes, that did all other pas,
The outrage of his furious fit relented.

The account is anticipated in the preceding canto (IV.i.23.6–9), "And of the dreadfull discord, which did driue / The noble *Argonauts* to outrage fell, / That each of life sought others to depriue, / All mindlesse of the Golden fleece, which made them striue." The opening quatrain to Sonnet 44 imitates elements from both passages.

1. *Peres:* 1. companions; 2. those of equal *ciuill* standing.

2. *iar:* 1. disagree or fight; but 2. the sense of musical disharmony is also present.

4. *Orpheus:* The tale is recounted in Apollonius, *Argonautica* 1.492 ff. . That the golden fleece caused the strife in the *FQ* episode is a Spenserian addition. Here the strife is caused through pride.

*harp:* David's use of the harp to quell strife is in 1 Sam. 16.23: "And so when the euil spirit of God came vpon Saul, Dauid toke an harpe and plaied with his hand and Saul was refreshed, and was eased: for the euil spirit departed from him."

4–6 & 12. *strife . . . warre, / the which my selfe againt my selfe doe make* and *to battaile fresh against my selfe to fight:* The self-war replicates the fighting of Paul in the second lesson at evening prayer, Col. 2.1, "I wolde ye knewe what great fighting I haue for your sakes."

5. *ciuill warre:* a common sonneteers' metaphor, e.g., Sidney, *AS* 39.7, "O make in me those civil wars to cease."

7. *passions:* In Whitney 186, *Orphei Musica*, the harp "makes them yeelding passions feele, that are by nature fierce."

    *warreid are:* warrayed are, are made war upon.

8. The two components of the line are duplicative; *skill:* 1. reason; 2. musical expertise.

    *stint:* 1. cause to cease; 2. assuage or *aslake* pain.

    *reason can aslake:* Orpheus's wisdom by contrast was most effectual — see Whitney, *Orphei Musica*, "besides his skill, he learned was, and wise."

9. *tunelesse harp:* 1. discordant, like the alarums of war; 2. without tune, silent.

10. *foes:* See morning prayer Ps. 30, 1, "I will magnifie thee, O Lord, for thou hast ... not made my foes to triumphe ouer me."

13. *to settle peace:* See Luke 18.39, "he shulde holde his peace (Vulgate, *taceret* = be silent, as in *tuneless* [9])."

14 (& 2). *malice* (& *pride*): contrary to the sidenote to Luke 18.17, "Signifying that they oght to lay aside all malice and pride."

**Thursday 7 March:** *Morning Prayer:* Pss. 30–31, Luke 18; *Evening Prayer:* Pss. 32–34, Col. 2.

### Sonnet 45

Sonnet 45, a mirror sonnet, has been diversely considered to embody a Platonic doctrine or not. Some (Harrison 135, Bhattacherje 184), attracted by its line, *the fayre Idea of your celestiall hew* (7), have argued that it incorporates stages of the Neo-Platonic ladder. Others have countered that the meaning is not Platonic at all and that *"Idea* means only *mental image"* (Renwick 200–201; see Ellrodt 42). Companion sonnets are Sonnet 78, which works the conceit of the *ymage* (11) in a slightly different and preoccupied way, and Sonnet 88, although its conclusion is decidedly anti-Platonic.

1–14. The *topos* of the mirror and its image exactly reflects the use of the term εἰκών in the second lesson at evening prayer for Friday 8 March, Col. 3.9–10, "seing that ye haue put of the olde man with his workes, And haue put on the newe, which is renewed in knowledge after the image of him that created him" (koiné, εἰς ἐπίγνωσιν κατ'εἰκόνα τοῦ κτίσαντος αὐτον = in knowledge according to the image of the creator). Compare the use of εἰκών as an image in a mirror in Plato, *The Republic*, 402. B: "Οὐκοῦν καὶ εἰκόνας γραμμάτων, εἴ που ἦ ἐν ὕδασιν ἦ ἐν κατόπτροις ἐμφαίνοιντο, οὐ πρότερον γνωσόμεθα πρὶν ἂν αὐτα γνῶμεν" (Is it not true that, if there are images of letters reflected in water or in mirrors, we shall not know them until we know the originals?). Plato applies the same metaphor to the eyes of lovers in *Phaedrus* (255. D), which compares the lover to one that has caught a disease of the eye from another but cannot discover its cause, not understanding that his love is like a mirror in which he beholds himself: "ἀλλ'οἷον ἀπ'ἄλλου ὀφθαλμίας ἀπολελαυκὼς πρόφασιν εἰπεῖν οὐκ ἔχει, ὥσπερ δὲ ἐν κατόπτρῳ ἐν τῷ ἐρῶντι ἑαυτὸν ὁρῶν λέληθεν." The context of the passage in *The Republic* clearly identifies εἰκών as an image associated with the original ἰδέα (Idea), which is the true image in the mind (see Shorey, ed., *The Republic*, 260 n.). The Pauline phrase, although not Platonic, is reminiscent of the eternal forms in the (creator's) mind, which constitute Plato's Ideas (see lines 5–8 note; both Paul and Plato qualify their use of εἰκὼν by listing a series of virtues necessary for true discernment).

1. The instruction to stop viewing her face in the mirror also matches the day's morning prayer Ps. 36.1, "there is no feare of God before his eyes. For he flattereth him selfe in his own sight."

   glasse: not then a "*Venus* looking glas" so prominent in *FQ* (e.g., III.i.8.9; III.ii.18–21). The mirror conceit, widespread both in England and on the continent, was developed variously, e.g., Shakespeare, Sonnet 3: "Looke in thy glasse"; or Richard Barnfield, *Cynthia with Certaine Sonnets*, Sonnet 11.10–11: "Looke in this glasse (quoth I) there shalt thou see / The perfect forme of my felicitie." Among the conceit's continental exponents both Petrarch (*Rime*, 45.10–11, "non dovea specchio farvi per mio danno, / a voi stessa piacendo, aspra e superba") and Tasso (*Rime*, 2.251.169, "Qual da cristallo lampeggiar si vede Raggio") treat it similarly (see Tasso, 2.316, 9–10, "Vede se stessa nel cristallo eterno / Quasi 'n ispecchio, e vede a sè sembianti . . ."). The observation by Renwick 201, who cites Serafino da Aquila, Tebaldeo, Marot, Scève and Desportes as possible sources, that "This is a fair specimen of the "source problem" of the *Amoretti*" is exact.

4. *semblant*: 1. normally appearance, particularly that which might mislead (see *Am.* 88 headnote for a discussion of φάντασμα = semblance); but 2. here true image (= εἰκών) – see line 1 note, Tasso, "sembianti."

5–8. The ἰδέαι of Plato were ideal forms, of which all created things were the imperfect images. They were conceived as the eternal forms of being (echoed in *remaines immortally* [8]), in opposition to their material forms, as subjects of thought but not of sight. The contrast between the lady's *celestial hew*, to be discovered within the poet, and her *earthly* resemblance, to be discerned by sight, corresponds to the instruction in Col. 3.2, "Set your affections on things which are aboue, *and* not on things, which are on the earth."

7. *hew*: 1. shape; 2. complexion or color (see *Am.* 3.8 note).

9. *dimmed and deformd*: Reflecting the opaque and flawed nature of sixteenth century glass, and hinting at Plato's world of shadows and material forms.

11. *visnomy*: physiognomy, but Spenser always uses the contracted form; 1. technically, the face read as an index to someone's nature or character (φύσις = nature + γνώμων = judge from γνῶσις = judgement or knowledge) – hence corresponding to the detail of Col. 3.10 (koiné, ἐπίγνωσις = judgement or knowledge); 2. reflection in a mirror (*OED* 3b).

13. *your selfe in me ye playne will see*: The poet's intention that the lady should see her light in the light within himself corresponds precisely to the day's morning prayer Ps. 36.9, "For . . . in thy light shall we see light."

14. *remoue the cause by which your fayre beames darkned be*: strictly the cause is the lady's *cruelty* (8), but there is a probable echo of Paul's forthright advice, Col. 3.5, to "Mortifie therefore your members which are on the earth" – a proper Lenten thought for assistance in subduing the passions. One of two alexandrines in the sequence (see *Am.* 10.14.)

Friday 8 March: *Morning Prayer*: Pss. 35–36, Luke 19. *Evening Prayer*: Ps. 37, Col. 3.

## Sonnet 46
Attributing fault to the heavens was proverbial (see Smith, *Proverb Lore*, 4). Here Spenser has drawn on earlier occasions in *FQ* when the heavens are held blameworthy, notably Meliboe's advice to Calidore (VI.ix.29.3) and Artegall's calling upon

the heavens to attest his innocence (V.xi.41.6–9). (Presumably departure is on a horse or in an open carriage, for hidden in the sonnet is the figure of a horse who will not *obay* [5], whom the poet must *raine* [14] and *hold back* [10], and to whose gait (*wrack* [12]) he also alludes.)

1. *abodes:* 1. stay, visit; 2. the sense of foreboding or ominous as in storm-clouds is also present.

    *prefixed time:* a time already set.

2. *cruell fayre:* A standard Petrarchan and Petrarchist epithet, see Petrarch *Rime*, 126.29, "fera bella" and 23.149, "fera bella e cruda." The epithet is used only in *Amoretti* and then 5 times within the space of 10 sonnets, *Am.* 46–56.

    *straight:* 1. without delay; 2. frankly.

    *wend my way:* Compare morning prayer Ps. 39.1 & 15 for Saturday 9 March, "I will take heede to my wayes," and "O spare me a litle, that I may recouer my strength: before I go hence."

3. *most hideous stormes:* Compare evening prayer Ps. 42.9, "all thy ... stormes are gone ouer me." Shakespeare begins Sonnet 34 with the same complaint.

4. *willing me against her will:* See evening prayer Ps. 41.2, "deliuer not thou him into the will of his enemies," and Ps. 40.10, "that I should fulfil thy wil."

5. *Whom then shall I or heauen or her obay?:* The dilemma matches that faced by the scribes and elders in the second lesson at morning prayer, Luke 20. Having questioned Christ as to the source of his authority to be obeyed, they were asked: "I also wil aske you one thing: tell me therefore: The baptisme of Iohn was it from heauen, or of men?" (vv. 3–4). Where the scribes subsequently debated among themselves, "If we shal say from heauen, he wil say, Why then beleued ye him not? But if we shal say, Of men, all the people wil stone vs" (vv. 5–6), so Spenser spends the rest of his sonnet discussing his own dilemma. The *divisio* is the third of three in close proximity, see *Am.* 41 & 43. *heauen:* monosyllabic throughout.

6. *the heauens know best what is the best for me:* Meliboe's advice to Calidore is identical (*FQ* VI.ix.29.1–3):

        In vaine (said then old *Meliboe*) doe men
            The heauens of their fortunes fault accuse,
            Sith they know best, what is the best for them.

8. *lower heauen:* 1. *lower* in contrast to *higher* heaven — the lady; 2. through its homonym lour, (louring / lowering), a gloomy, dark, threatening sky; 3. by transference, the forbidding looks or frown of the lady.

10. *hold me backe:* 1. restrain me; 2. rein me in, as one might a horse.

12. *wrack:* 1. torture; 2. ruin; but 3. *wrack*, through its homonym rack, suggests the storm-clouds which rack up before the wind; 4. the equine context of rack, intending a horse's gait as the poet departs, cannot be ignored.

14. *raine:* 1. rain; 2. homonymically, rein, and then an echo of morning prayer Ps. 39.2, "I will keepe my mouth as it were with a bridle"; the pun completes the sonnet's equine allusions.

**Saturday 9 March:** *Morning Prayer:* Pss. 38–40, Luke 20. *Evening Prayer:* Pss. 41–43, Col. 4.

### Sonnet 47

Spenser evidently was an enthusiastic angler, the fishing *topos* being one of his more popular images. Sonnet 47's dominant simile of the fish corresponds to the incident, when "*Iesus fedeth fiue thousand men with fiue loaues and two fishes*" recounted in the Gospel for the Fourth Sunday in Lent, 10 March, John 6.1–15.

1. *Trust not:* Similar cautions punctuate the second lesson at morning prayer, Luke 21, e.g., "be not deceiued" (v. 8).

   *smyling lookes: oeillades:* amorous glances which the lady bestows on the poet without ever intending they be requited; see Shakespeare, Sonnet 137.4–8, with its range of sexual undertones: "If eyes corrupt by ouer-partiall lookes, / Be anchord in the baye where all men ride, / Why of eyes falsehood hast thou forged hookes, / Whereto the iudgement of my heart is tide?" Like Shakespeare, Spenser recasts the seamstress' hook-and-eye.

2. *guylefull traynes:* snare, lures. Luke 21.35 counsels awareness "lest that day come on you at vnwares. For as a snare shal it come on all them" (with its Geneva version sidenote, "To catch and intangle them").

4 *foolish fish:* See headnote, John 6, and the subsequent detail, "two fishes" (v. 9) and "fishes" (v. 11). For the foolishness of such fish, see evening prayer Ps. 49.12–14, where man "may bee compared vnto the beastes that perishe.... This is their foolishnes" (see v. 10). The image was proverbial (see Smith, *Proverb Lore*, 37 & 266).

   *bayts:* At the end of Castiglione, *The Courtier*, 4 (Everyman, 308), one of Bembo's companions points out: "There be also many wicked men that have the comlinesse of a beautifull countenance, and it seemeth that nature hath so shaped them, because they may bee the readier to deceive, and that this amiable looke were like a baite that covereth the hooke."

6. *loue:* a possible play on words: *loue* = Italian *amo*, but *amo* = hook also in Italian.

   *decay:* death.

9. *her bloody hands them slay:* Recalls John's prophecies that, "they shal lay their hands on you" (v. 12), and "*some* of you shal they put to death" (v. 16), as well as morning prayer Ps. 44.22, "slayne."

10. *louely:* 1. beautiful; 2. lovingly.

13. *O mighty charm:* 1. the lady's eyes which enchant or captivate; 2. paradoxically a *charm* was an amulet or decoration used to deter evil, such as the cross on the Red Cross Knight's shield (*FQ* I.ii.18.1–4; see I.xi.36.9).

Sunday 10 March, Fourth Sunday in Lent: *Epistle:* Gal. 4.21–31. *Gospel:* John 6.1–15. *Morning Prayer:* Pss. 44–46, Luke 21. *Evening Prayer:* Pss. 47–49, 1 Thess. 1.

## Sonnet 48

Dodge 222 suggests the sonnet may reflect an actual incident; more probably it is the working of an infrequent conceit — e.g., Desportes, *Diane* 2.75.

1. *Innocent:* 1. without guilt; 2. unharmful (*in-nocens* = not-harming).

   *paper:* an unusual Spenserian term; 1. a paper was identified with the preferring of a suit, e.g., those at the "Princes Court," who "poore Sutors papers do retaine" (*Col* 741); it introduces a range of legal vocabulary in the sonnet; 2. possibly a written poem.

2. *matter:* 1. excuse; 2. legally, something presented to be tried or proved.

3. *cause:* in its pregnant sense, a proper ground for legal action.

4. *did sacrifize vnto the greedy fyre:* Compare the action of Peter, in the second lesson at morning prayer for Monday 11 March, Luke 22, who denied the cause of his "Master" (see line 8 note), when seated around a fire, "And when they had

kindled a fyre . . . a certeine maide behelde him as he sate by the fyre, and
hauing wel loked on him" (vv. 55–56).

> *sacrifice:* Peter's betrayal occured on the day "when the Passeouer must be
> sacrificed" (v. 7; see morning prayer Pss. 50.3, "there shall go before him a
> consuming fire"; 51.16, "For thou desirest no sacrifice . . . The sacrifice of God
> is a troubled spirit: a broken and contrite heart (O God) shalt thou not despise";
> and 50.5 & 8, "sacrifices").

5. *hyre:* recompense, payment.

6. *ordayned:* decreed; burning was the penalty for the heretic.

7. *treason didst conspire:* The theme of treason and betrayal matches that of Luke 22,
whose Geneva version headnote runs, "*Conspiracie against Christ . . . Iudas
treason,*" and which recounts how Judas "communed with the hie Priests, and
captaines, how he might betray him" (v. 4).

8. *plead:* (= pleaded) prosecute a legal action.

> *maisters:* unique occurrence in the sequence — see Luke 22.11, "Master."
> *payned:* 1. suffered; 2. punished — from its etymon *poena* = punishment (see
> Am. 10.14 note).

11. *complayned:* 1. lamented — see evening prayer Ps. 55, headnote (Geneva version), "Dauid . . . complaineth of the crueltie of Saul"; 2. legally, make a formal
statement of grievance before a competent authority, see Am. 12.13 note.

12. *the piteous passion of his dying smart:* In imitation of Luke 22.44, "agonie," with
its sidenote q, "Meaning, his death and passion."

14. *requite:* 1. repay (as in *hyre* [5]); 2. recompense or *auenge* (2) a wrong.

Monday 11 March: *Morning Prayer:* Pss. 50–52, Luke 22. *Evening Prayer:* Pss. 53–55, 1 Thess. 2.

## Sonnet 49

The sonnet is built around the conceit of the cockatrice or basilisk, the fabulous
reptile "brought forth of a Cockes egge" and hatched by a snake (see Topsell,
*Serpents* [1608] 119). The conceit matches Tuesday 12 March's morning prayer Ps.
58.3, "The vngodly are frowarde euen from their mothers wombe. . . . They are as
venemous as the poyson of a Serpent: euen like the deafe Adder that stoppeth her
eares." The poem's word-plays and etymological awarenesses make Spenser's
working of the conceit more complex than most.

1. *Fayre cruell:* a customary Petrarchan paradox, see Petrarch, *Rime,* 23.149, "quella
fera bella e cruda" (see Am. 46.2 note). Am. 7, which sustains an implied image
of the basilisk throughout, opens "Fayre eyes."

2. *your eyes haue powre to kill:* Pliny, *Nat. Hist.* 29.4.19.66 (in Holland's translation),
recounts of the cockatrice that "(by report) if he do but set his eye on a man, it
is enough to take away his life." Spenser's other reference to the cockatrice
occurs in *FQ* IV.viii.39.7–9: "Like as the Basiliske of serpents seede, / From
powrefull eyes close venim doth conuay / Into the lookers hart, and killeth farre
away." The conceit was generally worked in a stock manner — e.g., Drayton's
treatment of "That daungerous eye-killing Cockatrice," *Ideas Mirrour,* Amour
30.5–8.

3. *mighties iewell:* an etymological playing with βασῐλῐσκός, which primarily meant
kingly, mighty (see line 6 note, *imperious*) as well as basilisk. The cockatrice bore
a jewel-like mark on its forehead — see Bart. Angl. 350ᵛ, "[the Cockatrice] hath
a specke in his head as a precious stone."

3–4. *mercy . . . / greater glory thinke to saue, then spill:* Echoing the second lesson at morning prayer, Luke 23, "He saued others: let him saue him self" (v. 35), and, "If thou be the King of the Iewes, saue thy self."(v. 37). The sonnet's range of allusions to death, spilling of blood, mercy and saving correspond with the Lucan account.

4. *to saue, then spill:* Proverbial with classical origins, see Ovid, *Heroides* 12. 75–76, "Perdere posse sat est, siquem iuvet ipsa potestas; sed tibi servatus gloria maior ero." Spenser uses the adage of Mercy, "As it is greater prayse to saue, then spill" (*FQ* V.x.2.8; see *Am.* 38.11–12).

    *spill:* kill, destroy.

6. *imperious:* Another etymological pun on βασίλισκός 1. basilisk; 2. imperial, kingly.

8. *bend your force:* Compare Vulgate Ps. 58.6, *Intendit* (= bend) *arcum suum; arcus* in Ovid, *Met.* 3.42, is used also to describe the windings of a serpent.

10. *Cockatrices:* See headnote; morning prayer Ps. 58.3 was customarily identified with Ps. 91.13, "Super aspidem et basilicum ambulabis, / Et conculcabis leonem et draconem." Spenser has accepted the established association and construed the day's reference to "Serpent" and "Adder" as *Cockatrices.* (*Am.* 7 similarly associates Ps. 91.13 with Ps. 140.3.) He has also played on the Vulgate's *basilicum,* by taking up the etymology of *conculcabis* (= con + calco = to tread under foot) to render *basilicum* as "kokatrice." *Cockatrice* itself was thought to derive from *calcatrix* (= she who treads under foot), the feminine form of the noun from *calco.* The pun is echoed in *him that at your footstoole humbled lies.*

11–12. *footstoole . . . mercifull regard:* a rendering of Vulgate Ps. 56.7, *Ipsi calcaneum meum* (= my heel, foot) *observabunt* (= will regard), and an echo of Ps. 56.1, "Be mercifull vnto me, O God, for man goeth about to deuoure me" (Vulgate, *conculcavit me* = tread me under foot). Christ's triumph over death, recounted in Luke 23, was customarily seen as fulfilling Ps. 110.1, "vntill I make thine enemies thy footestoole."

12. *regard:* 1. a look or glance, in keeping with *eyes;* 2. attention, consideration for.
    *too:* 1611 & 1617 read *to.*

14. *admyred:* disyllabic by syncopation.

**Tuesday 12 March:** *Morning Prayer:* Pss. 56–58, Luke 23; *Evening Prayer:* Pss. 59–61, 1 Thess. 3.

## Sonnet 50

1–4. The sonnet's discourse upon the *topoi* of medicines, salves, and ointments directly corresponds to the opening incident of the second lesson at morning prayer for Wednesday 13 March, Luke 24, the account of the women who brought ointments to anoint the body of Christ and discovered the resurrection: "they came vnto the sepulchre, and broght the odores (Vulgate, *aromata*), which they had prepared" (v. 1; the verse expands the final verse of the preceding chapter, which specifies "odores, and ointments," while the parallel version of Mark (16.1) renders *aromata* as "swete ointments").

    The sonnet recalls the passage where Patience, the leech, cures the maladies afflicting the Red Cross Knight (*FQ* I.x.24):

        Who comming to that soule-diseased knight,
           Could hardly him intreat, to tell his griefe:
           Which knowne, and all that noyd his heauie spright

Well searcht, eftsoones he gan apply reliefe
Of salues and med'cines, which had passing priefe,
And thereto added words of wondrous might:
By which to ease he him recured briefe,
And much asswag'd the passion of his plight,
That he his paine endur'd, as seeming now more light.

Spenser's having recourse to the emblem of Patience matches in turn
morning prayer Ps. 62.5–6, "for my hope is in him (Vulgate, *Quoniam ab ipso
patientia mea*)." The leech or physician was a favorite Spenserian image.

1 & 10. *languishing . . . languour:* 1. disease, sickness; 2. by inference, woeful plight.
4. *medicines:* disyllabic by syncopation.
5. *priefe:* proven skill, experience.
6. *deep discouery of the mynds disease:* 1. profound; 2. secret — in direct imitation of
morning prayer Ps. 64.6–7, "they keepe secret among them selues, euery man in
the deepe of his heart . . . that they shall be wounded."
7–8. *hart . . . rules the members:* axiomatic.
            *members:* the limbs and organs of the body, in distinction from the heart
    — see *BCP*'s phrase (Collect for the Circumcision), "our hearts and all our mem-
    bers."
11. *ease:* 1. relief; 2. as an antonym to dis-ease, health.
12. *sweet cordialls:* medicines that restore the heart (from *cor* = heart). Belphoebe,
    by contrast, refuses Timias the "sweet Cordiall, which can restore / A loue-sick
    hart" (*FQ* III.v.50.6–7).
13. *my lyfes Leach:* 1. the lady who will cure the poet; 2. since the term was tradi-
    tionally applied to God and Christ from Tertullian onwards (its biblical analogue
    was Mark 2.17), the biblical subtext also suggests Christ, the lady being asked to
    manifest a like skill. (See Tertullian, *Adversus Marcum,* 3.17, "annunciari
    Christum medicatorem," and Chaucer, *S. T.,* 184, "God that is oure lyues
    leche." Spenser names Apollo, "King of Leaches" (*FQ* IV.12.25.4); Apollo also,
    having ravished Oenome, then taught her the "leaches craft" (*FQ* III.iv.41.3),
    even if Ovid, *Met.* 1.521, admits that love cannot be cured by herbs.)

**Wednesday 13 March:** *Morning Prayer:* Pss. 62–64, Luke 24. *Evening Prayer:* Pss. 65–67, 1 Thess. 4.

## Sonnet 51

The theme of artistic endurance, which the sonnet shares with Sonnet 69, is here
turned into recrimination against the lady's hardheartedness. The poet's desire to
soften her hardness echoes Ovid's account of the legend of Pygmalion (*Met.* 10.243–
94). Pygmalion, having made an ivory statue of Galatea, is able through Venus'
intervention to soften its hardness and bring it to life through his touch:

manibus quoque pectora temptat:
temptatum mollescit ebur positoque rigore
subsidit digitis ceditque, ut Hymettia sole
cera remollescit tractataque pollice multas
flectitur in facies ipsoque fit utilis usu.

(Golding, 10.307–12:

                                    and on her brest did lay
His hand. The Iuory wexed soft: and putting quyght away
All hardnesse, yeelded vnderneathe his fingars, as wee see

> A peece of wax made soft ageinst the Sunne, or drawen too bee
> In diuers shapes by chaufing it between ones handes, and so
> To serue to uses.)

The Ovidian metaphor for such softening, that of wax in the face of heat, corresponds exactly with the opening simile to morning prayer Ps. 68 for Thursday 14 March, "like as waxe melteth at the fire" (v. 2), the second time in the sequence that Spenser has been struck by the simile (see *Am.* 21)

2. *hardest Marble*: a frequent comparative detail of immortal verses, e.g., Whitney 197, *Pennae gloria perennis*, with its allusions to Homer and indebtedness to Pliny, (*Nat. Hist.* 7.16):

> Yea, thoughe some Monarche greate some worke should take in hand,
> Of marble, or of Adamant, that manie worldes shoulde stande,
> Yet, should one only man, with labour of the braine,
> Bequeathe the world a monument, that longer shoulde remaine.
> And when that marble waules, with force of time should waste;
> It should indure from age, to age, and yet no age should taste.

3-4. *for that*: so that.

    *ne*: 1. nor — *ne let* frequently introduces Spenserian orisons or invocations; 2. possibly an intentional echo of the Latin *ne* (as in evening prayer Vulgate Ps. 70.6, *ne moreris*) = *ut non* = so that . . . not; hence 'so that they should not fade.'

3. *endure*: The sonnet plays like *Am.* 6 on *endure* (= *in* + *durus* = hard), in *hardnes* (6), *hard* (8), *hard* (9), *endure* (12).

4. *moniment*: Like *Am.* 69, Sonnet 51 corresponds to a day following one for which a sonnet has been written to match a resurrection account. The common source lies with the Vulgate in which Mark, Luke, and John all use *monumentum* to describe the burial place of Christ; *moniment* is used elsewhere in the sequence only to commemorate the feasts of Easter Monday (*Am.* 69.10) and the Ascension (*Am.* 82.8), whose theme of penning immortal poetry finds an equivalent in Ps. 68.13's "feathers like golde" (Vulgate, *pennae . . . auri*).

5. *louers trade*: the craft of loving, the same as the "louely trade" of *FQ* III.xi.32.2. The phrase introduces a series of bawdy puns similar to that of *Am.* 6.

7-8. *neuer ought . . . assayde*: Proverbial, see Smith, *Proverb Lore*, 182 & 363 with the possible bawdy association of *neuer ought* = nought ( = vulva) ever (see *Am.* 6.1).

    *assayde*: 1. tried; see Ovid, "temptat: / temptatum mollescit ebur"; 2. attempted love-making; see Shakespeare, *VA* 608, "She hath assay'd as much as may be proved".

9-10. *Ne ought . . . to his will allure*: possibly extending the sexual innuendo: *Ne ought* = vulva; *will* = penis; *allure* = attract sexually.

10. *bend*: 1. yield — only something hard can bend, not something flaccid; 2. the archaic sense of bind or capture is also possible.

14. *but hauing her*: possessing sexually (see *1 Henry IV*, III.iii.132-33; Ralegh, *Nature, that washed her hands in milk*, 11).

**Thursday 14 March**: *Morning Prayer*: Ps. 68, John 1. *Evening Prayer*: Pss. 69-70, 1 Thess. 5.

## Sonnet 52

1-14. The poet as a melancholic lover, lamenting his absence from his beloved, has adopted the same role as Timias after his banishment by Belphoebe (*FQ* IV.vii.36–viii.2). Belphoebe's rejection is perceived with "sodaine glancing eye" (36.1). Timias, having rejected society and found a "fit solitary place" (38.4), discards his "wonted warlike weapons" and, when finally discovered by Arthur, refuses all relief:

> all he said and did, was vaine,
> Ne ought mote make him change his wonted tenor,
> Ne ought mote ease or mitigate his paine,
> He left him there in languor to remaine,
> Till time for him should remedy prouide,
> And him restore to former grace againe. (47.2–7)

Thereafter Timias "with penaunce sad / And pensiue sorrow pind and wore away" (viii.2.5–6). The sonnet finds little correspondence with any of the liturgical readings for Friday 16 March, although its turning present afflictions into penance is a proper lenten thought.

4. *despoiled*: stripped.

> *knowen shield*: 1. with its identifying device; 2. customary, wonted; see *FQ* IV.vi.5.5. "known armes."

7. *exylde*: Compare Petrarch, *Rime*, 21.10, "ne l'esilio infelice alcun soccorso."

8. *languor*: 1. sorrow, distresse — see *Am*. 50.10; 2. longing or ennui.

11. *dumps*: 1. fits of melancholy; 2. absence of mind; the only usage by Spenser, but see *Am*. 4.4, "dumpish spright." See Watson, *Hecatompathia*, 11: "a dumpe, or sounden extasie."

> *dreary*: melancholic, *sad*.

13. *absens*: Compare evening prayer Ps. 74.1, "O God, wherefore art thou absent from vs so long."

> *my penaunce make*: See lines 1–14 note, *FQ* IV.viii.2.5, "with penaunce sad."

**Friday 15 March**: *Morning Prayer*: Pss. 71–72, John 2. *Evening Prayer*: Pss. 73–74, 2 Thess. 1.

## Sonnet 53

1. *Panther*: Spenser accepted the received medieval and early Renaissance distinction between the leopard and panther (*FQ* I.vi.25.8 & 26.3). Here he also develops the accepted view that the panther attracted its prey by its spotted hide but hid its head because sight of it frightened the prey away. See Bart. Angl. 376[v]:

> And all foure footed beasts haue liking to beholde the diuerse coulours of the Panthera and Tygres, but they be a fearde of the horriblenesse of theyr heads, and therfore they hide their heads, and toll the beastes to them with fayrenesse of the other deale of the body, and take them when they come so tolled and eate them: and though he be a right cruel beast, yet he is not vnkind to them that helps and sucour him in anye wise.

2. *fray*: frighten.

3. *bush*: 1. shrub; 2. a place of concealment or ambush (*OED* 4 cites the phrase, "*thrust one's head in a bush*").

> *dreadfull head*: in *Am*. 31.5, such beasts have a "dreadfull countenaunce."

4. *pray*: The bestial *topos* matches morning prayer Ps. 76.4 (Geneva version) for Saturday 10 March: "Thou art more bright and puissant, then the mountaines

of pray," with its sidenote "he compareth the kingdomes . . . to the mountaines that are ful of rauening beasts."

5. *cruell fayre:* the standard Petrarchist epithet, see Petrarch, *Rime,* 23.149, "fera bella e cruda."

   *play:* toy with, as a large cat often does with its prey.

6–7. *with the goodly semblant of her hew, / she doth allure me:* See Am. 31.10, "through sweet allurement of her louely hew."

6. *goodly semblant:* countenance.

   *hew:* 1. shape, figure; 2. complexion, color; see Am. 31.10 note.

11. *embrew:* 1. primarily to stain; 2. here, in its pregnant sense, to pierce (*OED* 3).

12. Proverbial, see Smith, *Proverb Lore,* 339.

14. *as in theyr maker ye them best may see:* Compare the conclusion in Am. 9.13.

Saturday 16 March: *Morning Prayer:* Pss. 75–77, John 3. *Evening Prayer:* Ps. 78, 2 Thess. 2.

## Sonnet 54

The sonnet, opening with the theatrical *topos* and closing with the image of the stone, reverses the structure of Sonnet 18. Pageant, masque and spectacle are among Spenser's favorite conceits, although they are uncommon among sonneteers.

1. *Of this worlds Theatre:* The emblem corresponds to the opening image of the Epistle for the Fifth Sunday in Lent, 17 March, Heb. 9.11–16, which presents Christ as "a greater and a more perfite Tabernacle (koiné, σκηνῆς), not made with hands, that is not of this buylding." The koiné's σκηνή (Vulgate, *tabernaculum*), was used primarily by the Greeks as a technical term for a wooden stage on which actors performed. (See Am. 18.9–14 note.) Compare evening prayer Ps. 84.1 (Geneva version), "how amiable are thy tabernacles" (Vulgate, *Quam dilecta tabernacula tua*).

   *Theatre:* trisyllabic.

2. *ydly:* foolishly, even unconcernedly.

   *sits:* See morning prayer Ps. 80.1 & 14, where God "sittest vpon the Cherubins," and is called upon to "looke downe from heauen: beholde, and visite this vine."

3. *pageants:* 1. a play's individual scenes — such as are subsequently played out; 2. the drama of life itself, as in the phrase 'to play one's pageant'; 3. since *pageant* was used of the stage itself, an echo of σκηνή.

4. *disguysing:* 1. concealing; 2. masquing; *disguysing* was the old English word for masquing and Spenser frequently links the two — e.g., *FQ* III.iii.51.9, "to maske in strange disguise."

5. *fits:* befits; but a *fit* was 1. a strain of music associated with dancing and masquing; 2. a short period of time such as a *stay* (1); 3. a paroxysm, such as the poet's *troubled wits* (2).

6. *mask:* 1. masque; 2. mask, disguise.

8. *I waile:* See Am. 18.12.

   *Tragedy:* the theatrical *topos* is developed to accord with the peculiar pseudo-etymological detail provided by Heb. 9.11–12. Paul's σκηνή, "not made with hands," is distinguished from earlier σκηνή on which were enacted other performances "by the blood of goates" (v. 12; koiné, δι'αἵματος τράγων) and "the blood of bulles and of goates" (v. 13; koiné, τὸ αἷμα ταύρων καὶ τράγων). *Tragedy* ingeniously reflects the koiné's τράγος, which is its partial etymon.

11–12. *when I laugh she mocks, and when I cry / she laughes:* Imitating directly morning prayer Ps. 80.6, "our enemies laugh vs to scorne" (Vulgate, *subsannaverunt* = deride, mock, particularly in a pantomine or masque) and Ps. 79.4, with its context of onlookers, "We are become an open shame to our enemies: a very scorne (Vulgate, *subsannatio* = derision, mockery) and derision (Vulgate, *illusio* = a mocking, laughing) vnto them that are round about vs." (The Geneva version attaches to its rendering, "We are a reproche to our neighbours," the sidenote, "but thei . . . laughed at our miseries.") See *Am.* 18.12, corresponding to Ps. 52.7, "shall laugh him to scorne."

12. *hardens euermore her hart:* the same complaint occurs in *Am.* 18.6. See morning prayer Ps. 81.12 (Geneva version), "So I gaue them vp vnto the hardenes of their heart."

13. *merth nor mone:* a common poetic yoking – see *1 Henry IV*, II.iii.44.

14. *stone:* The Sunday's readings repeatedly associate temples with stones, see its Gospel, John 8.59, "Then toke they vp stones, to cast at him, but Iesus hid him self, and went out of the Temple," and morning prayer Ps. 79.1, "thy holy Temple haue they defiled, and made Hierusalem an heape of stones."

**Sunday 17 March, Fifth Sunday in Lent:** *Epistle:* Heb. 9.11–16. *Gospel:* John 8.46–59. *Morning Prayer:* Pss. 79–81, John 4. *Evening Prayer:* Pss. 82–85, 2 Thess. 3.

## Sonnet 55

The sonnet's *expeditio*, the third of the sequence and similar to Sonnet 9's, attempts to find a proper element with which to compare the lady's substance; it first eliminates the four elements of earth, water, air and fire, finally to arrive at a fifth element, the heavens. The paradoxical factors which cancel the four elements are they themselves in reverse order of their progression. The order and its contrary are given by Ovid, *Met.* 15.237–52 (Golding 15.262–75):

> This endlesse world conteynes therin I say
> Fowre substances of which all things are gendred. Of theis fower
> The Earth and Water for theyr masse and weyght are sunken lower,
> The other cowple Aire, and Fyre the purer of the twayne
> Mount vp, and nought can keepe them downe. And though there doo remayne
> A space between eche one of them: yit euery thing is made
> Of them same fowre, and intoo them at length ageine doo fade.
> The earth resoluing leysurely dooth melt too water sheere.
> The water fyned turnes too aire. The aire eeke purged cleere
> From grossenesse, spyreth vp aloft, and there becommeth fyre.
> From thence in order contrary they backe ageine retyre.
> Fyre thickening passeth intoo Aire, and Ayër wexing grosse,
> Returnes too water: Water eeke congealing intoo drosse,
> Becommeth earth. No kind of thing keepes ay his shape and hew.

1. *So oft as I:* see *Am.* 52.1, "So oft as . . . I."

3. *maruaile:* The only usage in *Amoretti* and echoing the double Joannine use in the second lesson at morning prayer for Monday 18 March, John 5.28, where Christ warns "Marueile not at this" and claims the Father "wil shewe . . . greater workes then these, that ye should marueile" (v. 20).

   *mould:* 1. earth, particularly that out of which the human body was formed – Ovid's "tellus"; 2. shape or hue – a sense sustained in *hye* (12).

5. *high thoughts:* 1. properly lofty; 2. proud, *haughty* (11).

    *heauenly:* disyllabic by syncopation.

6. *water:* Compare the detail of morning prayer Ps. 88.17, "They came round about me daily like water," evening prayer Ps. 89.10, "Thou rulest the raging of the sea," and John 5.3–7, *passim,* the pool of Bethesda with its "mouing of the water," "stirring of the water," "troubled the water" and "the water is troubled."

    *burne like fyre:* in direct imitation of Ps. 89.45, "burne like fire."

7. *light:* 1. having little weight in proportion to bulk; the syllogistic major, "that al light thynges contend vpwarde" (*OED* a 12), was standard — see headnote, Ovid, *Met.* 15.242–43, "gravitate carent ... alta petunt"; in the 16th century applied not only to air but to *water* (in the sense of pure) and *earth* (in the sense of friable); 2. by transference of women, wanton, unchaste.

    *rare:* 1. when used of the air, opposed to dense, with its particles widely dispersed, see headnote, Ovid, *Met.* 15.245–46), "tellus / in liquidas rarescit aquas" (= the earth rarefies [itself] into liquid waters); 2. uncommon; 3. splendid.

10–11. *skye ... heauen:* The concluding comparison corresponds to the exclamation in evening prayer Ps. 89.6, "For who is he among the cloudes: that shal be compared vnto the Lord ... that shall be like vnto the Lord?" Conventionally the sky lies beyond the fourth element, fire.

11. *haughty lookes:* 1. high-minded, exalted; 2. proud, disdainful.

    *aspire:* rise up as smoke or fire, see *Am.* 6.8. The word retained associations with 'spire,' to soar aloft, see headnote, Ovid, *Met.* 15.271, "spyreth vp aloft."

12. *immortall:* Compare the only biblical use of the adjective in the second lesson at evening prayer, 1 Tim. 1.17, "the King euerlasting, immortal, inuisible."

    *hye:* 1. Osgood, *Concordance,* 417 gives the reading high, although three consecutive qualifiers would be an unusual Spenserian construction; 2. more probably an older spelling of 'hue' (*OED* sb 1a) despite the difficulties of rhyme the reading would cause; see headnote, Ovid, *Met.* 15.252, "Nec species sua cuique manet" (Golding: "No kind of thing keepes ay his shape and hew") — in direct contrast to John 5.37, "nether haue ye sene his [God's] shape (Vulgate, *speciem eius*)."

Monday 18 March: *Morning Prayer:* Pss. 86–88, John 5. *Evening Prayer:* Ps. 89, 1 Tim. 1

### Sonnet 56

The sonnet's images of beast, tree and ship mirror the first three emblems of the six visions comprising Petrarch's "Standomi un giorno" (*Rime,* 323), each an allegory of Laura's death. Spenser had earlier translated Marot's rendering of the canzone for *A Theatre for Worldlings* and adapted it for *The Visions of Petrarch.* Here the role of Petrarch's "fera" is turned from hunted to hunter. The sonnet finds little close correspondence with any of the scriptural readings prescribed for Tuesday 19 March.

1, 5 & 9. *Fayre ye be sure:* The sonnet's structure imitates Tasso's "Voi set bella, ma ..." (*Rime,* 4.69.523).

    *Fayre ... but cruell:* a customary Petrarchan and Petrarchist paradox, see Petrarch, *Rime,* 23.149, "fera bella e cruda," and 126.29, "fera bella."

    *vnkind:* 1. uncharitable; 2. unnatural.

2. *Tygre:* See Petrarch, *Rime,* 323.4, "una fera m'apparve da man destra." In *Pet*

Spenser uses "Hynde" (4) from Marot's "Biche," itself an adaptation of Petrarch's "fera." Petrarch identifies the beast with the tiger in *Rime*, 152.1, "fera, un cor di tigre." The image is a Spenserian favorite, although uncommon among his predecessors, see *FQ* VI.x.34.4–6.

4. *felly:* fiercely.

7. *tree:* In *Pet* 29, the tree is the "Lawrell."

8. *ruinate:* bring ruin to.

10. *rocke amidst the raging floods:* See evening prayer Ps. 93.4–5 for Tuesday 19 March: "The floodes are rysen.... The waues of the sea are mightie, and rage horribly." The day's second lesson at morning prayer, John 6.16–21, tells of the disciples' ship tossed by a storm; it parallels the account in Luke 8.22–25 with which *Am.* 34, "Lyke as a ship," corresponds. See also *Pet* 21–24. Fletcher, *Licia*, Sonet 8.6–7, also associates the tiger and rock: "My sighes, that rocke, like wind it cannot rent, / Too Tyger-like you sweare, you cannot loue."

**Tuesday 19 March:** *Morning Prayer:* Pss. 90–92, John 6. *Evening Prayer:* Pss. 93–94, 1 Tim. 2 & 3.

## Sonnet 57

In preparation for the theme of mutuality and sanctification of the flesh which will mark subsequent sonnets, Sonnet 57 marks the end of the war.

1. *Sweet warriour:* The epithet places the poem within the tradition of similar epithets, e.g., Du Bellay, *L'Olive*, 70, "ô ma douce guerriere." The *locus classicus* was Petrarch, *Rime* 21, "Mille fiate, o dolce mia guerrera, / per aver co' begli occhi vostri pace." The poem resembles the warfare sonnet, *Am.* 11.1–4, with its epithet, "cruell warriour."

   *haue peace with you:* Petrarch's "per aver ... pace."

2. *High time:* Petrarch's "fiate."

3. *sue:* 1. pursue, prosecute; 2. secondarily, woo or court, the warfare is thus identified with the poet's courtship (see *Am.* 11.1 note).

4. *your incessant battry:* Reversing the direction of the "incessant battery" of *Am.* 14.10.

6. *should liue a iot:* the smallest bit (of time), whit (as in the second lesson at morning prayer for Wednesday 20 March, John 7.23, "euery whit").

7. *through launced euery where:* 1. lanced, pierced throughout — compare 1611 emendation, "through-launced"; 2. the association of arrows being launched or discharged is also present.

8. *thousand arrowes, which your eies haue shot:* transferred from Petrarch's "mille fiate," although the number of a thousand arrows was standard, e.g., Petrarch, *Rime*, 86.2, "mille strali"; see *Am.* 8.5–6 & 12.1 notes.

10. *stoures:* 1. assaults, even 'death-struggle' (*OED* sb. 2); 2. times of conflict — a Spenserianism.

11. *what glory can be got:* The question reflects the misplaced glory cited by Christ in John 7.18, "He that speaketh of him self, seketh his owne glorie: but he that seketh his glorie that sent him, the same is true."

12. *in slaying him ... :* The lady's incessant attempts to slay the poet reflect the attempts to kill Christ, recounted in John 7, "for the Iewes soght to kil him" (v. 1), and the repeated question, "Is not this he, whome they go about to kil?" (v. 25; see vv. 19, 20).

13. *timely grace:* 1. in short time; 2. in good time; see John 7.6 & 8, "My time is not yet come: but your time is alway readie."

14. *little space:* space of time — see John 7.33. "Yet am I a litle while with you" (koiné, μικρòν χρόνον = smallest time).

**Wednesday 20 March:** *Morning Prayer:* Pss. 95–97, John 7. *Evening Prayer:* Pss. 98–101, 1 Tim. 4.

### Sonnets 58 and 59

The vanity of the world was a frequent topic of meditation and Sonnet 58 and its adversative, Sonnet 59, reflect the proper assessment of the world made elsewhere in *Van* 152–54:

> Why do vaine men mean things so much deface,
> And in their might repose their most assurance,
> Sith nought on earth can chalenge long endurance?

Both sonnets reflect the full range of scriptural readings for Thursday 21 and Friday 2 March, each corresponding to the readings for both days.

### Sonnet 58

1. *By her that is most assured to her selfe:* The superscription, unique in the sequence, is the sequence's only instance of visual imaging. The final verse of 1 Tim. 4, the chapter preceding the second lesson at evening prayer for Thursday 21 March, 1 Tim. 5, with which Sonnet 58 corresponds, has attached to it a long sidenote, the last part of which, to avoid its extending down beyond the bottom of the chapter, has in frequent Geneva Bibles been run across between the chapters as a one-line extension. There thus appears in many Geneva Bibles a line above 1 Tim. 5, in a different font and with the appearance of a short superscription, which runs "*which is an assurance of thy saluation.*" Spenser's own superscription mirrors the apparent Geneva version one.

   *By her:* 1. concerning; Martz 163 cites as evidence Gascoigne, *A Hundreth Sundrie Flowers* (ed. C. T. Prouty [1942]) 114.10 & 115.12, "He began to write by a gentlewoman" and "Another Sonet written by the same Gentlewoman vppon the same occasion," with its masculine signature, "Si fortunatus infoelix"; 2. written by; if so, then the lady is presented as author of the sonnet, who signs herself, *most assured* (see line 14 note). The following adversative *Am.* 59 is the poet's reply.

2. *Weake is th'assurance that weake flesh reposeth:* The judgement concerning the flesh corresponds to the incident of the woman taken in adultery, whom Christ refuses to judge, in the second lesson at morning prayer, John 8, "Ye iudge after the flesh: I iudge no man. And if I also iudge, my iudgement is true" (vv. 15–16; see *FQ* I.x.1.1–2, "What man is he, that boasts of fleshly might, / And vaine assurance of mortality"). The lady is likewise cautioned not to judge wrongly (lines 13–14). *assurance* (*assurd*): 1. self-confidence, self-reliance; 2. theologically, the assurance of salvation; 3. a betrothal (see *Am.* 42.12 and note).

2–3. *her:* flesh's (*caro* is feminine).

4–5. *that soonest fals whenas she most supposeth / her selfe assurd:* See *Van* 167–68, and *Pet* 79–81.

6. *All flesh is frayle:* Proverbial, see Smith, *Proverb Lore*, 267, Whitney 217, *Omnis caro foenum*, and *FQ* VI.i.41.7, "All flesh is frayle." The aphorism reflects specifically the thrice repeated metaphor of man as grass in morning prayer Ps. 102, "My heart is smitten downe, and withered like grasse" (v. 4), "My dayes are gonne like a shadow: and I am withered like grasse" (v. 11) and Ps. 103.15

(with its headnote gloss in the Geneva Version, "*The frailtie of mans life*"), "The dayes of man are but as grasse: for he florisheth as a flowre of the fielde." Grass is identified as flesh in Isa. 40.6–7, "All flesh *is* grasse, and all the grace thereof *is* as the floure of the field. The grasse withereth, the floure fadeth, because the Spirit of the Lord bloweth vpon it" with its sidenote, "The Spirit of God shal discouer the vanitie in all that seme to haue anie excellencie of them selues." (See 1 Pet. 1.24, "For all flesh *is* as grasse, and all the glorie of man *is* as the flower of grasse. The grasse withereth, and the flower falleth away.")

*vnstayd*: unsupported; in *Am.* 59.11, "the stay of her owne stedfast might" is commended.

7. *like a vaine bubble*: See Van 152. Paralleling the second lesson at evening prayer for 22 March, 1 Tim. 6, "vaine bablings" (v. 20) and "he is pufte vp and knoweth nothing" (v. 4). Proverbial, see Whitney 217, *Omnis caro foenum*, 3–4, "like bubbles small," and Smith, *Proverb Lore*, 79 who cites Varro, *De Re Rustica*, I.1.1, "si est homo bulla (= bubble, trifle, or vanity)." The line is probably suggestive — as indeed are the poem's references to *nought* (see *Am.* 51.7–8 note), *bulla* being associated both with φύλλον = a flower petal and φαλλός = phallus (bubble's associative bauble/babble was used bawdily of a phallus, see Shakespeare, *RJ* II.iii.95, "to hide his bauble in a hole").

*blowen vp with ayre*: SC Feb., 87, "For Youngth is a bubble blown vp with breath," is glossed, appositely for Spenser and his betrothed, as "A verye moral and pitthy Allegorie of youth, and the lustes thereof, compared to a wearie wayfaring man."

8. *deuouring tyme . . . prayd*: Ovid's "Tempus edax rerum" (*Met.* 15.234) was proverbial; see morning prayer Ps. 102.3, "For my dayes are consumed awaye lyke smoke."

10–11. *Ne none so rich or wise, so strong or fayre, / but fayleth trusting on his owne assurance*: The admonition corresponds to Paul's advice, 1 Tim. 6.17, "Charge them that are riche in this worlde, that they be not high minded, and that they trust not in vncerteine riches."

14–15. *misdeeme so farre, / that to your selfe ye most assured arre*: The pharisees' misjudgement is similarly condemned in John 8.15–16.

15. *ye most assured*: 'yours assured' was a common closing to sixteenth century letters.

**Thursday 21 March**: *Morning Prayer*: Pss. 102–103, John 8. *Evening Prayer*: Ps. 104, 1 Tim. 5.

## Sonnet 59

The adversative sonnet to Sonnet 58 extends the correspondence with the second lessons at evening prayer for 21 and 22 March, 1 Tim. 5 and 6. It similarly identifies the disorder of the flesh and the natural disorder of the raging seas that is allegorically developed in *FQ* III.iv.8–10. The motif of the ship tossed by a storm is elsewhere used to describe temperance (*FQ* II.ii.24). The sonnet, like Shakespeare's Sonnet 36, is punctuated throughout with references from the *BCP*, marriage service.

1–2. *Thrise happie she . . . setled so in hart*: Compare the happiness of the Red Cross Knight at his marriage, "Thrise happy man the knight himselfe did hold, / Possessed of his Ladies hart and hand" (*FQ* I.xii.40.6). The ceremony is concluded with a nautical metaphor not unlike that here (see *FQ* I.xii.42).

1/9. *assured / assurance:* See *Am.* 58.2 note 3: betrothed; compare *BCP,* marriage service, "For be ye well assured...."

3–4. *for better ... / with worse:* See *BCP,* marriage service, "for better, for worse."

4. *start:* depart (*OED* 4e).

5–6. *steddy ship ... / the raging waues:* Contrasting happiness with the dangers of sea-faring reflects the imagery in Paul's claim, 1 Tim. 6.8–9, "let vs therewith be content. For they that wil be riche, fall into tentation and snares, and into many foolish and noysome lustes, which drowne men in perdition and destruction" (6.8–9).

7. *depart:* 1. deviate from; 2. secondarily, separate, put asunder, thus continuing the *BCP*'s marriage service association, "till death vs depart."

8. *false delight:* Compare Duessa's false claim, "For Loue is free, and led with selfe delight" (*FQ* IV.i.46.8).

9–10. *need not feare the spight / of grudging foes:* See 1 Tim. 6.2, "let them not despise them." In *FQ* IV.ix.14, Poena, having reformed her "lewd loues and lust intemperate" (7), is married to the lowlie Squire and thenceforth "ne spite of enemis / Could shake the safe assuraunce of their state."

10. *fauour seek of friends:* The societal precondition to marriage, see *FQ* II.iv.21.3, "Accord of friends, consent of parents sought."

11. *stay:* 1. continuance; 2. reliance, even self-reliance; 3. nautically, the ropes which support a mast.
    *stedfast:* firmly fixed like a pillar or mast.

12. *bends:* inclines; nautically the stays keep the mast upright and unbending towards either side.

13. *rest:* 1. is settled; 2. is reposed — see *Am.* 58.2, *reposeth.*

14. *such one:* ambiguous: either 1. *one* is the subject of *loues,* hence the poet is *most happy* because she (such a one) loves him best; or 2. *one* is the object of *loues,* hence the poet is *most happy* because he *loues* such a (*Most happy*) one. Or it is both — hence the complementarity of the betrotheds' assurance is underscored.

Friday 22 March: *Morning Prayer:* Ps. 105, John 9. *Evening Prayer:* Ps. 106, 1 Tim. 6.

## Sonnet 60

Sonnet 60 takes stock of the year passed, Spenser choosing the penultimate day of the year to commemorate its passing, because 24 March, the final day, was the feast of Palm Sunday in 1594 and required a festive sonnet. Reckonings of time were frequent among sonneteers. Spenser's numberings here have since the eighteenth century been used to calculate the year of his birth (see line 8 note). His knowledge of astronomy was not, as Harvey indicated of his earlier work, a limited one, but, as the calendrical niceties of *Epith.* show, complex and precise.

1. *They that in course of heauenly spheares are skild:* Harvey in his copy of Dionysius Periegetes' *Surveye of the World* (1572) complains of Spenser's culpable ignorance of astronomy, "Pudet ipsum Spenserum, etsi Sphaerae, astrolabiique non plane ignarum; suae in astronomicis Canonibus, tabulis, instrumentisque imperitiae" (*Marginalia* [ed. Moore Smith] 162). Evidently his expertise had grown by the time *Epith.* came to be written.
    *course:* passage; see *Am.* 62.2, "compast course."

2. *sundry:* separate, individual; possibly chosen because of its suggestive association with sun.

4. *Mars:* in the Ptolemaic system, where the normal form of a planet's orbit was thought circular, that of Mars was observed to be the most eccentric, see *FQ* VII.vii.52.1–4. Dodge (cited in *Variorum, Minor Poems,* 2.440) writes, "The planetary "yeare" to which Spenser refers is apparently the period of "restitution," that during which a planet, leaving a given position with regard to the sun, will return to that same position; the period, in other words, during which the revolutions of the planet in its epicycle and of the sun in its orbit will bring both back to the same relative position (of course, only approximate). For Mars, Ptolemy reckons this period at 79 years." (See Yale 636 which cites *Almagest* 9.3.) In fact, the earth, sun, and Mars are again in a straight line after 60.19 years. The numeral 60 coincides with the sonnet's number; this is the last of the martial sonnets, suggesting that Mars has indeed run his course.

5. *winged God:* Cupid.
> *his planet cleare:* a reference to the brightness of Venus.

6. *one year is spent:* Petrarch likewise takes stock in the penultimate sonnet of the *Rime,* the 364th out of 365:
> Tennemi Amor anni ventuno ardendo
> lieto nel foco e nel duol pien di speme;
> poi che Madonna e 'l mio cor seco inseme
> saliro al ciel, dieci altri anni piangendo.

8. *then al those fourty which my life outwent:* If the number forty is in any way accurate, it suggests 1553/54 as the year of Spenser's birth. Such a date would also fit well the date of his matriculation at Cambridge University, 20 May 1569 (see *Variorum, Minor Poems,* 2.439–40).

9. *louers books:* Associated with Lechery in *FQ* I.iv.25.8, "read in louing bookes."
> *inuent:* 1. discover; 2. devise or even fabricate.

10–11. Proverbial, see Smith, *Proverb Lore,* 461.

13. *my loues fayre Planet:* Venus occurs again in *Epith.* 282, "Hast thee O fayrest Planet to thy home."
> *short:* Spenser's only usage as a verb: 1. shorten her orbit, reduce the time of the coming earth year; 2. advance the date of; 3. mathematically, be short when calculating.

14. *this yeare ensuing:* this approaching year.
> *or else short my dayes:* Possibly reflecting evening prayer Ps. 109.7, "Let his dayes be fewe." Otherwise the sonnet bears little comparison with any of the proper psalms or lessons for Saturday 23 March.

**Saturday 23 March:** *Morning Prayer:* Ps. 107, John 10. *Evening Prayer:* Pss. 108–09, 2 Tim. 1.

## Sonnet 61

The sonnet, which commemorates Palm Sunday, 25 March in 1594, intervenes between sonnets acknowledging the year past and the year to come, and Spenser has called upon an earlier episode which celebrates the same occasion in *FQ* II.ii.40–42. There Elizabeth I's annual bestowing of the Order of Maidenhood is recorded: "An yearely solemne feast she wontes to make / The day that first doth lead the yeare around" (42.6–7). The queen is addressed as the "Great and most glorious virgin Queene aliue, / That with her soueraigne powre . . . (40.3–4) / In her the richesse of all heauenly grace / In chiefe degree are heaped vp on hye / And all that else this worlds enclosure bace . . . (41.1–3) / Adornes the person of her

Maiestie; / That men . . . / Do her adore with sacred reuerence, / As th'Idole of her makers great magnificence." (41.5–9).

1–2. *glorious image of the makers beautie . . . Idoll of my thought:* See headnote, *FQ* II.ii.41.9. The epithets establish the lady as of heavenly making — thus contrary to the associations of evening prayer Ps. 115.4, "Their idoles are siluer and golde: euen the worke of mens hands."

2. *My souerayne saynt:* See headnote, *FQ* II.ii.40.3, & IV. Pr.4.2, where Elizabeth I is addressed as, "that sacred Saint my soueraigne Queene."

3. *dare not henceforth aboue the bounds of dewtie / t'accuse of pride, or rashly blame for ought:* An instruction to the poet himself (identified in line 14 as among the *men of meane degree*), which gives the poem a sense of future resolve. He may, seemingly, *accuse* or *blame* her when it is his duty, but not otherwise, such as on those prior occasions when poetic convention or hyperbole allowed.

5. *diuinely wrought:* 1. the manner of her being made; 2. the divine origin of her being made.

6. *of the brood of Angels heuenly borne:* See the description of Una, "the Virgin borne of heauenly brood," Belphoebe, "So was this virgin borne," and Cambina, who "seemed borne of Angels brood" (*FQ* I.iii.8.7; III.vi.3.6 & IV.iv.39.7).

    *brood:* 1. of the family or lineage of angels; 2. the implied sense, 'of angelic contemplation' (brood), cannot be discounted.

    *heuenly:* as in *diuinely* (5), both 1. the manner of her being *borne*; and 2. the heavenly origin of her birth.

    *borne:* 1. brought forth into existence, generated; 2. in a transferred sense, of a heavenly condition — as in the phrase, 'a born Englishman'; 3. homonymically, carried, sustained.

    The line also uses morning prayer Ps. 110.3, "the deawe of thy birth is of the wombe of the morning," an Old Testament analogue for the conception and birth of Christ announced to the Blessed Virgin by an angel (see Roche 105–6), by drawing on the passage that narrates the conception and birth of Belphoebe for which the psalm verse also provided the basis (*FQ* III.vi.3.1–7): "Her berth was of the wombe of Morning dew, / And her conception of the ioyous Prime, / And all her whole creation did her shew / Pure and vnspotted from all loathly crime, / That is ingenerate in fleshly slime. / So was this virgin borne, so was she bred, / So was she trayned vp." Significantly for the eve of Christ's conception (25 March) Spenser has celebrated the lady's conception as an analogue of Christ's (see *Am.* 1.11 note).

7. *vpbrought:* 1. raised and educated; 2. homonymically, as in *borne* (6), raised up, "exalted" (see lines 13–14 note).

9. *The bud of ioy, the blossome of the morne:* See Ps. 110.3 "the deawe of thy birth is of the wombe of the morning." Johnson, "*Amoretti* and the Art of the Liturgy," 55 notes that Palm Sunday was also known as Blossom Sunday and Flowering Sunday.

11–12. *Scorn / base things:* The phrase (*Fuge turpia*) was proverbial — see *Am.* 5.6 & 13.9–19.

13–14. *Such heauenly formes . . . men of meane degree.* In the first instance *heauenly formes* retains its Neo-Platonic associations, but the sonnet's claim about the lady's heavenly origin corresponds exactly to that of the feast's Epistle, the hymn of Phil. 2.5–12, which acclaims the "glorie" of Christ, who "being in the forme of God, thoght it no robbery to be equal with God" (v. 6; the thought is

evident earlier in *diuinely wrought* (5) and *heuenly borne* [6]). The paradox
between *heauenly formes* and *men of meane degree* (= not gently born, servants)
further corresponds with that, acclaimed in Philippians, which contrasts Christ
"being in the forme of God" with his action when he "made him self of no
reputation, and toke on him the forme of a seruant, and was made like vnto
men" (v. 7).

   *worshipt:* exactly matching the purpose of the paradox in Phil. 2.9–10,
"Wherefore God hathe also highly exalted him, and giuen him a Name aboue
euerie name, That at the Name of Iesus shulde euerie knee bowe," with its
Geneva version sidenote g, "Worship, and be subiect to him." See also Ps.
110.3, "holy worship."

**Palm Sunday 24 March:** *Epistle:* Phil. 2.5–12. *Gospel:* Matt. 26.1–27.57. *Morning Prayer:* Pss.
110–13, John 11. *Evening Prayer:* Pss. 114–15, 2 Tim. 2.

## Sonnet 62

Sonnet 62 celebrates the change from the old to the new year on March 25, a
commencement date debated by Spenser in the Generall Argument to SC, "For it
is wel known and stoutely mainteyned with stronge reasons of the learned, that the
yeare beginneth in March. For then the sonne reneweth his finished course, and the
seasonable spring refresheth the earth." The annual return of the year becomes a
pattern of the seasonable return to grace for the poet and his betrothed. (Yale 637
notes that if the 89 *amoretti,* the 9 anacreontic verses, and the 24 stanzas of *Epithalamion* are totalled, numerically Sonnet 62 marks the beginning of the volume's
second part.)

   In structure the sonnet anticipates the Cranmerian prayer structure of Easter
Sunday's *Am.* 68. Like *Am.* 68 it uses the first person plural pronoun as the subject
of the prayer — its first occurrence in the sequence.

1. *yeare:* By coincidence the Epistle for the Monday before Easter, Isa. 63, contrasts
   the "olde time" with the present and celebrates the new year to come, "the
   yere of my redemed is come" (v. 4).
2. *compast course:* circular passage or progress; that which can be described with
   compasses — matching the repeated detail in morning prayer Pss. 116.3, "compassed me round about," and 118.10, "compassed me rounde about." It is a
   term of temporal measurement in *Am.* 60.1, "the course of heauenly spheares,"
   in *FQ* III.vii.55.3 & *Ro* 22.9.
4. *betokening:* signifying, one of only two usages by Spenser; the word looks forward
   to the rewards of Easter.
5. *So let vs:* the pronoun occurs only 3 times in the sequence, see *Am.* 68.13 (for
   Easter Sunday) and *Am.* 87.7 (for Expectation Sunday).
6. *chaunge eeke our mynds:* A prayer proper to Lent and a translation of μετανοέω
   = to change the mind, to be converted, to repent (the Geneva Bible's normal
   rendering). The equivalent instruction is frequent in the day's readings, see Isa.
   63.17, "Returne (Vulgate, *convertere*) for thy seruants sake," the day's second
   lesson at morning prayer, John 12.40, "and shulde be conuerted" (Vulgate,
   *convertantur*), and Ps. 116.7, "Turne againe then vnto thy rest, O my soule
   (Vulgate, *convertere anima mea*)."
10. *into the glooming world his gladsome ray:* See John 12.46, "I am come a light into
    the worlde . . . darknesse" (see also vv. 35–36).
    *glooming:* appearing dark.

11. *blend:* blinded, blemished. In imitation of the prophecy of Isa. 6.9, appealled to in John 12.40, "He hathe blinded their eyes ... that they ... and shulde be conuerted" (koiné, ἐπιστάφῶσιν = to turn oneself away from, an equivalent to μετανοέω; the two terms were often yoked together, see Acts 3.19). Spenser apparently knew that the verb was used traditionally to describe the circular course of the heavenly bodies, see Homer, *Od.* 5.274.

12. *timely:* 1. in time; 2. seasonably or opportunely, see *Am.* 4.9.

13–14. See *Am.* 4.3–4, "and bidding th'old Adieu, his passed date / bids all old thoughts to die in dumpish spright."

13. *heauy spright:* The change of adjective from *Am.* 4.4, "dumpish sprite," fits the repeated detail of the day's Gospel, Mark 14.34, "My soule is verie heauie" (see v. 38, "the spirit in dede is readie," & v. 40), and evening prayer Ps. 119.28, "My soule melteth away for very heauines."

**Monday 25 March, Monday afore Easter:** *Epistle:* Isa. 63.1–19. *Gospel:* Mark 14.1–72. *Morning Prayer:* Pss. 116–118, John 12. *Evening Prayer:* Ps. 119.1–32, 2 Tim. 3.

## Sonnet 63

The sonnet continues the theme of a change in weather, established in Sonnet 59 with its steady ship which parts the "raging waues and keepes her course aright," and sustained in Sonnet 62, with its images of a course run and storms turned to calm.

1–4. The *topos* of the storm-tossed bark was commonplace (see *Am.* 34 & 59), as was its steering a course towards the safety of port, e.g., Petrarch, *Rime,* 151.1–4, "Non d'atra e tempestosa onde marina / fuggìo in porto già mai stanco noc-chiero, / com' io dal fosco e torbido pensero / fuggo ove 'l gran desio mi sprona e 'nchina." (Compare Ariosto, *Lirica,* 3.28, "O sicuro, secreto e fidel porto," du Bellay, *Les Regrets,* 34, "Comme le marinier que le creul orage," and Ronsard's version, *Amours Diverses,* 13.) The conceit echoes Paul's statement in the second lesson at evening prayer for the Tuesday before Easter 26 March, 2 Tim. 4.6–7, "the time of my departing is at hand. I haue foght a good fight, and haue finished *my* course." Like the Palmer's benediction, in a passage also drawing on 2 Tim. 4.6–7 ("Must now anew begin, like race to runne; / God guide thee, Guyon, well to end thy warke, / And to the wished hauen bring thy weary barke" [*FQ* II.i.32.7–9]), the poet presents his completed course as a bark safely arriving at a haven. (For the image of departing and arriving see the day's Epistle, Isa. 50.5–11, "nether turned I backe" (v. 5), its second lesson at morning prayer, John 13, "Whither I go, can ye not come" (v. 33 and passim) and "he shulde departe out of this worlde" (v. 1), and in 2 Tim. 4.9, "Make spede to come vnto me atonce," and 21, "Make spede to come before winter.") *assay:* trial, test.

2. *endured:* See morning prayer Ps. 119.89, "O Lorde, thy woorde: endureth for euer in heauen."

4. *silly:* 1. defenseless; 2. weak, poor — contrasting with *deare and daynty* (8).

7. *soyle:* land, often one's proper homeland.
   *fraught:* 1. filled; 2. nautically of a ship, laden.

8–9. *happy ... rest:* Compare the poet's "happy rest" in *Am.* 76.13.

8. *daynty:* 1. tenderly beautiful; 2. from its etymon *dignitatem,* worthy, precious.

9. *Most happy he:* Recalling *Am.* 59.13–14, "most happy she ... / but he most happy."

12. *remembrance:* The only occasion Spenser uses the word in *Amoretti* and match-ing morning prayer Ps. 119.59, "I called mine owne wayes to remembrance."

14. *sorrowes:* The poet's sorrow reflects the biblical archetype of the sorrowful servant, celebrated in the day's Epistle, Isa. 50.11, "ye shal lie downe in sorowe."

**Tuesday 26 March, Tuesday afore Easter:** *Epistle:* Isa. 50.5–11. *Gospel:* Mark 15.1–47. *Morning Prayer:* Ps. 119.33–72, John 13. *Evening Prayer:* Ps. 119.73–104, 2 Tim. 4.

## Sonnet 64

The sonnet's opening reference to kiss is the only overtly physical reference in a sequence otherwise devoid of physical touch. Its flowers, moreover, are not chosen because of their particular odors, but are fashioned to hide a series of love-knots and word-plays. The sonnet thereby differs from the popular *blason*, whose conventions Spenser observed exactly in Sonnet 15.

1. *Comming to kisse her lyps:* The conceit corresponds to the biblical *topos* of Judas' kiss, recounted in the Gospel proper to the Wednesday before Easter, Luke 22.1–71: "he that was called Iudas one of the twelue, went before them, and came nere vnto Iesus to kisse him. And Iesus said vnto him, Iudas, betrayest thou the Sonne of man with a kisse?" (vv. 47–48). The betrayal takes place in the Garden of Gethsemane.

   *grace:* 1. pleasantness of taste or smell; 2. favor, goodness.

1–2. *(such grace I found) . . . a gardin of sweet flowres:* The sonnet by not celebrating an act of perfidy but its opposite, *grace*, and by singing of *a gardin of sweet flowres*, reflects the day's special first lessons at morning and evening prayer, Hos. 13 and 14, chosen because Hosea, having condemned false prophets who offer false sacrifices, "Let them kisse the calues" (13.2), asks that a song be on Israel's lips, "receiue *vs* graciously: so wil we render the calues of our lippes" (14.2). His song is of a sweet-smelling garden: "I wil be as the dewe vnto Israel: he shal growe as the lilie and fasten his rootes as *the trees* of Lebanon. His branches shal spreade, and his beautie shalbe as the oliue tre, and his smel as Lebanon . . . they shal reuiue *as* the corne, and florish as the vine: the sent thereof *shalbe* as the wine of Lebanon" (vv. 5–7). The items in Spenser's sweet-smelling garden generally differ from Hosea's corn, vine, olive and fir tree, the exception being "lilie."

2. *smelt:* See line 1 note, Hos. 14.6–7, "smel . . . sent." Medieval and Renaissance tropology linked and identified Hosea's Israel-garden, the chosen people, the elect, the Song of Solomon's *hortus inclusus* ("My sister, my spouse *is as* a garden inclosed. . . . Thy plantes *are as* an orcharde of pomegranates with swete frutes . . . let my welbeloued come to his garden, and eat his pleasant frute" [4.12–16]), and sweet-smelling flowers. See Trapp 266, commenting upon Hos. 14.6–8, "by *flowers* . . . are vnderstood . . . the first fruits of the Spirit, whereby the Elect giue a pleasant smell."

5–10. *Gillyflowers . . . Pincks . . . Cullambynes:* Compare the only other occasion when Spenser invokes these flowers, SC April, 136–37, "Bring hether the Pincke and purple Cullambine, / With Gelliflowres."

5. *Gillyflowers:* 1. a plant with flowers scented like a clove; 2. probably also *gill* = a giddy young woman (*OED* 4) + *flower*.

7. *browes lyke budded Bellamoures:* (*bel* = fair + *amour* = love); the only certain use of the word as a flower, although see *FQ* II.vi.16.7, where Belamoure is possibly

a flower. Either 1. the "floure Armour," which Hill 105 describes as "like to an ear of corne"; or 2. *Bellamoures* are no flowers at all but loving glances identical to belgards (Italian, *bel* = beautiful + *guardo* = look) — see *FQ* II.iii, 25, 2–3, "Vnder the shadow of her euen browes, / Working belgards." Fowler, *Conceitful Thought*, 96 contends that Bellamoure is not a flower "but a love glance, which will bloom as the young lady's budded brow opens."

8. *eyes lyke Pincks:* Pink — the general name of the species Dianthus, which has variegated sweet-smelling flowers. Dianthus = δι-ανθής = double-flowering, a flower appropriate to the eyes.

9. *Strawberry bed:* more physical than emblematic, although strawberries were omnipresent in medieval and Renaissance iconography.

10. *neck . . . bounch of Cullambynes:* an extended etymological pun: 1. *collum* = neck + *bynde* = bunch (OED bind 9); but 2. also *columbine:* like a dove (= *columba*) or of the color of a dove's neck (OED 3).

11. *lillyes:* See lines 1–2 note, Hos. 14.5, "he shal growe as the lilie."

12. *Iessemynes:* Jasmine or Gethsamine (see Turner, *Herbal*, 2.19.b, "Iesemin or Gethsamine"). The only occurence in Spenser and a probable ultimate cryptogram, the *locus* of the day's reading being the Garden of Gethsemane.

**Wednesday afore Easter, 27 March:** *Epistle:* Heb. 9.16–28. *Gospel:* Luke 22.1–71. *Morning Prayer:* Ps. 119.105–144, Hos. 13, John 14; *Evening Prayer:* Ps. 119.145–176, Hos. 14, Tit. 1.

## Sonnet 65

The sonnet's argument, one of the weightier and more complex of the sequence, affirms the betrotheds' perfect love and sets the nature of their forthcoming marriage within the context of the new covenant of grace. As such, it befits the Thursday before Easter, Maundy Thursday, whose second lesson at morning prayer in 1594, John 15, celebrates the institution of the new covenant, a feature of which is Christ's *mandatum*, "As the Father hathe loued me, so haue I loued you: continue in my loue. . . . This is my commandement, that ye loue one another, as I haue loued you. Greater loue then this hathe no man, when any man bestoweth his life for his friends" (John 15.9 & 12–13; Kaske, " 'Amoretti' 68," 518 wrongly appoints John 15 as the second lesson at morning prayer for March 27). For the coincidence of readings for the feast days of Maundy Thursday and St. Barnabas, June 11, see Introduction, p. 46. Maundy Thursday was also associated with marriage in 1594 through Ps. 128, one of the day's psalms at evening prayer, which was also read during the marriage service.

1–4. The captive lover is a common enough Petrarchist conceit, as indeed is the poet's reassuring the lady that she will, in contrast, gain a further liberty by ensnaring that of the poet (e.g., Amoret's "wished freedome" [*FQ* IV.x.37.5]). But Spenser's idea that through marriage two new liberties are gained is poetically unusual: both partners will share the new freedom that the holiness of marriage sanctions, although paradoxically, the poet concludes, he, who once was afeared of being bound, will thereby be bonded.

1. *misdeeme:* wrongly judge.

2. *fondly:* foolishly — see the day's second lessons at evening prayer Tit. 3.9, "But stay foolish questions . . . and contentions . . . for thei arre vnprofitable and vaine."

*feare:* Perfect love is beyond fear in John's amplification of the day's *mandatum*, "There is no feare in loue, but perfect loue casteth out feare: for feare hathe painfulnes: and he that feareth, is not perfect in loue" (1 John 4.18).

  *loose:* See the day's Gospel, Luke 23.16, "let him lowse" (see vv. 17, 22 & 25, "he let lowse vnto them him that . . . was cast into prison").

5. *bands:* 1. fetters; 2. the sense of a betrothal or engagement is also present (see Am. 1.3); 3. band was also used of a covenant or *league* (*OED* 12), see *Epith.* 396.

6. *constraynt:* See morning prayer Ps. 120.4, "Wo is me, that I am constrained."

7. *gentle bird:* Corresponding to the metaphor in morning prayer Ps. 124.6, "Our soule is escaped, euen as a birde out of the snare of the fouler: the snare is broken, and we are deliuered (Vulgate, *liberati sumus* = gain liberty [3])."

  *captiuity:* See evening prayer Ps. 126.5, "Turne our captiuitie, O Lord."

8. *nor discord spill:* Compare the day's Epistle, 1 Cor. 11.18, Paul's complaint, "I heare that there are dissensions among you."

  *discord:* disharmony, with hearts apart (*dis* = apart + *cor* = heart), but with an implied sense of musical disharmony. The concord-discord antithesis was firmly rooted in Spenser's conception of the nature of things (see *Variorum* 4.311), with concord nourishing virtue in the individual (e.g., *FQ* II.ii.33.8-9).

  *feeds her fill:* Proverbial, see Smith, *Proverb Lore*, 256; see Am. 72.8, where the bird desires "to feed his fill."

9-14. The sestet argues for the rightfulness of physical pleasure in marriage. Perfect love, because it is beyond the reach of pride, retains a prelapsarian goodness similar to that of the golden age, which is also "withouten . . . pride," and of which Spenser treats in *FQ* IV.viii.30:

> But antique age yet in the infancie
>> Of time, did liue then like an innocent,
>> In simple truth and blamelesse chastitie,
>> Ne then of guile had made experiment,
>> But voide of vile and treacherous intent,
>> Held vertue for it selfe in soueraine awe:
>> Then loyall loue had royall regiment,
> And each vnto his lust did make a lawe,
> From all forbidden things his liking to withdraw.

Spenser similarly portrays the marriage of Una and the Red Cross Knight (*FQ* I.xii.20ff.) in edenic terms, drawing upon its customary biblical analogues, Revelations (19.7, "the mariage of the Lambe") and the Song of Solomon.

10. *league:* covenant – a term reflecting a specific application of Protestant covenantal thought to marriage. Compare the impediment declared by Duessa before the marriage of the Red Cross Knight and Una, "Withhold, O soueraine Prince, your hasty hond / From knitting league with him, I you aread" (*FQ* I.xii.28.3-4).

11. *simple:* 1. pure; 2. single – counterbalanced by *mutuall*; 3. by transference, *simple* was also used of a *wound* (12) without complications.

  *mutuall good will:* Compare the plighting of the Red Cross Knight and Guyon, "With right hands plighted, pledges of goodwill" (*FQ* II.i.34.2), and contrast the reprehensible egocentric "freewill" of Am. 10.4, and the proper "goodwill" of Am. 67.13.

12. *to salue each othes wound:* hereafter wounds are not found in the sequence.

13-14. Faith, appropriately in convental theology, renders an "indifferent" thing a *spotlesse pleasure*, and by remedying the lust of the flesh, absorbs its difficulties into the freedom awarded by the covenant of grace; see *Epith.* 192.

13. *fearelesse:* See line 2 note, 1 John 14.

      *brasen:* of brass, therefore strong, such as the "brasen towre" in which Una's parents are imprisoned (*FQ* I.xi.3.2).

      *towre:* Recalls the day's special first lesson at evening prayer, Jer. 31, where the prophet, writing of the re-establishment of the Old Testament covenant, makes of it a covenant between husband and wife ("I was an housband vnto them, saith the Lord" [v. 32]), and sees as a sign of its faithfulness and duration a tower and a new city: "the citie shalbe buylt to the Lord from the tower of Hananeel, vnto the gate of the corner" (v. 38).

14. *spotless pleasure:* In the *locus amoenus* of love-making, the Temple of Venus, where the edenic associations are clear, pleasure is also without sin, "Their spotlesse pleasures, and sweet loues content" (*FQ* IV.x.26.2). See *HL* 287.

**Thursday afore Easter, 28 March:** *Epistle:* 1 Cor. 11.17–34. *Gospel:* Luke 23.1–56. *Morning Prayer:* Pss. 120–125, Dan. 9, John 15. *Evening Prayer:* Pss. 126–131, Jer. 31, Tit. 2 & 3.

## Sonnet 66

The sonnet, which corresponds to the feast of Good Friday, 29 March, is, like the preceding Sonnet 65, preoccupied with marriage, initially in a humorous vein, although its good-natured bantering cedes place to the weighty reciprocity of its final couplet. The primary notion of *disparagement* (3) as a marriage to one of baser rank, the secondary notion of *paragon* (5) as a consort in marriage, together with *mate* (6), *matchable* (7), *sorted* (10) and *pere* (10) all contribute to the marital theme. The final paradox of light and dark is an appropriate contrast for Good Friday, when the light of Christ is opposed, in the gospel's phrase, to "darkenes ouer all the land." Because the lady's light has illumined the poet, his light will reflect back on her and, because each will enhance the other, a mutuality accrues to both. (If the poem is construed as an address to Christ, then the *light* of the final couplet is also Christ's light which has *enlumind* the poet. As in the conclusion to *Am.* 68, the reflection between Christ and the poet is emphasized, as well as the reflection between the poet and the lady. The light, of course, is the same.)

1–2. *blessings / heauen:* Compare morning prayer Pss. 134.4, "The Lord that made heauen and earth: giue thee blessing," and 133.3–4, "For there the Lorde promised his blessing: and life for euermore."

2. *thrown:* The sense of lots being thrown or cast down by fortune's (or providence's) hand is implied (see line 10 note, *sorted*, and *Am.* 82.2 note, "lot").

3. *disparagement:* 1. The disgrace of a marriage to one of inferior, non-gentle, rank, see *FQ* VI.x.37.5, "base disparagement"; 2. a lowering of dignity or esteem, despisedness (see *HB* 162–165) – such as afflicted the suffering "seruant" in the day's special first lesson at evening prayer for the feast, Isa. 53.3, who "was dispised and we estemed him not."

4. *so meane a one:* Reflecting both Isaiah's suffering "seruant" (53.11) and the day's second lesson at evening prayer, Phil. 1.16, "Not now as a seruant, but aboue a seruant, euen as a brother beloued, specially to me." (In *Am.* 61.14, "men of meane degree," corresponds to Phil. 2.6, "the forme of a seruant," read for Palm Sunday 24 March.)

5. *paragon:* 1. a pattern of excellence; 2. a mate, consort in marriage – see *FQ* VI.ix.11.5, "To be a Princes Paragone esteemed."

6. *fit:* 1. worthy; 2. made (see *Am.* 22.1 note).

      *mate:* 1. companion; 2. spouse.

7. *Matchable to none:* 1. unequalled; 2. not joinable in marriage — a secondary connotation.

5/8. *high worths / lowly state:* In contrast to evening prayer Ps. 138.6, "For though the Lorde be high, yet hath hee respect vnto the lowly."

8. *why did ye stoup vnto so lowly state?:* A probable echo of Heb. 10.12-13, which makes the same comparison, "But this man . . . sitteth for euer at the right hand of God, And from hence forthe tarieth, til his enemies be made his fotestole," itself a coincidental echo of the psalm verse read at morning prayer Ps. 132.7, "fal low on our knees before his footestole."

9. *gate:* had got; unusual and here for rhyme.

10. *sorted with:* 1. consorted with as a companion or mate — a unique usage in Spenser; 2. etymologically associated with heavenly fortune, fate, lot (= *sors*). A feature of the crucifixion account is the fulfilling of Isaiah's prophecy, "and on my coate did cast lottes" (Vulgate, *sortem*).

   *peer:* 1. equal in rank; 2. wife (OED sb 3).

11. *it selfe dilate:* expand out from itself; see Nature's judgement with its Aristotelian sense of fulfillment, *FQ* VII.vii.58.5, "But by their change their being doe dilate."

12. *darknesse:* 1. recalls the crucifixion, when "there was a darkenes ouer all the land.... And the sunne was darkened" (Luke 23.44-45); 2. retains its Neo-Platonic sense of a shadow which is related to reality as the phenomenal world is related to the world of heavenly ideas, and thus echoes Good Friday's Epistle, Heb. 10.1, "For the Lawe hauing the shadowe of good things to come, and not the very image of the things."

13. *enlumind:* illuminated, enlightened.

14. *reflex:* 1. only used here and technically: the reflection of light from the sun, particularly as it rebounds from a region of darkness back into light (OED sb 1); 2. Neo-Platonically, the dilating of the lady's light will illumine the poet, who, once illumined, will by *reflex* continue to enlarge — and fulfill — her light, see HB 176-82.

**Good Friday 29 March:** *Epistle:* Heb. 10.1-25. *Gospel:* John 18.1–19.42. *Morning Prayer:* Pss. 132-135, John 16. *Evening Prayer:* Pss. 136-38, Phil. 1.

### Sonnet 67

Sonnet 67 comprises a web of related *topoi,* drawn from disparate sources, but all proper to the Evening before Easter, 30 March, and to the poet's forthcoming marriage-covenant (see Prescott, "Deer," 33-76 and Dasenbrock 43-44 for extensive treatments of the cervine *topos*).

1. Spenser has taken cognizance of the ancient liturgical tradition associated with Easter Evening, the procession of the catechumens to the font to be baptized, during which Ps. 42.1-2 was sung, "Like as the hart desireth the water brookes (Vulgate, *ad fontes aquarum*): so longeth (Geneva Bible, so panteth) my soule after thee, O God. My soule is a thirst for God, yea, euen for the liuing God: when shall I come to appreare before the presence of God?" The sonnet echoes the psalm's phrases in *Lyke as* (1), *thirst* (8), *next brooke* (8), and its transference of the Geneva version's "so panteth" to the *panting hounds* (4).

2. The sonnet belongs to the tradition of the chase, preserved in Petrarch's "Una candida cerva" (*Rime,* 190), and imitated by many of his successors, including Tasso, "Questa fera gentil" (*Rime,* 2.429.1). Spenser echoes the spirit of the

convention rather than the letter. He ignores, for example, the collar about the deer's neck and the only specific element he shares with either precedent is the "cangiato voler" of Tasso's gentle beast.

3. Rather, Spenser has resorted to the cervine tradition's *locus classicus*, the account in Ovid, *Met.* 10.106–42, of Cyparissus, who, like Ps. 42, would lead his deer to water brooks: "[cervum] tu liquidi ducebas fontis ad undam" (122; Golding, (10.129), "thou to water springs him led"; like Petrarch's deer, Ovid's also has about its neck a collar inset with jewels [113]). From Ovid Spenser has also drawn the details of the *fearelesse* (10) nature of the deer, as well as the sonnet's *shady place* (3).

4. Throughout the sonnet, and particularly through its pun on *deare*/deer, the hart remains an image of the spouse, whom the poet takes in hand and who is bound by *her owne goodwill* (12). The biblical analogue whose cervine association links marriage with baptism and thus underwrites the conceit was Prov. 5.18–19, "Let thy fountaine be blessed, and reioyce with the wife of thy youth. *Let her be as* the louing hinde and pleasant roe: let her breasts satisfie thee at all times, and delite in her loue continually."

1. *Lyke as:* See headnote, Ps. 42.1; the custom of singing the canticle *Sicut cervus* during the procession of the catechumens to the font at the Easter Vigil had its roots in the early church. It was common to all pre-reformed Easter Vigil rites and was accepted into the 1570 Roman Missal of Pius V.

1 & 3. *weary ... shady place:* Reminiscent of the detail provided by Ovid, *Met.* 10.128–29, with its action of the weary deer returning to the brook and its being accidentally discovered by the Cyparissus, "fessus (= *weary*) in herbosa posuit sua corpora terra / cervus et arborea (= *shady*) frigus ducebat ab umbra." Spenser uses the episode of Cyparissus, who of course killed the deer, in *FQ* I.vi.17.5–6.

3. *sits downe:* Compare morning prayer Ps. 139.1, "O Lord thou hast searched me out, and knowen me: thou knowest my downe sitting...."

4. *beguiled:* cheated; different from *beguyld* (14) which intends charmed or diverted.

7. *gentle deare:* the association of hunting and marriage (here underwritten by the pun on *deare* = 1. dear; 2. deer) was commonplace, and is used by Spenser in the account of Amoret and Scudamour, *FQ* IV.x.55.6–8, "but I which all that while / The pledge of faith, her hand engaged held, / Like warie Hynd within the weedie soyle." In *FQ* Scudamour is both the hunter who has ambushed Amoret, and also the hunted deer whose refuge Amoret is. The same image is used at their reunion, "Like as a Deare, that greedily embayes / In the coole soile, after long thirstinesse, / Which he in chace endured hath, now nigh breathlesse." (*FQ* (1590), III.xii.44.7–9). See also Tasso, *Rime*, 2.429.1.1–8:

> Questa fera gentil, ch'in si crucciosa
> > Fronte fuggia pur dianzi i vostri passi
> > Fra spini e sterpi, e dirupati sassi,
> > Strada ad og'nor prendendo erta, e dubbiosa;
> Or, cangiato voler, d'onesta posa
> > Vaga, discende ai sentier piani e bassi,
> > E, quasi ogni durezza indietro lassi,
> > Incontro vi si fa lieta e vezzosa.

Spenser identifies the "fera gentil" as a deer when he translates Petrarch's "fera gentil" (*Rime*, 323.8) as "a Hynde" in *Pet* 4 & 9.

8. *beholding:* seeing, looking, but its origin, 'be + hold,' is reflected later in *in her hand . . . tooke* (11).

   *thirst:* See headnote, Ps. 42.2, and compare evening prayer Ps. 143.6, "my soule gaspeth vnto thee as a thirstie land."

10. *sought not to fly:* See evening prayer Ps. 142.5, "I had no place to flee vnto."

   *fearelesse:* The deer in Ovid's account of Cyparissus shows the same fearless nature, allowing men to take it and soothe it with their hands, "isque metu vacuus naturalique pavore / . . . mulcendaque colla / quamlibet ignotis manibus praebere solebat" (*Met.* 10.117–19; Golding, 10.124–26, "This goodly Spitter beeing voyd of dread, as hauing quyght / Forgot his natiue fearefulnesse, . . . / Would suffer folk . . . to coy him with theyr hand."

11. *in hand . . . her tooke:* See morning prayer Ps. 139.9, "Euen there also shall thy hande leade me: and thy right hand shall hold me." In *Epith.* 238–39 a similar hesitancy occurs.

   *halfe trembling:* trembling is generally quivering brought on by fear or apprehension. The qualifier's antecedent remains open, implying mutuality: either 1. the *deare* is the lady, and because it is now *fearelesse*, the shaking, in its diminished form, appears as a continuing after-effect; or 2. the poet, consequent upon his own weariness, is *halfe trembling*.

11–12. *hand . . . goodwill:* See *FQ* II.i.34.2, the leave-taking of the Red Cross Knight and Guyon, "With right hands plighted, pledges of good will." The sonnet's *goodwill* contrasts with the reprehensible (and pre-Lenten) "freewill" of *Am.* 10.4.

14. *her owne will beguyld:* Corresponding to Tasso's "cangiato voler" (= changed will); see line 7 note.

   *beguyld:* charmed, or diverted (from a course of action).

**Holy Saturday 30 March:** *Epistle:* 1 Pet. 3.17–22. *Gospel:* Matt. 27.57–66. *Morning Prayer:* Pss. 139–41, John 17. *Evening Prayer:* Pss. 142–43, Heb. 1.


### Sonnet 68

The sonnet's opening liturgical reference to Easter Sunday, 31 March 1634, and its celebration of Christ's *triumph ouer death and sin* (2), introduces a poem, shaped after the manner of a formal prayer with invocation, relative clauses, and petition. The sonnet's tone is joyous and forthrightly personal as it anticipates the forthcoming marriage. It is addressed both to God and to the poet's betrothed who are allied in the poem's parallel epithets, *deare Lord* (5) and *deare loue* (13). For the moment the covert is laid aside, while the explicit mutuality of the common pronoun *vs* and the verb *entertayne* is precise.

1–14. The structure reflects the Cranmerian style of the *BCP*'s Collects (and the Latinate structure of the original Collects of the pre-reformed rites), its opening bearing some resemblance to the Collect for Easter Sunday, "Almightie God, which through thy onely begotten Sonne Iesus Christ hast ouercome death, and opened vnto vs the gate of euerlasting life. . . ." Cranmer omits the pre-reformed Latin's *hodierna die*, which Spenser's *on this day* acknowledges, "*Deus, qui hodierna die per Unigenitum tuum aeternitatis nobis aditum devicta morte reserasti. . .*"

   Ponsonby's claim (*Complaints*, To the *Gentle Reader*) that Spenser had once translated "The howers of the Lord," which contain at least seven such prayers, suggests some familiarity with the formulaic conventions of a Collect. (Kaske,

"'Amoretti' 68," 518–19 traces the discovery of the prayer structure back to James A. Noble in 1880.)

1. *Lord of lyfe:* A seasonably appropriate address deriving from Acts 3.15, "And killed the Lord of life, whome God hathe raised from the dead"; see *FQ* II.iv.62.6.

2. *triumph ouer death and sin:* Reflecting the Geneva version sidenote (see Prescott, "Deer," 43) to Eph. 4.8, "led captiuitie captiue" (see lines 3–4), "to triumph ouer . . . death and sinne," as well as the liturgical *topos* of the feast's specially chosen second lesson at morning prayer, Rom. 6.9–11, which contrasts sin and death with life (verses that were also read as one of two special anthems that were substituted on Easter Sunday for morning prayer's opening Ps. 95): "Knowing that Christ being raised from the dead, dyeth no more: death hath no more dominion ouer him (Bishops' Bible, "no power vpon him"). . . . Likewise thinke ye also, that ye are dead to sinne, but are aliue to God in Iesus Christ our Lord." Paul later acclaims the freedom from captivity that the resurrection buys, "But now being freed from sinne . . . ye haue your frute in holines, and the end, euerlasting life. For the wages of sinne is death; but the gifte of God *is* eternal life" (v. 22–23). The second anthem at morning prayer was drawn from 1 Cor. 15.20, "Christ is risen againe, the first fruites of them that sleepe." (Compare the Geneva version's sidenote to the chapter, "*O death, where is thy victorie!*")

3. *harrowd hell:* robbed hell; after his death Christ descended into hell to release those held captive by Satan. The image is rooted in 1 Pet. 3.19, read during the Epistle for Easter Evening, "By the which he also went, and preached vnto the spirits that were in prison."

3–4. *didst bring away / captiuity thence captiue vs to win:* Imitating Eph. 4.8 (& Ps. 68.18), "he led captiuitie captiue."

5. *This ioyous day, deare Lord, with ioy begin:* Compare the acclamation in the day's special Psalm at evening prayer, Ps. 118.24, "This is the day which the Lord hath made: we will reioyce and be glad in it." The verse is echoed in *Epith.* 115–16, "Fit for so ioyfull day, / The ioyfulst day that euer sunne did see."

7. *with they deare blood clene washt from sin:* Compare Rev. 1.5, "him that loued vs, and washed vs from our sinnes in his blood," and 1 John 1.7, "the blood of Iesus Christ his Sonne clenseth vs from all sinne."

    *deare:* 1. beloved; 2. costly, precious.

9. *weighing worthily:* valuing highly; it introduces the sestet's mercantile trope.

10. *likewise loue thee:* See Rom. 6.11, "Likewise thinke ye."

11. *that all lyke deare didst buy:* who bought all those who are dear to you – an explicit echo of 1 Cor. 6.20, "For ye are boght for a price (Bishops' version, "For ye are dearly bought").

    *buy:* a seasonal commonplace, deriving from Christ's accomplishing redemption at Easter (*red* = back + *emere* = buy). Ps. 111 was read on Easter Sunday for its phrase, "He sent redemption vnto his people" (v. 9).

12. *with loue may one another entertayne:* A prayerful resolution to the earlier instruction of Am. 4.14, "prepare your selfe new loue to entertaine" (see note).

    *entertayne:* 1. engage, but 2. hold mutually between ourselves, (*inter* = between + *tenere* = hold). The line's syntax is ambiguous: either 1. that Christ and those who are dear to him may embrace each other; or 2. that those who are dear to Christ may embrace each other; or 3. both meanings, thus underscoring the covenantal nature of love.

12–14. In obedience to the exhortation in 1 John 4.7 & 11, "Beloued, let vs loue
one another: for loue cometh of God. . . . Beloued, if God so loued vs, we oght
also to loue one another."

13. *So let vs:* The second of three occasions in the sequence when the personal
pronoun occurs — see *Am.* 62.5 note.

　　　*ought:* 1. are obliged, because love is Christ's lesson; 2. secondarily, owed,
echoing the Easter theme of redemption (see line 11 note); *ought* opens and
shuts the Lenten section of *Amoretti* (see *Am.* 22.2).

**Easter Sunday 31 March:** *Epistle:* Col. 3.1–8. *Gospel:* John 20.1–11. *Morning Prayer:* Pss. 2, 57,
111, Rom. 6. *Evening Prayer:* Pss. 113, 114, 118, Acts 2.

## Sonnet 69

The second occasion when a sonnet's principal theme is one of poetic immortality,
see *Am.* 27.9–12, 75.4–12 (for Low Sunday), & 82 (for the feast of the Ascension).
The theme fits exactly the liturgical *topos* associated with Easter Monday, 1 April,
the sepulchre (Vulgate, *monumentum*, koiné, μνημεῖον = memorial or record) or
monument from which Christ arises. Mention of the monument occurs in both the
day's Gospel, Luke 24.24, "certeine of them . . . went to the sepulchre" (Vulgate,
*monumentum*) and the special second lesson at morning prayer, Matt. 28.8, "they
departed quickely from the sepulchre" (Vulgate, *monumento*).

2. *Trophees:* Among the Greeks, either 1. a monument comprising a tree (ξύλον),
from which spoils of victory were hung, which corresponds with the tree of
Christ's victory acknowledged by Peter in the day's Epistle, Acts 10.39, "hanging him on a tre" (koiné, ξύλου); or 2. a structure erected to commemorate a
victory and adorned with spoils. Since trophy derives from τρέπω = to turn,
from which trope also derives, Spenser, etymologically, is anticipating line 9's
*verse* (from *vertere* = to turn).

　　　*Vsed:* were accustomed to.

3. *records:* accounts preserved for memory, monuments.

　　　*enrold:* 1. inscribed in a roll or register; 2. recorded.

4. *emprize:* a pun: 1. an enterprise of chivalric nature; but 2. an inscription (Italian,
*impresa* = a stamped motto) on a monument.

5. *trophee:* In *Col* 951, the poet's death, recorded in verse, is a "simple trophe" of
Rosalind's conquest.

　　　*most fit:* qualifies either *trophee* or *deuize.*

7. *of my loues conquest:* 1. primarily the conquest of my love, that is, my betrothed;
but 2. secondarily the conquest of my, the poet's, love, or even 3. the conquest
by my love, my betrothed, or the conquest by my, the poet's, love.

8. *honour, loue, and chastity:* See *Epith.* 191–92, "There dwels sweet loue and constant chastity, / Vnspotted fayth and comely womanhood." Both passages echo
the *BCP*, marriage service, "loue her, comfort her, honour and keepe her."

9. Poetic immortality was prominent from classical times onwards; see Horace, *Odes*,
3.30.1–9, beginning, "Exegi monumentum aere perennius" (I have built a
monument more lasting than bronze), and Ovid's conclusion to *Met.* 15.871 &
878–79, "opus exegi . . . perque omnia saecula fama . . . vivam," which introduces a passage echoed in *Am.* 27. (See Whitney 131, *Scripta manent.*) Compare
the intimations of immortality, Matt. 28.20, "I am with you always, vntil the
end of the worlde (Vulgate, *ad consummationem saeculi*), Amen."

10. *moniment:* (*monere* = to record, remember — see *memory* [6]); either 1. an erec-

tion intended to commemorate a person; 2. a written document or record — see *View* 92.1385. The poet is following the instruction given to Moses in the day's specially chosen first lesson at evening prayer, Exod. 17.14, "And the Lord said to Moses, Write this for a remembrance in the boke (Vulgate, *scribe hoc ob monumentum in libro*), and rehearse it to Ioshua." See Shakespeare Sonnet 81.9–11, with its indebtedness to the same passage, "Your monument shall be my gentle verse, / Which eyes not yet created shall ore-read, / And tougs to be, your beeing shall rehearse."

12. *rare*: 1. uncommon; 2. splendid.

13–14. Proverbial, see Smith, *Proverb Lore*, 655.

13. *happy purchase*: 1. the seizing (after the chase) of spoil or prey; 2. the buying — which recalls the preceding sonnet, *Am.* 68.11, "all lyke deare didst buy." See *Am.* 27.11–12.

   *spoile*: recalling the tree (trophy) on which spoils were hung.

14. *gotten*: 1. obtained; 2. won in victory, captured as spoils (*OED* v 4–5); 3. memorized (*OED* v 8).

   *toyle*: 1. labor; 2. battle, thus concluding the sonnet's associations with war (see *Am.* 11.6 note).

Easter Monday 1 April: *Epistle*: Acts 10.34–44. *Gospel*: Luke 24.13–36. *Morning Prayer*: Pss. 1–5, Matt. 28. *Evening Prayer*: Pss 6–8, Acts 3.

## Sonnet 70

The second sonnet in the sequence to celebrate the coming of spring, the other being Sonnet 19. Here the sonnet's occasion *topos* corresponds to the readings for the feast of the Annunciation, which, because the feast's normal date, 25 March, fell in the week before Easter in 1594, was transferred in that year to the first open day after Easter, the Tuesday of Easter Week, 2 April.

1. *herald*; messenger, envoy — see *Am.* 19.1, "messenger of Spring." The epithet matches the Gospel for the feast of the Annunciation, Luke 1.26, "the Angel (koiné, ἄγγελος = herald, envoy) Gabriel."

2. *cote armour*: 1. in heraldry, a vest of rich material embroidered with devices and worn by heralds; 2. the flowers announcing love's king.

5. *Goe to my loue*: in imitation of Solomon's instruction which opens the special first lesson at morning prayer for the Annunciation, Eccles. 2, "Go to now, I wil proue thee with ioye: therefore take thou pleasure in pleasant things." The poem's celebration of the spring flowers corresponds to Solomon's, "I haue planted me vineyards. I haue made me gardens and orchardes (with its Geneva version sidenote, "paradises"), and planted in them trees of all frute" (Eccles. 2.4–5).

   *careless*: without cares.

5–8. Barroway 42 sees in the quatrain reminiscences of Ecclesiastes' garden's parallel in the Song of Sol. 2.7 & 10–12, "nor waken my loue, vntil she please. . . . My welbeloued spake and said vnto me, Arise, my loue, my faire one, and come thy way. For beholde, winter is past: the raine is changed, and is gone away. The flowers appeare in the earth. . . ." The Geneva Bible closely identified the virgin of the Annunciation and the beloved of the Song of Solomon, the virgin being addressed by the angel, "Haile thou *that art* freely beloued" (v. 28).

6. *awake*: Corresponding to Paul's summoning in the second lesson at morning prayer for 2 April, 1 Cor. 15.3, "Awake to liue righteously." By coincidence 1

Cor. 15.3 is a gloss to Eccles. 2 (see Geneva Bible sidenote to the verse) and Paul makes frequent reference to those who are asleep, "the first frutes of them that slept" (v. 20; see vv. 6, 18 & 51).

8. *by the forelock take:* 'To take time by the forelock,' was proverbial (see Smith, *Proverb Lore*, 777), although this is its only explicit usage by Spenser; its *locus classicus* was Phaedrus, *Fabulae*, 5.8, "Calvus, comosa fronte, nudo occipio.... Occasionem rerum significat brevem."

The sonnet's theme of *carpe diem* matches directly the feast's first lesson at evening prayer, Eccles. 3.1–8 passim, "To all things *there is* an appointed time," with its apposite phrases, "A time to plant," "A time to speake," "A time to loue" and "He hathe made euerie thing beautiful in his time."

10. *louely:* 1. loving; 2. beautiful.

11. *make:* mate; a rime equivoque with line 9.

12. *amearst:* punished; the only use of the word by Spenser.

   *dew:* see 1 Cor. 15.8, "due time."

13. *whilest it is prime:* Compare the associated *carpe florem* of the Bower of Bliss, *FQ* II.xii.75.6–9:

> Gather therefore the Rose, whilest yet is prime,
> For soone comes age, that will her pride deflowre:
> Gather the Rose of loue, whilest yet is time,
> Whilest louing thou mayst loued be with equall crime.

The conceit was a traditional one, although in Spenser's case directly connected to Tasso, *Gerusalemme Liberata*, 16.15.5–8, "Colgiam la rosa in su'l mattino adorno / Di questo dì, che tosto il seren perde: / Colgiam d'Amor la rosa: amiamo hor, quando / Esser si puote riamato amando," which Fairfax (with Eccles. 3.2 & 8 in mind, "a time to plucke vp that, which is planted," "a time to embrace," and "a time to loue") translates: "Gather the rose of loue, while yet thou mast / Louing, be lou'd; embrasing, be embrast." The preceding line to the passage from Tasso gives the passage a temporal context by explicitly acknowledging the passing nature of April and its non-return, "Né perche faccia indietro April ritorno," which Spenser has evidently recalled when composing *Am.* 70 for 2 April.

   *prime:* 1. spring; 2. the moment of greatest perfection.

14. *none can call againe the passed time:* Compare Solomon's axiom in Eccles. 3.15, "What is that that hathe bene? that is now: and that that shalbe, hathe now bene: for God requireth that which is past," with its sidenote, "God onelie causeth that, which is past, to returne."

Annunciation: *Epistle:* Isa. 7.10–15. *Gospel:* Luke 1.26–38. *I Morning Prayer:* Eccl. 2. *I Evening Prayer:* Eccl. 3. **Tuesday 2 April, Easter Tuesday:** *Epistle:* Acts 13.26–42. *Gospel:* Luke 24.36–49. *Morning Prayer:* Pss. 9–11, Luke 24.1–12. *Evening Prayer:* Pss. 12–14, 1 Cor. 15.

## Sonnet 71

Dundas 13 has pointed out that the sonnet's apparent conceit, the drawn-work, seemingly encloses a further code, the B of *Bee* being a cypher for Boyle and the S or Sp of *Spyder*, a cypher for Spenser, the "spinner and therefore maker of allusions." In the bands of the drawn-work's network the embroidered bee is held fast. The net's *locus classicus* was Ovid, *Met.* 4.170ff., where Venus and her lover are imprisoned by a net/snare ("retiaque et laqueos") like to a spider's web. The incident, in Golding's translation (4.205–6), associates drawn-work with the spider's web: "This piece of worke was much more fine than any handwarpe oofe / Or that whereby the Spider hanges in sliding from the roofe."

1. *drawen work:* drawn-thread work, ornamental work done on a woven fabric by drawing out threads from the warp and woof (oof) to form a patterned network. Needlework can then be added. Although the sonnet apparently works an occasional conceit, the second lesson at morning prayer for Wednesday 3 April, John 21.18, reinforces its intimacy by associating bands and cords with the difference between the young and the old, "When thou wast yong, thou girdedst thy self ... but when thou shalt be olde ... another shal girde thee," to which the Geneva version attaches the sidenote, "In steed of a girdle, that shalt be tyed with bands and cordes: and where as now thou goest at libertie, then thou shalt be drawen to punishment." (Compare also the earlier trope in John 21.6, where the disciples, "Cast out the net [Vulgate, *rete* − see headnote, Ovid, "retia"] on the right side of the ship ... So they cast out, and they were not able at all to drawe it....")

2. *Bee:* rarely used elsewhere by Spenser, which reinforces its use here as a secret token. The Spider and the Bee were frequently treated emblematically, e.g., Whitney 51, who presents them under the inscription, "*Vitae, aut mori.*"

3. *Spyder:* elsewhere an emblem of touch (*FQ* II.xi.13.3).

3–4. *doth lurke / in close awayt:* In direct imitation of morning prayer Ps. 17.11–12, "They lie waiting in our way on euery side ... lurking in secret places."

5. *Right so:* a common colloquialism, e.g., *Am.* 53.5.

   *snare:* a concern also of evening prayer Ps. 18.4, "the snares" (Vulgate, *laquei* − identical, then, to Ovid's phrase, "retiaque et laqueos").

6. *thralled:* held in bondage, made captive.

7. *streight bands:* 1. strait, tightly drawn together bands; but 2. (from *strictus* = drawn out − of a sword) streit, drawn out, hence imprisoned in the interstices left by the drawn threads.

8. *remoue:* move from, escape.

10. *woodbynd:* (wood + bind = band) woodbine is a climbing plant like ivy and thus suitable for the sides and top of embroidery. It was known as "ladies bower" (Gerard, *Herbal*, Table of Names).

   *fragrant Eglantine:* see *Am.* 26.3. Eglantine (from *acus* = needle, *aculeus* = prickle) is an appropriate flower for needlework. It is "pleasant to smel to" (Turner, *Herbal*, 2. N.vi.a); see *FQ* II.v.29.4.

14. *gentle:* of an animal 1) well-bred; 2. easily managed.

**Wednesday 3 April:** *Morning Prayer:* Pss. 15–17, John 21. *Evening Prayer:* Ps. 18, Heb. 5.

## Sonnet 72

Sonnet 72 is a loose translation of Tasso's "L'alma vaga di luce e di bellezza" (*Rime*, 2.98. 67). Spenser's decision to translate it for Thursday 4 April fits neatly with the account of Christ's ascension into heaven contained in Acts 1, the day's second lesson at morning prayer. Both Spenser's sonnet and Tasso's original reflect a twofold movement, to heaven and back to earth:

> L'alma vaga di luce e di bellezza,
> Ardite spiega al Ciel l'ale amorose;
> Ma sì le fa l'umanità gravose,
> Che le dechina a quel, ch'in terra apprezza.

E de' piaceri alla dolce esca avvezza,
Ove in sereno volto Amor la pose
Tra bianche perle e mattutine rose,
Par che non trovi altra maggior dolcezza.
E fa quasi augellin, ch' in alto s' erga,
E poi discenda alfin ov' altri il cibi;
E quasi volontario s'imprigioni.
E fra tanti del Ciel graditi doni,
Si gran diletto par che in voi delibi,
Ch' in voi solo si pasce, e solo alberga.

1-8. The ascension account in Acts 1 opens "while they behelde, he was taken vp: for a cloude toke him vp out of their sight" (v. 9). The disciples, having "loked stedfastly towarde heaven," are then instructed to direct their gaze earthwards, "And while thei loked stedfastly towarde heauen, as he went, beholde, two men stode by them in white apparel, Which also said, Ye men of Galile, why stand ye gasing into heauen? This Iesus which is taken vp from you into heauen, shal so come, as ye haue sene him go into heauen" (vv. 10-11).

1. *spred her bolder winges:* Spenser makes comparative the 'Ardite' of Tasso's "Ardite spiega . . . l'ale." The emblem of the soul taking wings to itself was a Petrarchist favorite, e.g., Petrarch, *Rime*, 362, "Volo con l' ali de' pensieri al cielo." Whitney 152 has a device with verses like Spenser's — see line 11, "with heauie clogge of care" — while Prescott, *Spenser's Poetry*, 616 cites Alciati 121, an emblem of a winged figure with a clog (a weighted chain). See Casady 101-2.

2. *in mind to mount up to the purest sky:* See HHB 134-40, for a similar Neo-Platonic ascent; the passage there does not reverse its progress towards the earth.
    *in mind to:* see Tasso's "vaga" = desirous, intending.

4. *clogd with burden of mortality:* see Tasso, "sì le fa l'umanità gravose."

5. *where:* on earth. Spenser differs from his Petrarchist peers in asserting that he finds contentment on earth, for his spirit, having gazed upon the lady's beauty here, forgets its earlier striving towards heaven.

6. *resembling heauens glory:* Compare morning prayer Ps. 19.1, "The heauens declare the glorie of God."

7. *sweet pleasurs bayt:* See Tasso, "E de' piaceri alla dolce esca avvezza."

10. *mantleth:* a hawking term, suggested by Tasso's metaphor, "quasi augellin, ch' in alto s' erga, / E poi discenda"; the exercise of stretching out alternate wings over the corresponding leg.

9-12. 1) the poet's fancy finds fulfillment on earth, no longer requires the *other heauen*, but seeks only to please his heart's desire; this reading requires that *her* refer either to *fancy* or to *spirit*; 2. if *her* refers to *souerayne beauty*, then the heart that the fancy seeks to please is the lady's. The pun on *Hart* reinforces the second reading: the *fancy* seeks to please the desire of her hart and the sestet's references to *bath*, *full delight*,and *Hart* all echo the marriage imagery proper to Prov. 5.18-19, "Let thy fountaine be blessed, and reioyce with the wife of thy youth. *Let her be as* the louing hinde and pleasant roe: let her breasts satisfie thee at all times, and delite in her loue continually."

13. *Hart:* 1. if heart, the advice is self-advice; 2. if hart, the reference is to the poet's betrothed and the advice is equally directed at her; 3. if both, the advice is mutual advice.

13-14. A couplet contrary to anything found in Tasso and a markedly Spenserian affirmation. Because the lady's presence remains bound to earth, hers is not the traditional Petrarchist angelification which Spenser's peers often embraced.

Thursday 4 April: *Morning Prayer:* Pss. 19–21, Acts 1. *Evening Prayer:* Pss. 22–23, Heb. 6.

### Sonnet 73

Sonnet 73 is the second successive — and more faithful — translation of a Tasso sonnet, "Donna, poichè fortuna empia mi nega" (*Rime*, 2.319.222), although Spenser avoids using Tasso's opening two lines. Tasso's sonnets are linked by the common phrases, "E fa quasi augellin, (che l'ali spiega)" which seeks a "dolce esca." Sonnet 73 continues the bird simile implicit in *Am*. 72, retaining a common vocabulary, *spy* (5/5), *hart* (13/7), *back doth fly / flyes backe* (7/8), while Tasso's "dolce esca" becomes in Sonnet 73, *desired food*. Spenser also adopts the conclusion to the prior Tasso original as the concluding couplet to Sonnet 73.

> Donna, poichè fortuna empia mi nega
> Seguirvi, e cinge al piè dure catene;
> Almen per le vostre orme il cor ne viene,
> Cui laccio, oltre i bei crini, altro non lega.
> E fa quasi augellin, che l'ali spiega
> Dietro ad uom, che dolce esca in man ritiene,
> Che di cibarsi ne' vostri occhi ha spene,
> E questa è la cagion ch'ognor vi sega.
> Prendetel voi, e dentro al vostro seno
> Riponetel benigna, e quivi poi
> Felice prigionero i giorni spenda.
> Forse avverà, che i dolci affanni suoi
> Canti, e'l bel vostro nome, e'l suono intenda,
> Quanto cingon d'intorno Adria, e Tirreno.

The sonnet corresponds to none of the readings proper to Friday 5 April.

1. *Being:* disyllabic.
    *captyued:* trisyllabic.
    *care:* sorrow, suffering. In *FQ* IV.viii.5.5, a gentle bird comforts the suffering knight.
2. *none:* none other.
    *seruile:* like a slave.
3. *but the fayre tresses of your golden hayre:* See Tasso, "oltre i bei crini." See *Am*. 37.
5–12. Spenser's translation is here closest to Tasso's original.
8. *to feed his fill:* Proverbial (Smith, *Proverb Lore*, 256). See *Am*. 65.7–8.
10. *gently encage:* a rendering of Tasso's less specific "Riponete."
14. *lodging in your bosome to haue lent:* Compare the conclusion to Tasso's "L'alma vaga di luce e di bellezza," *Am*. 72 headnote, "Ch' in voi solo si pasce, e solo alberga."

Friday 5 April: *Morning Prayer:* Pss. 24–26, Acts 2. *Evening Prayer:* Pss. 27–29, Heb. 7.

### Sonnet 74

1–14. In celebrating the three Elizabeths in whom the poet is blessed, his mother, his queen and his betrothed, the sonnet imitates closely the second lesson at morning prayer for Saturday 6 April, Acts 3, in which Peter blesses the threefold God of glory who has upheld Christ, "The GOD of Abraham, and Isaac, and Iacob, the GOD of our fathers hathe glorified his Sonne Iesus" (v. 13).

1. *happy:* a synonym for blessed — see Am. 1.11–12 note.

 *fram'd:* 1. fashioned, shaped; 2. more particularly *fram'd* was used of the fetus in the womb (see Am. 8.9 note), taken up in *from mothers womb* (6); 3. specifically, letters shaped into words (*OED* 8a).

 *trade:* practice.

2. *that happy name:* See Acts 3.16, where the threefold God is upheld through the name of Christ, "And his Name hathe made this man sounde, whom ye se, and knowe, through faith in his Name."

 *desynd:* indicated.

3. *three times thrise happy:* See FQ IV.ii.41.5–6, where Agape's giving birth is similarly acclaimed, "Thrise happie mother, and thrise happie morne, / That bore three such, three such not to be fond." (The *Most happy letters*, being *three times thrise*, equal nine letters, the number in the name *Elizabeth*.)

5. *kind:* nature — a rime equivoque with line 7 where it carries the meaning, most benevolent; see Am. 70.9–11. This first happiness echoes the blessing announced in Acts 3.25, "in thy sede shal all the kinreds of the earth be blessed."

6. *from mothers womb:* An exact correspondence with the cause of Peter's blessing in Acts 3.2, the healing of the man crippled "from his mothers wombe."

 *deriu'd:* obtained (an origin or lineage).

 *by dew descent:* 1. by generation or by proper lineage; but 2. etymologically, words were considered to 'descend' from their root (*OED* v 8c).

8. *richesse:* wealth. In the Folio editions, "riches."

10. *my spirit out of dust was raysed:* See morning prayer Ps. 30.10, "Shall the dust giue thankes vnto thee." The phrase, and its associated Ps. 113.7 (Geneva version), "He raiseth the nedie out of the dust," was commonplace, see SC Oct., 39 and *View* 168.3552.

11. *to speake her prayse:* Likewise evening prayer Ps. 34.1 sings, "his praise shall euer be in my mouth."

14. *three such graces:* On one level the three gifts of nature, grace and glory. The three graces are the handmaids of Venus, their dance being described in FQ VI.x.15, where they "to men all gifts of grace do graunt." They are Αγλαΐα (= ornament [9]), Θάλια (= richness (*richesse* [8]) and Εὐφροσύνη (= merriment). To the three Spenser adds a fourth, Elizabeth I. He may also have had in mind the "three sundry Actions in liberalitye" of SC April, 109 Gloss.

**Saturday 6 April**: *Morning Prayer:* Pss. 30–31, Acts 3. *Evening Prayer:* Pss. 32–34, Heb. 8.

## Sonnet 75

The sonnet's opening combines a possible occasion of writing in the sand only to be washed away with further references to water, washing, naming and eternal life which fit well with the liturgical *topoi* of the First Sunday after Easter, Sunday 7 April, known as Low Sunday or *Dominica in albis [depositis]*, which acknowledges the neophytes who, having been washed in the waters of Baptism and received their names, are required no longer to wear their white vestments.

As Ovid brings the *Metamorphoses* to a conclusion with the conceit of poetic immortality, so *Am.* 75 seemingly was intended temporarily to bring the sequence to a close.

1. *wrote her name:* See the day's Epistle, 1 John 5.13, "These things haue I written vnto you, that beleue in the Name of the Sonne of God," and its second lesson at morning prayer, Acts 4, with its repeated reference to *name*, as the apostles, "preached in Iesus *Name* the resurrection from the dead" (v. 2; see vv. 7, 10, 12, 17, 18, 30).

    *strand:* strictly, the stretch of shore that lies between the tide-mark.

2. *washed:* See the references to water in 1 John 5.6 & 8, including the sidenote to verse 6, "The water . . . declare that we haue our sinnes washed by him"; see also the second lesson at evening prayer, Heb. 9.23.

5. *Vayne man . . . in vaine assay:* reflecting the imaginings of Acts 4.25, "Why did . . . the people imagine vaine things?"

10–11. *liue by fame: / . . . eternize:* The court of Elizabeth I is full of "knights of noble name, / That couet in th'immortall booke of fame / To be eternized" (*FQ* I.x.59.4–6).

    *fame:* see Ovid, *Met.* 15.878, "perque omnia saecula fama" (Golding, 15.994–96, "and time without all end / . . . My life shall euerlastingly bee lengthened still by fame"). On the conceit of poetic immortality, see *Am.* 27, 69.9–14 & 82.5–8.

10. *dy in dust:* Compare morning prayer Ps. 35.5, "Let them be as the dust before the wynde."

11. *my verse your vertues rare shall eternize / and in the heuens wryte your glorious name:* Matching the purpose of John's writing, 1 John 5.13, "These things haue I written vnto you, that beleue in the Name of the Sonne of God, that ye may knowe that ye haue eternal life." Likewise Acts 4.12, "for among men there is giuen none other name vnder heauen." See Ovid, *Met.* 15.876, "nomenque erit indelibile nomen" (Golding, 15.990–91, "And all the world shall neuer / Be able for too quench my name").

    *vertues . . . name:* similarly linked in Acts 4.7, "By what power (Vulgate, *virtute*), or in what Name haue ye done this?"

    *rare:* 1. uncommon; 2. excellent.

13. *shall all the world subdew:* An exact rendering of Ovid, *Met.* 15.877, "domitis terris" (= the subdued world), and in contrast to 1 John 5.4 (and passim), "all that is borne of God, ouercometh the worlde."

14. *later life renew:* probably the "heauenlie" life which the betrothed will finally enjoy.

**Sunday 7 April, First Sunday after Easter:** *Epistle:* 1 John 5.4–13. *Gospel:* John 20.19–24. *Morning Prayer:* Pss. 35–36, Acts 4. *Evening Prayer:* Ps. 37, Heb. 9.

## Sonnet 76

Sonnets 76 and 77 variously draw upon and adapt Tasso's sonnet, "Non son sì belli i fiori onde natura" (*Rime*, 3.133.94). Spenser has chosen to reflect a range of epithets provided by Tasso's sonnet to mark the occasion of the conception and indwelling of Christ in the womb of the Blessed Virgin, recounted in Matt. 1, the first chapter of the new round of New Testament second lessons at morning prayer that began on 3 May. (Its temporal reference to *early fruit in May*, a departure from Tasso's "april," also fits neatly with a sonnet composed in early May.) Sonnet 76 draws especially on Tasso's second quatrain for its opening litany of praise, while Sonnet 77 expands and elaborates his sestet. (For an extended contrast, see Scott, "Sources," 192 and Lever 110.)

Non son sì belli i fiori onde natura
Nel dolce april de' vaghi anni sereno
Sparge un bel volto, come in real seno
E bel quel ch'a l'autunno Amor matura.
Maraviglioso grembo, orto e cultura
D'Amore e paradiso mio terreno!
Il mio audace pensier chi tiene a freno
Se quello onde si nutre a te sol fura?
Quel che i passi fugaci d'Atalanta
Volser dal corso, o che guardò il dragone,
Son vili al mio desir ch' in te si pasce:
Né coglie Amor da peregrina pianta
Pomo ch'in pregio di beltà ti done
Ché nel tuo sen sol di te degno ei nasce.

Sonnets 76 and 77 are two of the most physical of the *amoretti*, although their easy flow and confident elegance contrast with the tense control of Tasso.

1. *Fayre bosome*: Tasso's "Maraviglioso grembo"; the chest cavity as well as the enclosure formed by the chest and arms in an embrace; "grembo," in contrast to "seno," was used more specifically as bosom, lap, or even womb. See morning prayer Ps. 17.14, "whose bellies (Vulgate, *venter* = womb) thou fillest with thy hid treasure." Because Spenser drops Tasso's temporal opening which embellishes the contrast between nature and love, he can recast his eulogy in a mode which hints at the unfallen quality of *the paradice of pleasure* (3).

   The association between paradise, the garden in the Song of Solomon and the Annunciation was customary, the angel identifying the Virgin in the Geneva version as the beloved: "Haile thou *that are* freely beloued . . . blessed *art* thou among women," to which Elizabeth adds, "because the frute of thy wombe (Vulgate, *ventris*) is blessed" (Luke 1.28 & 42). The phrases echo the description of the beloved in the Song of Solomon, "He shal lye betwene my brests" (1.12), and "vnder his shadow had I delight . . . and his fruit was sweet vnto my mouth . . . comfort me with apples" (2.3–5; see its archetypical *blason*, 7.1–9).

   *fraught*: laden, as a vessel.

3. *the bowre of blisse*: See FQ II.xii.42.ff.

   *paradice of pleasure*: Not unlike the "Elysian fields" of the Temple of Venus, FQ IV.x.23.2–3, described as "a second paradise to ghesse, / So lauishly enricht with natures threasure"; *bosome* was associated with paradise through Luke 16.22, "Abrahams bosome," which the Geneva Bible glosses as paradise.

4. *the sacred harbour of that heuenly spright*: the only epithet in the opening quatrain that finds no correspondence in Tasso, but one that could equally be applied to the Blessed Virgin.

   *harbour*: 1. lodging, dwelling-place; 2. since *harbour* was a frequent sixteenth century spelling of arbor, *bowre*.

5. *louely*: 1. beautiful; 2. loving.

7. *diuing*: plunging — the only time Spenser uses the word.

   *insight*: internal sight, in contrast to the external *louely sight* (5).

9. *And twixt her paps like early fruit in May*: Because Spenser has dropped Tasso's temporal contrast between April and autumn, he is free to change April to May. Compare Belphoebe, FQ II.iii.29.7–9, whose "daintie paps . . . like young fruit

in May / Now little gan to swell," a phrase which Upton, quoting Ariosto's description of Alcina (*Orl. Fur.* VII.14.3), "due pome acerbe," identifies as two unripe apples or young fruit in May.

   *paps*: 1. Tasso's "seno" which intends more particularly 'mamillae'; 2. secondarily, hills (*OED* 2b) — thus where the poet's thoughts will find *happy rest* (13); see morning prayer Ps. 15.1, "who shall rest vpon thy holy hill?"

   *early fruit in May*: by hypallage, "fruit in early May."
11. *wanton winges*: Not found in Tasso, but corresponding to the feature of morning prayer Ps. 17.8, "Keepe me as the apple of an eye: hyde me vnder the shadowe of thy wings."

   *loosely ... wanton*: The poet's thoughts are identified with the winged Cupid's wantonness.

**Friday 3 May**: *Morning Prayer*: Pss. 15–17, Matt. 1. *Evening Prayer*: Ps. 18, Rom. 2.

## Sonnet 77

Sonnet 77 completes the indebtedness to Tasso's "Non son sì belli i fiori onde natura" (see headnote, *Am.* 76), Spenser here concentrating on its sestet.
1. *dreame*: the dream motif changes Tasso's classical spirit and gives it a surreal quality. The modulation accords with the dream *topos* of Matt. 2, the second lesson at morning prayer for Saturday 4 May, which contains four accounts of dreams. The "Wisemen from the East," who "opened their treasures" to Christ were "were warned of God in a dreame" (v. 12), and Joseph, on three occasions, was instructed by an angel, who "appeared in a dreame" (vv. 13, 19, 22). The dreamlike quality absolves Spenser's poem of the seasonal changes which were an integral part of Tasso's sonnet.
2. *table*: see evening prayer Ps. 23.5, "Thou shalt prepare a table before me."

   *pure yuory*: See Ovid's account of Atalanta, whose skin is described as being of ivory, "terga eburnea" (*Met.* 10.592; see lines 7–8 note, *Atalanta*). The emblematic tradition associating breasts with ivory derived from Song of Sol. 5.14, "his bellie (Vulgate, *venter*) is as bright iuorie." Compare Belphoebe's forehead, *FQ* II.iii.24.1–2, "Her iuorie forhead ... / Like a broad table did it selfe dispred"; the passage draws on Ariosto (who is also indebted to the Song of Solomon), *Orl. Fur.* VII.11–16, which compares Alcina's breasts to young apples made of pure ivory, "due pome acerbe, e pur d'avorio fatte" (14.3; see Lynche, *Diella*, 31.1, "Faire Iuorie browe, the bord Loue banquets on").
3. *iuncats*: dainty sweetmeats. Spenser uses the term only once elsewhere, *FQ* V.iv.49.8–9, "And beare with you both wine and iuncates fit, / And bid him eate." The lines recall paradise through "bid him eat" which suggests Eve bidding Adam to eat the forbidden fruit (see Hamilton, *Faerie Queene*, 557).
4. *pompous*: 1. full of pomp, magnificent; 2. ostentatious.
6. *golden*: Corresponding to Hippomenes' "aurea poma" of Ovid, *Met.* 10.650, and echoing Matt. 2.11, where the Wise Men offered "euen golde."
7–8. The eleventh labor of Hercules was to obtain the apples which Juno received at her marriage and which she entrusted to the guardianship of the Hesperides on Mt. Atlas. The Hesperides were assisted in their task by the dragon Ladon (see Tasso, *il dragone*), which Hercules slew. The emblematic comparison between breasts and the Hesperides was frequent, e.g., Lynche, *Diella*, 22.9, "her breastes two aples of Hesperides." Atalanta was surpassed in running by Hippo-

menes of Euboea who threw down the apples (in his case three), which Atalanta
paused to pick up (See Ovid, *Met.* 10.560–680). Spenser connects the two myths
in *FQ* II.vii.54.5–9.

7. *far passing:* Recalls the manner in which Atalanta was surpassed by Hippomenes.

9. *Exceeding sweet:* Despite Barroway's willingness (41–42) to see here a reference to
Song of Sol. 4.11, compare morning prayer Ps. 19.10, "More to be desired are
they then gold: yea then much fine golde: sweeter also then honie, and the
hony combe."

    *Exceeding:* In imitation of Matt. 2.10 & 16, "exceading great ioye," and
"exceading wroth."

    *yet voyd of sinfull vice:* Spenser's apples, because *brought from paradice*,
change the nature of love, which in Tasso is a temporal force, to a love of
prelapsarian origin.

13–14. *Her brest that table:* Echoing in part evening prayer Ps. 22.9, "But thou art
hee that tooke me out of my mothers wombe: thou wast my hope when I
hanged yet vpon my mothers breasts." 'Write them vpon the table of thine
heart' was a stock metaphor (from Prov. 3.3) for 'keep in mind.'

14. *thoughts . . . fedd:* Tasso's "mio desir ch' in te si pasce." Compare evening prayer
Ps. 23.2. "He shall feede me (Vulgate, *in loco pascuae*)."

**Saturday 4 May:** *Morning Prayer:* Pss. 19–21, Matt. 2. *Evening Prayer:* Pss. 22–23, Rom. 3.

## Sonnet 78

The first sonnet of a number explicitly concerned with the lady's absence. Castiglione, *The Booke of the Courtier,* 4 (Everyman, 316–17), explains how absence
should be turned to the lover's advantage, "The lover therefore that considereth
onely the beautie in the bodie, loseth this treasure and happinesse, as soone as the
woman beloued with her departure leaueth the eies without their brightnesse. . . .
The Courtier by the helpe of reason must full and wholy call backe againe the
coueting of the bodie to beautie alone . . . and frame it within his imagination
sundred from all matter."

    The sonnet corresponds with Rogation Sunday, the Fifth Sunday after Easter, 5
May, the first of a series of days of fast leading up to the feast of the Ascension. The
days were marked by the ancient custom of 'beating the bounds' – a procession or
perambulation which went from place to place through the fields establishing the
bounds of the parish. Signs were left and decked with garlands (MacMichael, 114)
and, in its Reformed rite, "in the . . . going about the minister shall use none other
ceremony than to say in English the two psalms . . . the hundred and third psalm
and the hundred and fourth psalm. . ." (Grindal, 141). The psalms were chosen
particularly for the verse "Thou hast set them their boundes, which they shall not
passe" (104.9). Details of the two psalms persist through the sonnets for both
Rogation Sunday and Rogation Monday.

1–14. The poem's argument of the poet going his way, having looked upon his
beloved's natural face, corresponds to the metaphor in day's Epistle, James 1.22–
27, of the man, who, having looked upon his natural face in a mirror, goes his
way: "he is like unto a man, that beholdeth his natural face in a glasse (koiné,
τὸ πρόσωπον τῆς γενέσεως αὐτοῦ ἐν ἐσόπτρῳ = the face of his birth in a
mirror). For when he hathe considered him self, he goeth his way, and forget-
teth immediately what maner of one he was." (The poet, of course, continues

to carry his lady's image freshly in his mind.) *Am.* 45 corresponds to a like metaphor and thence uses Plato's image in a mirror (*The Republic*, 402B; see *Am.* 45.1–14 note) to construct its Platonic argument. Sonnet 78, corresponding to a matching mirror image, constructs its argument along similar lines.

1. *I go from place to place:* Reflecting the perambulation of 'Rogationing the Boundaries.' See Petrarch, *Rime*, 35.1–4:

> Solo e pensoso i più deserti campi
> vo mesurando a passi tardi e lenti,
> e gli occhi porto per fuggire intenti
> ove vestigio uman la rena stampi.

2. *hynd:* The simile corresponds exactly to the unique psalter reference in the day's evening prayer Ps. 29.8, "The voyce of the Lorde maketh the Hindes to bring foorth yong, and discouereth the thicke bushes" (Geneva Version, "forests"; see its sidenote f, a parallel to Petrarch's "i più deserti campi," "In places most desolate, where as semeth there is no presence of God.")

3. *seeke each where, where last I sawe her face:* Imitates the repeated detail in evening prayer Ps. 27.9–10, "seeke yee my face: thy face Lord will I seeke. O hide not thou thy face from me," and morning prayer Ps. 24.6, "this is the generation of them that seeke him: euen of them that seeke thy face, O Iacob."

5–7. *I seeke ... / ... nor ... can fynd:* Spenser's failure to find the lady's face runs counter to Christ's instruction in the day's Gospel, John 16.24, "aske, and ye shal receiue" (in all parallel accounts [Matt. 7.7, Luke 11.9], "Aske, and it shalbe giuen you: seke, and ye shal finde.").

5. *synd:* echoing the signs of the day's perambulation; 1. bearing her imprint, footstep; 2. sealed as her own.

6. *deckt:* corresponding to the action of decking the landmarks with flowers and the detail of perambulation Ps. 104.2, "Thou deckest thy selfe with light."

11. *trew obiect:* Platonically, the true reality, not the imperfect image, beheld in the mind and not in the sight.

12. *fancies:* 1. used technically by neo-Platonists for the faculty which forms mental representations of things not present to the senses; 2. as a contraction of fantasy, a deceived or delusive imagination − in contrast to *trew obiect* (11; see *Am.* 45.4, *Am.* 3.12 note, and *Am.* 88 headnote, for a fuller discussion of Plato's use of φάντασμα = semblance).

14. *behold her selfe:* In imitation of James 1.23, "beholdeth his natural face." See *Am.* 45.13.

**Rogation Sunday 5 May, Fifth Sunday after Easter:** *Epistle:* James 1.22–27. *Gospel:* John 16.23–33. *Morning Prayer:* Pss. 24–26, Matt. 3. *Evening Prayer:* Pss. 27–29, Rom. 4. Perambulation Psalms 103–4.

## Sonnet 79

Sonnet 79, written for Rogation Monday, 6 May, treats at greater length Sonnet 59's aphorism "All flesh is frayle," its distinction between fleshly beauty and true beauty which is of heavenly seed making it of one of the most apparently Platonic arguments of the sequence. Its argument of fleshly frailty draws on perambulation Ps. 103.14–16, "For he knoweth whereof we be made: he remembreth that we are but dust. The dayes of man are but as grasse: for he florisheth as a flowre of the fielde. For as soone as the winde goeth over it, it is gone: and the place thereof shall knowe it no more." Like Sonnet 58 it also draws upon the associated passages 1 Pet.

1.22–24 and Isa. 40.3–8 (see *Am.* 58.6 for further detail). The simile of the flesh as
a flower that fades was a popular Spenserian one, frequently with Petrine and Isaian
echoes (e.g., *FQ* V.ii.40.4–5 and VI.x.44.5–7).

1–14. The sonnet's division between *frayle corruption* and *true beautie* reflects the
   contrast made in Rom. 5.17, the day's second lesson at evening prayer, where
   Paul distinguishes between the corruption introduced into the world by Adam
   and the grace and perfection bought by Christ: "For if by the offence of one,
   death reigned through one, muche more shal they which receiue the abundance
   of grace . . . reigne in life through one, *that is* Iesus Christ."

1. *credit:* give credibility to or evidence of it; a unique Spenserian usage as a verb.

4. *much more praysed:* hyperbolically exceeding the praises of God that open both
   perambulation psalms, Ps. 103.1 & 2, Ps. 104.1, "Prayse the Lorde, O my
   soule."

6. *glorious:* imitating perambulation Ps. 104.1, "thou art become exceeding glorious."

8. *frayle corruption:* as above, reflecting perambulation Ps. 103.15 (with its headnote
   gloss in the Geneva Version, "*The frailtie of mans life*"), "The dayes of man are
   but as grasse"; grass is identified as corrupt flesh in Isa. 40.6–7, "All flesh *is*
   grasse."

   *that doth flesh ensew:* Imitating evening prayer Psalm 34.13, "seeke peace,
   and ensue it," the only occasion the word occurs in Coverdale which is not
   found in the Geneva version.

10. *diuine and borne of heauenly seed:* See 1 Pet. 1.23, "Being borne a new, not of
   mortal sede, but of immortal, by the worde of God."

11. *fayre Spirit:* Compare the day's second lesson at morning prayer, Matt. 4.1 where
   "Iesus [is] led aside of the Spirit into the wildernes"; see Isa. 40.7.

12. *proceed:* Compare Matt. 4.4, "But by euerie word that procedeath (koiné,
   ἐκπορευομένῳ) out of the mouth of God." (ἐκπορεύμα was the proper
   theological term for the trinitarian procession of the Spirit.)

14. *All other fayre lyke flowres untymely fade:* see headnote perambulation Ps. 103.14–
   16. See its associated passages, Isa. 40.6–7, "All flesh *is* grasse, and all the grace
   thereof *is* as the floure of the field. The grasse withereth, the floure fadeth,
   because the Spirit of the Lord bloweth vpon it," and 1 Pet. 1.24, "For all flesh
   *is* as grasse, and all the glorie of man *is* as the flower of grasse. The grasse
   withereth, and the flower falleth away."

**Monday 6 May**: *Morning Prayer:* Pss. 30–31, Matt. 4. *Evening Prayer:* Pss. 32–34, Rom. 5.
Perambulation Psalms 103–4.


## Sonnet 80

The sonnet's argument strongly suggests that the first six books of *The Faerie Queene*
were completed by the spring of 1594, although they were not published until 1596,
and that Spenser intended to continue the poem. The exhaustion the work caused
him is the subject of frequent asides throughout the work (*FQ* I.xii.1.42, II.x.1–2 &
VI. Pr.1–2), although the simile of the steed is unique to *Amoretti*.

   The sonnet shows little correspondence with any of the proper psalms or either
of the second lessons for Rogation Tuesday 7 May.

1. *race as I a haue run:* Spenser's resolve will be the same as the Palmer's to Guyon,
   who "Must now anew begin, like race to runne" (*FQ* II.i.32.7).

2. *compile:* which, heaped or piled together, make up its composition — suggesting the tedium of the work. Spenser is echoing Vergil, who was known as the *compilator* (*compilare* = to steal or plunder) by his reproachful rivals, because he imitated (or stole from) Homer.

3. *giue leaue to rest me:* Calidore, seeking a place of retirement, makes a similar plea to Meliboe, *FQ* VI.ix.31.3–4.

    *halfe fordonne:* 1. half done before; 2. exhausted (*OED* 11c), and since Spenser normally uses the prefix 'fore' as an intensifier, more exhausted (see *FQ* VI.xi.35.5).

4. *new breath:* 1. new life and refreshed vigor; 2. new inspiration, the classical and scriptural *divinus inflatus*, see Col 823–24.

5–6. *steed . . . prison:* The simile was a classical one from Vergil, *Aen.* 11.292–3, "Qualis ubi abruptis fugit praesepia vinclis / Tandem liber equus campoque potitus aperto. . . ." See Homer, *Il.* 6.506 and Tasso, *Gerusalemme Liberata,* 9.75. The day's second lesson at morning prayer, Matt. 5.25, warns "Agre with thine aduersarie quickely, . . . lest . . . thou be cast into prison."

5. *toyle:* 1. hard labor, exertion; but 2. a suggestion of an enclosure in which an animal is trapped is also retained.

7. *assoyle:* 1. discharge myself of the task; but 2. from the prison also.

9. *mew:* 1. a place of secret retirement, a study or den, (*OED* 3c); 2. a *prison* (6); 3. secondarily, a cage in which hawks and falcons were kept — the falconine image recurs later in the sonnet (see line 12 note); 4. finally, a stable, associated with *steed* (5; when the king's stables were built on the site of the royal falcons' mews at Charing Cross, by association they were called the Royal Mews).

10. *sport my muse:* enliven, recreate (as in *gather to my selfe new breath*), but note the homonym, *muse*/mews.

11. *heauenly hew:* 1. Neo-Platonically, a heavenly form or shape — see *Am.* 3.8 note; 2. possibly an oblique equine reference, a steed, when it knocks its legs together, being said to *hew* them (*OED* 8).

12. *higher pitch:* 1. to a more intense or higher degree; 2. to a higher musical pitch — continuing the image of *sing* (10); 3. when connected with *mew* (9), the highest point of flight of a hawk or falcon before swooping (*OED* 18).

13. *low and meane:* 1. literarily, an unadorned, plain style (*OED* a 1 II 3c) — an echo of the affected modesty of the opening stanza to *FQ*, "Me, all to meane, the sacred Muse areeds" (I. Pr.i.7); 2. musically, the degree in descant between the treble and base parts (*OED* a 2 1b).

Tuesday 7 May: *Morning Prayer:* Pss. 35–36, Matt. 5. *Evening Prayer:* Ps. 37, Rom. 6.

## Sonnet 81

Lee 197 describes Sonnet 81 as "little better than a literal translation" of Tasso's "Bella è la donna mia, se del bel crine" (*Rime,* 2.25.17):

    Bella è la donna mia, se del bel crine
    L'oro al vento ondeggiar avvien ch' io miri,
    Bella, se volger gli occhi in vaghi giri,
    O le rose fiorir tra neve e brine.
    È bella, dove poggi, ove s'inchina;
    Dov' orgoglio l'inaspra a' miei desiri,
    Belli sono i suoi sdegni, e quei martiri,

> Che mi fan degno d'onorato fine.
> Ma quella, ch' apre un dolce labro, e serra,
> Porta de' bei rubin si dolcemente,
> È beltà sovra ogn' altra altera ed alma.
> Porta gentil della prigion dell' alma,
> Onde i messi d'Amor escon sovente,
> E portan dolce pace, e dolce guerra.

Spenser, while following Tasso's *distributio* or *merismos* (Rix 48), has as usual selected some of Tasso's details and omitted others. The sonnet bears no resemblance to the coincident scripture readings for Wednesday 8 May.

1. *fayre golden heares*: A common feature of Petrarchist Ladies, e.g., Belphoebe's hair, *FQ* II.iii.30.1.
2. *loose wynd ye wauing*: The *locus classicus* of hair waving in the wind was Vergil, *Aen.* 1.318, "comam diffundere ventis."
3. Where Tasso's roses are generally white, Spenser customarily presents cheeks as red roses, e.g., Belphoebe, *FQ* II.iii.22.5–6.
5–6. An element of Spenser's not found in the original. Spenser nowhere else compares the breast with a bark.
7–8. Compare the chiaroscuro of Ariosto, *Orl. Fur.* VII.12.2–3, "son duo negri occhi, anzi duo chiari soli, / pietosi a riguardare, a mover parchi."
8. *with smiles she driues away*: Contrast *Am.* 21.12, "her smile me drawes, her frowne me driues away."
10–12. Spenser has added to Tasso's "Porta de' bei rubin" the standard association of pearls from Rev. 21.21, "And the twelue gates *were* twelue pearles, and euerie gate *is* of one pearle," see *Am.* 15.8–9 & *FQ* II.iii.24.6–8 (with its reference to Song of Sol. 4.11), "And when she spake, / Sweet words ... / ... twixt the perles and rubins softly brake." The association was standard among Petrarchists, e.g., Lynche, *Diego and Gynevra*, 74–76.
12. *the message of her gentle spright*: Tasso's "Porta gentil ... dell' alma, / Onde i messi d' Amor escon sovente," although "gentil" has been transferred from *gate* to *spright*.
13–14. Spenser's own conclusion and a departure from Tasso.

**Wednesday 8 May**: *Morning Prayer*: Pss. 38–40, Matt. 6. *Evening Prayer*: Pss. 41–43, Rom. 7.

### Sonnet 82

For the feast of the Ascension, Thursday 9 May, Spenser has chosen to celebrate the lady's heavenly name. The poet's lowliness and poetic inadequacy echoes his similar plaint and question in *FQ* II.x.1.1–5:

> Who now shall giue vnto me words and sound,
> Equall vnto this haughtie enterprise?
> Or who shall lend me wings, with which from ground
> My lowly verse may loftily arise
> And lift it selfe vnto the highest skies?

This is the third time the theme of poetic immortality has been used in the sequence (see *Am.* 27.9–12 & *Am.* 75.4–12).

1. *Ioy*: The poet's joy reflects the feast's special morning prayer Ps. 21.6, "For thou shalt giue him euerlasting felicitie: and make him glad with the ioy of thy countenance." It is also reminiscent of the address in *FQ* II.i.31.1–3, "Ioy may

you haue, and euerlasting fame, . . . For which enrolled is your glorious name /
In heauenly Registers aboue the sunne." The thought was a poetically familiar
one, e.g., Sidney, *AS* 69.1, "O ioy, too high for my low stile to show."

2. *I blesse my lot:* Corresponding to Ps. 21.3, "For thou shal preuent him with the
blessings of goodnesse," and in line with *Am.* 66.1, "To all those happy blessings which ye haue, / with plenteous hand by heauen vpon you thrown."

    *lot:* 1. the marked piece used in the contest of chance to determine an out-
come − the image is continued in *so lucky placed;* 2. fate, fortune (= *sors;* see
note *Am.* 66.9); 3. providential plan, (so identified in *Am.* 84.14, "blesse your
fortunes fayre election") − in contrast to Spenser's "luckelesse lot" as he
embarks on *FQ* Book III (see III. Pr.3.4). See Ariosto, *Orl. Fur.* III.2.2, "dal ciel
sortiti."

    *placed:* in *Am.* 66.2 the lots are "thrown."

4-8. See headnote, *FQ* II.x.1.1-5. The lines are a translation of Ariosto, *Orl. Fur.*
III.1.1-6:

> Chi mi darà la voce, e le parole
> Convenienti à sì nobil soggetto?
> Chi l'ale al verso pristerà, che vole
> Tanto ch' arivi à l'alto mio concetto?
> Molto maggior di quel furor, che suole,
> Ben or convien, che mi riscaldi il petto.

    Ariosto's "furor" is found in Sonnet 82's closest companion, *Am.* 85.11,
"heauenly fury."

5. *equall heuens:* impartial, even − as in an even lay or *lot* (= *aequus;* see headnote,
*FQ* II.x.1.2). A common expression, e.g., Greene, *Groatsworth of witte,* 42,
"Equal heauen hath denied that comfort."

6-7. *inuent / som heuenly wit:* discover; an inversion, for invention is generally the
result of wit; invention, as the first part of rhetoric, is the first of the five inward
wits (*OED* 1d). The thought's *locus classicus* is Ovid, *Met.* 15.878-79, with its
sense of prophecy, "perque omnia saecula fama, / siquid habent veri vatum
presagia, vivam."

    *wit:* 1. mind, intelligence; 2. poet.

7. *enchased:* 1. enshrined as a relic (= French *enchasser*); 2. set as a jewel in gold,
replicating Ps. 21.3, "For thou . . . shalt set a crowne of pure golde vpon his
head" (Vulgate, *coronam de lapide pretioso* = a crown of precious stones); 3.
engraved − a meaning used elsewhere by Spenser (e.g., *FQ* IV.x.8.7-8), and
hence a possible echo of the day's special first lesson at evening prayer, 2 (4)
Kings 2.7, "Send me now therefore a cunning man that can worke in golde . . .
and that can graue in grauen worke," and 14, "and he can skill to worke in
golde . . . and can graue in all grauen workes, and broder in all broydred worke."

8. *glorious name:* Reflecting the praises of Ps. 8.1 & 9, "how excellent is thy name
in all the worlde: thou that hast set thy glory aboue the heauens." Compare
*Am.* 75.12, "and in the heuens wryte your glorious name."

    *golden moniment:* See *Am.* 69.9-10, "Euen this verse vowed to eternity, /
shall be thereof immortall moniment," and compare evening prayer Ps. 68.13,
"her feathers like golde," a verse reflected in the "golden quill" of the associated sonnet, *Am.* 85.10.

12. *setting your immortall prayses forth:* Compare the repeated use of the word in Ps.
21.3, Ps. 15.4, & Ps. 8.1 & 9, "set," and "setteth," together with Ps. 68.4,

"sing praises vnto his name . . . praise him in his name, yea, and reioyce before
him."

13. *lofty argument:* In exact imitation of the opening detail to the feast's Epistle,
Acts 1.2 (Vulgate), *in multis argumentis* (koiné, ἐν πολλοῖς τεκμηῄοις =
conclusive or lofty arguments). See headnote, *FQ* II.x.1.4, "My lowly verse may
loftily arise," and Ariosto, *Orl. Fur.* III.1.4, "l'alto mio concetto."

13–14. *vplifting me, shall lift you vp:* Imitating morning prayer Ps. 24.7 & 9, "Lift vp
your heades, O ye gates, and be ye lift vp ye euerlasting doores"; see headnote,
*FQ* II.x.1.5).

14. *vnto an high degree:* Continues the Ascension imagery, see Ps. 68.18, "Thou art
gone vpon high."

Thursday 9 May, Ascension: *Epistle:* Acts 1.1–12. *Gospel:* Mark 16.14–20. *Morning Prayer:* Pss.
8, 15, 21, Deut. 10, Matt. 7. *Evening Prayer:* Pss. 24, 68, 108, 2 (4) Kings 2, Rom. 8.

## Sonnet 83

Sonnet 83 is a virtual repetition of Sonnet 35. It bears no correspondence with any
of the proper psalms or any of the second lessons for Friday 10 May or Saturday 11
May.

6. *seeing:* the only change from *Am.* 35.6: "hauing."

Friday 10 May / Saturday 11 May: *Morning Prayer:* Pss. 50–52 / 56–58, Matt. 8 / 9. *Evening
Prayer:* Pss. 53–55 / 59–61, Rom. 9 / 10.

## Sonnet 84

Sonnet 84's conclusion gives thanks for the poet's election, an appropriate conclusion to a sonnet written for Expectation Sunday, 12 May, whose second lesson at
evening prayer in 1594 was Rom. 11, the principal scriptural account of the
doctrine of election: "Euen so then at this present time is there a remnant through
the election of grace. And if *it be* of grace, it is no more of workes; or els were grace
no more grace" (vv. 5–6). The sonnet's structural distinction between *sensuall desyre*
(3) and *pure affections* (5), and its final imputation of election to the poet's spiritual
part corresponds exactly with Paul's ascribing election not to the realm of the flesh
but of grace. The poet also observes Paul's link between election and love, "as
touching the election, they are beloued for the fathers sakes" (v. 28).

1–14. The octet's syntax is ambiguous, see Osgood (*Variorum, Minor Poems*, 2.452):
   " 'Affections' and 'thoughts' seem to be vocative, and 'goe' imperative, unless
   some influence of 'Let' lingers about it to make it infinitive. And what is the
   antecedent of singular 'your selfe' — 'affections,' thoughts,' or an implied 'eyes'?
   Perhaps it is a sonnet conceived as embodying all these." It is clear, however,
   that the poet is addressing his two selves, his carnal, which he calls to suppress
   itself, and his spiritual, the *pure affections* (5) and *modest thoughts* (6), which he
   admonishes to [let] *goe visit* (7).

1 & 7. *Let not* & *[let] goe visit:* The instructions imitate the repeated admonitory
   *formulae*, "Let vs . . . ," of the *Commination against sinners*, which was customarily read after morning prayer in churchs, "Upon one of the two Sundays next
   before the feast of Pentecost" (*Liturgical Services of the Reign of Queen Elizabeth*
   [1847] 239).
       *filthy lustfull fyre:* corresponding with the *Commination*'s omnipresent refer-
   ences to "fire and brimstone" and its instruction "Goe ye cursed into the fire
   euerlasting."

3–4. *ne one light glance of sensuall desyre / Attempt to work her gentle mindes vnrest:* See the similar aspiration, *Epith.* 198–99. *Epith.*'s 11th section bears some similarity with the themes of *Am.* 82 & 24.

5–6. *pure affections . . . modest thoughts:* Compare the *Commination*'s advice, "Turne you cleane," and its proper psalm, Ps. 51, throughout.

5. *pure affections:* In contrast to the "base affections" of *Epith.* 196, which are ruled over by "vnspotted faith."

    *spotlesse:* Compare the day's second lesson at morning prayer, Matt. 10.16, "innocent (koiné, ἀκέραιοι = spotless, uncontaminated) as doves."

12. *too constant stiffenesse:* The lady's undiscerning obstinacy corresponds to the plight of Israel, whose hardness prevented its election in Rom. 11.7, "Israel hathe not obteined that he soght: but the election hathe obteined it, and the rest haue bene hardened" (see v. 25, with its elective "secret" that "obstinacie is come to Israel," and its sidenote q, "Meaning stubbernes and induration." The day's *Commination* also condemns "obstinate sinners" and the "stubbernesse of their hearte").

13. *rare perfection:* See *Am.* 24.2 note.

14. *blesse your fortunes:* See *Am.* 82.2, "I blesse my lot," where "lot" derivately intends providence.

**Sunday 12 May, Sunday after Ascension:** *Epistle:* 1 Pet. 4.7–12. *Gospel:* John 15.26–16.4. *Morning Prayer:* Pss. 62–64, Matt. 10. *Evening Prayer:* Pss. 65–67, Rom. 11.

## Sonnet 85

1–14. Sonnet 85, which corresponds to the Monday of Expectation Week, 13 May, opens with an indirect reference to the secret nature of election with which Sonnet 84 concludes. Its distinction between the unilluminated judgement of the world and the poet's true appraisal corresponds to that of Matt. 11, the day's second lesson at morning prayer, between those to whom true judgement has been given and those of the world to whom it has not, "I giue thee thankes, ô Father, Lord of heauen and earth, because thou hast hid these things from the wise and men of vnderstanding" (v. 25; the sidenote to the parallel verse, Luke 10.21, explains, "He attributeth it to the free election of God, that the wise and worldings knowe not the Gospel, and yet the poore base people vnderstand it.").

3. *Cuckow:* See *Am.* 19.1, "Cuckow, messenger of Spring." In Matt. 11.10 it is the prophet John who is the messenger, "Beholde, I send my messenger (koiné, ἄγγελόν = messenger, see *Am.* 70.1 note, "herald") before thy face."

    *Mauis:* the song-thrush; see *Epith.* 81.

4. *witlesse:* In contrast to *heauenly fury* (11) and the "heuenly wit" of *Am.* 82.7.

    *clatter:* talking idly or emptily; the cuckoo was known for its repetition of the same sound without variation.

5–6. *But they that skill not of so heauenly matter, / all that they know not:* echoes the claim about secret and heavenly knowledge in Matt. 11.27, "no man knoweth the Sonne, but the Father: nether knoweth any man the Father, but the Sonne."

8. *not to deeme of her desert aspyre:* observes the Pauline admonition in the day's second lesson at evening prayer, Rom. 12.3, "that no man presume to vnderstand aboue that which is mete to vnderstand."

    *desert:* excellence, worth.

9–14. The secret nature of the poet's divine inspiration corresponds to the nature and origin of the elects' secret knowledge, the sidenote to Matt. 11.26 stating, "Faith cometh not of mans wil or power, but by the secret illumination of God."

9. *Deepe ... parts entyre*: Contrast *Am.* 6.11, "deepe ... parts entire"

    *closet*: 1. the secret and most private part; 2. physically, associated with the heart and the pericardium (see La Primaudaye 2.221) and the breast or womb.

10. *written with a golden quill*: either 1. the feather of a bird formed into a pen, corresponding to morning prayer Ps. 68.13, "and her feathers like gold" (Vulgate, *pennae ... auri*); or 2. the hollow stem of a reed in its transferred sense of a pen or quill, corresponding to Matt. 11.7, "A reed shaken with the winde" (Vulgate, *harundinem*; see also Vulgate Psalm 68.30, *arundinis*, a psalm shared with Sonnet 82, see *Am.* 82.8 note); 3. secondarily, a reed pipe, echoing Matt. 11.16–17, "we haue piped vnto you" (koiné, Ηὐλήσαμεν = we have played on a reed instrument), which is expanded later in *her shrill trump shal thunder* (13). In *FQ* II.x.3.1–9 the classical quill of Homer is out-blazoned by the trumpet.

11. *heauenly fury*: the prophetic rage with which the poet-magus is inspired from above, corresponding to the Plato's μανία as used in *Phaedrus*, 245A, the other variety of which is earlier associated with prophecy ("ἡ μανία ἐγγενομένη καὶ προφητεύσασα" [*Phaedrus*, 244D]). The term had been defined by Cicero, *De Divinatione*, 1.31.66, "ea [praesagitio] si exarsit acrius, furor appellatus, cum a corpore animis abstractus divino instinctu concitatur," and popularized by Ficino, whose 1482 translation of Plato's *Ion* bore the subtitle, *De Furore Poetico*; see Sidney, *Apologie*, L3ʳ, "they are so beloued of the Gods, that whatsoeuer they write, proceeds of a diuine fury." It is the same as the "heauenly fury" with which Artegal interprets Britomart's dream (*FQ* V.vii.20.9) and the "halfe extatick stoure" of Merlin (deriving from Ariosto, *Orl. Fur.* III.9.4, "il profetico spirito di Merlino"), when he prophesies about Elizabeth's reign. Like *Am.* 82 Sonnet 85 owes something to Ariosto, *Orl. Fur.* III.1.5–6, "Molto maggior di quel furor, che suole, / Ben or convien, che mi riscaldi il petto."

    The sonnet's prophetic inspiration finds a correspondence with Matt. 11.9, speaking of John, "A Prophet? Yea ... more then a Prophet," and Rom. 12.6, "whether we *haue* prophecie, *let vs prophecie* according to the proportion of faith." The whole sonnet is in keeping with the heavenly inspiration whose arrival is awaited during Expectation Week.

13. *her shrill trump shal thunder*: Compare *Am.* 29.12, and the cuckoo in *Am.* 19.1–2, with whom the "trompet shrill" is also associated.

**Monday 13 May**: *Morning Prayer*: Ps. 68, Matt. 11. *Evening Prayer*: Pss. 69–70, Rom. 12.

## Sonnet 86

An unusual sonnet in its recrimination, although in part an adversative poem to the *Am.* 85's "heauenly fury." Such maledictions often find at least one place in sonnet sequences, e.g., Petrarch, *Rime*, 206, "S' i' 'l dissi mai," where the poet, accused of disturbing his beloved by loving another, condemns the slander and false lies after the manner of an Old Testament prophet. Spenser concludes the first six books of *FQ* on a similar recriminatory note (VI.xii.41).

1. *Venemous toung tipt with vile adders sting*: Reflects the malediction in the second lesson at morning prayer for Tuesday 14 May, Matt. 12.34–37, "O generacions of vipers (with its Geneva version sidenote, *Or, broodes*), how can you speake

good things, when ye are euil? . . . an euil man out of an euil treasure, bringeth forth euil things. But I say vnto you, that of euerie idle worde that men shal speake, they shal giue acounte thereof at the day of iudgement. . . . by thy wordes thou shalt be condemned" (see Am. 2.1, "Vnquiet thought," which corresponds to the Matthew's condemnation when it was read for Thursday 24 January). Allecto, the first Fury (Vergil, Aen. 7.351), exudes similar poisonous viperous thoughts, "viperam inspirans animam."

2. *Furies:* The three avenging goddesses with snakes twined in their hair, "the Authours of all euill and mischiefe" (Gloss to SC Nov., 164; see Vergil, Aen. 7.346).

The allusion recalls the figure of *Ate*, Discord, who "was borne of hellish brood, / And by infernall furies nourished" (FQ IV.i.26.7–8, see Homer, Il. 19.91–94, 126–31). The conceit's *locus classicus*, where Agamemnon invokes the Furies to condemn slander and perjury occurs later, Il. .258–65, "ἐρινύες, αἴ θ᾽ ὑπὸ γαῖαν / ἀνθρώπους τίνυνται, ὅτις κ᾽ ἐπίορκον ὀμόσσῃ, / . . . εἰ δὲ τι τῶνδ᾽ ἐπίορκον, ἐμοὶ θεοὶ ἄλγεα δοῖεν / πολλὰ μαλ᾽, ὅσσα διδοῦσιν, ὅτις σφ᾽ ἀλίτηται ὀμόσσας" (Chapman, 19.251–57, "ye Furies vnder earth that euery soule torment / Whom impious periury distaines . . . and let my plagues be such / As are inflicted by the gods, in all extremitie / of whomsoeuer perjur'd men, if godlesse periury / In least degree dishonor me"); Spenser has taken cognisance of the passage later, see lines 5 and 7 notes.

In imitation of Petrarch Spenser has more particularly drawn upon a range of matching detail in the Old Testament psalmic curse, Ps. 140, "Deliuer me, O Lord, from the euil man," which Christ's condemnation of the scribes and pharisees in Matt. 12.34–37 was traditionally accepted as paralleling. He paraphrases the Geneva Bible version of the psalm, including its condemnation of slanderers, "Thei haue sharpened their tongues like a serpent: adders poyson *is* vnder their lippes" (v. 3), see *toung* (1), *vile adders* (1), *poysoned* (4). Such men "make warre continually" (v. 2; Coverdale, "stirre vp strife"; compare *stirre vp* [8]). The sonnet's *coles of yre* (8) and *vpon thee fall* (6) reshape the psalm's curse "Let coles fall vpon them" (v. 10); *fyre* (9), and *hell* (5), appear in the curse's continuation, "let him cast them into the fyre, and into the depe pittes," (a synonym for *hell*). The concluding condemnation, *mischiefe thy reward, / dew to thy selfe that it for me prepard*, replicates the psalm's condemnation, "let the mischief of their owne lippes come vpon them" (v. 9; Coverdale, "fall vpon the head of them"). The sonnet's details also find a correspondence with the psalm's sidenotes: *Let all the plagues* (5) with the note, "Gods plagues shal light vpon him," and *false forged lyes . . . / . . . let kindle* (7–9) with the further note, "by their false . . . lies thei kindle the hatred of the wicked against me."

Spenser had, in FQ IV.viii.26.8–9, already identified the figure of slander with the asp through the association with Ps. 140, "For like the stings of Aspes, that kill with smart, / Her spightfull words did pricke, and wound the inner part." Likewise Detraction, who was "neare to Enuie" is pictured using the same psalmic verse in V.xii.36.3–5, "her cursed tongue full sharpe and short / Appear'd like Aspis sting, that closely kils, / Or cruelly does wound, whom so she wils."

*fell:* 1. fierce, dreadful — in imitation of Vergil, Aen. 2.337, "tristis Erinys"; 2. deadly (particularly when used of poison); 3. in a transferred sense, rancorously, as with gall; 4. possibly a fell of hair — a reference to the Furies' hair.

3. *combe:* 1. dress their heads; but 2. reminiscent of a cockscomb.

4. *poysoned words:* Reflecting the "idle worde" of Matt. 12.37.

    *spitefull speeches:* Spenser, in contrast to many medieval writers who commend jealousy as a means of enhancing love, generally denounces it as a threat to true love, see *FQ* III.11.1–2, where jealousy "that turnest loue diuine / To ioylesse dread" is addressed as "O Hatefull hellish Snake, what furie furst / Brought thee from balefull house of Proserpine."

5. *horrid paines of hell:* a translation of Homer's "ἄλγεα ... πολλὰ μαλ'" (which Chapman [19.254] translates as "plagues," and Pope as "horrid woes"). Tisiphone, the third Fury, appears with a scourge of snakes as the portress to hell in Vergil, *Aen.* 6.57–74.

7. *false forged lies:* corresponding to Homer's "ἐπίορκον ὀμόσσῃ."

11. *conspire:* See Matt. 12.14, where the pharisees, who slandered Christ, "consulted against him, how they might destroye him."

13. *shame be thy meed:* See *FQ* IV.vi.6.1. "Honi soit qui mal y pense," the motto of the Knights of the Garter. Contrast the intent of morning prayer Ps. 71.11 & 22, "My tongue also shall talke of they righteousnesse ... for they are ... brought vnto shame that seeke to do me euill."

**Tuesday 14 May:** *Morning Prayer:* Pss. 71–72, Matt. 12. *Evening Prayer:* Pss. 73–74, Rom. 13.

## Sonnet 87

The first of three concluding sonnets lamenting the lady's absence and seeking consolation for it. The conjunction of *reascend* (8) and *expectation* (9) associate it with the period after the Ascension and leading up to the feast of Pentecost, which "is called Expectation-week for now the Apostles were earnestly expecting the fulfilling of that promise of our Lord, *If I go away, I will send the Comforter to you, S. John 16.7*" (Sparrow 170).

1–14. The poet's preoccupation with the slow passing of night and day reflects the observation of Paul in the second lesson at evening prayer for Wednesday 15 May, Rom. 14.5, "This man estemeth one day aboue another, and another man counteth euerie daye a like." (The verse expands one from the preceding chapter, "The night is past, and the day is at hand.")

    The sonnet's extended reverse aubade, caused by the absence of the poet's beloved, is like the psalmist who, in "heauinesse" and lacking "comfort," laments the Lord's absence in the day's morning prayer Ps. 77.2–7, "In the time of my trouble I sought the Lord ... in the night season.... Thou holdest mine eyes waking ... in the night I commune with mine owne heart and search out my spirits. Will the Lord absent him selfe for euer?"

2. *long weary dayes:* For the *locus classicus* of the weariness of day succeeding night and night day, see Ovid, *Met.* 15.188, "Cum lassa quiete" (Golding, 15.206–09, "We see that after day commes nyght and darks the sky, / And after nyght the lyghtsum Sunne succeedeth orderly. / Like colour is not in the heauen when all things weery lye / At midnyght sound a sleepe."

    *outworne:* 1. worn out; 2. a sense of exhaustion is also implied. Compare *FQ* III.v.61.1, Arthur's complaint against the night, "Thus did the Prince that wearie night outweare."

4. *protract:* its only Spenserian usage; prolongation, both of time (*from euening vntill morne*) and space (from west to east).

5–8. The antithetical thought was frequent among poets, e.g., Shakespeare, Sonnet
    27.13–14.

6. *noyous:* annoying.

7. *forlorne:* 1. forsaken; 2. secondarily, forlorn hope or expectation.

8. *reascend:* The only occasion Spenser uses the word.

9. *expectation:* See headnote, Expectation Week. The same temporal association may
    underly Sidney's lament, *AS* 21.7–11, "least else that friendly foe, / Great
    expectation, weare a traine of shame. / For since mad March great promise made
    of me, / If now the May of my years much decline, / What can be hoped my
    haruest time will be?"

10. *fain:* 1. wish, desire; 2. a possible pun on 'feign,' fashion.
    *beguile:* to distract the attention from pain.

11. *term:* 1. period; 2. the condition of grief (*weary dayes* and *many nights*).
    *his:* its = grief's.

12. *minute:* the shortest period of time for the Elizabethan.
    *myle:* 1. mile; 2. homonymically, moil (= toil, drudgery; see Shakespeare,
    Sonnet 50.4–6); *minute* and *myle* recall the temporal and spatial of *from euening
    vntill morne* (4).

**Wednesday 15 May:** *Morning Prayer:* Pss. 75–77, Matt. 13. *Evening Prayer:* Ps. 78, Rom. 14.

## Sonnet 88

Sonnet 88's use of technical Platonic terms, particularly its *Idaea playne* (9), is the
most consistent and, apparently, most conscious of all the *amoretti*. But any explicit
adherence to Platonic doctrine, as some have discerned (Lee xcviii, Casady 288),
runs contrary to the anti-Platonic direction of the final couplet. Rather Spenser has
turned Plato's terminology into a conceit of his own devising. The poet's mind may
be sustained by contemplating the image of the heavenly ray as revealed in the lady,
the true Idea of beauty itself, but the paradoxical starving of his body is insisted
upon with down-to-earth reality.

The poet's lack of light fits properly with the liturgical perspectives of Expectation Week. As well, the proximate comfort of the Holy Spirit's coming at Pentecost
has been fused with the details of the second lesson at morning prayer for Thursday
16 May, Matt. 14, a combination of liturgical theme and distinctive scriptural
imagery which occurred only in 1594. Matt. 14 recounts that, when the disciples
saw Christ walking on the water, they cried out in fear, "It is a spirit" (v. 26;
Vulgate, *phantasma*, koiné, φάντασμά). Φάντασμα was used by Plato to indicate
an image presented to the mind as an object. He associates it (*Phaedo*, 64. D) with
the darkness and shadows of the visible world and sees it as a portion of the visible
still remaining with the spiritual. He elsewhere differentiates it from εἰκών (*Sophist*,
236. B-C), defining it a as semblance (= φάντασμα) rather than an original
likeness (= εἰκών). As in *Am.* 45, where Spenser adopted the Platonic εἰκών to
fulfill a liturgical correspondence, so here he has also chosen to write a sonnet of
Platonic cast to correspond with the day's uncommon scriptural use of φάντασμα.

1–4. The vocabulary of sonnet's opening quatrain, *comfort, affrayd, night* and *dangers*,
    all reflect Matt. 14, when Christ, who "in the fourth watch of the night"
    walked towards the disciples' boat endangered by a storm, said, "Be of good
    comfort. It is I: be not afraied" (v. 27). (Peter is also reported as "afraied" [v.
    30], which the Geneva version glosses, "he must nedes fall in danger.")

3. _I wander as in darkenesse:_ Compare evening prayer Ps. 82.5, "walke on still in darkenesse."

5–6. 1. physically, when others look upon their shadows in full daylight; 2. philosophically, an allusion to the Platonic world of shadows.

6. _shadowes vayne:_ The Platonic phenomenal world of which φαντάσματα are part was differentiated from the true world of ἰδέαι; compare _Am._ 35.13–14, a sonnet also coinciding with an account of the feeding of 5000 (see line 12 note). The phrase is often used by Spenser in a non-Platonic way to commend the simple life, e.g., _FQ_ VI.ix.27.3–6, and to condemn the busy life at court (VI.x.2.7–8).

8. _whereof some glance doth in mine eie remayne:_ Exactly rendering the notion behind Plato's φάντασμα (see headnote).

7. _th'onely image of that heauenly ray:_ See _Am._ 45.11, "ymage" (= εἰκών) and _Am._ 78.4, "ymage." The same thought occurs in _HB_ 184–88, "It you behoues to loue, and forth to lay / That heauenly riches, which in you ye beare, / That men the more admyre their fountaine may, / For else what booteth that celestiall ray, / If it in darknesse be enshrined euer." Renwick 156 cites Bembo, _Rime,_ f. 31ᵛ, "La bella immagin sua veduta in parte / Il digiun pasce, e i miei sospiri acqueta."

9. _Idaea:_ the ἰδέα of Plato, undarkened by the dross of physicality, and in contrast to φαντάσματα; see _Am._ 45.7, "the fayre Idea of your celestial hew."

_playne:_ 1. clear, in contrast to _clearest day_ (5); 2. possibly a trace of Latin _plenum_ (French _plein_) = full.

10. _through contemplation:_ See _HHB_ 134–37, "Thence gathering plumes of perfect speculation, / To impe the wings of thy high flying mynd, / Mount vp aloft through heauenly contemplation, / From this darke world," where the direction is clearly an ascension. Here, however, the object of the poet's contemplation, although absent, remains on earth.

12. _feed my loue-affamisht hart:_ see Matt. 14, where "_Christ fedeth fiue thousand_" (vv. 13–21). Spenser's distinction between spiritual and bodily nourishment matches the Geneva version's sidenote to the account, "Christ leaueth them not destitute of bodelie noourishment, which seke the fode of the soule."

_loue-affamisht:_ a unique occurrence in Spenser.

**Thursday 16 May:** _Morning Prayer:_ Pss. 79–81, Matt. 14. _Evening Prayer:_ Pss. 82–85, Rom. 15.

## Sonnet 89

Sonnet 89 is associated with Pentecost through its image of the _Culuer_ and its allusion to the liturgical occasion of the coming of Holy Spirit, the heavenly comforter. No marked correspondence exists between the sonnet and any of the proper psalms or either of the second lessons for Friday 17 May. Spenser may have had in mind Tasso's "O vaga tortorella" (_Rime,_ 4.50.399), although any reference to widow would have been inappropriate.

> O vaga tortorella
> tu la tua compagnia
> ed io pianago colei che non fu mia.
> Misera vedovella,
> tu sovra il nudo ramo,
> a piè del secco tronco io la richiamo:
> mal'aura solo e 'l vento
> risponde mormorando al mio lamento.

The poet's plaint anticipates the solitary notes which begin *Epith.*, "So I vnto my selfe alone will sing" (17).

1. *Culuer:* Dove, and emblem of the Holy Spirit. In *FQ* IV.viii.3–12 the dove, by leading Belphoebe back to Timias overcomes their separation. Thus by implication the separation of the lovers here will also be overcome.

   *bared bough:* see Tasso, "il nudo ramo," & *TM* 245–46, where the poet associates his plaint with the lament of Euterpe, the muse of lyric poetry and inventor of the double flute:

   All comfortlesse vpon the bared bow,
   Like wofull culuers doo sit wayling now.

3. *wishful vow:* 1. a vow full of wishes; 2. wished-for vow. In *Epith.* 385–87 the vow is one full of wishes only, the wished-for vow having already been exchanged.

9. *that vnder heauen doth houe:* 1. *linger* (4), expect; 2. hover — which sustains the bird simile and recalls the description of the culvers in Vergil, *Aen.* 6.191, "ipsa sub ora viri caelo venere volantes"; 3. pass on, pass by (*OED* 3).

10. *comfort:* See morning prayer Ps. 86.4, "Comfort the soule of thy seruant."

11. *aspect:* aspéct. Her face is hauntingly absent in *Am.* 78.8.

    *God:* here, at the conclusion, the only occasion in the sequence when God is specifically mentioned.

12. *vnspotted pleasauns:* Spenser for the greater part of *FQ* uses the noun only with a negative association (Duessa [I.ii.30.1], the House of Pride [I.iv.38.2], the Red Cross Knight's fall [I.vii.4.2], Phaedria [II.vi.6.9], the Bower of Blisse [II.xii.50.3] and Cupid's masque [III.xii.18.1]). Only late in Book VI (x.5.4), does he associate *pleasauns* with the unfallen.

**Friday 17 May**: *Morning Prayer:* Pss. 86–88, Matt. 15. *Evening Prayer:* Ps. 89, Rom. 16.

## [Anacreontics]

The classical precedent for Spenser's placing before his *Epithalamium* a series of three fescennine anacreontic verses lies with the model set by Claudian, whose *Epithalamium de nuptiis Honorii Augusti*, wherever it is found in extant Latin manuscripts, is preceded by four short fescennine verses. (See Birt, cxxix–cxxxiii, who establishes among the manuscripts six orders of Claudian's major poems. In the five series which contain the *Epithalamium* it is preceded always by the *Fescinnina*.) Renaissance editors of Claudian adopted the same poetic order of placing the *Fescinnina* immediately prior to the *Epithalamium*, beginning with the Vicenza edition of 1482, and subsequently in those of Venice (1500), Vienna (1510), Florence (1519), Paris (1530), and particularly that of Basil (1534) which places the *Fescennina* before both Claudian's *Epithalamium de nuptiis Honorii Augusti* and a relocated *Epithalamium dictum Palladio . . . et Celerinae*. This linking was observed in the subsequent editions of Lyon (1535 & 1551) and Antwerp (1571) (see Birt clxxxiv–cxciv).

Spenser's inclusion before his *Epithalamion* of anacreontic verses, whose questionable nature caused some earlier commentators to doubt his authorship — and apparently caused Sidney on his deathbed to disown his Anacreontics (see Duncan-Jones, "Sidney's Anacreontics," 226) — thus observes the classical model provided by Claudian. The Anacreontics also bear a resemblance to the theme of Claudian's fourth and concluding *Fescennina*, whose *topos* is that of the bee defending its honey from stealing. The genial context given by Claudian to Theocritus' Κηριοκλέπτης had already been adopted by Spenser in *Am.* 26.

James Hutton 106–31 has demonstrated the widespread development of the Κηριοκλέπτης motif following the publication in 1485 of the Aldine Theocritus and the 1554 Paris edition of the *Anacreontis Teii odae* by Henri Estienne. The invention, found in Theocritus' *Idyll* 19, was ascribed originally to him, although latterly to Bion or Moschus. Facets of the invention are found in *Anacreontea, 35*, but the matter of the two poems is so closely allied that their influence can only be traced together. Hutton identifies some 130 workings of the motif in a list that concludes with the end of the 18th century and which contains such names as Tasso, Alciati, Ronsard, de Baïf, Estienne, Scaliger, Belleau and Whitney (147, "*Fel in melle*"), any of which Spenser could have read. He identifies "certain divergent traits" which distinguish the two Greek models, but concludes that Spenser's Anacreontic verses, like many neo-Latin, French and Italian versions, are a syncretic compilation of the two sources and manifest features whose proximate origins are finally indeterminable.

Some of the verses' features do, however, find a kinship with elements particular to both Theocritus and Anacreon, as well as Claudian, Tasso, Marot and Watson. Evidence exists to suggest that Spenser was familiar with the Greek versions of Theocritus and Anacreon, for he had apparently already translated Moschus' Idyll, Ἔρως δραπέτης (*Amor Fugitivus* or The Fugitive Love), with which the Κηριοκλέπτης invention was closely identified. E. K.'s gloss to *SC* March, 79, notes, "... Moschus his Idyllion of wandring loue, being now most excellently translated into Latine by the singuler learned man Angelus Politianus: whych worke I haue seene amongst other of thys Poets doings, very wel translated also into Englishe Rymes." Spenser later recounts Venus' search for the fugitive Cupid as a prelude to the Garden of Adonis in *FQ* III.vi.11–26. The *Anacreontea* would have been available to him, as they were to Sidney, in Estienne's 1554 Greek edition with Latin verse translations. The theme was popular amongst Spenser's contemporaries and can be found among others in Lynche, *Diella*, 18.

Prescott, *Spenser's Poetry*, 623–24 has recently identified two reworkings of epigrams by Marot: Spenser's second anacreontic verse, "As Diane hunted on a day," being a loose rendering of Marot's "L'Enfant Amour n'a plus son arc estrange," and the third verse, "I Saw in secret to my Dame," a translation of Marot's "Amour trouua celle qui m'est amere." In the fourth series of anacreontic verses Hutton 106–31 identifies three strains: the first two stanzas are a rendering of Tasso's madrigal, "Mentre in grembo," the second two draw upon the classical models of Theocritus and Anacreon, while the final two stanzas are Spenser's own invention, although they share the conceit of Cupid's being cured with the conclusion to Watson's *Hecatompathia*, 53.

The following are the two classical models:

*Theocritus. Idyll* 19.

Τὸν κλέπταν πότ' Ἔρωτα κακὰ κέντασε μέλισσα
κηρίον ἐκ σίμβλων συλεύμενον, ἄκρα δὲ χειρῶν
δάκτυλα πάνθ' ὑπένυξεν. ὃ δ' ἄλγεε καὶ χέρ' ἐφύση
καὶ τὰν γᾶρ ἐπάταξε καὶ ἄλατο, τᾷ δ' Ἀφροδίτᾳ
δεῖξέ τε τὰν ὀδύναν καὶ μέμφετο, ὅττί γε τυτθόν
θηρίον ἐστὶ μέλιςςα καὶ ἁλίκα τραύματα ποιεῖ.

χά μάτηρ γελάσασα· τί δ'; οὐκ ἴσος ἐσσὶ μελίσσαις
ὡς τυτθὸν μὲν ἴης, τὰ δὲ τραύματα ἀλίκα ποιεῖς;

(Love the thief was once stung by a wicked bee, as he filched a honeycomb from the hive, and all his finger-tips were pricked. It hurt, and he blew on his hand, stamped the earth, and skipped about; and he showed his hurt to Aphrodite, complaining that the bee is but a tiny creature, but it causes such wounds. And his mother laughed: "What! are you not like the bees, you who are also little, but cause such great wounds?" [Hutton, 109])

Anacreon. 35.

Ἔρως ποτ' ἐν ῥόδοιϲι
κοιμωμένην μέλιτταν
οὐκ εἶδεν, ἀλλ' ἐτρώθη·
τὸν δάκτυλον παταχθεὶς
τᾶς χειρὸς ὠλόλυξε.
δραμὼν δὲ καὶ πετασθεὶς
πρὸς τὴν καλὴν Κυθήρην
'ὄλωλα, μῆτερ, 'εἶπεν,
'ὄλωλα κἀποθνήσκω·
ὄφις μ' ἔτυψε μικρὸς
Πτερωτός, ὃν καλοῦσιν
μέλιτταν οἱ γεωργοί.'
ἁ δ'εἶπεν· 'εἰ τὸ κέντρον
πονεῖ τὸ τᾶς μελίττας,
πόσον δοκεῖς πονοῦσιν,
Ἔρως, ὅσους σὺ βάλλεις;'

(Love once failed to notice a bee that was sleeping among the roses, and he was wounded: he was struck in the finger, and he howled. He ran and flew to beautiful Cythere and said, "I have been killed, mother, killed. I am dying. I was struck by the small winged snake that farmers call 'the bee.'" She replied, "If the bee-sting is painful, what pain, Love, do you suppose all your victims suffer?" [Loeb Classics, trans. David Campbell, 107–9])

1–82. The verses comprise 9 stanzas (of which 1–2 are awarded one page and the subsequent 7 a single page), 3 rhyme schemes (1, 2–3, 4–9), and 4 metrical patterns (1, 2, 3, & 4–9). All end with a tetrameter couplet. Only lines 1–2 strictly observe the short hemiambics of the *Anacreontea*: ˆ—ˆ—ˆ— —.

1–6. The stanza develops the Κηριοκλέπτης invention with a series of bawdy puns and imitates the associated honey-stealing of Claudian's *Fescinnina*, 4.7–8, "non quisquam . . . / Hyblaeos latebris nec spoliat favos," to which Whitney alludes in his emblem, "*Post amara dulcia*" (165). The *topos* was frequent even among English sonneteers, e.g., Barnes, *Parthenophil and Parthenophe*, Ode, 16.39–52, and Barnfield, *Cynthia*, 8.6–11, "Ah foolish Bees (thinke I) that doe not sucke / His lips for hony . . . Kisse him, but sting him not, for if you doe, / His angry voice your flying will pursue."

1. *waxed*: 1. grew; but 2. clearly the word has been chosen for its association with wax and honey.

2. *Venus baby*: Cupid.

3. *cunning*: 1. deceitful art; 2. as a bawdy pun (from *cunnus* = female pudenda), knowledge of the sexual type.

7–14. Compare Marot, "L'Enfant Amour n'a plus son arc estrange," *Oeuvres*,
  4.169.132,

>  L'Enfant Amour n'a plus son arc estrange,
>  Dont il blessoit d'hommes & cueurs & testes:
>  Auec celuy de Diane a faict change
>  Dont elle alloit aux champs faire les questes.
>  Ilz ont changé, n'enfaictes plus d'enquestes;
>  Et si on dict: à quoy le congnois tu?
>  Ie voy qu'Amour chasse souuent aux bestes,
>  Et qu'elle attainct les hommes de vertu.

15–22. A translation of Marot, "Amour trouua celle qui m'est amere," *Oeuvres*,
  4.193.157,

>  Amour trouua celle qui m'est amere,
>  Et ie y estoys, i'en sçay bien mieulx le compte:
>  "Bon iour (dict-il), bon iour Venus ma mere."
>  Puis tout à coup il veoit qu'il se mescompte,
>  Dont la couleur au visage lui monte
>  D'auoir failly: honteux, Dieu sçait combien:
>  "Non, non, Amour (ce dis ie) n'ayez honte;
>  Plus cler voyantz que vous f'y trompent bien."

23–42. A rendering of Tasso's madrigal, "Mentre in grembo," *Rime*, 2.341,

>  Mentre in grembo a la madre Amore un giorno
>  Dolcemente dormiva,
>  Una zanzara zufolava intorno
>  Per quella dolce riva,
>  Disse allor, desto a quel susurro, Amore:
>  Da sì picciola forma
>  Com' esce sì gran voce e tal rumore
>  Che sveglia ognun che dorma?
>  Con maniere vezzose
>  Lusingandogli il sonno col suo canto
>  Venere gli rispose:
>  E tu picciolo sei,
>  Ma pur gli uomini in terra col tuo pianto
>  E 'n ciel desti gli Dèi.

Spenser imitates both Tasso's opening lines and their rhythm, although he
changes Tasso's gnat into a bee.

25. *trumpet:* used elsewhere by Spenser also of the gnat, see *FQ* II.ix.16.3.

32. *corage:* 1. bravery; 2. lust.

33. *closely:* secretly or inwardly.

51–52. *The fly that I so much did scorne, / hath hurt me with his little horne:* An echo
  of Cupid's exclamation in Anacreon, "ὄφις μικρὸς Πτερωτός" (= little
  winged serpent).
  
  *horn:* assists the poem's bawdy associations.

54. *of his griefe complayned:* Cupid's complaining of his grief is specifically mentioned
  only by Theocritus, see 19.5, "τὰν ὀδύναν καὶ μέμφετο."

55. *could not chose but laugh:* Venus laughing is not contained in Anacreon and is a
  feature of Theocritus, 19.8, "χὰ μάτηρ γελάσασα" Hutton 123, however,
  indicates that Spenser's continental antecedents generally imitate the detail: "in

Ronsard Venus smiles ('se sourit'), in Baïf she begins to laugh ('se prenant à rire')."

57–58. *Think now . . . dost wound:* Such an admonition concludes the poems of both Anacreon and Theocritus, although Spenser's is closer to that of Anacreon, 35.13–16, "ἁ δ'εἶπεν· 'εἰ τὸ κέντρον / πονεῖ τὸ τὰς μελίττας, / πόσον δοκεῖς πονοῦσιν, / "Ἔρως, ὅσους σὺ βάλλεις;'"; see Theocritus, 19.7–8, "τί δ'; οὐκ ἴσος ἐσσὶ μελίσσαις / ὡς τυτθὸν μὲν ἴης, τὰ δὲ τραύματα ἁλίκα ποιεῖς;."

59. *pricked:* 1. wounded; but 2. *prick* also retains suggestive overtones.

63–82. The theme of the last two stanzas, the cure of Cupid, is an elaboration not found in the two classical antecedents. The closest model to Spenser could have been Watson's *Hecatompathia*, 53, whose conclusion, Love's cure by Aesculapius, is Watson's own invention. Like Spenser, Watson concludes his working of the *topos* by applying it to the self, the gradual disclosure of identity also being a feature of Claudian's concluding *Fescennina*. Watson shows his awareness of a number of translations of Theocritus' idyll in his argument prefixed to his versions, "The two first partes of this Sonnet, are an imitation of certaine Greeke verses of *Theocritus;* which verses as they are translated by many good Poets of later dayes, so moste aptlye and plainely by C. *Vrcinus Velius* in his Epigrammes":

> Where tender *Loue* had laide him downe to sleepe,
> A little Bee so stong his fingers end,
> That burning ache enforced him to weepe
> And call for Phebus Sonne to stand his frend,
> To whome he cride, I muse so small a thing
> Can pricke thus deepe with suche a little Sting.
> Why so, sweet Boy, quoth Venus sitting by?
> Thy selfe is yong, thy arrowes are but small
> And yet thy shotte makes hardest harts to cry:
> To Phebus Sunne she turned therewithall,
> And prayde him shew his skill to cure the sore,
> Whose like her Boy had neuer felt before.
> Then he with Herbes recured soone the wound,
> Which being done, he threw the Herbes away,
> Whose force, through touching *Loue,* in selfe same ground,
> By haplesse hap did breede my hartes decay:
> For there they fell, where long my hart had li'ne
> To waite for *Loue,* and what he should assigne.

64. *smock:* a female undergarment, but suggestive also of immorality (OED 3b).

68–70. *salue of soueraigne might: / And then she bath'd him in a dainty well / the well of deare delight:* The cure of Aesculapius ("Phoebus sunne") in Watson's *Hecatompathia* is obtained through the application of herbs. The customary herb against the bee-sting was thyme, see Hill 61, "And the hearb healeth the sting of the Bee, if the same be laid vpon it." In *FQ* I.xi.48. 1–3 a sovereign balm flows from the first tree as from a well to cure the knight: "From that first tree forth flowd, as from a well, / A trickling streame of Balme, most soueraine / And daintie deare." Here the analogy is devoid of any Christian perspective and explicitly suggestive.

*well:* 1. literally, a spring; 2. bawdily, the female sexual organ.

73. *boy ... wel recured:* See lines 63–82 note, Watson, *Hecatompathia*, 53.12–13, "Boy ... recured soone the wound."

81. *languish:* A frequent complaint in the preceding *amoretti*, see *Am.* 50.1 & 10, 36.3, 52.8 & 60.11.

## Epithalamion

1. *Ye learned sisters:* In imitation of Ovid's "doctas sorores" (*Met.* 5.255; Golding (5.294) "the learned sisters nine"; see *Fasti*, 6.811). The invocation was a conventional opening, see *Am.* 1.10's reference to *Helicon*, where the Muses dwelt. Catullus likewise opens his epithalamial verses, *Carmen* 61, "Collis o Heliconii / cultor" (O inhabitant of Mount Helicon), as does Statius, *Epithalamion in Stellam et Violentillam*, 3–5, "procul ecce canoro / demigrant Helicone deae quatiuntque novena / lampade solemnem thalamis coeuntibus ignem" (Behold, far away the goddesses descend from Helicon and brandish with ninefold torch the fire that hallows the wedding bed). (See Buttet, *Epithalame Aux Nosses de Philibert de Savoie*, 61–62, "Les neuf Muses, ses seurs, toutes à sa naissance, / Laissant leur mont Olympe.") The invocation was frequent from Homer onwards. Although originally three in number, by the time of Hesiod they were nine (*Theogony*, 77ff.), and Spenser invokes all nine in *TM* 1, "ye sacred Sisters nine."

2. *others to adorne:* See the dedications to *FQ* (e.g., Ded. Son. xvi.8, "adorne these verses base") and Spenser's common use of the phrase in *FQ* IV.ii.34.8, where Cambridge is "adorn'd ... with many a gentle Muse."

3. *gracefull:* conferring honor or grace.
      *rymes:* verses.

7–11. *when ye list your owne mishaps to mourne:* The lament, given its similarities with the lament of the Muses in *TM*, probably refers to that poem (see Grosart 1.189; Welsford 173). The Muses who sit beside the "Springs of *Helicone*" are asked to recount their lamentations upon the decayed state of the arts and neglect of learning, for since the death of Phaeton, "Of you his mournfull Sisters was lamented, / Such mournfull tunes were neuer since inuented" (11–12). *Epith.*'s introduction is thus a Spenserian *contaminatio*, because such lamentation properly belongs to Phaeton's sisters, the Heliades (see Ovid, *Met.* 2.333–66), and not to the Muses.

10–11. *teach the woods and waters to lament / Your dolefull dreriment:* A pastoral convention, deriving from Vergil, *Eclogues*, 1.4–5, "Tu Tityre ... resonare doces Amaryllida silvas," and found also in *SC* June, 95–96 & *FQ* IV.xi.41.9.

10. *woods and waters:* See *TM* 21 & 25, "th' hollow hills ... The trembling streames."

12. *sorrowfull complaints:* a Spenserian pleonasm.
      *complaints:* Possibly a reference to *The Teares of the Muses* and other poems which were published in 1591 under the title, "Complaints. *Containing sundrie small Poemes of the Worlds Vanitie.*" Such complaints were a medieval tradition and Spenser is fond of incorporating them in *FQ*, e.g., the "piteous plaintes" at IV.xii.6–8. The solitary Cuddie similarly complains in *SC* Aug., 151–52.

15. *enuide:* envied.

16. *Orpheus:* Both Vergil (*Georgics,* 4.453–527) and Ovid (*Met* 10.1–147) recount the story of Orpheus, whose wife Eurydice, having been killed by a snake-bite, was won from Hades by Orpheus' music. Ovid begins with Orpheus inviting Hymen to his wedding, though in vain ("nequiquam"). It is the Vergilian account, however, that includes the detail that Orpheus sang to himself a lament upon his wife's absence — at the rising, and the declining, of the day, "ipse cava solans aegrum testudine amorem / te, dulcis coniunx, te solo in litore secum, / te veniente die, te decedente canebat" (he [Orpheus], seeking to soothe his sorrowful love with his hollow shell, sang of you, his sweet wife, to himself alone on the shore, as day arose and day declined; Claudian opens his *Epistula ad Serenam* with Orpheus' wedding, "Orphea cum primae sociarent numina taedae / ruraque compleret Thracia festus Hymen" [When Orpheus' marriage-torch was first kindled and festive Hymen filled the Thracian countryside]). Loewenstein 291 points to the extensive influence of Vergilian (and Orphean) paradigms on the construction of *Epithalamion.*

18. *The woods shall to me answer and my Eccho ring:* A refrain conflating classical epithalamial and pastoral conventions: Claudian concludes his *Praefatio* to *Epith. Honorii* with a similar cry, "frondoso strepuit felix Hymenaeus Olympo; / reginam resonant Othrys et Ossa Thetim" (the happy cry of Hymen rings o'er leafy Olympus and Othrys and Ossa resound with the name queen Thetis); see his *Epith. Palladio,* 23–25, "Celerina per omnes / Italiae canitur montes omnisque maritum / Palladium resonabat ager" (the name Celerina is sung through all the hills of Italy and every field resounds with that of her husband Palladius). Compare also Ps. 96.12, "Let the fielde be ioyfull, and all that is in it: then shall all the trees of the wood reioyce before the Lord," a verse closer to *Epith.*'s second refrain (35–36).

Spenser elsewhere constantly uses the pastoral tenor of the refrain, echoing Vergil, *Eclogues,* 10.8, which sings of an absent mistress, "non canimus surdis, respondent omnia silvae" (we sing not to deaf ears; the woods echo every [note]) — see SC June, 52; TM 19–22; FQ I.iii.8.2; I.vi.14.2; I.viii.11.9; II.iii.20.8–9; VI.viii.46.1–4; VI.x.10.5; VI.xi.26.6; VII.vi.52.8–9; *Proth* 112–13.

The refrain in differing forms concludes the first twenty-three stanzas of *Epith.,* each form appropriately shaped to respond to the lines that immediately precede it and to mark the progress of the marriage-day. The form here, given the poet's solitude, incorporates the only use in the series of the personal pronoun *me.* Later, once night has descended and outside voices are no longer required, the refrain is couched in the negative, *The woods no more shal answere, nor your echo ring* (314). After the couple are conjoined, the plural of the first person pronoun is used, *Ne let the woods vs answere, nor our Eccho ring* (389).

*Eccho:* Mirroring the complaint of Narcissus, Ovid, *Met.* 3.507, "planxerunt dryades: plangentibus adsonat Echo" (Golding 3.632–33, "The Wood nymphes also did lament. And *Echo* did rebound / To euery sorrowfull noyse of theirs with like lamenting sound").

19–20. *Early before the worlds light giuing lampe, / His golden beame vpon the hils doth spred:* Statius opens *Epith. in Stella* with Phoebus distributing garlands, "Phoebus . . . serta ferunt" (17–19).

22. *ye:* technically an instruction to the sisters, but calling upon maidens to awaken the bride is a feature of classical epithalamia, see Catullus, *Carmen* 61.36–40, "vosque item simul, integrae / virgines, quibus advenit / par dies, agite in

modum / dicite "o Hymenaee Hymen, / o Hymen Hymenaee." (you also, at the same time, unwedded maidens, for whom a similar day approaches, go and in like measure say, "O Hymenaeus Hymen, O Hymen Hymenaeus")."

*fresh lusty hed:* (= lustihead); 1. refreshed vigor after sleep, without carnal associations; 2. lustfulness (see *FQ* II.i.41.7).

23–25. *Go to the bowre of my beloued loue, / My truest turtle doue, / Bid her awake:* strongly reminiscent of the spouse's words in the Song of Solomon, "My welbeloued spake and said vnto me, Arise, my loue, my faire one.... The flowers appear in the earth ... the voice of the turtle is heard in our land" (2.7–12 passim) and "I slepe, but mine heart waketh, *it is* the voyce of my welbeloued that knocketh, *saying*, Open vnto me, my sister, my loue, my dooue" (5.2). The turtle dove, from biblical times, signified marital fidelity. The solitariness of the poet, who like a dove lamented the absence of his mate in *Am.* 89, is about to be overcome.

26. *maske to moue:* a retinue of masked persons, accompanied by torch-bearers, musicians and dancers and lead by a presenter. Hymen frequently figures as a presenter of wedding masques in Renaissance epithalamia.

27. *Taed:* (*taeda* = wedding torch); associated with Hymen and a feature of epithalamia, see Claudian, *Epith. Honorii*, 229, "taedasque parari" (the torches are being prepared), and Catullus, *Carmen* 61.14–15, addressing Hymen, "manu / Pineam quate taedam" (shake the pine torch with your hand).

*flake:* 1. a fragment of ignited matter thrown off a burning object; 2. since the etymon of *flake* is cognate with the Old Norse *flóke*, a lock of hair, an exact translation of the metaphor of hair ("comas") used later by Catullus of the taed, *Carmen* 61.77–78, "viden ut faces splendidas quatiunt comas?" (Spenser pleonastically uses the etymology during the nuptials of the Red Cross Knight and Una, *FQ* I.xii.37.6, "At which the bushy Teade a groome did light," and I.xi.26.4, "A flake of fire, that flashing in his beard.")

29. *fresh garments trim:* The noun between two adjectives imitates classical constructions.

31. *the wished day is come:* See *FQ* II.iv.22.1. The expression was classical, see Claudian, *Epith. Honorii*, 45, "Optatusne dies aderit?" (will the wished day ever come?), and Catullus, *Carmen* 64.31–32, "Quis simul optatae finito tempore luces / Advenere" (once that wished day in time fulfilled had come; see Claudian, *Epistula ad Serenam*, 51).

33. *vsury:* interest rather than usury, as in Una's pledge to Arthur (*FQ* I.viii.27.89–9), "Behold what ye this day haue done for mee / And what I cannot quite, requite with vsuree." Interest is a minor feature of classical epithalamia, see Claudian, *Epith. Honorii*, 37–38, "... cui Mariam debes. faenus mihi solve paternum" ("you do owe Maria to me. Pay back to me the interest due to the father"). The thought is repeated at 317–18 where the poet prays that his labors and cares be *sumd in one, and cancelled for aye.*

36–39. *That all the woods may answer and your eccho ring. / Bring with you all the Nymphes that you can heare / Both of the riuers and the forrests greene: / And of the sea:* Nymphs inhabit, *inter alia*, all epithalamia, both classical and Renaissance. See Claudian, *Epith. Honorii*, 159 & 171, *Fescennina*, 22–24, and *Epith. Palladio*, 7 & 17; Statius, *Epith. Stellam*, 115–16; Catullus, *Carmen* 61.29–30, "Nympha quos super irrigat / frigerans Aganippe," adopted in detail by Buttet, *Epithalame*, 91–98; Belleau, *Epithalame du Duc de Lorraine*, 9–16. Spenser identifies here the nymphs of the rivers, the Naiades, of the forests, the Dryades (from the oak, their favorite tree — see *Am.* 6.5 note), and the sea, the Nereides.

The connection between the nymphs and *Epith.*'s second refrain had already been established in *FQ* VI.x.10.4–5, where the dancing feet of the nymphs and graces are heard to beat the ground: "And many feete fast thumping th' hollow ground, / That through the woods their Eccho did rebound" (see Catullus, *Carmen* 61.12–15). Since the primary Greek sense of nymph was a bride or a marriageable maiden (see E. K.'s note, *SC* April, 120, "For the word Nymphe in Greeke signifieth . . . a Spouse or Bryde"), *Nymphes* was an appropriate term to include in an epithalamium.

37. *al the Nymphes that you can heare: you* is the object of *heare.*

39. *the sea that neighbours to her neare:* possibly a reference to the sea near Yougal. The house of Elizabeth Boyle's brother-in-law, Sir Richard Smith, stood on the estuary where the river Blackwater, of which the Awbeg (the Mulla [see 156 note]) was a tributary, flowed into the sea. Welsford 175 suggests that Elizabeth Boyle was married from the house.

40. *gay girlands:* a favorite Spenserian phrase; *gay girlands goodly,* reflects the frequent rhetorical repetition in Catullus, *Carmen* 61.19, "bona cum bona," and 44, "bonae Veneris, boni." In most classical and neo-Latin epithalamies the bride is bedecked with garlands of flowers; Spenser is closest to Statius, *Epith. in Stella,* 23, "tu modo fronte rosas, violis modo lilia mixta excipis . . ." (now roses, now lilies mixed with violets, do you receive upon your brow).

44. *blew:* In *Proth* 30, the violet is identified as "pallid blew"; see Catullus, *Carmen* 61.6–7 and 64.282–83. The *riband* (ribbon) binding the flowers comprises a knot symbolizing the spouses' wedding vows (see *Am.* 6.14).

45–47. *And let them make great store of bridale poses, / And let them eeke bring store of other flowers / To deck the bridale bowers:* A further feature of classical (and neo-Latin) epithalamia was the decking of the bridal chamber with flowers, specifically roses and violets; *great store* imitates Claudian's "calathos largos" (*Epith. Palladio,* 116–19),

> Ut thalami tetigere fores, tum vere rubentes
> desuper invertunt calathos largosque rosarum
> imbres et violas plenis sparsere pharetris
> collectas Veneris prato . . .

(As they reached the doors of the bridal bower, they empty great baskets full of red flowers, pouring forth showers of roses and scattering from their full quivers violets gathered in Venus' meadow . . .).

48–49. *And let the ground whereas her foot shall tread, / For feare the stones her tender foot should wrong:* A possible echo of Ps. 91.12, where the angels "shall beare thee in their handes: that thou hurt not thy foote against a stone." But compare the detail, and marital context, of the verse's parallel, Deut. 28.56, "The tender and deintie woman among you, which neuer wolde venture to set the sole of her fote vpon the grounde (for her softnes and tendernes) shalbe grieued at her housband. . . ."

51. *diapred lyke the discolored mead: diapred,* with the ground adorned with a fretwork pattern; *diapred* derives from διά + ἄσπρος = white — like *lillyes* (43) — interwoven with another color; *discolored* retains its older sense of variously colored, particolored, rather than uncolored or pale.

54. *song:* probably the song mentioned at line 35.

56. _Ye Nympes of Mulla:_ Invoking local nymphs was a well-established convention both in classical and continental epithalamia, see Buttet, _Epithalame_, 167 & 172, who invokes the nymphs of both the Seine and the Marne, while Belleau, _Epithalame_, 4, invokes those of the Seine. The Mulla is Spenser's name for the river Awbeg which flowed through his estate at Kilcolman and thence into the Blackwater (in Spenser's day the Broadwater). The name derived from Kilne-mullah, the older name for the district now Buttevant. Spenser evidently also has in mind the Latin _mullus_ = a fish of the mullet family.

    _carefull heed:_ another pleonasm.

57–58. _trouts ... pikes:_ Details provided by an enthusiastic and knowledgeable fisherman (see _Am._ 47). There are evidently good trout and pike in the river still (see _Variorum, Minor Poems_, 2.464).

60. _rushy lake:_ Renwick 205 observes that, "The _rushy lake_ is a stone's-throw from Kilcolman tower, which stands on the northern rim of a saucer of land draining northward into it."

62. _Bynd vp the locks the which hang scatterd light:_ See the instruction, SC April, 133, Claudian, _Epith. Honorii_, 122 ("crines festina ligat"), and Belleau, _Epithalame_, 1–4.

64. _your faces as the christall bright:_ See SC June, 25–30, where the "lighfote Nymphes" will be kissed by Pan, "And Pan himselfe to kisse their christall faces." The association was standard , see Gn 898 & _Am._ 45.1–2.

67. _lightfoot mayds: lightfoot_ occurs eleven times in Spenser, on five occasions being applied to nymphs or fairies, beginning with the reference immediately above, SC June, 26.1) The Nereides, who are associated with both river-waters and the sea and who from classical times were described as _light_ (see Horace, _Odes_, 1.1.29, "Nympharum leves ... chori"); Cymothoe (= light on the waters, from κῦμα = billows on the river-waters + θόη = light or swift), is listed among them at FQ VI.xi.49.4 (see TM 31, "The ioyous Nymphes and lightfoote Faeries"); 2. the nymphs of Diana, which are seen as inhabiting the Arlo, identified in FQ VII.vi.36, as the hill on which the Mulla (Awbeg) rises.

    _deere: 1595_ and _F12_ all have _dore_, which, if only for reasons of rhyme, should be amended to _deere_. The Old English _deor_ and Middle English _dere_ or deere were used to signify any kind of wild four-legged animal as well as deer.

67–70. Apart from the lines' topical references, wolves being common in Ireland until 1700, the lines illustrate Spenser's syncretic wit. The nymphs of the mountains were the Νύμφαι ὀρεστιάδες or ὀρεάδες, from ὀρεινός = mountain. But ὀρεινός was also used of wild wolves (see _Od._ 10.212). The two meanings of the Greek original are present, as the mountain nymphs (the agents of Diana, the _nympha nympharum_ and protector of women as well as wild animals especially deer) are called upon to keep the wild wolves far from the bride.

68. _towre:_ probably 1. stand aloft or outlined against the sky (see FQ II.xii.30.5); rather than 2. the falconry term, soar or perch aloft (see FQ VI.x.6.8–9), because _deere_ did not ordinarily include birds.

70. _steele darts:_ the weapons of Diana were customarily silver.

74. _Wake, now my loue, awake:_ Compare the instruction of Song of Sol. 2.7 (3.5 & 8.4), "nor waken my loue."

75–76. _The Rosy Morne long since left Tithones bed, / All ready to her siluer coche to clyme:_ A standard expression originating with the Homeric epithet, ῥοδοδάκτυλος 'Ηώς = rosy-fingered dawn, see *Il.* 21.1 & *Od.* 2.1. The description finds a place in Vergil, whose details Spenser has conflated, *Aen.* 4.585, "Et iam prima novo spargebit lumine terras / Tithoni croceum linquens Aurora cubile" (And already early Dawn, leaving Tithonus' golden bed, spreads the earth with new light), and 7.26, where the detail of her coach is included, "et aethere ab alto / Aurora in roseis fulgebat lutea bigis" (from the high heaven rose-colored Morning shone in her rosy coach). See Statius, *Epith. Stellam*, 44–45, "nec si alma per auras / te potius prensum aveheret Tithonia biga" (unless Dawn had rather seized you and in Tithonus' coach carried you through the air).

75. *Tithones:* consort of Aurora, who was granted immortality but not eternal youth.

76. *siluer coche:* traditionally her coach was golden, but then Diana's *darts* (69) were customarily *siluer.* Spenser generally uses *siluer* in *FQ* to connote purity (see VI.vii.19.8, "siluer slomber").

77. *Phoebus:* an epithet of Apollo (from φοῖβος= bright). Phoebus Apollo is the sun-god as well as leader of the Muses.

78–84. This small aubade conflates the traditional epithalamial dawn-song to awake the bride with a choric list of birds in the manner of a common medieval poetic convention, e.g., *Romance of the Rose,* passim, and Chaucer, *Parl. Foules,* 330–65, as well as the intricate medieval Bird Masses.

80. *Larke:* Although the lark is the messenger of dawn, it is not commonly found in the English aube, despite Chaucer's inclusion, *K. T.* 1491, "The bisy larke, messager of day."

*mattins:* (from *matutinas* = of the morning); the first of the canonical hours (earlier performed at midnight but occasionally at daybreak) and used by the Church of England since the reformation for morning prayer, which combines elements from both matins and lauds (= *praises* [79]).

81. *Mauis:* the song-thrush.

*descant:* the only Spenserian usage; from *des* = apart and *cantus* = song, part-singing; in plainsong a counterpoint motif sung above the basic melody (*cantus firmus*).

82. *Ouzell:* the blackbird.

*shrills:* see Puttenham 41 on epithalamial music, "the tunes of the songs were very loude and shrill."

*Ruddock:* the robin redbreast.

83. *consent:* confused in significance and spelling with concent (see *FQ* III.xii.5.7, "A lay of loues delight, with sweet concent," where *1596* has "consent"); so here both 1. consent = agreement or approval; and 2. concent (*con* = together + *cantus* = song) = a concord of voices singing together.

85–87. The lines echo the parable of the virgins who "went to mete the bridegrome" (Matt. 25.1–13). Awaiting his coming, they "slombred and slept," but were aroused by the cry, "Beholde, the bridegrome cometh: go out to mete him" (v. 6).

87. *T' awayt:* used often by Spenser to mean 'to keep watch for' (see *FQ* I.xi.52.4), and in imitation of Matt. 25.13 above, "Watche therefore: for ye knowe nether the day, nor the houre, when the Sonne of man wil come."

87. *make:* archaic form of mate — see *Am.* 70.11.

90. *ioy and pleasance:* recalling Euterpe (ἔυ = goodly + τέρψις = joy or pleasance), the muse of lyric poetry and inventor of the double flute, whom Spenser associates with choirs of birds in *TM* 235–46 (see *Am.* 89.1 note).

95. *Hesperus*: Hesperus, both the morning star and evening star, is an appropriate epithalamial feature; see Catullus, *Carmen* 62.33, and Claudian, who mentions Hesperus in connection with choruses now sung, "Septima lux . . . viderat exactos Hesperus igne choros" (*Praef.* to *Epith. Honorii*, 15–16 [seven times Hesperus had relit his lamp and seen the choirs complete their song]). In Rev. 22.16 the morning star is identified with Christ the bridegroom, "I Iesus . . . am . . . the bright morning starre" (see 2.28). Spenser had already combined the two sources to describe the preparation of Una for her betrothal feast (*FQ* I.xii.21.4–7).

96. *daughters of delight*: Identified as the Graces at *FQ* VI.x.15.1. Traditionally the Graces are the handmaids of Venus – see Natalis Comes 4.16.130a.48, where they represent delight – *hilaritas* and *laetitia* (*ioy and pleasance*, see line 90).

98–102. The Greek Ὥρα (Latin, *Hora*) are the goddesses of the seasons and represent periods governed by natural laws and revolutions. They are primarily personifications of natural laws and astronomical features, and hence causal powers who regulate, *allot*, the seasons and cause the change from night to day and even from birth to death (*Doe make and still repayre*). According to Hesiod (*Theogony*, 901–06) the hours are the daughters of Jove and Spenser accepts this parentage in *FQ* VII.vii.45.1–2, "Then came the *Howres*, faire daughters of high *Ioue*, / And timely *Night*." Here the lines suggest that Spenser has identified Jupiter and Day, thus making the hours the daughters of Day and Night. In Homer, *Hymn* 6, 1–13, they are described as χρυσάμπυκες (having golden fillets in their hair).

Here the hours are also presented as the divisions between day and night and are identified by Spenser with the sidereal hours of the Ptolemaic system. See Hieatt 31–59 for his reconstruction of *Epith.* according to the sidereal hours and its kinship with the Mutabilitie Cantos.

99. *In Ioues sweet paradice*: Spenser may be recalling Plato, *Symposium*, 203B, where Eros, the son of Poros (resource) and Penia (poverty), is conceived on Aphrodite's birthday in Jove's garden (εἰς τὸν τοῦ Διὸς κῆπον).

103. *ye three handmayds of the Cyprian Queene*: The three graces who attend Venus are Aglia, Euphrosyne, Thalia – often associated with the muses and hours. The specific function of Aglia (ἀγλαΐα = adornment) is reflected in the following two lines, to *adorne* / *addorne* the bride (see *Am.* 74.14 note). The graces were commonly present in epithalamia, e.g., Claudian, *Epith. Honorii*, 100–5 & 202–3, where they choose flowers for the feast, "tu, Gratia, flores / elige" (See *Epith. Palladio*, 9).

*Cyprian*: see *FQ* II.xii.65.3, "Cyprian goddesse."

110–13. *virgins*: See Catullus, *Carmen* 61.36–37, where *virgins* are called to visit the home with Hymen as he adorns the bride, "vosque item simul, integrae / virgines, quibus advenit / par dies, agite in modum" (you unwedded virgins, for whom a similar day is coming, come with me).

115. *so ioyfull day*, / *The ioyfulst day*: In direct imitation of Catullus, *Carmen* 61.11, "excitusque hilari die" (wakening on this *ioyfull day*; see Buttet, *Epithalame*, 7, "Ce jour fait solemnel soit à la France cher"), and echoing Ps. 118.24, "This is the day which the Lord hath made: we will reioyce and be glad in it" (see *Am.* 68.5, for Easter Sunday, "This ioyous day"). An example of the rhetorical device, *ploce*.

117–18. *Faire Sun, shew forth thy fauourable ray*, / *And let they lifull heat not feruent be*: Spenser, when recounting the conception of Belphoebe and Amoret makes allusion to the the sun's life-giving powers in "antique bookes" and acclaims the sun, "Great father he of generation / Is rightly cald, th' author of life and light" (FQ III.vi.9.1–2); see Natalis Comes 4.10.114a.15, "Hic [the sun] èst generationis et corruptionis unicus auctor" (the sun is the sole author of generation and corruption).

119–20. *For feare of burning her sunshyny face, / Her beauty to disgrace:* 1. disfigure; 2. dishonor, shame — a probable small joke, because 'to be under a cloud' in Spenser's time already meant 'to be in disgrace.'

121. *O fayrest Phoebus, father of the Muse:* Normally the Muses are the daughters of Jove (see Hesiod, *Theogony*, 77), but Spenser elsewhere makes Apollo their father (see TM 2; FQ I.xi.5.6 & III.iii.4.2). He probably accepted the idea from Natalis Comes 4.10.110a.13–15, "Fuerunt ... Musae in ejus tutela creditae quarum et dux et pater Apollo fuit existimatus" (the Muses were thought to fall under the protection of Apollo, who was considered their leader and father).

124. *simple:* 1. single; 2. straightforward.

> *boone:* prayer (to Apollo the sun-god for a fine — but temperate — day for his marriage, as recompense for past services done in his name as *father of the Muse*).

125. *let this day let this one day:* a rhetorical *ploce.* The prayer is reminiscent of the shape of the BCP's Collects (see 10th Sunday after Trinity, "Let thy merciful eares, O Lorde, be open to the prayers of thy humble seruants ...").

129–37. *Harke how the Minstrels ... But most of all the Damzels ... when they their tymbrels smyte ... Crying aloud with strong confused noyce:* The details imitate exactly the procession in Ps. 68.25, "The singers go before, the minstrels folowe after: in the midest are the damosels playing with the timbrels." (Compare 1 Macc. 9.39, "and beholde, there was a great noyce, and muche preparation: then the bridegrome came forthe, and his friends and his brethren met them with tymbrels.") Timbrels are a feature of classical epithalamia, e.g., Catullus, *Carmen* 63.7–8, "cepit manibus leve typanum, typanum, tubam Cybelles ..., quatiensque terga tauri teneris cava digitis / canere ..." (she took the light timbrel, timbrel, trumpet of Cybele ... and beating with soft fingers the hollow oxhide she sang ... ; see *Carmen* 63.29 & *Carmen* 64.261–64, with its hymeneal procession including timbrels ["tympana"], horns, ["cornua"] and pipe ["tibia"]).

131. *pipe:* a feature of Catullus, *Carmen* 63, where it is linked with the timbrel, "ubi tympana reboant, / tibicen ubi canit Phryx curvo grave calamo" (21–22; where the voice of the cymbals sounds, where timbrels resound, where the Phrygian piper sounds a deep note on his curved pipe).

> *tabor:* an early name for the drum, in the sixteenth century generally a small drum used principally to accompany a pipe or trumpet.

> *trembling Croud:* an ancient Celtic instrument of six strings, of which four were played with the bow and two by plucking with the fingers. Sidney, *Apologie*, F4ᵛ, comments that his heart was moved by it, even though it was a rough instrument, "and yet is it sung but by some blinde Crouder, with no rougher voyce, then rude stile."

> *trembling:* 1. the strings of the *Croud* vibrate to produce sound; 2. the tremulous sound of voices and music.

132. *That well agree:* pipe, drum and fiddle used in consort are an instance of Spenser's incorporating folkloristic and local detail into his epithalamium — a feature also of Buttet's *Epithalame*, 225–33.

136. *all the sences they doe rauish quite:* See FQ I.i.45.5 & VI.x.30.7.

137-40. *The whyles the boyes run vp and downe the street, / Crying aloud with strong confused noyce, / As if it were one voyce. / Hymen io Hymen, Hymen they do shout:* Spenser has here drawn on Homer's description of the epithalamial procession of maidens and boys through the streets (ἀνὰ ἄστυ), singing hymeneal chants and accompanied by both *pipe* and cither (φόρμιγγες), which he has converted to *Croud, Il.* 18.491-96,

> ἐν τῇ μέν ῥα γάμοι τ᾽ ἔσαν εἰλαπίναι τε,
> νύμφας δ᾽ἐκ θαλάμων δαΐδων ὕπο λαμπομενάων
> ἠγίνεον ἀνὰ ἄστυ, πολὺς δ᾽ὑμέναιος ὀρώρει,
> κοῦροι δ᾽ ὀρχηστῆρες ἐδίνεον, ἐ δ᾽ ἄρα τοῖσιν
> αὐλοὶ φόρμιγγές τε βοὴν ἔχον· αἱ δὲ γυναῖκες
> ἱστάμεναι θαύμαζον ἐπὶ προθύροισιν ἑκάστη.

> (The one did nuptials celebrate,
> Observing at them solemne feasts; the Brides from foorth their bowres
> With torches vsherd through the streets, a world of Paramours
> Excited by them; youths and maides in louely circles danc't,
> To whom the merrie Pipe and Harpe their spritely sounds aduanc't,
> The matrones standing in their dores admiring.
>                                                [Chapman, 18.445-50])

He has also replicated the hymeneal detail of Catullus, *Carmen* 61.117-23:

> tollite, o pueri, faces:
> flammeum video venire.
> ite, concinite in modum,
> "io Hymen Hymenaee io,
>     io Hymen Hymenaee."

> ne diu taceat procax
> Fescennina iocatio

(Lift up the torches, boys: I see the wedding veil coming. Go, sing in measure, "Io Hymen Hymenaeus io, io Hymen Hymenaeus." Let not the fescennine jesting be silent long.)

The same hymeneal chant is sung by the graces at *FQ* I.i.48.6, while a like procession occurs at V.xi.34.1-4

140. *io:* a monosyllable and the equivalent of the exclamation, 'oh.'

143. *To which the people standing all about:* See lines 137-40 note, Homer, "αἱ δὲ γυναῖκες / ἱστάμεναι θαύμαζον ἐπὶ προθύροισιν ἑκάστη" (*Il.* 18.495-96; "the matrones standing in their dores admiring").

145. *laud:* 1. praise; 2. possibly lauds, the office following matins, sung also during early morning.

148-50. *Loe where she comes along with portly pace / Lyke Phoebe from her chamber of the East, / Arysing forth to run her mighty race:* In exact imitation of Ps. 19.5, "In them hath he set a tabernacle for the sunne: which commeth foorth as a bridegrome, out of his chamber (Vulgate, *ut sponsus de thalamo*), and reioyceth as a Gyaunt to runne his course" (Geneva Version, "and reioyceth like a mightie man to runne his race"; the Geneva Version gives Spenser warrant to transfer the metaphor to the bride through its gloss to "chambre": "Or vaile. The maner was that the bride and bridegrome shulde stand vnder a vaile together, and after come forthe with great solemnitie and reioycing of the assemblie."). In imitating Ps. 19 Spenser is following directly the instruction of Puttenham who in his description of the epithalamium lays down (in Puttenham's case after the wedding night), "In the morning . . . the bride must within few hours arise and apparrell her selfe . . . and . . . must by order come forth *Sicut sponsa de thalamo*, very demurely and stately to be sene" (42).

Spenser, in keeping with the general principle in *Epith.* of identifying the bridegroom with the sun and the bride with the moon, converts the psalm's sun to moon — *Phoebe*.

148. *portly:* dignified, stately; see *Am.* 13.1 note & *FQ* III.ii.24.6–8, where it is Phoebus who is *portly*.

149. *Phoebe:* the feminine form of Phoebus and a title of Artemis, the twin sister of Phoebus Apollo, in her role as moon goddess.

151. *Clad all in white, that seemes a virgin best. / So well it her beseemes that ye would weene / Some angell she had beene:* Most virgins in *FQ* are dresssed in white, e.g., Una's espousal garment is "all lilly white, withouten spot" (I.xii.22.7), Belphoebe wears a "Camus lylly whight" (II.iii.26.4), while Alma "in robe of lilly white . . . was arayd" (II.ix.19.1). Here Spenser has, conventionally, conflated the raiment of the bride in Revelation's Marriage of the Lamb, who is described as "araied with pure fyne linen and shining" (19.8) with that of the seven Angels who are "clothed in pure and bright linnen" (15.6). White was customarily associated with angels — at the ascension "two men stode . . . in white apparel" (Acts 1.10), which the Geneva Bible glosses, "Which were Angels in mens forme."

154. *Her long loose yellow locks lyke golden wyre:* See *Am.* 81.1, "fayre golden heares" (a translation of Tasso's "del bel crine / L' oro"). Many of Spenser's heroines in *FQ* (twelve occasions in all) have golden hair, including Belphoebe (II.iii.30.1) and Alma (II.ix.19.6). Both Catullus (*Carmen* 64.63, "non flavo retinens subtilem vertice mitram" [she does not keep the delicate headband on her golden hair]) and Claudian (*Epith. Honorii*, 242, "nunc flavam niveo miratur vertice matrem" [the snowy neck and yellow hair of the mother] and 266, "non crines aequant violae" [wall-flowers are no more yellow than your hair]), use the epithet.

*lyke golden wyre:* the simile was used from medieval times onwards, Spenser using it at least six times.

155. *Sprinckled with perle, and perling flowres a tweene:* Compare Arthur's helmet, *FQ* I.vii.32.3.

*perle . . . perling:* a false polyptoton; *perling*, from purl = twist, meant to embroider or entwine with gold or silver threads, hence *a tweene*, a favorite Spenserian archaism.

The description of the bride runs contrary to the Pauline instruction, read during the *BCP*'s marriage service, 1 Tim. 2.9, "Likewise also the women, that thy arraye them selues in comelie apparel, with shamefastnes and modestie, not with broyded heare, or gold, or pearles, or costlie apparel," which the Geneva Bible glosses, "The worde signifieth to plat, to crispe, to broyde, to folde, to bush, to curle, or to lay it curiously."

159–61. *Her modest eyes abashed to behold / So many gazers, as on her do stare, / Vpon the lowly ground affixed are:* Modesty was enjoined upon brides (see 1 Tim. 2.9 above) and is a repeated feature of classical epithalamia, see Statius, *Epith. in Stellam*, 11–12, "ipsa manu nuptam genetrix Aeneia duxit / lumina demissam et

dulci probitate rubentem" (the mother of Aeneas [Venus] with her own hand
leads forth the bride, with eyes abashed and blushing with chaste modesty);
Claudian, *Epith. Honorii*, 268–69, "miscet quam iusta pudorem / temperies nimio
nec sanguine candor abundat" (how just the mixture that comprises your modesty, your fairness not over-endowed with too much blushing; see *Fescennina*,
4.3, "iam nuptae trepidat sollictus pudor" [anxious modesty now alarms the
bride]); and Catullus, *Carmen* 61.79, "tardet ingenuus pudor" (noble shame
delays).

167–79. An extended blason, with elements in common with Sonnet 15, as well as
the lengthy portrait of Belphoebe, *FQ* II.iii.22–30. The blason's emblematic
details drew frequently from the Song of Solomon, the whole passage concluding
with a reference to the lady's inner perfection. Elements of the blason imitate
Claudian, *Epith. Honorii*, 264–70:

> qui dignior aula
> vultus erit? non labra rosae, non colla pruinae,
> non crines aequant violae, non lumina flammae.
> quam iuncti leviter sese discrimine confert
> umbra supercilii! . . .
> Aurorae vincis ditos umerosque Dianae

(What countenance could better befit a palace? Your lips are redder than roses,
your neck whiter than snow, your hair more golden than the wall-flower, your
eyes brighter than fire. How well the shadow of your even brows meets upon
your forehead . . . your fingers out-do those of Aurora,
your shoulders out-do those of Diana.)

167. *Tell me ye merchants daughters:* An example of epithalamial local coloring, the
mercantile contrasting with the regal and noble characters who populate
classical epithalamia. See *Am.* 15.1, "Ye tradefull Merchants."

170. See *FQ* V.iii.23.2 & VI.viii.2.2.

171–77. An example of the rhetorical figure, *icon* (see Rix 56).

171. *Her goodly eyes lyke Saphyres shining bright:* See *Am.* 15.7. A standard simile,
particularly among Italian sonneteers.

172. *Her forehead yuory white:* See *Am.* 15.10 and *FQ* II.iii.24.1 (of Belphoebe),
"Her iuorie forhead."The *locus classicus* was Ovid, *Heroides*, 20.57, "eburnea
cervix."

173. *Her cheekes lyke apples which the sun hath rudded:* A conflation of the detail of
the Song of Sol. 2.3, "Like the apple tre among the trees of the forest: so *is* my
welbeloued," and 5.10, "My welbeloued is white and ruddy," with the *locus
classicus* of Ovid, *Met.* 4.331, "hic color aprica pendentibus arbore pomis /
aut ebori tincto est aut sub candore rubenti" (Golding, 4.405–6, "For in his face the
colour fresh appeared like the same / That is in Apples which doe hang vpon
the Sunnie side: / As Iuorie shadowed with a red").

174. *Her lips lyke cherryes charming men to byte:* a commonplace, e.g., Shakespeare,
*MND* II.ii.139–40, "Thy lips, those kissing cherries."

175. *vncrudded:* uncurdled.

176. *Her paps lyke lyllies budded:* See Song of Sol. 2.1–2, "I am the rose of the field,
and the lilie of the valleis. Like a lilie among the thornes. . . ."

177. *Her snowie necke lyke to a marble towre:* See Song of Sol. 4.4, "Thy necke is as
the towre of Dauid," and 7.4, "Thy necke is like a towre of yuorie."

185–87. The lines, of a strong Neo-Platonic character, complete the strict require-ments of the blason by elaborating the lady's inner perfection. They repeat the argument of *Am*. 45, where the poet discerns within his "inward selfe" the lady's true worth, "the fayre Idea of your celestiall hew." Guyon sings of Belphoebe in a similar vein, *FQ* II.iii.41.1–2.

189. *red*: read, in its obsolete sense of seen or observed (found only in Spenser — see *FQ* III.ix.2.3).

189–90. *And stand astonisht lyke to those which red / Medusaes mazeful hed*: As a punishment from Minerva, Medusa, one of the Gorgons, had her hair turned into a maze of serpents and her eyes were given the power to turn into stone anyone who observed her head (see Ovid, *Met*. 4.802, "attonitos formidine terreat hostes" [she affrights her astonisht enemies with dread]).

> *astonisht*: Spenser is either 1. playing with the spurious derivation of astonied from 'stony'; or 2. has in mind Ovid's "attonitos" (= astonied or stunned), its actual etymon.

> *mazeful*: 1. amazed, *astonisht*, astonied; 2. like a maze — such as that formed by the serpents on Medusa's head; see *Am*. 7.1, "mazed hart," which corre-sponds with a reference to serpents.

191. *There dwels*: interiorly, with her *inward beauty*.

191–93. For discussion of the various conjugal virtues listed here, see *Am*. 65 and 69 notes, passim. Here Spenser lists seven *heauenly guifts: loue, chastity, fayth, comely womanhed, honour, modesty, vertue*; they are akin to, but not identical to the seven virtues, faith, hope, charity, prudence, justice, fortitude and temperance.

> *Vnspotted*: echoing both the homeric epithet, ἀμύμων (= spotless; see *Od*. 1.29) and the Song of Sol. 4.7, "there is no spot in thee" (used of Una [*FQ* I.xii.22.7] and Belphoebe [II.iii.22.3]), as well as the Pauline advice to spouses to be without "spot or wrinkle ... holie and without blame" (Eph. 5.27, a phrase adopted by the *BCP*'s marriage service).

192. *comely womanhed*: 1595 and F12 all have *womanhood*, but rhyme requires *womanhed*. Compare Col. 3.18, also found in the *BCP* marriage service, "Wiues, submit your selues vnto your housbands, as it is comelie in the Lord."

194–99. Throughout the passage Spenser is reflecting the common Neo-Platonic doctrine that love is the desire for beauty and that virtue shows itself in beauty, as well as its distinction between the types of love, the heavenly, human and bestial. In *FQ* III.iii.1 he distinguishes between heavenly love, that is "ykindled first aboue" and "doth true beautie loue, / And choseth vertue for his dearest Dame," and that "which doth base affections moue / In brutish minds, and filthy lust inflame." In *Am*. 8.6 he distinguishes love of heavenly origin from "base affections," and in *Am*. 84.5, "filthy lustfull fyre," from, "pure affections bred in spotlesse brest."

204. *Open the temple gates vnto my loue*: A customary epithalamial cry, see Catullus, *Carmen* 61.76–77, "Claustra pandite ianuae / Virgo adest" (Open the bindings of the door. The bride comes) and Statius, *Epith. in Stellam*, 17, "pande fores!" (open the gates). Compare also the cry when the bridegroom comes in the parable of the virgins, Matt. 25.11, "Lord, open [the gate] to vs."

207–08. *And all the postes adorne as doth behoue, / And all the pillours deck with girlands trim*: Adorning the house with garlands was a feature of classical epithalamia but is here transposed to the church (*temple*) in which the marriage ceremony will be performed. Adorning the door-posts is common to Statius, *Epith. in Stellam*, 230–

31, "Iam festa fervet domus utraque pompa. / Fronde virent postes" (each house glows with festive pomp. The posts are green with garlands), and Catullus, *Carmen* 64.292–93, "Haec circum sedes late contexta locavit, / Vestibulum ut molli velatum fronde vireret" (These [green trees] he [Peneus] placed amply around their house, that the veiled portal might flourish with soft leafy garlands). In *SC* May, 11–14, Spenser has both the door-posts of the houses and the church pillars garlanded during the Mayday festivities in such a way as to please a *Saynt*.

210. *trembling*: tremulous, fearful. The bride throughout the passage remains physically retiring and bashful.

215. *high altar*: a peculiar phrase for Spenser, because use of the term was contentious in the 16th century, having been supplanted by, among others, 'Lords table.'

216–17. *The sacred cermonies there partake, / The which do endlesse matrimony make*: Echoing Paul, 1 Cor. 9.13, writing of ceremonies, "They which wait at the altar, are partakers with the altar." Spenser seems to have identified the marriage rite itself with the actual state (and indissoluble, *endlesse*, nature) of marriage; see *FQ* II.iv.22.5–6, "There wanted nought but few rites to be donne, / Which mariage make."

217. The middle line of *Epith.*, whose middle words, *endlesse matrimony*, anticipate and parallel its final line's final words, *endlesse moniment*.

220. *hollow throates*: not empty, but reverberating as a shout of exultation or a reverberating sound in a hollow, see *FQ* II.xii.25.3, "hollow rumbling rore."

221. *Antheme*: deriving from *antiphona*, a composition sung responsively by a divided choir; possibly a reference to Ps. 128 (or 67), which the *BCP* lays down should be said or sung during the marriage service.

223–27. Only here, in the wedding ceremony, is the physical first acknowledged. The physical closeness of the priest's benedictory imposition of hands, a form of blessing used also in the coronation and all ordination rites, causes the bride to blush.

226–27. *How the red roses flush vp in her cheekes, / And the pure snow with goodly vermill stayne*: In Statius, *Epith. in Stellam*, 22–23, both the bridegroom and bride are so described, "tu modo fronte rosas, violis modo lilia mixta / excipis et dominae niveis a vultibus obstas" (Now you receive roses on your brow, now lilies mixed with violets, as you protect the snowy looks of your lady).

227. *Like crimsin dyde in grayne*: the Kermes or Scarlet Grain (*granum = grayne*) insect was originally thought to be a berry. Dried out they were used for dyeing scarlet.

229–30. *That euen th' Angels which continually, / About the sacred Altare doe remaine / Forget their seruice and about her fly*: Depicting the presence of angels at weddings was sanctioned by common tradition. Perkins 1.613.2, quotes Tertullian as proof of the ancient belief that marriage is "*that coniunction which was made by the Church, consecrated by prayers and solemne seruice, [and] witnessed by the Angels.*" The *locus biblicus* for the belief lies with Rev. 8.3, where angels are presented as surrounding the altar, "And I saw the seuen Angels, which stode before God ... Then another Angel came and stode before the altar." The verses contribute to the apocalyptic context of *Epith.* and are used also to construct the account of Mercilla's palace (*FQ* V.ix.28–29) and to provide detail for the temple (and altar) of the Temple of Venus (*FQ* IV.x.42.1–5).

234. *sad:* serious and sober. Spenser uses the word to indicate the noble mood of the Red Cross Knight ("too solemne sad" [*FQ* I.i.2.8]), Guyon ("Still solemne sad" [II.vi.37.5]) and Arthur ("somwhat sad, and solemne" [II.ix.36.8]).

238–39. *Why blush ye loue to giue to me your hand, / The pledge of all our band?:* The first physical touch of the poem and reflecting the *BCP*'s marriage service rubric prior to the exchange of vows, "the Minister receiuing the woman at her father or friendes handes, shall cause the man to take the woman by the right hande, and so either to giue their troth to the other" (see the detail of the following prayer, "pledged their troth either to other").

240. *Sing ye sweet Angels, Alleluya sing:* During the apocalyptic Marriage of the Lamb, Rev. 19.6–7, like exclamations are sung, "And I heard like a voyce of a great multitude (in heauen) . . . saying, Hallelu-iah: for our Lord God almightie hathe reigned. Let vs be glad and reioyce, and giue glorie to him: for the Mariage of the Lambe is come." The verses are echoed in the epithalamial song during Una's espousal ceremony, *FQ* I.xii.39.3–4.

242. *Now al is done:* A further apocalyptic association, recalling the Marriage of the Lamb, where John sees the "holie citie" descending, "prepared as a bride trimmed for her housband," and hears the great voice exclaim: "It is done. I am α and ω, the beginning and the end" (Rev. 21.2 & 6).

243. *triumph of our victory:* Into the procession back to the bridal home, which this stanza introduces, Spenser allusively incorporates details of the Roman triumph or solemn procession and entry of the victorious general into the city. The procession included the spoils and gains of the campaign (*glory of her gaine* [244]); for the occasion a *coronea triumphalis* (triumphal coronal) was awarded (*coronall* [255]), while the general wore the *tunica palmite*, a tunic embroidered with vines and palms, (*wreathes of vine* [255]). In adopting the military conceit Spenser has imitated Claudian, *Epith. Honorii*, 186–97, where the soldiers are called upon to distance themselves from the god of war and lay down their arms.

245. *ioyance:* a Spenserian coinage.

249. *This day for euer to me holy is:* a repeated refrain, see lines 125 & 263.

251. *belly full:* either 1. full wine-skin, its sense in Old English; or 2. all that the bellies of the guests will hold.

252. *wull:* will or want.

253–54. *And sprinkle all the postes and wals with wine, / That they may sweat, and drunken be withall:* an allusion to the Roman custom of anointing the door-posts of the house to which the bride is brought, see Claudian, *Epith. Honorii*, 208–10, "hi nostra nitidos postes obducere myrto / contendant; pars nectareis adspergite tecta / fontibus et flamma lucos adolete Sabaeos" (let these hasten to weave our sacred mytle about the shining door-posts. Sprinkle the house with drops of nectar and burn a whole grove of Sabaean incense). Spenser had already drawn on the passage for the espousal feast of Una, *FQ* I.xii.38.1–5:

> Then gan they sprinckle all the posts with wine,
>> And made great feast to solemnize that day;
>> They all perfumde with frankincense diuine,
>> And precious odours fetcht from far away,
>> That all the house did sweat with great aray:

*sweat:* either 1. an echo of Claudian's *nitidos* = plump and fat as well as shiny; or 2. as in *FQ* above, where *sweat* alludes to sprinkled perfumes.

255–57. *Crowne ye God Bacchus with a coronall, / And Hymen also crowne with wreathes of vine, / And let the Graces daunce vnto the rest:* directly imitating Claudian, *Epith. Honorii,* 216–17, where the military imagery (see line 243 note) cedes place to instructions to Hymen, the Graces and Concord: "Tu festas, Hymenaee, faces, tu Gratia, flores / elige, tu geminas, Concordia, necte coronas" (You, Hymen, choose the festive torches, you, the Graces, choose the festive flowers, you, Concord, weave twin coronals). The crowns are to be as rich as that which the Bacchae wove with the mantling vine, "opaco palmite Bacchae" (217).

> *Graces daunce:* for the graces dancing, see *SC* April, 109–12 & *FQ* VI.x.14–16.

> *Bacchus:* the god of both wine and fertility.

265–66. *This day the sunne is in his chiefest hight, / With Barnaby the bright:* The feast of St. Barnabas, 11 June. According to the old style Julian calendar, 11 June was also the summer solstice. The lines echo the proverb, 'Barnaby bright, Barnaby bright, / the longest day and the shortest night.'

267. *declining daily by degrees:* 1. little by little; 2. astronomically, after the summer solstice.

269. *Crab:* The zodiacal Cancer, which the BCP calendar ordains for 12 June.

273–74. *Yet neuer day so long, but late would passe. / Ring ye the bels, to make it weare away:* A possible echo of the current proverb, "For though the day be neuer so longe / At last belles ryngeth to euensonge," found, *inter alia,* in Hawes, *Pastime of Pleasure* 208.5479–80.

> *late:* finally.

275. *bonfiers make all day:* A possible echo of the cry in Statius, *Epith. in Stellam,* 231, "effulgent compita flammis" (the cross-roads are bright with fires), but more probably a general call to rejoicing.

278–79. *Ah when will this long weary day haue end / And lende me leaue to come vnto my loue?:* See *Am.* 87.2. Such complaining is a feature of most epithalamia, see Claudian, *Epith. Honorii,* 14–15, "incusat spes aegra moras longique videntur / stare dies" (sad hope complains at the delay and the long days seem to stand still), and 288, "calet obvius ire / iam princeps tardumque cupit discedere solem" (the prince burns to go to meet her and desires the tardy sun descend); see also Catullus, *Carmen* 62.1–2, "Vesper adest, iuvenes, consurgite: Vesper Olympo expectata diu vix tandem lumina tollit." (Evening has come, youths rise up: Vesper from Olympus is now at last just raising his expected light).

282–84. *Hast thee O fayrest Planet to thy home / Within the Westerne fome: / Thy tyred steedes long since haue need of rest:* A frequent poetic image; e.g., *FQ* I.v.44.7–9, where night "backe returning tooke her wonted way, / To runne her timely race, whilst Phoebus pure / In westerne waues his wearie wagon did recure."

282. *O fayrest Planet:* in the Ptolemaic universe the sun was accounted a planet.

285–90. The lines are close to Bion's hymn to Hesperus, *Idyll* 10.1–6 & 10, the *locus classicus* of such hymns,

Ἕσπερε, τᾶς ἐρατᾶς χρύσεον φάος Ἀφρογενείας,
Ἕσπερε κυανέας ἱερὸν φίλε νυκτὸς ἄγαλμα,
τόσσον ἀφαυρότερος μήνας, ὅσον ἔξοχος ἄστρων,
καῖρε φίλος, καί μοι ποτὶ ποιμένα κῶμον ἄγοντι
ἀντὶ σελαναίας τὺ δίδου φάος . . .
ἀλλ' ἐράω· καλὸν δέ τ'ἐρασσαμένῳ συναρέσθαι

(Hesperus, golden lamp of the loving daughter of the foam, beloved Hesperus, glorious crown of the dark blue night, that much gloomier than the moon as you are bright among the stars, greetings friend. And as I lead the joyous procession to the shepherd's abode, grant me your light in place of the moon's. ... I am a lover and it is good to make lovers content.)

The hymn was frequently imitated (see Ronsard, *Oeuvres* 2.345. *Ode* 20.1–9), although the *nightes dread* (290) is more specifically available in Bion than anywhere else, "καλὸν δέ τ᾽ ἐρασσαμένῳ συναρέσθαι" (it is good to protect lovers).

285. *gloome:* gloam, become dusk, possibly reflecting Bion's ἀφαυρότερος = glooming.

286. *with golden creast:* a delicate rendering of Bion's "χρύσεον ... ἄγαλμα" (golden ... crown or crest). In *FQ* I.xii.2.3, the flaming "creast" belongs to Phoebus.

288. *glorious lampe of loue:* the planet Venus, but see Bion, *Idyll* 10.1, "῞Εσπερε, τᾶς ἐρατᾶς χρύσεον φάος ᾽Αφρογενείας" (Hesperus, golden lamp of the loving daughter of the foam). Compare also Buttet's working of Bion's *Idyll* 10, *Epithalame*, 539–40, "Dieu te gard, ô flambeau, ô joieuse lumiere, / Digne de luire au ciel sus toutes la premiere."

290. *through the nights sad dread:* 1595 has *nights dread*, which a hand in the British Museum copy has amended to *th/o/rough the nights dread*, while *F12* amends it to *nights sad dread*, clearly for the sake of scansion. Some modern editors prefer *nightés*, but, given the precedent in *Am.* 87.3–4, "many nights ... theyr sad protract," and Spenser's frequent description of night as *sad* (e.g., *FQ* I.i.39.9), the Folios' emendation seems an informed one. (Possibly the *8o* compositor, misreading the closing and opening ...s s... and the closing and opening ...d d... of 'nightes sad dread,' mistakenly dropped the middle word.)

291–92. *How chearefully thou lookest from aboue,* / *And seemst to laugh:* an echo of Spenser's favorite Homeric epithet, "φιλομμειδής ᾽Αφροδίτη" (loving-to-smile Venus; see *Hom. Hymn*, 5.65.155 and passim; see *Am.* 39.1–2 note).

296–97. *Now ceasse ye damsels your delights forepast;* / *Enough is it:* matches Catullus' conclusion to *Carmen* 61.227–28, "Claudite ostia virgines. / Lusimus satis" (Maidens, shut the doors. We have played enough).

298. *Now day is doen, and night is nighing fast:* / *Now bring the Bryde into the brydall boures:* Imitating the repeated refrain of Catullus, *Carmen* 61.90–91 (and passim), "abit dies: / prodeas, nova nupta" (the day is done; new bride, you may come forth).

300. *Now night is come:* the phrase is apposite and exact. Occurring a quarter way through Stanza 17, it indicates that 16 1/4 hours have already passed, thus matching the almanacal observation that in southern Ireland daylight on 11 June, the mid-summer solstice, extends for 16 1/4 hours (see Hieatt passim).

302. *Lay her in lillies and in violets:* In Statius, *Epith. in Stellam*, 22, the bridegroom protects his bride from the shower of lilies and violets: "violis modo lilia mixta / excipis" (intercept the lilies mixed with violets).

303–4. *And silken courteins ouer her display,* / *And odourd sheetes, and Arras couerlets:* Spenser, in observing the epithalamial convention of describing the bridal bed, is closest to Claudian, *Epith. Honorii*, 210–213, where the graces are called upon to employ all their arts in decorating the marriage bed with yellow silks from China and tapestries from Sidon, and to perfume the house with Sabaean

incense, "flamma lucos adolete Sabaeos; / pars infecta croco velamina lutea
Serum / pandite Sidoniasque solo prosternite vestes / ast alii thalamum docto
componite textu." Catullus (*Carmen* 64.50–51) paints a similar picture of the
marriage bed with its coverlet embroidered with details of ancient heroes and
their deeds.

306. *proud humility*: a daring oxymoron; 1. splendid *humility* (see *FQ* V.vii.3.7, "great
humility"); 2. the connotation of tumescent or desirous is also present.

307–10. A Spenserian *contaminatio*. Properly Maia inhabited Mount Cyllene in
Arcadia and the god Mercury, conceived by Jove, was born there rather than in
the vale of Tempe, which was location of Jove's pursuit of Daphne. Spenser has
associated Maia with Venus and numbered her among Venus' attendants, even
if the *Alcidalian brooke* is in Boeotia and it is there that the graces bathe with
Venus – see Natalis Comes 4.15.129a.34–35, "nam saepius ad Orchomenios has
lotum ire solitas ad fontem Acidalium dixerunt antiqui" (for the ancient authors
state that these [the graces] were accustomed to go to Orchomenum to the
Acidalian brooke to bathe; see Servius, *ad Aen.* 1.720, "fonte Acidalio qui est
in Orchomeno Boeotiae civitate, in quo se Gratiae lavant, quas Veneri constat
sacratas" [the Acidalian brook which is in Orchomenum in Boeotia, in which
the graces bathed themselves, who are sacred to Venus]). The dance of the
graces on Mount Acidale in *FQ* VI.x.6ff. is based partly on the same passage.

308. *Tempe*: Compare the epithalamial associations of *Tempe* in Catullus, *Carmen*
64.285–86, "viridantia Tempe, / Tempe, quae silvae cingunt super impendentes
/ ... linquens Doris celebranda choreis" (leaving verdant Tempe, Tempe
surrounded with hanging forests, to be haunted by Dorian dances).

311. *ye damsels may be gon*: The dismissal of spectators and outsiders to the marriage
rites allows Spenser to change the stanzas' refrain at line 314 to the negative.

316. For the epithalamial feature of interest and debt, see line 33 note. The sum of
the poet's labors during the day (and pains during courtship – see *Am.* 63) are
cancelled for ever.
   *labour*: 1. toil; 2. pain; 3. the latinate use of *labor* meaning an eclipse
   cannot be discounted, thus night that eclipses the day (see Vergil, *Aen.* 1.742).

322–39. *From feare of perill and foule horror free. / Let no false treason seeke vs to
entrap*: Introduces a series of prayers, seemingly shaped after the manner of an
exorcism, against the offspring of night. Spenser's list in part is very close to
that of Natalis Comes 3.12.72b.47–73a.1 (see Hesiod, *Theogony*, 211–15), "qui
a Genealogis antiquis sic nominantur, Amor, Dolus, Metus, Labor, Invidentia,
Fatum, Senectus, Mors, Tenebrae, Miseria, Quaerela, Gratia, Fraus, Pertinacia,
Parcae, Hesperides, Somnia, quos omnes Erebo et Nocte natos fuerunt" (who
from ancient genealogies are thus named, Love, Deceit [*dolefull* (334)], Fear
[*feare of perill* (322) and *hidden feares* (336)], Labor [or pain, *labour* (316)],
Jealousy, Fate, Old Age, Death [*damned ghosts* (347)], Darkness, Misfortune,
Lament [*lamenting cryes* (334)], Falsehood [*false treason* (323) and *false whispers*
(335)], Obstinacy, the Fates, Parcae and Hesperides, Dreams [*deluding dreames*
(338)], all of whom were born of Erebus and Night).

323. *Let no false treason seek vs to entrap*: See *Am.* 12.4.

328–29. *Lyke as when Ioue with fayre Alcmena lay, / When he begot the great Tirythian
groome*: Jove gained access to Alcmena by disguising himself as her absent
husband Amphitryon. He delayed the sun's rising so that his night with Alcmena was extended to three nights. The fruit of their love-making was Hercules.

Compare Chaucer, *T. & C.* 3.1427–28, "O nyght, allas! why nyltow ouer vs houe, / As longe as whan Almena lay by Ioue?" and Buttet, *Epithalame*, 25–26, "descendance certene / Du grand Tirynthien, fils de la belle Alcmene."

329. *Tirynthian groome:* Hercules who was brought up in Tiryns.

　　*groome:* either 1. bridegroom; or 2. one who attends horses, with the suggestion of Hercules' labor in the stables of Diomedes.

330–31. Seemingly a Spenserian innovation, Majesty customarily being thought the daughter of Honor and Reverentia (see Ovid, *Fasti*, 5.23–25).

334–39. Such imprecations against the spirits of the night are a familiar feature of both classical and Renaissance epithalamia, e.g., Statius, *Epith. in Stellam*, 26–30, prays, "cedant curaeque metusque, / cessent mendaces obliqui carminis astus, / Fama tace ... / ... consumpta est fabula vulgi" (let anxieties and fears cede place, let crafty hints of false stories cease. Rumor be silent ... the gossip of the vulgar kind is finished). Compare the call for peace and calm in Claudian, *Epith. Honorii*, 191–93, "Procul igneus horror / Thoracum, gladiosque tegat vagina minaces. / Stent bellatrices aquilae saevique dracones" (Let the fiery horror of breastplates be distant, let the scabbard ensheath the threatening swords, let the martial standards and savage dragons stand still).

334. *lamenting cryes:* see Puttenham 41, where epithalamial music and noise-making is designed "to diminish the noise of the laughing lamenting spouse."

　　*dolefull:* an extended pun: 1. full of grief, from *dolor* = grief; 2. full of deceit, from *dolus* = deceit − see lines 322–23 note; 3. possibly an echo also of dole = divided, hence *within nor yet without* (335).

335. *within nor yet without:* An allusion to the epithalamial conventions of noise-making. The first four lines of the stanza refer to factors within the marriage chamber (such as the *lamenting* of the spouse); the subsequent lines to factors from outside it. Conventionally such noise was both music and "the casting of pottes full of nuttes round about the chamber vpon the hard floore or pauement ... so as the Ladies and gentlewomen should haue their eares so occupied what with Musicke, and what with their handes wantonly scambling and catching after the nuttes, that they could not intend to harken after any other thing" (Puttenham 41, who draws upon Catullus, *Carmen* 61.124, "neu nuces pueris neget").

337. *misconceiued:* wrongly conceived.

340. *helpelesse harmes:* harms that defeat help.

341. *Pouke:* (*ponke* in 1595 as well as *F12*; Old Irish *púca*, Middle English, *pouke* [identified with the devil]), a malicious sprite or goblin, who under the name Robin Goodfellow appeared at weddings to ridicule them with his tricks.

345. *shriech Oule:* An instrument of night and ignorance in *TM* 283–84, "In stead of them fowle Goblins and Shriekowles, / With fearfull howling do all places fill," and a sign of desolation in Isa. 34.14, where it is a translation of the Hebrew *lilith*, either a female demon associated with night, storms, and unclean ghoulish creatures or a succuba (see Jeffrey 454). It is the "messenger of death" in *FQ* I.v.30.6 (following Ovid, *Met.* 10.453, "funereus bubo," and Chaucer, *Parlement of Foules*, 343, "of deth the bode bryngeth").

　　*Storke:* Compare Ovid, *Met.* 6.97, where making noises like a stork is the punishment for Antigone's jealousy, "ipsa sibi plaudat crepitante ciconia rostro" (Golding, 6.117, "and with a bobbed Bill [of a Stork] bewayle the cause of hir missehap"; Lev. 11.19, numbers the stork amongst its birds of abomination).

346. *Nor the night Rauen that still deadly yels:* Compare the June Eclogue of *SC*,
"Here no night Rauens lodge more black then pitche / . . . nor gastly owles doe
flee" (23–24) and E. K.'s gloss, "by such hatefull byrdes, hee meanenth all
misfortunes (whereof they be tokens) flying euery where"; see *FQ* II.xii.36.4–5,
where the "hoars Night-rauen" is described as the "trump of dolefull drere."

347. *damned ghosts:* such ghosts, who inhabit "that darke dreadfull hole of Tartare
steepe" at *FQ* II.xii.6.4–5, are associated at VI.xii.35 with Cerebus whom
Hercules, the "Tirythian swaine," dragged from hell to the upper world as a
lesson to Pluto and "other damned ghosts."

349–50. *Ne let th' vnplesant Quyre of Frogs still croking / Make vs to wish theyr choking:*
A conflation of classical sources with local detail, see Vergil, *Georgics*, 1.378,
"et veterem in limo ranae cecinere querellam" (in the mire the frogs croak their
ancient lament; frogs are associated with jealousy or *Invidia* [= to look askance]
through an extended etymological pun on *limus* [= both looking askance and
mire]). But the irritation Spenser felt at the frogs' nocturnal croaking in the
Irish bog is also evident both here and also in *FQ* V.x.23.8.

353. *But let stil Silence trew night watches keepe:* Not the silence of the prior stanza
which was the mere absence of noise, but creative (and continuing) silence
which constitutes peace. Spenser retains the Latin sense of the word, where
*silentium* intends perfectness and the *silenda* were mysteries or secrets.

    *trew:* either 1. 'still and true silence' − a Latinism, see line 29 note; or 2.
'true night watches.'

354. *assurance:* 1. confidence; 2. the *assurance* of salvation; 3. by inference, a
betrothal (see *Am.* 42.12 note & *FQ* I.ii.27.1, "Henceforth in safe assuraunce
may ye rest," which words constitue the plighting of a troth).

355. *tymely sleep:* 1. opportune sleep, at this time; 2. sleep that occurs for this
moment of time.

356. *poure his limbs forth:* a Latinism, from *fundere* = to pour out, but meaning to
stretch out when used of the body (see Vergil, *Aen.* 5.837), thus imitating
exactly Catullus, when describing the spouses' forthcoming sleep, *Carmen*
64.330–31, "quae tibi flexanimo mentem perfundat amore / languidulosque
paret tecum coniungere somnos" (which pours (spreads) onto your soul heart-
swaying love and prepares to join to you languid sleep).

    *playne:* either 1. the military imagery of *night watches* (353) is being retained
− 'to take the plain' being the equivalent of 'to take the field' − thus the
marriage bed is being equated with a battlefield; see Statius, *Epith. in Stellam*, 59,
"fessa iacet stratis" (tired she lies upon the bed / plain); or 2. obliquely, plaint
or moan, see *FQ* III.v.39.8–9.

357–59. Winged cupids and Venus' doves are included in most epithalamia, see
Statius, *Epith. in Stellam*, 54, "toros deae tenerum premit agmen Amorum" (a
band of tender loves swarms about her bed), and Claudian, *Epith. Honorii*, 153,
who depicts Venus accompanied by a broad company of winged loves, "prose-
quitur voluver late comitatus Amorum," describing them later as a "pennata co-
hors" (204; winged band). See Du Bellay, *Epithalame*, 307–10, "Et les petits A-
mours / Y volettent sans cesse / Autour de la Princesse / En mille et mille tours."

357. *hundred:* Although the customary classical number of winged loves is a thousand, a hundred is used by Spenser to suggest a full number, see *FQ* III.iv.21.1
& IV.iv.31.6.

    *little . . . loues:* reminiscent of *amoretti*.

360. *secret dark:* Statius, *Epith. in Stellam,* 59–60, writes of the bed of Venus yielding its guilty secrets, "conscia culpae." Spenser is at pains to urge the lack of guilt and the propriety of the conjugal proceedings – *which none reproues.*

362. *snatches of delight:* 1. delights that have been grasped – also with sexual undertones (OED 6b), see FQ II.v.34.6, "to steale a snatch of amorous conceipt"; 2. short spells or periods of delight; 3. entanglements or *snares.*

364. *Ye sonnes of Venus, play your sports at will:* Cupid sporting with his brothers is a feature of Claudian, *Epith. Honorii,* 72–73, "mille pharetrati ludunt in margine fratres, / ... gens mollis Amorum" (a thousand brother loves with quivers play round about the margin ... a tender company of loves). The instruction exactly corresponds to that given the lovers in Catullus, *Carmen* 61.206, "Ludite ut libet" (sport at will).

365. *pleasure:* personified here, as it is again in HL 280–90, in a passage which strongly echoes this stanza:

> There thou them placest in a Paradize
> Of all delight, and ioyous happie rest,
> Where they doe feede on Nectar heauenly wize,
> With *Hercules* and *Hebe,* and the rest
> Of *Venus* dearlings, through her bountie blest.
> And lie like Gods in yuorie beds arayd,
> With rose and lillies ouer them displayd.
> There with thy daughter *Pleasure* they doe play
> Their hurtlesse sports, without rebuke or blame,
> And in her snowy bosome boldly lay
> Their quiet heads, deuoyd of guilty shame

367. *albe it good or ill:* An unenforced aside concerning the joys of sexual pleasure and a properly protestant assertion, e.g., Perkins, 3.689.1, is at pains to assert that the marriage act was "neither good nor bad" (a point Spenser makes in *Am.* 65), "The mariage bed signifieth that solitarie and secret societie which is betweene man and wife alone. And it is a thing of its owne nature indifferent; neither good nor bad."

368. *play:* suggesting sexual pleasures – see FQ III.vi.50.1, where *Pleasure* is the daughter of Cupid and Psyche.

369. *For it will soone be day:* See Buttet, *Epithalame,* 601–02, "entrés au désiré sejour, / Car je croi que demain il sera trop tôt jour."

372. The appearance of the moon – as an omen – is a common detail in Renaissance epithalamia, see Buttet, *Epithalame,* 534–36, "Et d'où vient ce grand feu? Page, ouvre la fenestre: / Sans plus nous retarder, si faut-il le savoir. / Hà! c'est l'astre pieux qui flamme sur le soir."

374–96. The invocation imitates directly Statius, *Epith. in Stellam,* 268–273, in which Cynthia and Juno (Lucina = the one who brings to light) are addressed and asked to bless the woman with off-spring, yet not to cause her discomfort,

> acceleret partu decimum bona Cynthia mensem,
> sed parcat Lucina precor; tuque ipse parenti
> parce, puer, ne mollem uterum, ne stantia laedas
> pectora; cumque tuos tacto natura recessu
> formarit vultus, multum de patre decoris,
> plus de matre feras.

(May goodly Cynthia hasten the tenth month for the childbirth, but spare her, Lucina, I pray. And you, child, spare your mother and do not injure her tender womb or swelling breasts. And when nature in that secret recess has shaped your features, may you draw much beauty from your father and more from your mother.)

374. *Cinthia:* the goddess Diana, called Cynthia on account of her birth on Mount Cynthus. She was patroness of virginity, but as goddess of the moon also the protector of married women, especially those in childbirth.

379–81. *And for a fleece of woll, which priuily, / The Latmian shephard once vnto thee brought, / His pleasures with thee wrought:* The moon-goddess, having fallen in love with the shepherd Endymion, descended night after night to enjoy his favors. (See E. K.'s gloss to *SC* July, 64, "The Shepheard is Endymion, whom the Poets fayne, to haue bene so beloued of Phoebe.s. the Moone, that he was by her kept a sleepe in a caue by the space of xxx. years, for to enioye his companye.") According to Vergil, *Georgics,* 3.391–93, the *fleece of woll* was given to the moon by Pan and not by Endymion, but Spenser may have known Servius' commentary on Vergil's lines, "mutet fabulam: nam non Pan sed Endymion ammasse dicitur Lunam" (he is changing the fable: for it is not Pan but Endymion who is said to have loved the Moon). Customarily the legend recounts that Pan beguiled Luna by changing himself into a ram with a beautiful white fleece. That version of the legend is alluded to in Claudian, *Epith. Honorii,* 183, "lanigeri suis ostentantia pellem" (with its device of the fleece-covered pelt of the ram). Scaliger 151 writes at length on the necessary appearance of wool in epithalamia.

379. *priuily:* secretly; possibly an echo of Catullus's *furtim, Carmen* 64.5–6, "ut Triviam furtim sub Latmia saxa relegans / dulcis amor gyro devocet aerio" (how sweet love allures Diana from her airy circuit, banishing her secretly to the rocky Latmian cave).

383–87. Classical epithalamia generally conclude by asking the blessing of children, see Claudian, *Epith. Honorii,* 340–41, "sic uterus crescat Mariae; sic natus in ostro / parvus Honoriades genibus considat avitis" (so may the womb of Maria grow big; so may little Honorius, born in the purple, rest in his grandfather's lap); and Catullus, *Carmen* 61.207–10, "brevi liberos date. non decet / tam vetus sine liberis / nomen esse, sed indidem / semper ingenerari" (bring forth children soon; it is not proper that such an old name should be without children, but that they should be ever born from the same stock; see 61.212–16).

383. *wemens labours:* the pains of childbirth.

384. *generation goodly dost enlarge:* either 1. does bless liberally with generating (*OED* 7); or 2. since Spenser often uses *enlarge* of the human race or kind (see *HL* 105, & *HHL* 52), the continuance of the human race, succeeding generations.

*goodly:* either an adjective qualifying *generation* or an adverb governing *enlarge.*

385. *Encline thy will:* used technically of prayers, see *FQ* VI.vii.26.2, "That to his prayer nought he would incline," and *Am.* 22.2, "Men to deuotion ought to be inclynd." The verb derived from the oft-repeated biblical (and psalmic) orison, "let my prayer enter into thy presence, encline thine eare vnto my calling" (Ps. 88.1).

*wishfull vow:* a vow full of wishes; the spouses' conjoining will overcome the lament of *Am.* 89.3, "and in her songs sends many a wishfull vow."

386. *informe:* shape inwardly — see *Am.* 8.9 note.

    *timely seed:* 1. opportune; 2. occurring within the course of time (see line 404 note).

390–91. *great Iuno, which with awful might / The lawes of wedlock still dost patronize:* Juno was the protector of women and the goddess of lawful and fruitful marriage, see Vergil, *Aen.* 4.59, "Iunoni ante omnis, cui vincla iugalia curae" (great Juno, under whose patronage are the bonds of wedlock).

    *awful:* a direct translation of Statius, *Epith. in Stellam,* 239–40, "dat Iuno verenda / vincla" (Juno brings the awful bonds). Buttet, *Epithalame,* 589–94, invokes, in a similar manner, Venus, Juno and Hymen:

> La pudique Venus, qui voz deuc cueurs attise,
> Et la saincte Junon de sa main vous conduise;
> Le bien heureux Hymen qui ce triomphe a fait,
> Vous étregne à jamais d' un saint vouloir parfait;
> Une agreable paix, une amour mutuelle,
> Couchant avecques vous, i soit perpetuelle;

*patronize:* defend or protect.

392–93. The common distinction between the betrothal and the wedding ceremony is present here: Una is betrothed but not married to the Red Cross Knight at the conclusion to *FQ* I.

    *religion:* 1. from *religio* = *re* + *ligo,* to bind together; the same root as *lex* = law, and used by classical authors occasionally to mean the same as *obligatio;* hence the binding together that plighting troth involves; 2. synonymously, *rites* (*OED* 3), hence the rites of betrothal which are solemnized by the rites of marriage.

    *solemnize:* to celebrate marriage with proper ceremonies.

398. *Genius:* (from *gigno* = beget or produce); the procreative force, a titular deity of a person. The *genius* was a masculine principle, the guardian spirit of a woman being her Juno — see Natalis Comes 4.3.92b.31–35, "Crediderunt siquidem antiqui singulos homines, statim atque nati fuissent, daemones duos habere, alternum malum, alternum bonum, quorum nos sub tutela essemus, quos ambos Genios vocarunt, et putarunt nobiscum esse natos. Dictus est autem Genius, vt placuit Latinis, a gignendo, vel quia nobiscum gignatur, vel quia illi procreandorum cura diuinitus commissa putaretur" (The ancients believed that each person, immediately they were born, had two spirits, one bad, one good, under whose guardianship we lie, both of whome they called Genius, and they thought they were born with us. Genius is so called, according to the Latins, from *gignendo,* either because he is born with us, or because the guardianship of generation is thought to be committed to him from the gods). For Spenser's definition of *Genius,* see *FQ* II.xii.47.

398–99. *Genius . . . gentle . . . genial:* a Latinate polyptoton.

399. *genial bed:* the *lectus genialis,* the Latin technical term for the marriage bed, being dedicated to *Genius.*

404. *timely fruit:* 1. appropriate; but 2. see *FQ* I.vi.23.3, "with timely fruit her belly sweld," with its connotations of early ripening (*OED* 1; see *FQ* VI.x.38.5). Compare Buttet, *Epithalame,* 600–602, "Allés donque, allés ô bien heureux amans, / Et, avecques tout l' heur que le Ciel vous presente, / Recevés le doux fruit de votre longue attente."

405. *Hebe:* the goddess of youth (see Natalis Comes 2.5.44b.46, "quam Latini Iuventatem vocarunt"). She was given in marriage to Hercules by Juno. Spenser associates them with *Pleasure* in *HL* 282–84. She was considered the principle of fruitfulness and ripeness — see Natalis Comes 2.5.45a.45: through her "omnia herbarum, arborumque genera pullulant, et pubescunt . . . verumetiam omnia nata conservent" (every type of plant and tree springs forth and ripens . . . indeed everything that is born is conserved).

   *Hymen free:* Hymen's work is now accomplished.

413. *all ye powers:* either 1. the classical *virtus* (= heavenly power, as in the phrase *deorum virtute* = by the power or aid of the gods); or 2. a reference to angels, the sixth order of angels being the 'Powers' (see Col. 1.16) — if so, then Spenser is alluding to the neo-Platonist idea that angels inhabit and guard each sphere in the Ptolemaic scheme of the heavens and govern human destinies, see *HHB* 78–86.

414. *fayne:* imagine or conceive.

417–22. *large posterity . . . there inherit:* See Matt. 5.5, "for they shal inherite the earth," and Ps. 37.22 & 30, "the blessed of God, shal possesse the land . . . the righteous shal inherite the land." That children are ultimately for the populating of heaven was orthodox contemporary marriage doctrine, e.g., Smith, *A Preparative to Mariage* 105, "Therefore in Psalm 127.4. ["Loe children and the fruite of the wombe: are an heritage and gift that commeth of the Lorde"] children are called the heritage of the Lord, to shewe that they should bee trained as though they were not mens children but Gods, that they may have Gods heritage after."

420. *haughty pallaces:* high rather than proud.

421. *guerdon:* reward.

423–25. *blessed Saints . . . tymely ioyes:* For the idea of (poetic) immortality, see *Am.* 82.1–8 note, citing *FQ* II.i.31.1–4. The idea of immortality being gained through children moves easily to the possibility of poetic immortality in *Epith.*'s final envoy.

424. Requires a further (hexametric?) line to complete its rhyme. Some editors have concluded that the compositor has dropped a line (see *Variorum, Minor Poems,* 2.493–94), although Hieatt 68 proposes a numerological argument that the line is deliberately omitted "so as to create a situation that can be "recompensed" in his [Spenser's] *tornata,* in accordance with his manner of resolving his other symbolic schemes."

427. *duly:* see *your dew time* (430).

429. *hasty accidents:* occurrences (beyond human control) happening in time — see *FQ* VI.xii.20.2–4.

430. *stay:* halt, arrest.

432–33. *Be vnto her a goodly ornament, / And for short time an endlesse moniment:* The idea of poetic immortality is traditional, although not customary in epithalamia. Spenser is fond of the conceit, see *RT* 405–6, "Rome liuing, was the worlds sole ornament, / And dead, is now the world sole moniment," a translation of du Bellay, "Rome vivant fu l'ornement du monde, / Et morte elle est du monde le tumbeau." The conceit had occurred regularly among the *amoretti,* see *Am.* 27, 69.9–12, 75.9–10 & 82.4–8. Spenser often had in mind both the conclusion to Ovid's *Met.* 15.878–79 and Horace, *Odes,* 3.30.1–9, which began, "Exegi monumentum aere perennis," which E. K. cites as apposite in the Envoy to *SC.*

*short time:* A complex phrase, whose ambiguity contributes markedly to the envoy's richness. 1. While time endures, equivalent, then, to the classical βραχύς χρόνος (see Plato, *Timaeus*, 75B) and *breve tempus* to indicate the span of time. This sense is confirmed by its context in *FQ* VII.viii.1.9, "Short *Time* shall soon cut down with his consuming sickle." 2. The short time of the marriage day which this poem will eternise — Spenser would have known the Pauline marriage instruction, 1 Cor. 7.29 & 31, "And this I say, brethren, because the time is short, hereafter that bothe they which haue wiues, be as thogh they had none ... for the facion of this worlde goeth away." 3. Hieatt advances the case that *Epithalamion* is a *moniment* in that it celebrates the cyclical divisions created by the sun and numerologically discernible in the poem as the year, days and hours. He also proposes that *short time* is sidereal time which, when compared to the sun's completion of an orbit, is caught *short*, is incomplete (see Hieatt passim).

# Textual Notes

## The Text

The text selected as copy-text is the 1595 octavo edition of *Amoretti and Epithalamion*, held at the Wrenn Library, University of Texas, which contains the fewest errors of all extant copies of the edition; in the textual notes eight of the eleven known extant copies of the edition are collated with it.

The 1595 edition of *Amoretti and Epithalamion*, apart from its punctuation, is generally printed accurately. Since the sonnets, as printed, correspond with a chronological order, the printer has presumably taken care to duplicate the order of the manuscript as sent. The edition contains some faults but the extant copies reveal most of its sheets to be without major error. Verbal (not literal) differences between the 1595 octavo and the 1611 first folio edition and the 1617 second folio edition of the *Collected Works* have been recorded in the textual notes. Most verbal emendations of 1595 that were required had already been made in the folio editions.

The punctuation of 1595 edition of *Amoretti and Epithalamion*, however, particularly when compared with the careful punctuation of the 1590 and 1596 editions of *The Faerie Queene*, must be characterized as idiosyncratic. The compositors, possibly with a rigid metrical structure in mind, have attempted to provide each sonnet with a uniform pattern of punctuation. Generally each of the sonnet's lines are concluded with the following pattern: for each quatrain ", : , . (or :)" with a final couplet ", ." . Clearly such rigidity could not be maintained: not only did it confuse meaning, it frequently verged on the ridiculous. Thus the pattern was sometimes moderated and even, occasionally, abandoned.

The 1611 first folio *Collected Works* attempted to remedy the octavo's punctuation. But its attempts to punctuate logically rather than metrically, or at least to punctuate less rigidly, eventually proved too great a task. The compositors' efforts became half-hearted and the ensuing mix of punctuative styles is not very successful. Generally, however, punctuation occurs more frequently within a line and the more blatant idiosyncratic marks are removed.

The proposed edition, in line with editorial convention, has accepted the punctuation of the 1595 octavo edition. Changes have been made only where the edition is clearly faulty or where the punctuation would mislead or confuse a reader. Often the emendations made accord with the 1611 and 1617 folio editions, particularly where these editions have disregarded the octavo's attempts to punctuate metrically. Other variants in accidentals between editions have not been registered.

The modern practice in the use of ∫ / s, VV / W and ligatures has been adopted. The same modern practice has been observed when quoting from all printed works. Abbreviations (ampersand and tilde), which occur in the octavo edition only to compress a line which would otherwise have been crowded off, have been silently expanded. Italics have been preserved. Catchwords have been omitted. Faulty spacing and turned and wrong-font letters have been corrected.

## Description

*Entry in Stationers' Register*: xix° die Nouembris (1594) William Ponsonby. Entred for his Copie vnder thandes of the Wardens, A booke entituled Amoretti and Epithalamion written not longe since by Edmund Spencer . . . . . . . . vjd

*Title Page*: AMORETTI / AND / Epithalamion. / Written not long since / by Edmunde / Spenser. Device (Mackerrow 278, *ut infra*) Printed for William / Ponsonby. 1595.

*Colophon*: *Imprinted by P. S. for Wil*- / liam Ponsonby.

*Collation*: Octavo, but on cut-down sheets. A–H in eights, with a half-sheet of 4 leaves signed ¶ between A1 and A2. Of 68 leaves unnumbered.

*Contents*: A1ʳ Title-page. A1ᵛ blank.¶1ʳ–2ʳ The Epistle Dedicatory. ¶2ᵛ blank. ¶3ʳ G: W. senior, to the Author. ¶3ᵛ blank. ¶4ʳ G. W. I [to the Author]. ¶4ᵛ blank. A2ʳ–F6ʳ Sonnets I–LXXXIX. F6ᵛ–G2ʳ Untitled [Anacreontic verses]. G2ᵛ blank. G3ʳ Title-page: Epithalamion. Device *(ut infra)*. G4ʳ–H7ᵛ Epithalami-on. H8ʳ Colophon. H8ᵛ blank.

One sonnet and one stanza of *Epithalamion* per page. The top and bottom of each page is adorned with an ornamental band. The top band is a line of 9 pieces of sickle pattern set symmetrically but in no regularly consistent pattern. The bottom band is an intricate arrangement of 16 sections of sickle pattern, set in fours in a line and generally set pied.

*Device*: (40.5 x 35 mm.) The device is framed by the motto, "ET VSQVE AD NVBES VERITAS TVA." which is taken from Psalm 57.11 and replicates Psalm 36.5, "Et veritas tua usque ad nubes" ("*and* thy faithfulnes [ô Lord, *reacheth*] vnto the cloudes" [Coverdale and Geneva versions].). The device comprises a bell and a hand reaching down from the clouds which upholds a dove. The dove in turn trails from its beak bands from which hang an opened book surrounded by the sun's rays. Below, the initials P. S. for Peter Short (master-printer 1589–1603).

*Catchwords*: on every page except ¶2–4 and C8ʳ. The following differ from the first words of the following page: A4ᵛ Faire] Fayre; A8ʳ Returne] Retourne; A8ᵛ In] Ye; B8ᵛ See] Ah; C8ᵛ Thrust] Trust; G8ʳ Lacking] Lackyng; H1ʳ Behould] Behold.

*Copies examined*: *British Library*, formes C°, Cⁱ, Hⁱ uncorrected. *Bodleian, Oxford*, lacks title page A1, ¶1–4, A8, H1, H8; formes Cⁱ, Hⁱ uncorrected. *Edinburgh University Library* formes ¶°, B°, Bⁱ, Hⁱ uncorrected; *Folger Shakespeare Library*

forme H[i] uncorrected. *Huntington Library* forme H[i] uncorrected. *Harry Ransom Humanities Research Centre, University of Texas* (Pforzheimer) formes E°, H[i] uncorrected. *John Rylands Library, Manchester* formes A°, A[i], B°, B[i], C[i], D°, D[i] contain frequent instances where the ink hasn't taken or where (particularly sheet D) the text has been inked in; forme H[i] uncorrected. *Trinity College, Cambridge* (Capell 18) lacks ¶1–4; forme H[i] uncorrected. *Wrenn Library, University of Texas.*

THE / FAERIE QUEEN: / THE / Shepheards Calendar: / *Together* / WITH THE OTHER / Works of England's Arch-Poët, / EDM. SPENSER: / ¶ *Collected into one Volume, and / carefully corrected.* / Printed By *H. L.* for *Mathew Lownes.* / Anno Dom. 1611.

With its title: AMORETTI / AND / EPITHALAMION. / VVritten by *Edmunde Spenser.* Device. AT LONDON / Printed by *H. L.* for *Mathew Lownes.* 1611.

THE / FAERIE QUEEN: / THE / Shepheards Calendar: / *Together* / WITH THE OTHER / Works of England's Arch-Poët, / EDM. SPENSER: / ¶ *Collected into one Volume, and / carefully corrected.* / Printed By *H. L.* for *Mathew Lownes.* / Anno Dom. 1617.

With its title: AMORETTI / AND / EPITHALAMION. / VVritten by *Edmunde Spenser.* Device. AT LONDON / Printed by *H, L.* for *Mathew Lownes.* 1617.

## Textual Notes

The following symbols relating to textual matters appear below.

]   The reading to the left of the bracket is that of all witnesses not mentioned to the right of the bracket.

^   A caret indicates the absence of punctuation.

~   A wavy dash replaces a word where punctuation alone differs.

### Amoretti

A1 *senior:* ~, *8°F12* ‖ 5 landes] lande *8°(Edinburgh)F12* ‖ 11 neighboures] neighoures *8°* ‖ 14 reede.] ~, *8°*

A2 1 *plaine,*] ~. *8°* ‖ 2 *roundelaies*] roudelaies *8°* ‖ 3 *vaine*] ~, *8°F12* ‖ 4 *daies:*] ~. *8°* ‖ 6 *quill,*] ~. *8°* ‖ 8 *skill,*] ~. *8°:* ~: *F1* ‖ 12 *meede.*] ~, *F2* ‖ Signature G. W. I.] G. W. I. *F12*

I. 2 dead doing] dead-doing *F12* ∥ 9 brooke: ~, *8°F12*
II. 6 brood:] ~. *8° (Rylands)*
III. 13 write] ~, *8°*
V. 14 pride?: ~. *8°F12*
VI. 1 mind] ~, *8°* ‖ 9 desire: ~, *8°F12*

VII. 7 askew,] ~, *8⁰*

VIII. 5 guest] ~, *8⁰*  ‖  6 wound?: ~: *8⁰F12*

IX. 4 th' ymage] th ymage *8⁰ (Rylands)*

X. 2 be?] ~: *8⁰*  ‖  7 brings] bring *F2*

XI. 3 addresse] ~, *8⁰*  ‖  8 vnpittied] vnpitteid *8⁰*  ‖  11 turmoyle,] ~ ˄ *8⁰* *(Rylands)*

XII. 9 t' abide] t abide *8⁰ (Rylands)*  ‖  12 me kept] kept me *F12*

XIII. 5 majesty.] ~, *8⁰*  ‖  6 borne,] ~: *8⁰*

XIIII. 6 forts which] forces, *F12*

XV. 1 toyle: ~, *8⁰F12*  ‖  3 treasures] treasure *F12*  ‖  10 weene;] ~, *8⁰ (Rylands)*  ‖  12 sheene,] ~: *F12*

XVI. 3 amaze] a maze *F12*  ‖  4 delight,: ~. *8⁰*: ~; *F12*  ‖  11 when] whe *F2*

XVII. 6 guide] ~: *8⁰*  ‖  7 workmanship] wormanship *8⁰*

XVIII. 10 sayes teares] sayes, Teares *F12*  ‖  11 sayes] ~, *F12*  ‖  12 waile,] ~ ˄ *8⁰*

XX. 2 humbled] humble *F12*

XXI. 1–4 Art, . . . face, . . . grace?] Art? . . . face: . . . grace. *8⁰*  ‖  4 t' adorne] t adorne *8⁰ (Rylands)*  ‖  6 loues] loue *F12*  ‖  7 countenance] count'nance *F12*  ‖  8 impure.] ~, *8⁰F1*

XXIII. 4 vnreaue:] ~, *8⁰*

XXIIII. 2 goodly] godly *F2*  ‖  8 see,: ~. *8⁰*: ~; *F12*

XXV. 2 mysery?] ~: *8⁰*  ‖  9 hide] ~, *8⁰*

XXVI. 14 gaine?] ~. *8⁰F1*: againe. *8⁰ (Edinburgh)*

XXVIII. 2 giues] guies *8⁰*  ‖  8 attyre.] ~ ˄ *8⁰ (punctuation crowded off)*  ‖  10 flee] flie *8⁰F1*

XXIX. 1 damzell] damozell *8⁰ (Edinburgh)*  ‖  5 bay (quoth she)] bay, quoth she, *F12*

XXX. 12 deuyse?] ~. *8⁰*

XXXI. 11 bath] ~, *8⁰*

XXXII. 9 fit,] ~: *8⁰*

XXXIII. 3 faëry] faery *8⁰ (Rylands)*  ‖  6 it: ~, *8⁰F12*  ‖  9 wit: ~: *8⁰*; ~? *F1*: ~, *F2*  ‖  10 toyle?] ~, *8⁰F1*  ‖  11 sins] sith *F12*  ‖  fit: ~, *8⁰F12*

XXXIIII. 1 wyde: ~, *8⁰F12*  ‖  2 way] ~. *8⁰*  ‖  3 guyde,] ~. *8⁰*  ‖  4 astray:] ~. *8⁰*  ‖  5 ray: ~, *8⁰F12*  ‖  12 griefe.] ~, *8⁰*

XXXV. 1 couetize: ~, *8⁰F12*  ‖  6 hauing *8⁰ (Sonnet 35)*: seeing *8⁰ (Sonnet 83)*  ‖  8 poore.] ~ ˄ *8⁰ (punctuation crowded off)*

XXXVI. 4 release?: ~. *8⁰F12*  ‖  8 miseryes?] ~. *8⁰F1*  ‖  10 gayned] ~: *8⁰*: ~, *F12*

XXXVII. 1 tresses] ~,  ‖  7 enfold] ~, *8⁰*

XXXVIII. 2 into] in to *F2*  ‖  4 allur'd] allu'rd *8⁰*  ‖  6 skill: ~, *8⁰F12*

XXXIX. 6 sadnesse,] ~: *8⁰*  ‖  8 hart robbing] hart-robbing *F12*  ‖  9 Whylest] Whilst *F12*  ‖  12 meat: ~, *8⁰F12*

XL. 3 eyelid] eye-lid *F12*  |  appeare] ~, *8⁰*  ‖  6 sunshine] sun-shine *F2*  ‖  8 ray:] ~ ˄ *8⁰ (punctuation crowded off)*  ‖  10 fled,] ~: *8⁰*  ‖  13 storme beaten] storme-beaten *F12*  |  cheared: ~, *8⁰F12*  ‖  14 sunshine] sun-shine *F12*

XLI. 2 foe?] ~: *8⁰*  ‖  8 her] Wer *F2*  ‖  9 boast: ~, *8⁰F12*

XLII. 8 hart;] ~ ˄ *8⁰*  ‖  12 his] in *F12*  ‖  13 from] fron. *8⁰ (British Library)*

XLIII. 12 loue learned] loue-learned *F12*

XLIIII. 2 amongst] among *F12* ‖ 7 whilest] whilst *F12* | arre,] ~. *8°* ‖ 11/12 awake, to battaile] awake to battaile, *F12*

XLV. 5 shew] ~, *8°*

XLVI. 2 my way] away *F12* ‖ 5 obay?] ~, *8°* ‖ 11 she: ~, *8°F12* ‖ 13 sustaine] ~, *8°*

XLVII. 5 guyde] ~, *8°*

XLVIII. 1 hand] ~, *8°* ‖ 10 the anguish] th'anguish *8°* ‖ 11 complayned,] ~ ^ *F12*

XLIX. 10 kill] ~, *8°* ‖ 12 too] to *F12* ‖ 13 admyred] admyr'd *F12*

L. 2 griefe: greife: greife: *8°*: greife. *8°* (*Rylands*): griefe, *F12* ‖ 5 man (quod I)] man, quoth I, *F12* | priefe: ~: *8°* : ~, *F12* ‖ 8 please?] ~. *8°* ‖ 9 appease] ~, *8°*

LII. 2 field,] ~: *8°* ‖ 9 vaine: ~, *8°F12* ‖ 11 disdayne] ~, *8°*

LIII. 1 hyde] ~, *8°* ‖ 4 whylest] whilst *F12* ‖ 6 semblant] semblance *F12* hew,] ~: *8°*

LIIII. 1 worlds] wolds *F1*: world *F2*

LV. 5 heauenly] heu'nly *F12* ‖ 6 fyre] fy[r]e *8°* (*Rylands inked in*) ‖ 12 mind] loue *F12* | rest.] ~: *8°*

LVI. 7 finding] findin[s] *8°* (*Rylands inked in*) ‖ 8 beats on] bea[ts o]n *8°* (*Rylands inked in*)

LVII. 3 lenger] longer *F12* ‖ 7 through launched] through-launced *F12* ‖ 8 eies haue] eie[s h]aue *8°* (*Rylands inked in*) ‖ 10 stoures.] ~, *8°* ‖ 13 grace,] ~. *8°*

LVIII. 1 reposeth] ~, *8°* ‖ 3 supposeth] ~, *8°* ‖ 7 prayd: ~, *8°F12* ‖ 8 glories] gl[ori]es *8°* (*Rylands inked in*): glorious *F12* ‖ 14 arre?] ~. *8°F1*

LIX. 1 assured] assur'd *F12* ‖ 3 allured] allur'd *F12* ‖ 5 ship,] ~^ *8°* ‖ 8 delight] deli[gh]t *8°* (*Rylands inked in*) ‖ 9 spight] spight, *8°*: spigh[ht], *8°* (*Rylands inked in*) ‖ 13 assured] assur'd *F12*

LX. 4 spheare.] ~^ *8°* (*punctuation crowded off*)

LXI. 3 dewtie: ~, *8°F12* ‖ 11 scorne] ~, *8°*

LXII. 6 amend:] ~^ *8°* (*punctuation crowded off*): ~, *F12* ‖ 9 send] ~, *8°*

LXIII. 4 sore:] ~. *8°* ‖ 6 arriue:] ~, *8°* ‖ 9 atchyue] ~, *8°F1* ‖ 11 depriue] ~, *8°*

LXIIII. 12 Iessemynes:] ~, *8°*

LXV. 1 vaine,] ~^ *8°* (*punctuation crowded off*) ‖ 12 wound:] woûd ^ *8°* (*punctuation crowded off*)

LXVI. 2 thrown,] ~: *8°* ‖ 8 state?] ~. *8°* ‖ 13 enlumind] enlumin'd *F1*: enlightned *F2*

LXVII. 2 escapt away] escape away *F12* ‖ 4 pray,: ~. *8°*: ~: *F12* ‖ 12 goodwill] good will *F12*

LXVIII. 1 day: ~, *8°F12* ‖ 3 away] ~, *8°* ‖ 4 win:] ~. *8°* ‖ 6 thou] tbou *8°* ‖ 8 felicitie:] ~. *8°*

LXIX. 8 chastity?] ~. *8°F1*

LXX. 2 cote armour] coat-armour *F12* | displayd] ~, *8°* ‖ 4 arrayd:: ~. *8°F1*: ~; *F2* ‖ 9 make: ~, *8°F12* ‖ 11 make: ~, *8°F12* ‖ 13 whilest] whilst *F12*

LXXI. 3 lurke] ~, *8°* ‖ 9 aboue: about *8°F12* ‖ 13 see,] ~. *8°*

LXXIII. 2 tye,:] ~: 8°F12

LXXIIII. 8 richesse] riches F12

LXXV. 2 a way] away F12 ‖ 6 immortalize,] ~. 8° ‖ 9 (quod I)] quoth I, F12 | deuize] ~, 8° ‖ 11 name,:] ~. 8°F12 ‖ 12 whenas] when as F12

LXXVI. 1 richest] riches F12 ‖ 4 spright::] ~. 8°: ~; F12

LXXVII. 3 entertayne] ~, 8° ‖ 4 roialty?:] ~. 8°F12 ‖ 5 ly] ~, 8° ‖ 11 paradice] ~, F2 ‖ 12 by Loue *(indented)*] By loue 8° *(not indented to enable turnover of line 14's "fedd")* ‖ 13 spredd] speedd 8° *(Pforzheimer)*

LXXVIII. 7 her can] can her F12 ‖ 8 aspect.:, 8°: ~; F12 ‖ 14 mee.] ~: 8°

LXXX. 2 compile,] ~^ 8° *(punctuation crowded off)*

LXXXI. 4 does] doth F12 ‖ 9 display] ~, 8°F1 ‖ 12 spright:] ~, 8°

LXXXII. 11 spent: ~, 8°F12

LXXXIII. 1 couetize: ~, 8°F12 ‖ 4 complayne.] ~ ^ 8° ‖ 6 seeing 8° *(Sonnet 83):* hauing 8° *(Sonnet 35)*

LXXXIIII. 3 desyre: ~: 8°: ~, F12 ‖ 6 sprites,] ~^ 8° *(punctuation crowded off)* ‖ 8 angelick] Angel-like F12

LXXXV. 3 does] doth F12 ‖ 13 thunder,] ~^ 8° *(punctuation crowded off)*

LXXXVI. 4 well,: ~. 8°: ~; F12 ‖ 13 reward,] ~. 8°

LXXXVII. 3 moue] ~, 8°

LXXXVIII. 9 the Idaea] th' Idaea 8° ‖ 13 whylest] whylst F12

LXXXIX. 1 bough: ~, 8°F12 ‖ 3 vow] vew 8° ‖ 4 late,: ~. 8°: ~; F12 ‖ 8 doue:] ~^ 8° *(punctuation crowded off)* ‖ 9 houe: ~, 8°F12

[Anacreontic Verses]. 1 old,] ~. 8° ‖ 2 blynd] blinded F12 ‖ 18 shame] ~: 8° ‖ 20 other.] ~, 8°F2 ‖ 30 withall?] ~. 8° ‖ 49 alasse (he cryde)] alas, he cride, F12 ‖ 57 quod] quoth F12 ‖ 73 recured] ~, 8° ‖ 75 enured] ~, 8° ‖ 81 please] ~, 8°

**Epithalamion.** 6 prayse,: ~. 8°: ~; F12 ‖ 11 dreriment,: ~. 8°: ~: F12 ‖ 13 girland] girlands F12 ‖ 19 lampe] ~, 8° ‖ 22 lusty hed] lustiehead F12 ‖ 24 turtle doue] Turtle-doue, F12 ‖ 34 whylest] whilst F12 ‖ 41 hand] ~, 8° ‖ 44 trueloue wize] true-loue wise, F1: true-loue-wise, F2 ‖ 49 wrong,] ~^ 8° ‖ 61 take,] ~. 8° ‖ 67 dere: dore 8°F12 ‖ 70 neer,] ~^ 8° *(punctuation crowded off)* ‖ 81 replyes] replie F12 ‖ 88 louelearned] loue-learned F12 ‖ 89 among?: ~. 8°: ~: F12 ‖ 92 dreames: dreame 8°F12 ‖ 109 ring.] ~^ 8° *(punctuation crowded off)* ‖ 116 see.] ~^ 8° ‖ 118 lifull] life-full F12 ‖ 129 aloud] ~^ 8° ‖ 155 a tweene] atweene F12 ‖ 158 Queene.] ~, 8° ‖ 168 before?] ~^ 8° ‖ 184 ring?: ~^ 8° *(punctuation crowded off):* ~. F12 ‖ 185 ye] you F2 ‖ 192 womanhed: womanhood 8°F12 ‖ 209 you.] ~, 8° ‖ 211 vew:] ~, 8° ‖ 213 come 8° *(Edinburgh Pforzheimer Trinity Wren):* com e 8° *(British Library Folger Huntington Rylands)* ‖ 214 faces;] ~^ 8° ‖ 215 may] ~, 8° ‖ 218 play] ~; 8°: ~, F1 ‖ 220 throates] ~. 8° ‖ 222 ring.] ~^ 8° *(punctuation crowded off)* ‖ 229 th'Angels] the Angels F12 ‖ 234 fastened] fast'ned F12 ‖ 237 vnsownd.] ~, 8° ‖ 239 band?] ~, 8°: ~. F1 ‖ 241 ring.] ~^ 8° *(punctuation crowded off)* ‖ 248 liue long] liue-long F2 ‖ 249 is.] ~, 8°F1 ‖ 263 ye] you F12 | downe] dovvne 8° ‖ 272 weare:] ~. 8° *(British Library)* ‖ 278 weary] vveary 8° ‖ 280 How] Hovv 8°: Hovv. 8° *(Tudor and Stuart)* |

slowly] slovvly *8°* ‖ 281 does] doth *F12* ‖ 290 through] thˆrough / o *8°*
*(British Library)* | nights sad dread] nights dread *8°* ‖ 296 forepast;] ~, *8°*
*(British Library)* ‖ 297 is it,] it is ^ *F12* ‖ 300 Now night *8°* *(British Library*
*Huntington Rylands Wren)*: The night *8°* *(Bodleian Edinburgh Folger Trinity*
*Pforzheimer)* ‖ 304 couerlets.] ~, *8°* ‖ 310 brooke.] ~^ *8°* ‖ 314 ring.]
~^ *8°* *(punctuation crowded off)* ‖ 324 dread] drad *F12* ‖ 332 yongmen]
young men *F12* ‖ 341 Pouke: Ponke *8°F12* ‖ 343 hob Goblins] Hob-
goblins *F12* ‖ 345 shriech Oule] shriech-Owle *F12* ‖ 351 none *8°* *(British*
*Library Bodleian Folger Huntington Rylands Wren)*: n.ne *8°* *(Edinburgh Pforz-*
*heimer Trinity)* ‖ 356 poure *8°* *(Folger(?))*: poüre *8°* *(inked over, British Library*
*Bodleian Edinburgh Folger (?) Huntington Pforzheimer Trinity)*: ponre *8°* *(Ry-*
*lands Wren)* | your pleasant *8°* *(British Library Huntington Rylands Wren)*: the
pleasant *8°* *(Bodleian Edinburgh Folger Pforzheimer Trinity)* ‖ 359 your bed
*8°* *(British Library Huntington Rylands Wren)*: the bed *8°* *(Bodleian Edinburgh*
*Folger Pforzheimer Trinity)* ‖ 373 face, that] face which *F12* | bright?] ~,
*8°* ‖ 380 Latmian *8°* *(British Library Huntington Rylands Wren)*: Latinian *8°*
*(Bodleian Edinburgh Folger Pforzheimer Trinity)* ‖ 385 thy] they *8°* ‖ 399
remaine: ~, *8°F12* ‖ 401 delight] ~. *8°* *(British Library (?) Huntington)* ‖
411 clods,] ~: *8°*

# *Appendix*

The scripture readings and lessons prescribed by the
*Book of Common Prayer* for 1594 with corresponding Sonnets[1]

| No. | Day | Date / Feast | Liturgical Occasion | Scriptural Reference |
|-----|-----|--------------|---------------------|----------------------|
| 1. | Wed. | 23 January Hilary Term begins | Morning Prayer I Lesson II Lesson Evening Prayer I Lesson II Lesson | Psalms 110–13 Genesis 44 Matthew 21 Psalm 114–15 Genesis 45 1 Corinthians 5 |
| 2. | Thu. | 24 January | Morning Prayer I Lesson II Lesson Evening Prayer I Lesson II Lesson | Psalms 116–18 Genesis 46 Matthew 22/23 Psalm 119.1–32 Genesis 47 1 Corinthians 6 |
| 3. | Fri. | 25 January Conversion of St. Paul | Epistle Gospel Morning Prayer I Lesson II Lesson Evening Prayer I Lesson II Lesson | Acts 9.1–32 Matthew 19.27–30 Psalm 119.33–72 Wisdom 5 Acts 22.1–22 Psalm 119.73–104 Wisdom 6 Acts 26 |
| 4. | Sat. | 26 January | Morning Prayer I Lesson II Lesson Evening Prayer I Lesson II Lesson | Psalm 119.105–44 Genesis 48 Matthew 23 Psalm 119.145–76 Genesis 49 1 Corinthians 7 |

---

[1] Earlier editions of the *Book of Common Prayer* still retained the older names of the Old Testament books, particularly 1–4 Kings. Only in later editions, for example that of 1582 used here, were the new names employed, 1–2 Kings becoming 1–2 Samuel and 3–4 Kings becoming 1–2 Kings. Both versions are given in the table below.

| | | | | |
|---|---|---|---|---|
| 5. | Sun. | 27 January Septuagesima Sun. | Epistle | 1 Corinthians 9.24–27 |
| | | | Gospel | Matthew 20.1–17 |
| | | | Morning Prayer | Psalms 120–25 |
| | | | I Lesson | Genesis 1 |
| | | | II Lesson | Matthew 24 |
| | | | Evening Prayer | Psalms 126–31 |
| | | | I Lesson | Genesis 2 |
| | | | II Lesson | 1 Corinthians 8 |
| 6. | Mon. | 28 January | Morning Prayer | Psalms 132–35 |
| | | | I Lesson | Exodus 2 |
| | | | II Lesson | Matthew 25 |
| | | | Evening Prayer | Psalm 136–38 |
| | | | I Lesson | Exodus 3 |
| | | | II Lesson | 1 Corinthians 9 |
| 7. | Tue. | 29 January | Morning Prayer | Psalms 139–41 |
| | | | I Lesson | Exodus 4 |
| | | | II Lesson | Matthew 26 |
| | | | Evening Prayer | Psalm 142–43 |
| | | | I Lesson | Exodus 5 |
| | | | II Lesson | 1 Corinthians 10 |
| 8. | Wed. | 30 January | Morning Prayer | Psalms 144–46 |
| | | | I Lesson | Exodus 7 |
| | | | II Lesson | Matthew 27 |
| | | | Evening Prayer | Psalm 147–50 |
| | | | I Lesson | Exodus 8 |
| | | | II Lesson | 1 Corinthians 11 |
| 9. | Thu. | 31 January | Morning Prayer | Psalms 144–46 or 1–5 |
| | | | I Lesson | Exodus 9 |
| | | | II Lesson | Matthew 28 |
| | | | Evening Prayer | Psalm 147–50 or 6–8 |
| | | | I Lesson | Exodus 10 |
| | | | II Lesson | 1 Corinthians 12 |
| 10. | Friday | 1 February | Morning Prayer | Psalms 9–11 |
| | | | I Lesson | Exodus 11 |
| | | | II Lesson | Mark 1 |
| | | | Evening Prayer | Psalms 12–14 |
| | | | I Lesson | Exodus 12 |
| | | | II Lesson | 1 Corinthians 13 |
| 11. | Sat. | 2 February Purification | Epistle | 1 Corinthians 9.24–27 |
| | | | Gospel | Luke 2.22–27 |
| | | | Morning Prayer | Psalms 15–17 |
| | | | I Lesson | Wisdom 9 |
| | | | II Lesson | Mark 2 |
| | | | Evening Prayer | Psalm 18 |
| | | | I Lesson | Wisdom 12 |
| | | | II Lesson | 1 Corinthians 14 |
| 12. | Sun. | 3 February Sexagesima Sun. | Epistle | 2 Corinthians 11.19–33 |
| | | | Gospel | Luke 8.4–16 |
| | | | Morning Prayer | Psalms 19–21 |

| | | | I Lesson | Genesis 3 |
| | | | II Lesson | Mark 3 |
| | | | Evening Prayer | Psalms 22–23 |
| | | | I Lesson | Genesis 6 |
| | | | II Lesson | 1 Corinthians 15 |
| 13. | Mon. | 4 February | Morning Prayer | Psalms 24–26 |
| | | | I Lesson | Exodus 15 |
| | | | II Lesson | Mark 4 |
| | | | Evening Prayer | Psalms 27–29 |
| | | | I Lesson | Exodus 16 |
| | | | II Lesson | 1 Corinthians 16 |
| 14. | Tue. | 5 February | Morning Prayer | Psalms 30–31 |
| | | | I Lesson | Exodus 17 |
| | | | II Lesson | Mark 5 |
| | | | Evening Prayer | Psalms 32–34 |
| | | | I Lesson | Exodus 18 |
| | | | II Lesson | 2 Corinthians 1 |
| 15. | Wed. | 6 February | Morning Prayer | Psalms 35–36 |
| | | | I Lesson | Exodus 19 |
| | | | II Lesson | Mark 6 |
| | | | Evening Prayer | Psalm 37 |
| | | | I Lesson | Exodus 20 |
| | | | II Lesson | 2 Corinthians 2 |
| 16. | Thu. | 7 February | Morning Prayer | Psalms 38–40 |
| | | | I Lesson | Exodus 21 |
| | | | II Lesson | Mark 7 |
| | | | Evening Prayer | Psalms 41–43 |
| | | | I Lesson | Exodus 22 |
| | | | II Lesson | 2 Corinthians 3 |
| 17. | Fri. | 8 February | Morning Prayer | Psalms 44–46 |
| | | | I Lesson | Exodus 23 |
| | | | II Lesson | Mark 8 |
| | | | Evening Prayer | Psalms 47–49 |
| | | | I Lesson | Exodus 24 |
| | | | II Lesson | 2 Corinthians 4 |
| 18. | Sat. | 9 February | Morning Prayer | Psalms 50–52 |
| | | | I Lesson | Exodus 32 |
| | | | II Lesson | Mark 9 |
| | | | Evening Prayer | Psalms 53–55 |
| | | | I Lesson | Exodus 33 |
| | | | II Lesson | 2 Corinthians 5 |
| 19. | Sun. | 10 February | Epistle | 1 Corinthians 13.1–13 |
| | | Quinquagesima Sun. | Gospel | Luke 18.31–43 |
| | | | Morning Prayer | Psalms 56–58 |
| | | | I Lesson | Genesis 9 |
| | | | II Lesson | Mark 10 |
| | | | Evening Prayer | Psalms 59–61 |
| | | | I Lesson | Genesis 12 |
| | | | II Lesson | 2 Corinthians 6 |

| 20. Mon. | 11 February | Morning Prayer | Psalms 62–64 |
| | | I Lesson | Leviticus 19 |
| | | II Lesson | Mark 11 |
| | | Evening Prayer | Psalms 65–67 |
| | | I Lesson | Leviticus 20 |
| | | II Lesson | 2 Corinthians 7 |
| 21. Tue. | 12 February | Morning Prayer | Psalm 68 |
| | | I Lesson | Leviticus 26 |
| | | II Lesson | Mark 12 |
| | | Evening Prayer | Psalms 69–70 |
| | | I Lesson | Numbers 11 |
| | | II Lesson | 2 Corinthians 8 |
| 22. Wed. | 13 February | Epistle | Joel 2.12–18 |
| | Ash Wednesday | Gospel | Matthew 6.16–22 |
| | | Morning Prayer | Psalms 71–72 |
| | | I Lesson | Numbers 12 |
| | | II Lesson | Mark 13 |
| | | Evening Prayer | Psalms 73–74 |
| | | I Lesson | Numbers 13 |
| | | II Lesson | 2 Corinthians 9 |
| 23. Thu. | 14 February | Morning Prayer | Psalms 75–77 |
| | | I Lesson | Numbers 14 |
| | | II Lesson | Mark 14 |
| | | Evening Prayer | Psalm 78 |
| | | I Lesson | Numbers 16 |
| | | II Lesson | 2 Corinthians 10 |
| 24. Fri. | 15 February | Morning Prayer | Psalms 79–81 |
| | | I Lesson | Numbers 17 |
| | | II Lesson | Mark 15 |
| | | Evening Prayer | Psalms 82–85 |
| | | I Lesson | Numbers 20 |
| | | II Lesson | 2 Corinthians 11 |
| 25. Sat. | 16 February | Morning Prayer | Psalms 86–88 |
| | | I Lesson | Numbers 21 |
| | | II Lesson | Mark 16 |
| | | Evening Prayer | Psalm 89 |
| | | I Lesson | Numbers 22 |
| | | II Lesson | 2 Corinthians 12 |
| 26. Sun. | 17 February | Epistle | 2 Corinthians 6.1–11 |
| | First Sunday | Gospel | Matthew 4.1–12 |
| | in Lent | Morning Prayer | Psalms 90–92 |
| | | I Lesson | Genesis 19 |
| | | II Lesson | Luke 1.1–39 |
| | | Evening Prayer | Psalms 93–94 |
| | | I Lesson | Genesis 22 |
| | | II Lesson | 2 Corinthians 13 |
| 27. Mon. | 18 February | Morning Prayer | Psalms 95–97 |
| | | I Lesson | Numbers 25 |
| | | II Lesson | Luke 1.40–80 |

|  |  |  |  |  |
|---|---|---|---|---|
|  |  |  | Evening Prayer | Psalms 98–101 |
|  |  |  | I Lesson | Numbers 27 |
|  |  |  | II Lesson | Galatians 1 |
| 28. | Tue. | 19 February | Morning Prayer | Psalms 102–103 |
|  |  |  | I Lesson | Numbers 30 |
|  |  |  | II Lesson | Luke 2 |
|  |  |  | Evening Prayer | Psalm 104 |
|  |  |  | I Lesson | Numbers 31 |
|  |  |  | II Lesson | Galatians 2 |
| 29. | Wed. | 20 February | Morning Prayer | Psalm 105 |
|  |  |  | I Lesson | Numbers 32 |
|  |  |  | II Lesson | Luke 3 |
|  |  |  | Evening Prayer | Psalm 106 |
|  |  |  | I Lesson | Numbers 35 |
|  |  |  | II Lesson | Galatians 3 |
| 30. | Thu. | 21 February | Morning Prayer | Psalm 107 |
|  |  |  | I Lesson | Numbers 36 |
|  |  |  | II Lesson | Luke 4 |
|  |  |  | Evening Prayer | Psalms 108–109 |
|  |  |  | I Lesson | Deuteronomy 1 |
|  |  |  | II Lesson | Galatians 4 |
| 31. | Fri. | 22 February | Morning Prayer | Psalm 110–113 |
|  |  |  | I Lesson | Deuteronomy 2 |
|  |  |  | II Lesson | Luke 5 |
|  |  |  | Evening Prayer | Psalms 114–115 |
|  |  |  | I Lesson | Deuteronomy 3 |
|  |  |  | II Lesson | Galatians 5 |
| 32. | Sat. | 23 February | Morning Prayer | Psalms 116–118 |
|  |  |  | I Lesson | Deuteronomy 4 |
|  |  |  | II Lesson | Luke 6 |
|  |  |  | Evening Prayer | Psalm 119.1–32 |
|  |  |  | I Lesson | Deuteronomy 5 |
|  |  |  | II Lesson | 2 Corinthians 8 |
| 33. | Sun. | 24 February | Epistle | 1 Thessalonians 4.1–5 |
|  |  | 2nd Sunday in Lent | Gospel | Matthew 15.21–28 |
|  |  | (St. Matthias | Epistle | Acts 1.15–26 |
|  |  |  | Gospel | Matthew 11.25–30) |
|  |  |  | Morning Prayer | Psalm 119.33–72 |
|  |  |  | I Lesson | Genesis 27 |
|  |  | (St. Matthias | I Lesson | Wisdom 19) |
|  |  |  | II Lesson | Luke 7 |
|  |  |  | Evening Prayer | Psalm 119.73–104 |
|  |  |  | I Lesson | Genesis 34 |
|  |  | (St. Matthias | I Lesson | Ecclesiastes 1) |
|  |  |  | II Lesson | Ephesians 1 |
| 34. | Mon. | 25 February | Morning Prayer | Psalm 119.105–144 |
|  |  |  | I Lesson | Deuteronomy 6 |
|  |  |  | II Lesson | Luke 8 |

|  |  |  |  |  |
|---|---|---|---|---|
|  |  |  | Evening Prayer | Psalm 119.145–76 |
|  |  |  | I Lesson | Deuteronomy 7 |
|  |  |  | II Lesson | Ephesians 2 |
| 35. | Tue. | 26 February | Morning Prayer | Psalms 120–125 |
|  |  |  | I Lesson | Deuteronomy 8 |
|  |  |  | II Lesson | Luke 9 |
|  |  |  | Evening Prayer | Psalms 126–131 |
|  |  |  | I Lesson | Deuteronomy 9 |
|  |  |  | II Lesson | Ephesians 3 |
| 36. | Wed. | 27 February | Morning Prayer | Psalms 132–135 |
|  |  |  | I Lesson | Deuteronomy 10 |
|  |  |  | II Lesson | Luke 10 |
|  |  |  | Evening Prayer | Psalms 136–138 |
|  |  |  | I Lesson | Deuteronomy 11 |
|  |  |  | II Lesson | Ephesians 4 |
| 37. | Thu. | 28 February | Morning Prayer | Psalms 139–141 |
|  |  |  | I Lesson | Deuteronomy 12 |
|  |  |  | II Lesson | Luke 11 |
|  |  |  | Evening Prayer | Psalms 142–143 |
|  |  |  | I Lesson | Deuteronomy 15 |
|  |  |  | II Lesson | Ephesians 5 |
| 38. | Fri. | 1 March | Morning Prayer | Psalms 144–146 |
|  |  |  | I Lesson | Deuteronomy 16 |
|  |  |  | II Lesson | Luke 12 |
|  |  |  | Evening Prayer | Psalms 147–150 |
|  |  |  | I Lesson | Deuteronomy 17 |
|  |  |  | II Lesson | Ephesians 6 |
| 39. | Sat. | 2 March | Morning Prayer | Psalms 1–5 |
|  |  |  | I Lesson | Deuteronomy 18 |
|  |  |  | II Lesson | Luke 13 |
|  |  |  | Evening Prayer | Psalms 6–8 |
|  |  |  | I Lesson | Deuteronomy 19 |
|  |  |  | II Lesson | Philippians 1 |
| 40. | Sun. | 3 March | Epistle | Ephesians 5.1–15 |
|  |  | Third Sunday | Gospel | Luke 11.14–29 |
|  |  | in Lent | Morning Prayer | Psalms 9–11 |
|  |  |  | I Lesson | Genesis 39 |
|  |  |  | II Lesson | Luke 14 |
|  |  |  | Evening Prayer | Psalms 12–14 |
|  |  |  | I Lesson | Genesis 42 |
|  |  |  | II Lesson | Philippians 2 |
| 41. | Mon. | 4 March | Morning Prayer | Psalms 15–17 |
|  |  |  | I Lesson | Deuteronomy 22 |
|  |  |  | II Lesson | Luke 15 |
|  |  |  | Evening Prayer | Psalm 18 |
|  |  |  | I Lesson | Deuteronomy 24 |
|  |  |  | II Lesson | Philippians 3 |

| | | | | |
|---|---|---|---|---|
| 42. | Tue. | 5 March | Morning Prayer | Psalms 19–21 |
| | | | I Lesson | Deuteronomy 25 |
| | | | II Lesson | Luke 16 |
| | | | Evening Prayer | Psalms 22–23 |
| | | | I Lesson | Deuteronomy 26 |
| | | | II Lesson | Philippians 4 |
| 43. | Wed. | 6 March | Morning Prayer | Psalms 24–26 |
| | | | I Lesson | Deuteronomy 27 |
| | | | II Lesson | Luke 17 |
| | | | Evening Prayer | Psalms 27–29 |
| | | | I Lesson | Deuteronomy 28 |
| | | | II Lesson | Colossians 1 |
| 44. | Thu. | 7 March | Morning Prayer | Psalms 30–31 |
| | | | I Lesson | Deuteronomy 29 |
| | | | II Lesson | Luke 18 |
| | | | Evening Prayer | Psalms 32–34 |
| | | | I Lesson | Deuteronomy 30 |
| | | | II Lesson | Colossians 2 |
| 45. | Fri. | 8 March | Morning Prayer | Psalms 35–36 |
| | | | I Lesson | Deuteronomy 31 |
| | | | II Lesson | Luke 19 |
| | | | Evening Prayer | Psalm 37 |
| | | | I Lesson | Deuteronomy 32 |
| | | | II Lesson | Colossians 3 |
| 46. | Sat. | 9 March | Morning Prayer | Psalms 38–40 |
| | | | I Lesson | Deuteronomy 33 |
| | | | II Lesson | Luke 20 |
| | | | Evening Prayer | Psalms 41–43 |
| | | | I Lesson | Deuteronomy 34 |
| | | | II Lesson | Colossians 4 |
| 47. | Sun. | 10 March | Epistle | Galatians 4.21–31 |
| | | Fourth Sunday | Gospel | John 6.1–15 |
| | | in Lent | Morning Prayer | Psalms 44–46 |
| | | | I Lesson | Genesis 43 |
| | | | II Lesson | Luke 21 |
| | | | Evening Prayer | Psalms 47–49 |
| | | | I Lesson | Genesis 45 |
| | | | II Lesson | 1 Thessalonians 1 |
| 48. | Mon. | 11 March | Morning Prayer | Psalms 50–52 |
| | | | I Lesson | Joshua 3 |
| | | | II Lesson | Luke 22 |
| | | | Evening Prayer | Psalms 53–55 |
| | | | I Lesson | Joshua 4 |
| | | | II Lesson | 1 Thessalonians 2 |
| 49. | Tue. | 12 March | Morning Prayer | Psalms 56–58 |
| | | | I Lesson | Joshua 5 |
| | | | II Lesson | Luke 23 |
| | | | Evening Prayer | Psalms 59–61 |

|  |  |  |  |  |
|---|---|---|---|---|
|  |  |  | I Lesson | Joshua 6 |
|  |  |  | II Lesson | 1 Thessalonians 3 |
| 50. | Wed. | 13 March | Morning Prayer | Psalms 62–64 |
|  |  |  | I Lesson | Joshua 7 |
|  |  |  | II Lesson | Luke 24 |
|  |  |  | Evening Prayer | Psalms 65–67 |
|  |  |  | I Lesson | Joshua 8 |
|  |  |  | II Lesson | 1 Thessalonians 4 |
| 51. | Thu. | 14 March | Morning Prayer | Psalm 68 |
|  |  |  | I Lesson | Joshua 9 |
|  |  |  | II Lesson | John 1 |
|  |  |  | Evening Prayer | Psalms 69–70 |
|  |  |  | I Lesson | Joshua 9 |
|  |  |  | II Lesson | 1 Thessalonians 5 |
| 52. | Fri. | 15 March | Morning Prayer | Psalms 71–72 |
|  |  |  | I Lesson | Joshua 23 |
|  |  |  | II Lesson | John 2 |
|  |  |  | Evening Prayer | Psalms 73–74 |
|  |  |  | I Lesson | Joshua 24 |
|  |  |  | II Lesson | 2 Thessalonians 1 |
| 53. | Sat. | 16 March | Morning Prayer | Psalms 75–77 |
|  |  |  | I Lesson | Judges 1 |
|  |  |  | II Lesson | John 3 |
|  |  |  | Evening Prayer | Psalm 78 |
|  |  |  | I Lesson | Judges 2 |
|  |  |  | II Lesson | 2 Thessalonians 2 |
| 54. | Sun. | 17 March | Epistle | Hebrews 9.11–16 |
|  |  | Fifth Sunday | Gospel | John 8.46–59 |
|  |  | in Lent | Morning Prayer | Psalms 79–81 |
|  |  |  | I Lesson | Exodus 3 |
|  |  |  | II Lesson | John 4 |
|  |  |  | Evening Prayer | Psalms 82–85 |
|  |  |  | I Lesson | Exodus 5 |
|  |  |  | II Lesson | 2 Thessalonians 3 |
| 55. | Mon. | 18 March | Morning Prayer | Psalms 86–88 |
|  |  |  | I Lesson | Judges 5 |
|  |  |  | II Lesson | John 5 |
|  |  |  | Evening Prayer | Psalm 89 |
|  |  |  | I Lesson | Judges 6 |
|  |  |  | II Lesson | 1 Timothy 1 |
| 56. | Tue. | 19 March | Morning Prayer | Psalms 90–92 |
|  |  |  | I Lesson | Judges 7 |
|  |  |  | II Lesson | John 6 |
|  |  |  | Evening Prayer | Psalms 93–94 |
|  |  |  | I Lesson | Judges 8 |
|  |  |  | II Lesson | 1 Timothy 2 & 3 |
| 57. | Wed. | 20 March | Morning Prayer | Psalms 95–97 |
|  |  |  | I Lesson | Judges 9 |

|   |   |   |   |   |
|---|---|---|---|---|
| | | | II Lesson | John 7 |
| | | | Evening Prayer | Psalms 98–101 |
| | | | I Lesson | Judges 10 |
| | | | II Lesson | 1 Timothy 4 |
| 58. | Thu. | 21 March | Morning Prayer | Psalms 102–103 |
| | | | I Lesson | Judges 11 |
| | | | II Lesson | John 8 |
| | | | Evening Prayer | Psalm 104 |
| | | | I Lesson | Judges 12 |
| | | | II Lesson | 1 Timothy 5 |
| 59. | Fri. | 22 March | Morning Prayer | Psalm 105 |
| | | | I Lesson | Judges 13 |
| | | | II Lesson | John 9 |
| | | | Evening Prayer | Psalm 106 |
| | | | I Lesson | Judges 14 |
| | | | II Lesson | 1 Timothy 6 |
| 60. | Sat. | 23 March | Morning Prayer | Psalm 107 |
| | | | I Lesson | Judges 15 |
| | | | II Lesson | John 10 |
| | | | Evening Prayer | Psalms 108–109 |
| | | | I Lesson | Judges 16 |
| | | | II Lesson | 2 Timothy 1 |
| 61. | Sun. | 24 March<br>Palm Sunday | Epistle | Philippians 2.5–12 |
| | | | Gospel | Matthew 26.1–27.57 |
| | | | Morning Prayer | Psalms 110–113 |
| | | | I Lesson | Exodus 9 |
| | | | II Lesson | John 11 |
| | | | Evening Prayer | Psalms 114–115 |
| | | | I Lesson | Exodus 10 |
| | | | II Lesson | 2 Timothy 2 |
| 62. | Mon. | 25 March<br>Monday<br>before Easter | Epistle | Isaiah 63.1–19 |
| | | | Gospel | Mark 14.1–72 |
| | | | Morning Prayer | Psalms 116–118 |
| | | | I Lesson | Ecclesiastes 2 |
| | | | II Lesson | John 12 |
| | | | Evening Prayer | Psalm 119.1–32 |
| | | | I Lesson | Ecclesiastes 3 |
| | | | II Lesson | 2 Timothy 3 |
| 63. | Tue. | 26 March<br>Tuesday before<br>Easter | Epistle | Isaiah 50.5–11 |
| | | | Gospel | Mark 15.1–47 |
| | | | Morning Prayer | Psalm 119.33–72 |
| | | | I Lesson | Judges 19 |
| | | | II Lesson | John 13 |
| | | | Evening Prayer | Psalm 119.73–104 |
| | | | I Lesson | Judges 20 |
| | | | II Lesson | 2 Timothy 4 |
| 64. | Wed. | 27 March<br>Wednesday before<br>Easter | Epistle | Hebrews 9.16–28 |
| | | | Gospel | Luke 22.1–71 |
| | | | Morning Prayer | Psalm 119.105–144 |

|  |  |  | I Lesson | Hosea 13 |
|---|---|---|---|---|
|  |  |  | II Lesson | John 14 |
|  |  |  | Evening Prayer | Psalm 119.145–76 |
|  |  |  | I Lesson | Hosea 14 |
|  |  |  | II Lesson | Titus 1 |
| 65. | Thu. | 28 March | Epistle | 1 Corinthians 11.17–34 |
|  |  | Thursday before | Gospel | Luke 23.1–56 |
|  |  | Easter | Morning Prayer | Psalms 120–125 |
|  |  |  | I Lesson | Daniel 9 |
|  |  |  | II Lesson | John 15 |
|  |  |  | Evening Prayer | Psalms 126–131 |
|  |  |  | I Lesson | Jeremiah 31 |
|  |  |  | II Lesson | Titus 2 & 3 |
| 66. | Fri. | 29 March | Epistle | Hebrews 10.1–25 |
|  |  | Good Friday | Gospel | John 18.1–19.42 |
|  |  |  | Morning Prayer | Psalms 132–135 |
|  |  |  | I Lesson | Genesis 22 |
|  |  |  | II Lesson | John 16 |
|  |  |  | Evening Prayer | Psalms 136–138 |
|  |  |  | I Lesson | Isaiah 53 |
|  |  |  | II Lesson | Philemon 1 |
| 67. | Sat. | 30 March | Epistle | 1 Peter 3.17–22 |
|  |  | Holy Saturday | Gospel | Matthew 27.57–66 |
|  |  |  | Morning Prayer | Psalms 139–141 |
|  |  |  | I Lesson | Zachariah 9 |
|  |  |  | II Lesson | John 17 |
|  |  |  | Evening Prayer | Psalms 142–43 |
|  |  |  | I Lesson | Exodus 13 |
|  |  |  | II Lesson | Hebrews 1 |
| 68. | Sun. | 31 March | Epistle | Colossians 3.1–8 |
|  |  | Easter Sunday | Gospel | John 20.1–11 |
|  |  |  | Morning Prayer | Psalms 2, 57, 111 |
|  |  |  | I Lesson | Exodus 12 |
|  |  |  | II Lesson | Romans 6 |
|  |  |  | Evening Prayer | Psalms 113, 114, 118 |
|  |  |  | I Lesson | Exodus 14 |
|  |  |  | II Lesson | Acts 2 |
| 69. | Mon. | 1 April | Epistle | Acts 10.34–44 |
|  |  | Easter Monday | Gospel | Luke 24.13–36 |
|  |  |  | Morning Prayer | Psalms 1–5 |
|  |  |  | I Lesson | Exodus 16 |
|  |  |  | II Lesson | Matthew 28 |
|  |  |  | Evening Prayer | Psalms 6–8 |
|  |  |  | I Lesson | Exodus 17 |
|  |  |  | II Lesson | Acts 3 |
| 70. | Tue. | 2 April | Epistle | Isaiah 7.10–15 |
|  |  | Annunciation / | Gospel | Luke 1.26–38 |
|  |  | (Easter Tuesday | Epistle | Acts 13.26–42 |
|  |  |  | Gospel | Luke 24.36–49) |

|  |  |  |  |
|---|---|---|---|
|  |  | Morning Prayer | Psalms 9–11 |
|  |  | I Lesson | Ecclesiastes 2 |
|  | (Easter Tuesday | I Lesson | Exodus 20 |
|  |  | II Lesson | Luke 24.1–12) |
|  |  | Evening Prayer | Psalms 12–14 |
|  |  | I Lesson | Ecclesiastes 3 |
|  | (Easter Tuesday | I Lesson | Exodus 32 |
|  |  | II Lesson | 1 Corinthians 15) |

71. Wed. 3 April

| | Morning Prayer | Psalms 15–17 |
|---|---|---|
| | I Lesson | 1 Samuel (Kings) 10 |
| | II Lesson | John 21 |
| | Evening Prayer | Psalm 18 |
| | I Lesson | 1 Samuel (Kings) 11 |
| | II Lesson | Hebrews 5 |

72. Thu. 4 April

| | Morning Prayer | Psalms 19–21 |
|---|---|---|
| | I Lesson | 1 Samuel (Kings) 12 |
| | II Lesson | Acts 1 |
| | Evening Prayer | Psalms 22–23 |
| | I Lesson | 1 Samuel (Kings) 13 |
| | II Lesson | Hebrews 6 |

73. Fri. 5 April

| | Morning Prayer | Psalms 24–26 |
|---|---|---|
| | I Lesson | 1 Samuel (Kings) 14 |
| | II Lesson | Acts 2 |
| | Evening Prayer | Psalms 27–29 |
| | I Lesson | 1 Samuel (Kings) 15 |
| | II Lesson | Hebrews 7 |

74. Sat. 6 April

| | Morning Prayer | Psalms 30–31 |
|---|---|---|
| | I Lesson | 1 Samuel (Kings) 16 |
| | II Lesson | Acts 3 |
| | Evening Prayer | Psalms 32–34 |
| | I Lesson | 1 Samuel (Kings) 17 |
| | II Lesson | Hebrews 8 |

75. Sun. 7 April
Low Sunday

| | Epistle | 1 John 5.4–13 |
|---|---|---|
| | Gospel | John 20.19–24 |
| | Morning Prayer | Psalms 35–36 |
| | I Lesson | Numbers 16 |
| | II Lesson | Acts 4 |
| | Evening Prayer | Psalm 37 |
| | I Lesson | Numbers 22 |
| | II Lesson | Hebrews 9 |

*******************************************

76. Fri. 3 May

| | Morning Prayer | Psalms 15–17 |
|---|---|---|
| | I Lesson | 1 (3) Kings 11 |
| | II Lesson | Matthew 1 |
| | Evening Prayer | Psalm 18 |
| | I Lesson | 1 (3) Kings 12 |
| | II Lesson | Romans 2 |

| | | | | |
|---|---|---|---|---|
| 77. Sat. | 4 May | | Morning Prayer | Psalms 19–21 |
| | | | I Lesson | 1 (3) Kings 13 |
| | | | II Lesson | Matthew 2 |
| | | | Evening Prayer | Psalms 22–23 |
| | | | I Lesson | 1 (3) Kings 14 |
| | | | II Lesson | Romans 3 |
| 78. Sun. | 5 May | | Epistle | James 1.22–27 |
| | Fifth Sunday | | Gospel | John 16.23–33 |
| | after Easter | | Morning Prayer | Psalms 24–26 |
| | | | I Lesson | Deuteronomy 8 |
| | | | II Lesson | Matthew 3 |
| | | | Evening Prayer | Psalms 27–29 |
| | | | I Lesson | Deuteronomy 9 |
| | | | II Lesson | Romans 4 |
| | | | Perambulation | Psalms 103–104 |
| 79. Mon. | 6 May | | Morning Prayer | Psalms 30–31 |
| | | | I Lesson | 1 (3) Kings 17 |
| | | | II Lesson | Matthew 4 |
| | | | Evening Prayer | Psalms 32–34 |
| | | | I Lesson | 1 (3) Kings 18 |
| | | | II Lesson | Romans 5 |
| | | | Perambulation | Psalms 103–104 |
| 80. Tue. | 7 May | | Morning Prayer | Psalms 35–36 |
| | | | I Lesson | 1 (3) Kings 19 |
| | | | II Lesson | Matthew 5 |
| | | | Evening Prayer | Psalm 37 |
| | | | I Lesson | 1 (3) Kings 20 |
| | | | II Lesson | Romans 6 |
| 81. Wed. | 8 May | | Morning Prayer | Psalms 38–40 |
| | | | I Lesson | 1 (3) Kings 21 |
| | | | II Lesson | Matthew 6 |
| | | | Evening Prayer | Psalms 41–43 |
| | | | I Lesson | 1 (3) Kings 22 |
| | | | II Lesson | Romans 7 |
| 82. Thu. | 9 May | | Epistle | Acts 1.1–12 |
| | Ascension Thursday | | Gospel | Mark 16.14–20 |
| | | | Morning Prayer | Psalms 8, 15, 21 |
| | | | I Lesson | Deuteronomy 10 |
| | | | II Lesson | Matthew 7 |
| | | | Evening Prayer | Psalms 24, 68, 108 |
| | | | I Lesson | 2 (4) Kings 2 |
| | | | II Lesson | Romans 8 |
| 83. Fri. | 10 May | | Morning Prayer | Psalms 50–52 |
| | | | I Lesson | 2 (4) Kings 3 |
| | | | II Lesson | Matthew 8 |
| | | | Evening Prayer | Psalms 53–55 |
| | | | I Lesson | 2 (4) Kings 4 |
| | | | II Lesson | Romans 9 |

| 83. | Sat. | 11 May | Morning Prayer | Psalms 56–58 |
| | | | I Lesson | 2 (4) Kings 5 |
| | | | II Lesson | Matthew 9 |
| | | | Evening Prayer | Psalms 59–61 |
| | | | I Lesson | 2 (4) Kings 6 |
| | | | II Lesson | Romans 10 |
| 84. | Sun. | 12 May | Epistle | 1 Peter 4.7–12 |
| | | Expectation Sunday | Gospel | John 15.26–16.4 |
| | | | Morning Prayer | Psalms 62–64 |
| | | | I Lesson | Deuteronomy 12 |
| | | | II Lesson | Matthew 10 |
| | | | Evening Prayer | Psalms 65–67 |
| | | | I Lesson | Deuteronomy 13 |
| | | | II Lesson | Romans 11 |
| 85. | Mon. | 13 May | Morning Prayer | Psalm 68 |
| | | | I Lesson | 2 (4) Kings 9 |
| | | | II Lesson | Matthew 11 |
| | | | Evening Prayer | Psalms 69–70 |
| | | | I Lesson | 2 (4) Kings 10 |
| | | | II Lesson | Romans 12 |
| 86. | Tue. | 14 May | Morning Prayer | Psalms 71–72 |
| | | | I Lesson | 2 (4) Kings 11 |
| | | | II Lesson | Matthew 12 |
| | | | Evening Prayer | Psalms 73–74 |
| | | | I Lesson | 2 (4) Kings 12 |
| | | | II Lesson | Romans 13 |
| 87. | Wed. | 15 May | Morning Prayer | Psalms 75–77 |
| | | | I Lesson | 2 (4) Kings 13 |
| | | | II Lesson | Matthew 13 |
| | | | Evening Prayer | Psalm 78 |
| | | | I Lesson | 2 (4) Kings 14 |
| | | | II Lesson | Romans 14 |
| 88. | Thu. | 16 May | Morning Prayer | Psalms 79–81 |
| | | | I Lesson | 2 (4) Kings 15 |
| | | | II Lesson | Matthew 14 |
| | | | Evening Prayer | Psalms 82–85 |
| | | | I Lesson | 2 (4) Kings 16 |
| | | | II Lesson | Romans 15 |
| 89. | Fri. | 17 May | Morning Prayer | Psalms 86–88 |
| | | | I Lesson | 2 (4) Kings 17 |
| | | | II Lesson | Matthew 15 |
| | | | Evening Prayer | Psalm 89 |
| | | | I Lesson | 2 (4) Kings 18 |
| | | | II Lesson | Romans 16 |

# Bibliography of Works Cited

Alciati. *Emblemata*. Antwerp, 1581.

Allman, Eileen Jorge. "*Epithalamion's* Bridegroom: Orpheus-Adam-Christ." *Renascence* 32 (1979–80): 240–47.

Anacreon. "Anacreontea." In *Greek Lyric Poetry*. Trans. D. A. Campbell. LCL, 1987.

Anderson, Douglas. " 'Vnto My Selfe Alone': Spenser's Plenary Epithalamion." *SpS* 5 (1985): 149–66.

Apollonius Rhodius. *Argonautica*. Ed. H. Fränkel. Oxford: Clarendon Press, 1882.

Ariosto, Ludovico. *Orlando Furioso*. Ed. Dino Provenzal. Milan: B. U. R., 1955.

——. *Lirica*. Ed. Giuseppe Fatini. Bari: Laterza, 1924.

Bacon, Francis. *The Essayes or Counsels, Civill and Morall*. Ed. M. Kiernan. Oxford: Clarendon Press, 1985.

Barnes, Barnabe. *Parthenophil and Parthenophe. Sonnettes, Madrigals, Elegies and Odes*. London, 1593.

Barnfield, Richard. *Cynthia. With Certaine Sonnets, and the Legend of Cassandra*. London, 1595.

Baroway, Israel. "The Imagery of Spenser and the *Song of Songs*." JEGP 33 (1934): 23–45.

Bartholomaeus Anglicus. *Batman vppon Bartholome, his Booke De proprietatibus rerum*. London, 1582.

Belleau, Rémy. *Oeuvres Poétiques de Rémy Belleau*. Ed. Marty Laveaux. Geneva: Slatkine Reprints, 1965.

Bennett, Josephine Waters. "Spenser's *Amoretti LXII* and the Date of the New Year." *RQ* 26 (1973): 433–36.

Bernard, John D. "Spenserian Pastoral and the *Amoretti*." ELH 47 (1980): 419–32.

Berry, Henry F. "The English Settlement in Mallow under the Jephson Family." *Journal of the Cork Historical and Archaeological Society*. 2d ser., 12 (1906): 1–26.

Bhattacherje, Mohinimohan. *Platonic Ideas in Spenser*. London: Longmans, Green, 1935.

Bible (Bishops' Version). *The holie Bible ... Imprinted at London ... by Richarde Iugge*. London, 1572.

Bible (Geneva Version). *The Bible and Holy Scriptures conteyned in the Olde and Newe Testament ... Printed by Rouland Hall*. Geneva, 1560; facsimile ed. Lloyd E. Berry. Madison: Univ. of Wisconsin Press, 1969.

Bible (Geneva Version). *The Bible. Translated according to the Ebrew and Greeke, and conferred with the best translations in diuers languages ... Whereunto is added the Psalter of the common translation agreeing with the booke of Common prayer ... Imprinted at London by Christopher Barker.* London, 1578.

*Biblia Vulgata.* Ed. A. Colunga and L. Turrado. Madrid: Biblioteca de Autores Cristianos, 1959.

Bible: New Testament. *The Englishman's Greek New Testament; giving the Greek Text of Stephens 1550.* London: Samuel Bagster, 1877.

Bieman, Elizabeth. " 'Sometimes I ... mask in myrth lyke to a Comedy': Spenser's *Amoretti.*" *SpS* 4 (1983): 131–41.

*Book of Common Prayer ... Imprinted at London ... by Richarde Iugge.* London, 1572.

*The booke of Common prayer ... Imprinted at London by Christopher Barker.* London, 1578.

*The Booke of Common prayer ... Imprinted at London by Christopher Barker.* London, 1582.

Brown, James Neil. " 'Lyke Phoebe,' Lunar Numerical and Calendrical Patterns in Spenser's *Amoretti.*" *The Gypsy Scholar* 1 (1973): 5–15.

Bryskett, Lodowick. *A Discourse of Ciuill Life.* London, 1606; facsimile, Amsterdam: Theatrum Orbis Terrarum Ltd., 1971.

Buttet, Marc-Claude de. *Oeuvres Poétiques de M.-C. de Buttet.* Ed. Marty Laveaux. Geneva: Slatkine Reprints, 1969.

Casady, Edwin. "The Neo-Platonic Ladder in Spenser's *Amoretti.*" *PQ* 20 (1941): 284–95.

Case, Robert H. *English Epithalamies.* London: John Lane, 1896.

Castiglione, Baltissare. *The Book of the Courtier.* Trans. Sir Thomas Hoby. London: Dent, 1928.

Catullus, Tibullus and Pervigilium Veneris. *Poems.* Trans. F. W. Cornish. LCL, 1921.

Chaucer, Geoffrey. *The Complete Works of Geoffrey Chaucer.* Ed. W. W. Skeat. Oxford: Clarendon Press, 1963.

Cheney, Christopher R. *Handbook of Dates for Students of English History.* London: Royal Historical Society, 1945.

Chinitz, David. "The Poem as Sacrament: Spenser's *Epithalamion* and the Golden Section." *JMRS* 21 (1991): 251–68.

Claudian. *Works.* Trans. M. Platnauer. LCL, 1956.

Claudianus Claudius. *Carmina.* Ed. Theodore Birt. Berlin: Weidmann, 1961.

Clay, William Keatinge. *Liturgies and Occasional Forms of Prayer Set Forth in the Reign of Queen Elizabeth.* Cambridge: Cambridge Univ. Press, 1847.

Cleaver, Robert. *A Godlie Forme of Householde Gouernment.* London, 1598.

Constable, Henry. *Diana.* London, 1594; facsimile, Menston: Scolar Press, 1973.

Cummings, L. "Spenser's *Amoretti VIII*: New Manuscript Versions." *SEL* 4 (1964): 125–35.

Cummings, Peter. "Spenser's *Amoretti* as an Allegory of Love." *TSLL* 12 (1970): 163–79.

Daniel, Samuel. *Delia. Contayning certayne Sonnets: with the complaint of Rosamond.* London, 1592; facsimile, Menston: Scolar Press, 1969.

278 *Bibliography*

——. *The Civil Wars*. Ed. Laurence Michel. New Haven: Yale Univ. Press, 1958.

Dasenbrock, Reed Way. "The Petrarchan Context of Spenser's *Amoretti*." *PMLA* 100 (1985): 38–50.

Davies, John. *The Poems of Sir John Davies*. Ed. R. Krueger. Oxford: Clarendon Press, 1975.

DeNeef, A. Leigh. *Spenser and the Motives of Metaphor*. Durham: Duke Univ. Press, 1982.

Desportes, Philippe. *Les amours de Diane*. Ed. F. de Malberbe and V. E. Graham. Geneva: Librairie E. Droz, 1959.

——. *Cléonice Dernières Amours*. Ed. F. de Malberbe and V. E. Graham. Geneva: Librairie E. Droz, 1962.

Dodge, R. E. N. "A Sermon on Source-Hunting." *MP* 9 (1911): 214–22.

Drayton, Michael. *Ideas Mirrour. Amours in Quatorzains*. London, 1594.

Du Bellay, Joachim. *Oeuvres Poétiques*. Ed. Henri Weber. Paris: Librairie Marcel Didier, 1970.

Duncan-Jones, Katherine. "Was the 1609 *Shake-Speares Sonnets* Really Unauthorized?" *RES* 34 (1983): 151–71.

——. "Sidney's Anacreontics." *RES* 36 (1985): 226–28.

Dundas, Judith. *The Spider and the Bee: the Artistry of Spenser's Faerie Queene*. Urbana: Univ. of Illinois Press, 1985.

Dunlop, Alexander. "Calendar Symbolism in the *Amoretti*." *N&Q* 214 (1969): 24–26.

——. "The Unity of Spenser's *Amoretti*." In *Silent Poetry*, ed. Alastair Fowler. New York: Barnes and Noble, 1970, 153–69.

——. "The Drama of *Amoretti*." *SpS* 1 (1980): 107–20.

Eade, J. C. "The Pattern in the Astronomy of Spenser's *Epithalamion*." *RES* n.s. 23 (1972): 173–78.

Edwards, Calvin R. "The Narcissus Myth in Spenser's Poetry." *SPh* 74 (1977): 63–88.

Ellrodt, Robert. *Neoplatonism in the Poetry of Spenser*. Geneva: Librairie E. Droz, 1960.

Erasmus, Desiderius. *Opera omnia*. Ed. J. H. Waszink, L.-E. Halkin, C. Reedijk and C. M. Bruehl. Amsterdam: North Holland, 1969–83.

Fairfax, Edward. *Godfrey of Bulloigne, or The Recouerie of Ierusalem*. London, 1600. Ed. K. M. Lea and T. M. Gang. Oxford: Clarendon Press, 1981.

Ficino, Marsilio. *Commentary on Plato's Symposium: The text and a translation*. Ed. Sears Reynolds Jayne. Columbia: Univ. of Missouri Press, 1944.

Fletcher, Giles. *Licia, or Poemes of Loue ... Whereunto is added the rising to the Crowne of Richard the Third*. London, 1593.

Fowler, Alastair. *Spenser and the Numbers of Time*. London: Routledge and Kegan Paul, 1964.

——, ed. *Silent Poetry*. London: Routledge and Kegan Paul, 1970.

——. *Triumphal Forms. Structural Patterns in Elizabeth Poetry*. Cambridge: Cambridge Univ. Press, 1970.

——. *Conceitful Thought: The Interpretation of English Renaissance Poems*. Edinburgh: Edinburgh Univ. Press, 1975.

Fukuda, Shohachi. "The Numerological Patterning of *Amoretti and Epithala-mion.*" *SpS* 8 (1988): 33–48.

Gascoigne, George. *A Hundreth Sundrie Flowres.* London, 1573.

Gee, Alexander. *The Ground of Christianitie.* London, 1594.

Gerard, John. *The Herball, or General Historie of Plants.* London, 1597.

Golding, Arthur. *The xv. Bookes of P. Ouidius Naso, entytuled Metamorphosis, translated oute of Latin into English meeter.* London, 1567; facsimile, Amsterdam: Theatrum Orbis Terrarum, Ltd., 1977.

Gollancz, I. "Spenseriana." *Proceedings of the British Academy* (1908): 99–105.

Gottfried, Rudolf. "The 'G. W. Senior' and 'G. W. I.' of Spenser's Amoretti." *MLQ* 3 (1942): 543–46.

Greene, Robert. *Greenes Groatsworth of witte.* London, 1592.

Greene, Thomas M. "Spenser and the Epithalamic Convention." *Comparative Literature* 9 (1957): 215–28.

Griffin, Bartholomew. *Fidessa, more chaste then kinde.* London, 1596.

Grindal, Edmund. *Remains.* Ed. W. Nicholson. Cambridge: Parker Society, 1843.

Hamilton, A. C. *Essential Articles for the Study of Edmund Spenser.* Hamden: Archon Books, 1972.

Hamilton, A. C., Cheney, D., Blisset, W. F., Richardson, D. H. and Barker, W. W., eds., *The Spenser Encyclopaedia.* Toronto: Univ. of Toronto Press, 1990.

Hardison, O. B., Jr. "*Amoretti* and the *Dolce Stil Nuovo.*" *ELR* 2 (1972): 208–16.

Harrison, John S. *Platonism in English Poetry.* New York: Columbia Univ. Press, 1915.

Harvey, Gabriel. *Marginalia.* Ed. G. C. Moore Smith. Stratford-upon-Avon: Shakespeare Head Press, 1913.

Hawes, Stephen. *The Pastime of Pleasure.* London. 1517.

Hesiod. *Theogony.* Trans. M. L. West. Oxford: Clarendon Press, 1988.

Hieatt, A. Kent. *Short Time's Endless Monument.* New York: Columbia Univ. Press, 1960.

——. "A Numerical Key to Spenser's *Amoretti* and Guyon in the House of Mammon." *YES* 3 (1973): 14–27.

Hill, Thomas. *The Arte of Gardening.* London, 1608.

Homer. *Hymns.* Ed. T. W. Allen, W. R. Halliday and E. E. Sikes. Oxford: Clarendon Press, 1936.

——. *Iliad.* Ed. D. B. Munro. Oxford: Clarendon Press, 1890.

——. *Odyssey.* Trans. A. T. Murray. LCL, 1919.

——. *Homer's Iliad and Odyssey.* Trans. George Chapman. London, 1616; repr. London: Chatto and Windus, 1892.

Hoopes, Robert. "God Guide Thee, Guyon: Nature and Grace Reconciled in *The Faerie Queene*, Book II." *RES* n.s. 5 (1954): 14–24.

Horace. *The Odes and Epodes.* Trans. C. E. Bennet. LCL, 1952.

——. *Satires, Epistles and Ars Poetica.* Trans. H. R. Fairclough. LCL, 1961.

Hoskins, Edgar. *Horae Beatae Mariae Virginis or Sarum and York Primers.* London: Longmans, 1906.

Hume, Andrea. *Edmund Spenser, Protestant Poet.* Cambridge: Cambridge Univ. Press, 1984.

Hunter, G. K. "Spenser's *Amoretti* and the English Sonnet Tradition." In *A Theatre for Spenserians*, ed. J.M. Kennedy and J. A. Reither. Toronto: Univ. of Toronto Press, 1973, 124–44.

——. " 'Unity' and Numbers in Spenser's *Amoretti*," *YES* 5 (1975): 39–45.

Hutton, James. "Cupid and the Bee." In *Essays on Renaissance Poetry*, ed. Rita Guerlac. Ithaca: Cornell Univ. Press, 1980, 106–31.

Jeffrey, David Lyle. *A Dictionary of Biblical Tradition in English Literature*. Grand Rapids, Mich.: Wm. B. Eerdmans Publishing Co., 1992.

Johnson, William C. "Rhyme and Repetition in Spenser's *Amoretti*." *Xavier University Studies* 9 (1970): 15–25.

——. "Spenser's *Amoretti* 6." *Explicator* 29, no.5 (1971): 38.

——. "Amor and Spenser's *Amoretti*." *ES* 54 (1973): 217–26.

——. "Spenser's *Amoretti* and the Art of the Liturgy." *SEL* 14 (1974): 47–62.

——. "Spenser and the Fine Art of Punning." *Neuphilologische Mitteilungen* 77, no.3 (1976): 376–86.

——. " 'Sacred Rites' and Prayer Book Echoes in Spenser's *Epithalamion*." *Ren. & Ref.* 12 (1976): 49–54.

——. *Spenser's Amoretti: Analogies of Love*. Lewisburg: Bucknell Univ. Press, 1990.

——. "Spenser in the House of Busyrane: Transformations of Reality in *The Faerie Queene* III and *Amoretti*." *ES* 73 (1992): 104–120.

——. "Spenser's 'Greener' Hymnes and *Amoretti*: 'Retraction' and 'Reform.' " *ES* 73 (1992): 431–43.

——. "Gender Fashioning and the Dynamics of Mutuality in Spenser's *Amoretti*." *ES* 74 (1993): 503–19.

Judson, Alexander Corbin. *Spenser in Southern Ireland*. Bloomington: The Principia Press, 1933.

——. *The Life of Edmund Spenser*. Baltimore: Johns Hopkins Univ. Press, 1945.

——. "Amoretti, Sonnet I." *MLN* 58 (1943): 548–50.

Kalil, Judith. " 'Mask in Myrth Lyke to a Comedy,' Spenser's Persona in the *Amoretti*." *Thoth* 13, no.2 (1973): 19–26.

Kaske, Carol V. "Another Liturgical Dimension of *Amoretti* 68." *N&Q* 24 (1977): 518–19.

——. "Spenser's *Amoretti and Epithalamion* of 1595: Structure, Genre, Numerology." *ELR* 8 (1978): 271–95.

Kastner, L. E. "Spenser's *Amoretti* and Desportes." *MLR* 4 (1908–9): 65–69.

Kellogg, Robert. "Thought's Astonishment and the Dark Conceits of Spenser's *Amoretti*." In *The Prince of Poets*, ed. John R. Elliot, Jr. New York: New York Univ. Press, 1968, 139–51.

King, John N. "The Godly Woman in Elizabethan Iconography." *RQ* 38 (1985): 41–94.

Klein, Lisa M. " 'Let us love, deare love lyke as we ought': Protestant Marriage and the Revision of Petrarchan Loving in Spenser's *Amoretti*." *SpS* 10 (1989): 109–37.

Kostic, Veselin. *Spenser's Sources in Italian Poetry*. Belgrade: Faculté de Philologie de l'Université de Belgrade, 1969.

Landrum, Grace Warren. "Spenser's Use of the Bible and His Alleged Puritanism." *PMLA* 41 (1926): 517–44.

Langland, William. *The Vision of William concerning Piers the Plowman*. Ed. W. W. Skeat. Oxford: Clarendon Press, 1953.

La Primaudaye, Pierre de. *The French Academie, Part I*. London, 1586.

——. *The French Academie, Part II*. London, 1594.

Lee, Sidney. *Elizabethan Sonnets*. London: Archibald Constable, 1904.

Lever, J. W. *The Elizabethan Love Sonnet*. London: Methuen, 1956.

Lodge, Thomas. *Phillis: Honoured with Pastorall, Sonnets, Elegies and amorous delights*. London, 1593.

Loewenstein, Joseph. "Echo's Ring: Orpheus and Spenser's Career." *ELR* 16 (1986): 287–302.

——. "A Note on the Structure of Spenser's *Amoretti*: Viper Thoughts." *SpS* 8 (1987): 311–23.

Lucretius. *De rerum natura*. Trans. W. D. H. Rouse. LCL, 1975.

Lynche, Richard. *Diella, Certain Sonnets, adioyned to the amorous Poeme of Dom Diego and Gineura*. London, 1596.

McKerrow, Ronald. B. *Printers' and Publishers' Devices in England and Scotland, 1485–1640*. London: The Bibliographical Society, 1913.

MacMichael, J. Holden. "Beating the Bounds." *N&Q* 10 (1904): 113–14.

McNeir, Waldo. "An Apology for Spenser's *Amoretti*." In *Essential Articles for the Study of Edmund Spenser*, ed. A. C. Hamilton. Hamden: Archon Books, 1972.

Maplet, John. *A Greene Forest or a Naturall Historie, Wherein may be seene . . . the most soueraigne Vertues in all . . . Stones and Mettals, . . . Plantes, Herbes . . . Brute Beastes*. London, 1567.

Marot, Clement. *Les Oeuvres de Clement Marot*. Paris: Jean Schemit, 1871–1931.

Martz, Louis. "The *Amoretti*: 'Most Goodly Temperature.'" In *Form and Convention in the Poetry of Edmund Spenser*, ed. William Nelson. New York: Columbia Univ. Press, 1961, 146–68.

Mazzola, Elizabeth. "Marrying Medusa: Spenser's *Epithalamion* and Renaissance Reconstructions of Female Privacy." *Genre* 25 (1992): 193–210.

Miller, Jacqueline. "'Love Doth Hold My Hand': Writing and Wooing in the Sonnets of Sidney and Spenser." *ELH* 46 (1979): 541–58.

Miola, Robert. "Spenser's Anacreontics: A Mythological Metaphor." *Studies in Philology* 77 (1980): 50–66.

Natalis Comes. *Mythologiae*. Venice, 1567. Ed. S. Orgel. New York: Garland, 1976.

Neely, Carol Thomas. "The Structure of English Renaissance Sonnet Sequences." *ELH* 45 (1978): 359–89.

Neuse, Richard. "The Triumph of Hasty Accidents: A Note on the Symbolic Mode of the 'Epithalamion.'" *MLR* 61 (1966): 163–74.

Nohrnberg, James Carson. *The Analogy of The Faerie Queene*. Princeton: Princeton Univ. Press, 1976.

Okerlund, Arlene N. "The Rhetoric of Love: Voice in the *Amoretti* and the Songs and Sonnets." *Quarterly Journal of Speech* 1 (1982): 37–46.

Osgood, Charles Grosvenor. *A Concordance to the Poems of Edmund Spenser.* Gloucester: Peter Smith, 1963.

Ovid, *Tristia, Ex Ponto.* Trans. A. L. Wheeler. LCL, 1924.

——. *Ars Amatoria.* Trans. A. S. Hollis. Oxford: Clarendon Press, 1977.

——. *Heroides, Amores.* Trans. G. P. Goold. LCL, 1977.

——. *Metamorphoses.* Ed. Hugo Magnus. New York: Arno Press, 1979.

——. *Fasti.* Trans. G. P. Goold. LCL, 1989.

Padelford, F. M. "Spenser and the Theology of Calvin." MP 12 (1914): 1–18.

Panofsky, Dora and Panofsky, Erwin. *Pandora's Box: The Changing Aspects of a Mythical Symbol.* London: Routledge and Kegan Paul, 1950.

Percy, William. *Sonnets to the fairest Coelia.* London, 1594.

Perkins, William. *The Workes of . . . M. William Perkins.* Cambridge, 1609.

Petrarch, Francesco. *Rime, Trionfi e Poesie Latine.* Ed. F. Neri. Milan: Riccardo Ricciardi, 1951.

Phaedrus. *Fabulae.* Trans. B. E. Perry. LCL, 1965.

Plato. *Platonis Opera.* Ed. J. Burnet. Oxford: Clarendon Press, 1901.

——. *The Republic.* Trans. Paul Shorey. LCL, 1956.

Plautus. *Works.* Trans. Paul Nixon. LCL, 1916–38.

Pliny. *Naturalis Historia.* Ed. C. Mayhoff. Stuttgart: Bibliotheca Scriptorum Graecorum et Romanorum, 1967.

Pollard, A. F. "New Year's Day and Leap Year in English History." EHR 55 (1940): 177–93.

Pollard, A. W. and Redgrave, G. R. *A Short-Title Catalogue of Books Printed in England, Scotland, & Ireland and of English Books Printed Abroad, 1475–1640.* 2nd ed. Rev. W. A. Jackson, F. S. Ferguson & K. F. Pantzer. London: The Bibliographical Society, 1976–1991.

Poole, Reginald Lane. *Medieval Reckoning of Time.* London: Society for Promoting Christian Knowledge, 1921.

——. "The Beginning of the Year in the Middle Ages." *Proceedings of the British Academy* 10 (1921): 113–37.

Prescott, Anne Lake. "The Thirsty Deer and the Lord of Life: Some Contexts for *Amoretti* 67–70." SpS 6 (1985): 33–76.

Puttenham, George. *The Arte of English Poesie.* London 1589; facsimile, Amsterdam: Theatrum Orbis Terrarum Ltd., 1971.

Quitsland, Jon A. "Spenser's *Amoretti* 8 and Platonic Commentaries on Petrarch." *Journal of the Warburg and Courtauld Institute* 36 (1973): 256–76.

Ricks, Don N. "Persona and Process in Spenser's *Amoretti*." Ariel 3 (1972): 5–15.

Rix, Herbert David. "Rhetoric in Spenser's Poetry." *The Pennsylvania State College Bulletin* no.7, Folcroft: The Folcroft Press, 1940.

Roche, Thomas P., Jr. *The Kindly Flame: A Study of the "Faerie Queene" III and IV.* Princeton: Princeton Univ. Press, 1964.

Ronsard, Pierre. *Oeuvres Complètes.* Ed. Paul Laumonier. Paris: E. Droz, 1924–59.

Scaliger, J. C. *Poetices libri septem.* 1561; facsimile, Stuttgart: Friedrich Frommann Verlag, 1964.

Scott, Janet G. "Sources of Spenser's *Amoretti*." MLR 22 (1927): 189–95.

——. *Les Sonnets Elizabéthains.* Paris: Champion, 1929.

Seneca, *Tragedies.* Trans. F. J. Miller. LCL, 1916–17.

Shaheen, Naseeb. *Biblical References in The Faerie Queene.* Memphis: Memphis State Univ. Press, 1976.

Shakespeare, William. *The Complete Works.* Ed. Peter Alexander. London: Collins, 1960.

——. *Shakespeare's Sonnets.* Ed. Stephen Booth. New Haven: Yale Univ. Press, 1977.

——. *The Sonnets and A Lover's Complaint.* Ed. John Kerrigan. Harmondsworth: Penguin Books, 1986.

Sidney, Philip. *The Poems of Sir Philip Sidney.* Ed. William A. Ringler, Jr. Oxford: Clarendon Press, 1962.

——. *An Apologie for Poetrie.* London, 1595; facsimile, Amsterdam: Theatrum Orbis Terrarum Ltd., 1971.

Smith, Charles G. *Spenser's Proverb Lore with Special Reference to His Use of the 'Sententiae' of Leonard Culman and Publilius Syrus.* Cambridge: Harvard Univ. Press, 1970.

Smith, Henry. *A Preparative to Marriage.* London, 1591.

——. *The Sermons of Maister Henrie Smith.* London, 1593.

Sparrow, Anthony. *A Rationale upon the Book of Common-Prayer of the Church of England.* London, 1676.

Southern, John. *Pandora, The Musyque or the beautie, of his Mistresse Diana.* London, 1584.

Spencer, Edmund. *The Complete Works in Verse and Prose of Edmund Spenser.* Ed. A. Grosart. London: Spenser Society, 1882–84.

——. *The Works of Edmund Spenser: A Variorum Edition.* Ed. E. Greenlaw, C. G. Osgood, F. M. Padelford, R. Heffner and H. G. Lotspeich. Baltimore: Johns Hopkins Univ. Press, 1932–49.

——. *Poetical Works.* Ed. J. C. Smith and E. de Selincourt. Oxford: Oxford Univ. Press, 1969.

——. *The Faerie Queene.* Ed. A. C. Hamilton. London: Longmans, 1977.

——. *Epithalamion.* Ed. R. Beum. Columbus: Merrill, 1968.

——. *Daphnaïda and Other Poems.* Ed. W. L. Renwick. London: Scholartis Press, 1929.

——. *The Yale Edition of the Shorter Poems of Edmund Spenser.* Ed. W. A. Oram, E. Bjorvand, R. Bond, T. H. Cain, A. Dunlop and R. Schell. New Haven and London: Yale Univ. Press, 1989.

——. *Edmund Spenser's Poetry.* Ed. Hugh MacLean and Anne Lake Prescott. New York: W. W. Norton, 1993.

Statius. *Works.* Trans. J. H. Mozley. LCL, 1928.

Tacitus. *Works.* Trans. M. Hutton, W. Peterson, M. Winterbottom and J. Jackson. LCL, 1914–37.

Tasso, Torquato. *Rime.* Ed. Angelo Solerti. Bologna: Romagnoli-dall'Acqua, 1898–1902.

——. *La Gerusalemme Liberata.* Ed. Ludovico Magugliani. Milan: B. U. R., 1950.

Tertullian. *Adversus Marcionem.* Trans. Ernest Adams. Oxford: Clarendon Press, 1972.

Thompson, Charlotte. "Love in an Orderly Universe: A Unification of Spenser's *Amoretti, Anacreontics*, and *Epithalamion.*" *Viator* 16 (1985): 277–335.

Tilley, Morris P. *A Dictionary of the Proverbs in England in the Sixteenth and Seventeenth Centuries.* Ann Arbor: Univ. of Michigan Press, 1950.

Topsell, Edward. *The Historie of Serpents.* London 1551.

Trapp, John. *A Commentary upon the Books of Proverbs, Ecclesiastes, and the Song of Songs.* London, 1650.

Turner, Myron. "The Imagery of Spenser's *Amoretti.*" *Neophilologus* 72 (1988): 284–99.

Turner, William. *A new Herball.* London, 1551.

Upton, John. *Notes on The Fairy Queen.* Ed. J. G. Radcliffe. New York: Garland, 1987.

Van Winkle, Cortlandt. *Epithalamion by Edmund Spenser.* New York: F. S. Croft & Co., 1926.

Vergil. *Aeneid VII–XII.* Trans. H. R. Fairclough. LCL, 1918.

——. *Aeneid.* Trans. Thomas Phaer and Thomas Twyne. London, 1584; ed. S. Lally. New York: Garland, 1987.

——. *Eclogues, Georgics, Aeneid I–VI.* Trans. H. R. Fairclough. LCL, 1916.

Wall, John N. *Transformations of the Word: Spenser, Herbert, Vaughan.* Athens: Univ. of Georgia Press, 1988.

Watson, Thomas. *The Hecatompathia or Passionate Centurie of Loue.* London, 1582.

Webb, George. *A Garden of spiritual Flowers.* London, 1610.

Wells, R. Headlam. "Poetic Decorum in Spenser's *Amoretti.*" *Cahiers Elisabéthains* 25 (1984): 9–21.

Welsford, E. *Spenser: Fowre Hymnes Epithalamion: A Study of Edmund Spenser's Doctrine of Love.* Oxford: Basil Blackwell, 1967.

Whitaker, Virgil K. *The Religious Basis of Spenser's Thought.* Stanford: Stanford Univ. Press, 1950.

White, Helen. *The Tudor Books of Private Devotion.* Madison: Univ. of Wisconsin Press, 1951.

Whitney, G. *A Choice of Emblemes, and other Devises.* Leyden, 1586; facsimile, Amsterdam: Theatrum Orbis Terrarum Ltd., 1969.

Wickert, Max A. "Structure and Ceremony in Spenser's *Epithalamion.*" *ELH* 35 (1968): 135–57.

Winstanley, Lilian. "Spenser and Puritanism–1." *MLQ* 3 (1900): 6–16.

Woodhouse, A. S. P. "Nature and Grace in *The Faerie Queene.*" *ELH* 16 (1949): 194–228.

——. "Spenser, Nature and Grace: Mr. Gang's Mode of Argument Reviewed." *ELH* 27 (1960): 1–15.

*Zepheria.* London, 1594.

# Index to the Commentary

This index makes no pretense to completion and is not a concordance, for which readers are referred to C. G. Osgood, *A Concordance to the Poems of Edmund Spenser* (Gloucester, 1963). It lists only those terms which are explicated in some detail. Scriptural references cited in the commentary are so numerous that listing them would serve little purpose; hence they are not indexed. The references are to *Amoretti* unless otherwise stated.

# Amoretti: Index of First Lines

Edmund Spenser's *Amoretti and Epithalamion* incorporates a significant literary discovery that has considerable ramifications not only for Spenser's other poetry but for Elizabethan poetry in general. *Amoretti* comprises eight-nine sonnets, written during Spenser's courtship of his second wife. The text shows that they observe a daily, sequential, and chronological order: that laid down by the liturgical calendar of the Church of England's *Book of Common Prayer*. Spenser draws upon the prescribed scripture readings for the sonnets' topics, imagery, vocabulary, and word-games. These scriptural associations also make a rather impenetrable and seemingly uninteresting cycle of poems a highly personal, very funny, and often risqué sequence. It also reveals that Spenser, when shaping *Amoretti and Epithalamion,* chose to present it as both a poetic and liturgical artefact.

**Kenneth J. Larsen** is a professor in the Department of English at the University of Auckland, New Zealand.

# ꭰRTS

ꭰꬲꭰιꭼꝟꝑꮮ & ꭱꭼꮑꭺιꮪꮪꭺꮑꮯꭼ ꭲꭼꭐꭲꮪ & ꮪꭲꭒꭰιꭼꮪ
is the publishing program of the
Arizona Center for Medieval and Renaissance Studies
at Arizona State University, Tempe, Arizona.

ꭰRTS emphasizes books that are needed —
texts, translations, and major research tools.

ꭰRTS aims to publish the highest quality scholarship
in attractive and durable format at modest cost.